This book is presented

to _____

on the _____ day of _____

by _____

with the prayer that
the Christ who lives on every page
may be the Head of your home,
the silent Listener to every conversation,
the unseen Guest at every meal,
and the unfailing Comforter in
every hour of need.

Daily Walk With God

Meditations for Every Day

Herman W. Gockel

Publishing House
St. Louis

Concordia Publishing House, St. Louis, Missouri
Copyright © 1982 Concordia Publishing House
Manufactured in the United States of America

Library of Congress Cataloging in Publication Data

Gockel, Herman William, 1906-
    Daily walk with God.
      1. Devotional calendars—Lutheran Church. I. Title.
BV4811.G52   242'.2   82-1486
ISBN 0-570-03298-9   AACR2
ISBN 0-570-03855-3 (pbk.)

---

3   4   5   6   7   8   9   10   IB   91   90   89   88   87   86   85

Contents

Preface

This is not a book on Christian theology. It is, rather, a book of Christian piety—based firmly on a Christian theology that is faithful to the Holy Scriptures. Its devotional units are well suited for quiet meditation either by the individual believer or in the Christian family circle.

It is recommended that the Bible (the actual, physical book) be used in connection with each devotion. The suggested Scripture readings indicated at the top of each page ordinarily give the broader context of the brief passages quoted above each meditation and lead to a fuller understanding of the entire devotion.

In these pages the author has tried to follow the example of the apostle Paul, who told the Corinthian Christians: "I determined not to know anything among you, except Jesus Christ, and Him crucified." As a result, a word of caution may be in order. This volume is meant to be read only one meditation a day. Anyone who tries to read this entire book in one sitting may experience a seeming repetitiousness, since, directly or indirectly, the crucified Christ is the motivating theme of almost every page. For this the author makes no apology. But to avoid the possible feeling of repetitiousness (the repeated references to the Saviorhood and Lordship of Christ in constantly varying contexts), he urges the reader to use this book according to its original intention—that is, one meditation each day.

The author has made use of various Bible translations, but he has leaned most heavily on the King James Version. While it is true that some modern translations are occasionally more accurate and make effective use of the contemporary idiom (and are therefore more useful in formal Bible Study), it is still true that the beauty of the King James Version frequently makes it more suitable for devotional reading. For instance, "Yahweh is my Shepherd, I will not lack anything" may be a more literal, or a more idiomatic, translation of Psalm 23, but for devotional reading and meditation who can match the beauty and warmth of the familiar "The Lord is my Shepherd, I shall not want"?

Whenever the King James Version is unclear or uncomfortable for the modern reader, the author has either explained the text in the body of the meditation or has made use of a more modern translation. (RSV is the abbreviation for the Revised Standard Version; NEB for the *New English Bible;* Phillips for *The New Testament in Modern English* by J. B. Phillips; and LB for *The Living Bible.)*

For obvious reasons it was impossible to follow the various emphases of the church year accurately, since it is impossible to match the church year with the calendar year. We have, however, tried to keep most meditations as closely in tune with the church year as possible.

May these family devotions help many to heed the Scriptural invitation: "Let the Word of Christ dwell among you richly in all wisdom; teaching and admonishing one another in psalms and hymns and spiritual songs, singing with grace in your hearts to the Lord" (Colossians 3:16).

Herman W. Gockel

Meditations
for
Each Day
of the
Year

Read Philippians 3:7-14   **January 1**

Just a Day at a Time

As thy days, so shall thy strength be. Deuteronomy 33:25

An anxious patient, lying on her sickbed, turned to her doctor and asked: "Doctor, how long will I have to lie here and suffer?" "Just a day at a time," replied the wise physician.

Just a day at a time! What a wonderful philosophy of life. Just a day at a time the new year will come to us with its new burdens, duties, hopes, and fears. As we stand today upon the threshold of a brand new year, which, if it continues the pace of the year now past, will record great changes in the history of our country, in the history of us as families and as individuals, let us not be discouraged or dismayed by the overwhelming greatness of its possibilities. Let us rather find comfort and encouragement in the fact that God has cut the coming year into smaller pieces, and we shall have to live it "just a day at a time."

We cannot live tomorrow today. Nor can we live next week tomorrow. But, with God's help, we can bear the burdens and the challenges that come to us *today.*

As our days, so shall our strength be. We have God's own assurance that each day throughout the coming year will find us equipped with that amount of strength that will be necessary to bear its burden, to endure its trial, to fight its battle through. We have this assurance because we have a Friend who has promised to be with us in His love and His omnipotence "even unto the end of the world"—Jesus Christ, our Lord and Savior.

Surely we have every reason on this very first day of another year to speak the pleading, yet confident prayer of the Christian poet:

> Lord, for tomorrow and its needs I do not pray,
> Keep me, my God, from stain of sin *just for today.*
> Where'er I fail, forgive for Jesus' sake, I pray;
> Let me be kind in word and deed *just for today.*
> Let me in season, Lord, be grave, in season gay,
> Let me be faithful to Thy grace *just for today.*

11

Safe in the Everlasting Arms

I will never leave thee nor forsake thee. *Hebrews 13:5*

It is inevitable that in our weaker moments we scan the horizons of the future with apprehension and foreboding. There is no doubt that the year which we have just entered *will* have its share of anxious hours: hours of sickness, perhaps death; sleepless nights; friendless, lonely hours; moments when that lump within our throat begins to swell and that teardrop in our eye refuses to be concealed; hours when our debts seem greater than our God, when our enemies seem closer than our Savior.

But as the redeemed of Christ we can place our hand into the hand of God and march courageously onward. For if our faith remains firmly grounded in His Word, then when days of sickness come to us in the year that lies ahead, we shall hear His voice whispering to us the comforting assurance: "I am the Lord that healeth thee." If the wings of the angel of death can be heard about our home before we close this year, we shall hear the voice of Him who sent that angel still proclaiming: "I am the Resurrection and the Life, he that believeth in Me shall never die." When that friendless, lonely hour will come to us in the year that stretches out before us, we shall feel His loving arm about us and His cheering voice: "*I* will never leave thee nor forsake thee." "Lo, *I* am with thee alway even unto the end of the world." In every hour of trial we will be fortified by the eternal promise: "The eternal God is thy Refuge, and underneath are the everlasting arms."

Are these merely the sentimental phrases of a commercial New Year's card? By no means. Each promise is taken directly from the inspired Word of God. What God promises God performs. Therefore we can sing with faith undaunted:

> What a peace is mine, what a joy divine,
> Leaning on the everlasting arms!
> What a blessedness, what a hope is mine,
> Leaning on the everlasting arms!

Numbering Our Days

So teach us to number our days, that we may apply our hearts unto wisdom. *Psalm 90:12*

Time, like money, is a gift of God for the "spending" of which we shall some day have to give an account. How are we *spending* our time? As faithful Christians we will, as it were, count out the few days and years which God has allotted to us and then resolve to spend them as wisely as we can.

As we move further into the new year, let us remember that it is not merely the tick of the clock or the swing of the pendulum that measures time, but it is the *deeds* which we crowd into it. It is not merely the changing of calendars that measures our years, but rather the deeds of service to God and man which we crowd into the fleeting moments as they flit and fly into eternity. A man may be 90 years old in hours but no more than six months old in the value he has been to God and to his fellow men.

Let us look upon our hours as gifts of God to be used in His service, to His honor, and to the welfare of our neighbor. As we look out over the year which lies ahead, let us budget our hours and especially set aside a generous portion of time to be spent for the things of God: our private devotions, our public worship, our church activities, our personal missionary endeavors, and our deeds of charity. These are but a few of the things which God expects us to purchase with the moments he allots us.

There are many more. If God grants us another year of time, it is inevitable that we will "spend" it; let us resolve today to "spend" it wisely—for Him, for our fellowman, and for our eternal welfare. To this end we pray:

> Take my life and let it be
> Consecrated Lord, to Thee;
> *Take my moments and my days,*
> Let them flow in ceaseless praise.
>
> Take my love, my Lord, I pour
> At Thy feet its treasure store;
> *Take myself,* and I will be
> Ever, only, all for Thee.

A Life Centered in Christ

For me to live is Christ, and to die is gain. Philippians 1:21

The Bible gives us good examples of two kinds of lives, one a life centered in *itself* and the other a life which is centered in *Christ*. The former we find in the well-known story of the rich man in the parable. His whole life consisted in the abundance of the things he had accumulated, in barns and bales and bank accounts. God placed His own verdict on that type of life when He said: "Thou fool!"

An example of the other type of life we find in the life of the apostle Paul. Those things upon which the rich man had hung his heart meant nothing to Paul, and the things which meant nothing to the rich man were the very things which, to Paul, made life worth living: *to know Christ* and to be made like Him. That was not only Paul's deepest satisfaction—it was his highest goal.

Paul had learned the secret of a truly happy life. He could put it in six short words: "For me to live is Christ." His entire life was wrapped up in the Savior and His Gospel of forgiveness. He was living *for* Christ now, and soon he would be living *with* Christ in the heavenly mansion. That is why he could say: "To die is gain." For Paul, life was grand, and death was glorious!

During the first week of a new year we might well ask ourselves: Can we say that for us to live is Christ? Have we found our deepest joy, the fulfillment of our every want and wish, in *Him?* Let us make sure every morning that we see *Christ* at the end of our road, and then let us walk that road courageously, cheerfully, gaining strength as we draw ever closer to Him who is standing at our journey's end.

> For me to live is Jesus, To die is gain for me.
> Whate'er my Savior pleases, That e'er my will shall be
> He is my highest Treasure, On earth and heav'n above.
> He is my highest pleasure, My Life, my Light, my Love.

Did Christmas Leave You Cold?

Make me to hear joy and gladness; that the bones which Thou hast broken may rejoice. *Psalm 51:8*

Another Christmas has come and gone. Did the voices of the children, the anthems of the church choir, and the sermons of the pastor fill our hearts with that warmth and joy of yesteryear? Or did this Christmas *"leave us cold"?*

That all depends. What was it in Christmas that we were looking for? Did we bring to the festive season the penitent and broken heart of David, who pleaded: "Make me to hear joy and gladness; that the bones which Thou has broken may rejoice"? Did we bring to the Christ Child hearts bleeding by reason of sin, pleading for the soothing ointment of forgiveness which only He could give?

He who has pleaded penitently with God: "Make me to hear *joy* and *gladness; that the bones which Thou hast broken may rejoice"* will never say that the message of the angels has left him cold.

Rather, he will exclaim with David who had experienced the essential joy of the Christmas Gospel: "Bless the Lord, O my soul, and all that is within me, bless His holy name. Bless the Lord, O my soul, and forget not all His benefits, who forgiveth all thine iniquities . . . who redeemeth thy life from destruction, who crowneth thee with loving kindness and tender mercies . . . He hath not dealt with us after our sins, nor rewarded us according to our iniquities. . . . As far as the east is from the west, so far hath He removed our transgressions from us." That is the Christmas message! Anything "cold" about that? Never! Only warmth, light, and joy!

It is not too late to catch the spirit of the 17th-century poet who wrote:

"O rejoice, ye Christians loudly, For our joy has now begun;
Wondrous things our God has done . . .
Joy, O Joy, beyond all gladness! Christ has done away with sadness!
Hence, all sorrow and repining, For the Sun of grace is shining!

The Christmas of the Gentiles

*There came wise men . . . saying, Where is He that is born King of the Jews?
Matthew 2:1-2*

Today is the festival of the Epiphany. Epiphany is a Greek word which means appearance, or "becoming public." The Epiphany festival commemorates the appearance of the Christ Child as the promised Savior to the Gentile nations, and thus to all the peoples of the world. That is why January 6 has become known as "the Christmas of the Gentiles."

Everything about Christmas has a distinctly Jewish aspect. The parents of Jesus, the town of Bethlehem, the shepherds, the circumcision, the temple scene—all combine to make a purely Jewish story. But this Child of Bethlehem was to be the Savior of *all* men of *all* lands and of *all* times. So the Christmas story is followed immediately by the story of the Epiphany.

Wise men in a distant land—not members of the Jewish race, not inhabitants of Palestine—see His star in *their* land, and by the divine operation of God's Holy Spirit they come to a living faith in the newborn Savior. Bethlehem's Child was *their* Redeemer, just as He was the Redeemer of Mary and Joseph and Simeon and Anna. That is why the poet exclaims: "Lift up thine eyes in wonder, See heathen nations yonder. They come from far to Thee!"

Let us thank God for this revelation. When Christ was born on that first Christmas, most of our ancestors were heathens who roved the plains of Europe. That we are Christians today we owe to the fact that Christ is the Savior of the Gentiles as well as of the Jews. In a sense, then, today is *our* Christmas. *We* are the Gentiles who have been brought into the safety of the fold by the Savior's all-embracing, matchless mercy. Let us never cease to praise Him for having called us out of darkness into the wonders of His marvelous light.

> As with gladness men of old, Did the guiding star behold!
> So most gracious Lord, may we, Evermore be led by Thee!

Arise . . . Shine!

Arise, shine; for thy light is come. Isaiah 60:1

The Old Testament text most closely associated with the Epiphany of our Lord is the one quoted above. "Arise, shine; for thy light is come, and the glory of the Lord is risen upon thee." How appropriate that each year we hear this Old Testament challenge while our hearts and homes are still basking in the afterglow of Christmas!

Our Light indeed has come. In the gross darkness which covers this groping, stumbling world we have once more seen the light: the Light from heaven, God's own Son come down to earth. With aged Simeon each of us has said (and continues to say): "Mine eyes have seen Thy salvation . . . a *Light* to lighten the Gentiles, and the glory of Thy people Israel."

What are we to do, now that we have seen the Light? "Arise, shine," says the prophet. We are to spread the light. We are to tell all, both near and far, about Him who has called us out of darkness into His marvelous light.

We are to engage in personal evangelism and to support our church's missionary program at home and abroad. We are to arise from our lethargy, our inactivity, our indifference, holding high the light of our salvation. Are we doing that?

There is always the danger, especially in our highly organized church life of today, that we literally "arise and shine" *vicariously*—that we restrict much of our Epiphany joy to reading of the "victories" on our church's mission fronts. We read glowing reports of the Gospel's steady progress "from Greenland's icy mountains to India's coral strand" and then feel that we have discharged our Epiphany obligations.

Let us rather, at this moment, look at our own record. How have *we* been proclaiming to all, near and far: "The Lord is come"?

Lord, grant me the Epiphany grace to share Your light with others. May I create opportunities to speak of my Savior to those who have not yet heard the message of His love and mercy. Amen.

Head Religion

And they said unto him, In Bethlehem of Judea; for thus it is written. *Matthew 2:5*

When Herod called the chief priests and scribes and inquired of them where the promised King of the Jews was to be born, they immediately answered with a Bible passage, "In Bethlehem of Judea, for thus it is written."

The scribes were good at quoting Bible passages, but in many instances that is where their "religion" stopped. Although they knew *where* the Christ child was to be born and could point to a specific Bible verse to prove their claim, they were not sufficiently interested to go and see if He actually *was* born. They had discharged their duty by locating the proper Bible reference.

We might well be warned by this tragic example of a purely "head" religion. Strange as it may seem, our very familiarity with the Gospel, if we are not constantly on our guard, can make us blind to its beauties and deaf to its pleadings. We begin to imagine that having a Bible passage in our memory is the same as having Christ in our heart, that having completed the Catechism is the same as having "finished the course."

No, let us implore God's Holy Spirit to grant us a genuine *heart* religion, a living faith in Jesus, our Redeemer. Let our heart glow daily in deep-felt gratitude to God for the marvelous salvation which is our in the message of the Gospel. If we have a *heart* religion, we will also have a *hand* religion; we will put our Bible passages into practice. We will do as the Wise Men did: Having heard the Word, they did not merely memorize the Scripture passage, but they *believed* the Word and went out and followed its directions. They found the Savior! May we always follow their example.

> As with joyful steps they sped To Thy lowly manger bed,
> There to bend the knee before Thee whom heav'n and earth adore,
> So may we with willing feet Ever seek Thy mercy seat.

Mine Eyes Have Seen

Lord, now lettest Thou Thy servant depart in peace, according to Thy word, for mine eyes have seen Thy salvation. *Luke 2:29-30*

Like a meteor that flashes across the midnight sky—now seen, now gone—Simeon, the patriarch of Jerusalem, appears only once in all the pages of the Bible. But the few words which he spoke on that one occasion have come down through the ages as a priceless legacy.

"Mine eyes have *seen*." At last, after years of patient waiting, he had beheld the Savior for whom his longing eyes had looked. For him the climactic hour had come. His eyes had *seen*, and now his heart could be at peace. His eyes had seen the Lord's salvation!

In these post-Christmas days, as we look out across a world of deepening darkness, how unspeakably grateful we should be that we, too, have shared in Simeon's great discovery. We, too, have *seen* our Lord's salvation.

For us the warmth and glow of Christmas is a permanent possession. No matter what the month, we are always living between two Christmases; and the peace and hope and joy we have found in the infant Savior shine before and after.

In the midst of a world of darkness, enshrouded by despondency, doubt, and despair, we can walk courageously into the gathering gloom and say: "Mine eyes have seen! Mine eyes have seen Thy salvation!"

We will have that courage in our lives if we have that Infant in our hearts. As we cradle Him in our arms of faith, may we repeat the words of the poet:

Jesus, the very thought of Thee With sweetness fills the breast;
But sweeter far *Thy face to see* And in Thy presence rest.

Nor voice can sing, nor heart can frame, Nor can the memory find
A sweeter sound than Thy blest name, O Savior, of mankind!

B.C. and A.D.

Lord, NOW lettest Thou Thy servant depart in peace, according to Thy Word.
Luke 2:29

There is a sense in which the life of the aged Simeon can be viewed as the life of the world in miniature. As in the history of the world, so also in the life of Simeon there were, no doubt, days of great significance. But if anyone had asked Simeon before he closed his eyes in their final sleep, which was the greatest day of his life, there can be no doubt as to his reply.

The greatest day in the life of Simeon was the day on which his eyes first beheld the Christ Child in the temple and held Him in his arms. The life of Simeon, like the life of the world, had only one date which, as it were, formed a great divide. For Simeon everything in his life happened either B.C. or A.D., either *before* he saw the Christ or *after*. (A.D. being the Latin for "in the year of our Lord.") No other date really mattered.

The "now" of his *Nunc Dimittis* was the red-letter date on the spiritual calendar of his life. It marked the end of long years of waiting and ushered in the golden sunset which God Himself had promised. "Lord, NOW"—after all these years of waiting—"*now* lettest Thou Thy servant depart in peace, according to Thy Word."

There is a red-letter day in the life of every Christian which divides his life into before and after, into B.C. and A.D. That is the day on which the eyes of our faith for the first time beheld the Son of God as Lord and Savior.

We may not be consciously aware of the very first time we laid believing eyes on Christ as our personal Redeemer. It may be a bright and shining moment which we will never forget, or it may be one of those many "ordinary" moments during which we received Christian instruction from a faithful pastor. No matter. The important thing is that we share in the same peace that filled the heart of aged Simeon. Do we—really?

The Cradle in the Shadow of the Cross

Yea, a sword shall pierce through thine own soul. *Luke 2:35*

These were strange words for the venerable Simeon to address to Mary, the happy young mother who had brought her infant Son to the temple: "A sword shall pierce through thine own soul." As Simeon held the "Salvation of the Lord" to his bosom, he could see, as it were, the grim arms of a rugged cross casting its gloomy shadow across the tiny form which he was holding.

Calvary, the cross, the crucifixion, the mother of Jesus weeping at His feet—all seem to sweep like a swiftly moving picture before the dimming eyes of Simeon. Mary must not yet know, and so he speaks in shadows: "yea, a sword shall pierce through thine own soul," Mary. Simeon could say, as few others in his day could, that he had seen the Lord's salvation—because he had seen "the cradle in the shadow of the cross."

The world during the past weeks has stood at the cradle. But did it see the cross? The *cross*, which stands behind the cradle and casts its shadow on the blessed manger scene: *that* gives the picture meaning. The Christ of Bethlehem would be of little value if it were not for the Christ of Golgotha and the Christ of Calvary.

For us the *Lamb of God* is born! The cross, the altar, awaits the precious sacrifice—the Lamb which was born to bear the sins of a fallen world. Let us rejoice that like Simeon of old our eyes have beheld the Christmas miracle in its true significance—that Calvary has given meaning to our Christmas. That is why we sing:

> In the Cross of Christ I glory, Tow'ring o'er the wrecks of time.
> All the light of sacred story Gathers round its head sublime.
> Bane and blessing, pain and pleasure, By the Cross are sanctified;
> Peace is there that knows no measure, Joys that thro' all time abide.

May it be given to everyone of us to see the infant Savior in the shadow of the cross. Amen.

A Sign Spoken Against

This Child is set . . . for a sign which shall be spoken against. *Luke 2:34*

Simeon follows up his joyful *Nunc Dimittis* with another somber reflection. Thus far the Christ Child had met with very little opposition, though the world had treated Him with coldness and indifference. But, says the aged patriarch, before long this cold indifference will be changed to active opposition, for "this Child is set for a sign which shall be spoken against."

Scarcely had those words been spoken when the forces of opposition began their evil work, which has not stopped to this very hour. The Child of Bethlehem was destined to become "despised and rejected of men, a man of sorrows and acquainted with grief." Down through the ages there were to be those who would curse and revile His memory.

Even today, while in the world He is still a sign that is spoken against, in large sections of the church He is merely a *sign,* though not always spoken against. He is merely a human Savior, a symbol of all that is good, but no more.

We therefore have every reason to praise God once more in the afterglow of the Christmas festival, that to us the Babe in the manger is still what He was to Simeon of old, namely, "the Lord's Salvation," "the Wonderful, the Counselor, the Mighty God, the Everlasting Father, the Prince of Peace." Not merely God's *sign* but God's *Son!* Not spoken against but worshiped and adored.

Let us praise Him with grateful hearts that as we leave another Christmas festival behind us we can truly say: "Lord, now lettest Thou Thy servant depart in peace, according to Thy word, for mine eyes have seen Thy salvation," my Savior and my Lord!

As we behold the infant Son of Mary with the eyes of faith and acknowledge Him as "the Lord's salvation," our promised Redeemer and promised Lord, our hearts can pray:

O dearest Jesus, Thee I pray: Within my heart now make Thy stay,
That I, like Simeon of old, By faith may gladly Thee behold. Amen.

The Revealer of Thoughts

. . . that the thoughts of many hearts may be revealed. Luke 2:35

With the Christ Child clasped tenderly in his arms, Simeon still is gazing intently upon the shadow of the cross. "A sword shall pierce through thine own soul," he says to Mary, *"that the thoughts of many hearts may be revealed."*

The *cross,* not merely the cradle, is to be the great revealer of men's thoughts. Standing around the manger, men's differences are not always apparent. But standing around the cross, *that* is where "the thoughts of many hearts" shall be revealed. Men who have been known to preach with almost angelic eloquence about the wonders of the stable birth have stuttered and floundered when it came to the preaching of the cross.

Thousands who during the past weeks have sung the joyful strains of jubilant Christmas carols will find themselves unable, a few months from now, to join the church in the singing of its Lenten hymns. Why? Because "the preaching of the *cross* is to them that perish foolishness." The preaching of the cross is the great divider, which clearly separates "them that perish" from those "which are saved."

How unspeakably grateful should we be that, while the world at large may play its Christmas melodies on a broken instrument, we can thrill in the wondrous harmony of the *complete* revelation of God. For us the manger is not empty, but in it lies that precious Sacrifice which God Himself prepared to take away our sins.

Let us not be ashamed of the cross of our Redeemer, with its message of full and free forgiveness. Rather let us look forward to the day when we will stand before the throne of Christ in robes that have been "washed and made white in the blood of the Lamb."

> Till then—nor is my boasting vain—
> Till then I boast a *Savior slain;*
> And oh, may this my glory be,
> That Christ is not ashamed of me!

Taking Christmas with Us

But Mary kept all these things, and pondered them in her heart. *Luke 2:19*

Can we still remember the joy that filled our hearts at Christmas? It was only a few weeks ago that we celebrated the birth of the Savior with songs of gladness. Now the sounds and sights of the season have faded and soon will become a distant memory. The trees have been untrimmed and consigned to the rubbish barrel. The sparkling ornaments have been packed and put away for another year. Christmas is past!

Is there no way of taking Christmas with us? No way of recapturing the thrill and charm of the past weeks and taking them with us out into our workaday world? That all depends upon what it is in Christmas that we wish to take along. The *true* glories of the Christmas season are the Christian's perennial and perpetual possession.

We are told that "Mary *kept* all these things." She took them with her. They were hers to keep. What were these "things" which Mary took along into the days that followed Christmas? They were the glorious assurances of the Christmas story, including the astounding promise of the angel Gabriel some nine months before. These she "kept," and these she "pondered in her heart."

We too may take our Christmas with us out across the threshold of another year. "These things"—peace, pardon, love, and joy—are ours; they are ours to keep. The tinsel of the Christmas season may fall like blossom petals to the ground, but its true fruit—the glorious assurance of sins forgiven and the resultant peace and joy—these are ours forever. These things, praise God, we shall take along with us. With the Christian poet we pray:

Redeemer, come! I open wide My heart to Thee; here Lord, *abide!*
Let me Thine inner presence feel Thy grace and love in me reveal;
Thy Holy Spirit guide us on Until our glorious goal is won.
Eternal praise and fame We offer to Thy name!

Don't Break the Habit

They went up to Jerusalem after the custom of the feast. *Luke 2:42*

"He just goes to church out of habit." How often this charge is leveled against the regular church attender. While God is surely displeased with purely mechanical worship, much can be said in favor of "going to church out of habit."

Of the holy family we are told that they went to Jerusalem every year at the time of the Passover "after the *custom* of the feast." Years later, when He visited Nazareth, Jesus attended the local synagog on the Sabbath "as His *custom* was." For Him it was the most natural thing to do. It was His "custom," His wholesome custom.

Breaking the wholesome custom of regular church attendance is rarely a conscious, rational decision. As a rule, it is an insidious process—with no rationale behind it. One simply misses a single Sunday for no apparent reason. Next month perhaps *two* Sundays find his (and his family's) church pew vacant. Again, this is more the result of non-decision than decision. Finally, almost unknown to the drifting member, the unlooked-for has happened. He has "broken" the habit.

We can break good habits such as regular church attendance only at great spiritual peril. Once such habits are broken, they will be replaced by the habits of non-attendance, non-fellowship, non-participation, and a dwindling source of spiritual nourishment. In that direction, ultimately, lies spiritual death.

If we are attending church merely out of habit, so be it. But let us continue to attend. Meanwhile we pray for the higher motivation of King David: "Lord, I have loved the habitation of Thy house, and the place where Thine honor dwelleth." He who hears God's Word regularly finds that one good habit leads to another.

Lord, let me never stray from Your church, nor from Your precious Word and sacraments. Amen.

"We Are All Beggars"

There is no difference, for all have sinned. Romans 3:22-23

The words which appear in large type at the top of this page take on special significance when we consider who wrote them and under what circumstances. They were the last words from the pen of Dr. Martin Luther. They were found scribbled on a scrap of paper next to the bed in which he died. In full, the note read: "We are all beggars, this is true."

How typical—both of the man and of his entire theology. A giant of church history, a world-historical figure, a man who had won the acclaim of his generation, yet his final words were a confession of his radical poverty. "We are all beggars!"

In a sense, these few words capture the whole of his theology. There is no difference between pope and peasant, prince and pauper, for *all* have sinned and deserve nothing but wrath and punishment at the hand of God. We dare come into His presence only as beggars—not asking for our just deserts but begging only for His mercy.

Luther hit upon the idea of "beggars before God," when he discovered the true meaning of the word "grace" when used in connection with the salvation of the sinner. In that context grace could mean only the unmerited mercy of a loving God in heaven. Again and again he used the word "grace" as the very opposite of "merit" or of "works" (see Romans 11:6). His constant refrain was the same as that of Paul: We are saved by grace and by grace *alone*—grace to the utter exclusion of merit (Romans 3:23-24).

What a comfort for you and me today, not only to know that we are beggars before God but also to know that the God from whom we beg is "full of compassion, and gracious, and plenteous in mercy and truth." In Christ He has forgiven us all our sin and made us rich beyond all measure. With the poet we can sing:

> Nothing in my hand I bring, Simply to Thy cross I cling;
> Could my zeal no respite know, Could my tears forever flow,
> All for sin could not atone; Thou must save and Thou alone.

The Anchor of the Line

Keep thy heart with all diligence; for out of it are the issues of life. *Proverbs 4:23*

In the strategy of war, certain cities are designated as "the anchors of the line." As long as these hold, the enemy cannot advance. But as soon as these fall, the whole line begins to crumble, and the hour of defeat is close at hand.

It was of such an "anchor city" that Solomon spoke when he said: "*Keep thy heart* with all diligence, for out of it are the issues of life." It is in the heart that the tide of battle in the Christian life is determined.

When faith has gone out of the heart, when convictions have become flabby, when carelessness and indifference have made their inroads, the citadel has fallen, and the whole line is doomed to crumble. But if the heart remains firm, rooted surely in the promises of God, undergirded by faith in the Gospel, and reinforced by daily prayer and close communion with our God, the whole line will hold—for the "anchor city" has proved impregnable.

How is it with us in this respect? Is our "anchor city" holding? Surely, we have no reason for smug complacency. Our anchor city is under fire. The devil, the world, and our flesh have conspired to unhinge its gates and to take its citadel by storm. Let us "watch and pray." Let us "be sober, be vigilant." Let us "put on the Gospel armor, each piece put on with prayer." Let us hold ever more firmly to the Word. God's Word is our defense. As long as we rely on His Word as our "shield and buckler," we can sing with Martin Luther:

> With might of ours can naught be done, Soon were our loss effected;
> But for us fights the Valiant One, Whom God Himself elected.
> Ask ye, Who is this? Jesus Christ it is, Of Sabaoth Lord,
> And there's none other God; *He holds the field forever!*

How important it is that we turn over the defense of our "anchor city" (our heart) to "Jesus Christ, of Sabaoth Lord." He'll keep it safe forever!

All the Days of My Life

Surely goodness and mercy shall follow me all the days of my life. Psalm 23:6

Did you notice how long David said the goodness and mercy of the Lord would follow him? Only today? Only this year? Only as long as David would be king and would occupy the royal palace? No! "Goodness and mercy shall follow me *all the days of my life.*"

The same goodness and mercy which had followed him when he was a shepherd boy on the fields near Bethlehem, which had preserved him when he was persecuted by Saul, which had elevated him to the highest position among God's people, which had reclaimed him when he had fallen and restored him to loving sonship with the Father, that same goodness and mercy would follow him *all the days of his life!*

Surely, God's promise to us is as sure as it was to David. His ability to provide is not diminished with the passing of the years. His goodness will not be *less* good tomorrow than it is today. His mercies which have been new to us every morning will not fail.

The advancing years may bring with them their multiplied reminders that "swift to its close ebbs out life's little day"—the waning strength, the fading vigor, the slowing step, the blurring vision—but they will also bring with them the multiplied assurances that "the eternal God is thy Refuge and underneath are the everlasting arms."

This will be true, even when all evidence seems to prove the contrary—when a long and painful terminal illness seems to belie the promises of God, when "sweet death" is delayed for reasons that defy all human reason. Even in the "dark valley of the shadow" (yes, especially then) we will walk by faith and not by sight.

Through every changing scene of life we have our Lord's assurance that our Savior, who is "the same yesterday, today, and forever" will be at our side, guiding, helping, and upholding. Can we be afraid of such a prospect?

Men Whose Eyes Have Seen the King

[John says:] We beheld His glory. *John 1:14*

Recently we read of a church society which featured as its speaker a Christian gentleman who had been born blind, but who after years of blindness had received his sight. In moving words he described the thrill which was his when after almost a lifetime of blindness he suddenly stepped out of the world of darkness into the world of light.

Every child of God has experienced a miracle very much the same as the speaker that evening had experienced. Perhaps, to a general audience, the gaining of *spiritual* sight, after spiritual blindness, may not seem as dramatic or spectacular—but, in reality, it is *more* miraculous. It is always an act of God, wrought by His Holy Spirit.

Again and again the Bible speaks of the miracle of conversion as stepping from darkness to light. Paul tells the Ephesian Christians that "ye were sometimes darkness but now are ye light in the Lord." What is more, he commissions them as "lecturers" who are to go out and tell about their glorious experience. Just as Peter told his new converts to go out and *talk* about the Lord "who had called them out of [spiritual] darkness into His marvelous light."

We who have seen the Lord's salvation in Bethlehem's manger have been commissioned to speak freely to our friends and fellowmen about the stirring events that we have seen. Are we being obedient to that charge?

Send Thou, O Lord, to every place Swift messengers before Thy face,
The heralds of Thy wondrous grace, Where Thou Thyself wilt come.

Send men *whose eyes have seen the King*, Men in whose ears the sweet words ring;
Send such Thy lost ones home to bring; Send them where Thou wilt come.

     O Lord, we have beheld Your glory. Enable us to spread the message of
Your glory throughout the world. Amen.

What Others Have Not Seen

Eye hath not seen, nor ear heard . . . the things which God hath prepared for them that love Him. 1 Corinthians 2:9

Some have misinterpreted this passage to refer to the glories which will be revealed to us in heaven. The fact is, however, that we have already seen these wondrous things. The very next verse continues: "But God *hath revealed* them to us by His Spirit." What are these unspeakably glorious things which no natural eye has seen but which we, as the children of God, already have beheld?

They are the treasures of Christ's Gospel: the wonderful assurance of peace with God through faith in Jesus; the assurance that the gates of hell have been forever closed behind us and the portals of heaven thrown open; the assurance that through Christ we have a loving Father in heaven and that, come what may, His hand will guide us and sustain us and bring us safely to the Father's house.

Do these sound like vaporous abstractions—a sort of heavenly bakery shop with assorted "pies in the skies"—a beautiful celestial island of never-never-land of which Christian people dream but which will disappear with the warmth of the rising sun?

By no means! They are the real-as-life spiritual realities which God has *already* placed before our enlightened eyes and of which He has assured us through the revelation of Word and Sacrament.

While it is true of the spiritually *unenlightened* world about us that "eye hath not seen, nor ear heard . . . the things which God hath prepared for them that love Him," God has *already revealed* them to us through His Spirit—through His spoken and written Word and through His divinely instituted sacraments. Indeed, our *eyes have seen!*

O Lord, I thank You for the revelation of Your love and grace through Jesus Christ, my Lord. Amen.

I Have Seen My Sin

My sin is ever before me. Psalm 51:3

A Christian housewife was trying to lead a troubled man to Christ. To her urgent entreaties the despairing man replied: "It's no use. I'm lost, I tell you, *I'm lost!*"

"Thank God for that!" the woman answered quietly. "Why?" exclaimed the poor man in astonishment. "Because," she replied, "the Bible tells us: 'The Son of Man is come to seek and to save that which is *lost.*' You say you're *lost.* Then you're just the man He's come to save!"

If our eyes are to see our Savior in all His love and beauty, they must first see our sin in all its ugliness. Before we can experience the "joy of salvation," we must know something of the enormity of our iniquity.

David's eyes had seen his sin in all its sordidness—including adultery and murder. "I acknowledge my transgressions, and my sin is ever before me," he exclaims. His eyes had seen something terrible, and he was praying God to rid him of the nightmare of his iniquity.

So, too, it is with us. We have sinned most grievously. Our eyes have seen the tremendous burden of our guilt. But, thank God, our eyes have seen that tremendous burden placed upon the cross of the Son of God and carried into the sea of God's forgetfulness. He assures us that, for Jesus' sake, He will remember our sin no more. With every penitent we must pray:

> All that I was, my sin, my guilt, My death was all my own;
> All that I am I owe to Thee, My gracious God, alone.
>
> All that I am, e'en here on earth, All that I hope to be,
> When Jesus comes with grace divine, I owe it, Lord, to Thee.

Do Your Best—Today

Whatsoever thy hand findeth to do, do it with thy might. Ecclesiastes 9:10

St. Francis of Assisi, while hoeing his garden one day, was asked what he would do if he were told that he was going to die at sundown. He replied: "I would finish hoeing my garden."

Significantly, a similar story is told about Martin Luther. One morning, while discussing points of theology with a group of friends, he was asked: "Father Luther, what would you do if you knew for sure that the Lord was coming tonight?" In his usual quick and impetuous manner, Luther replied: "I'd go out into my garden and plant an apple tree"—meaning he'd go about his ordinary business.

If only all of us in these unsettled days could emulate the attitude of these heroes of the faith. Because of the insecurity and uncertainty of our times too many of us are inclined to stop "hoeing our gardens." Many a young man asks: "Why go to college when an atomic war will soon be upon us?" Many a young woman wonders: "Why have a family when there's no guarantee of future happiness?" Why plan and work for a future which may never come?

The Christian has an answer to that question. God has given him a life to live. God has given him a task to do. As long as God gives him life and health and talent, he will go on "hoeing his garden" to the best of his ability.

"Whatsoever thy hand findeth to do, do it with thy might," the Scriptures tell us. The very certainty of His early death prompted the Savior to work with unflagging zeal and unabated diligence. "I must work the works of Him that sent Me, while it is day. The night cometh when no man can work."

God has asked us to make the best of the present. We can be sure that *He* will make the best of the future.

Lord, keep me faithful to my present tasks. Amen.

1 Corinthians 13

But the greatest of these is charity. *1 Corinthians 13:13*

There are some Bible passages which are so well-known that a mere reference to their location in the Scriptures will suffice to recall the entire content of the passage. Thus, for instance, John 3:16 has come to be known as the Gospel in a nutshell. The Twenty-Third Psalm calls to mind the entire shepherd scene, and Matthew 18 suggests the various stages of brotherly admonition.

Another such convenient label for an important Scripture teaching is *1 Corinthians 13*. This matchless chapter has become known as Paul's great "hymn of love." In language as simple as it is sublime, and eloquent as it is earnest, Paul in this chapter first proclaims the absolute necessity of Christian charity and then describes this Christian grace in action. The word *charity* is used throughout this chapter in the sense of genuine Christian love. *1 Corinthians 13*, therefore, is known as the Bible's chapter of love.

Could there be a chapter more important for the world in which we live, where the love of many has waxed cold? Could there be a chapter more important for our Christian congregations and Christian families where, in many cases, the milk of human kindness has gone sour and rancor and bitterness prevail?

Let us return again and again to the sweet waters of *1 Corinthians 13*. Let us remind ourselves repeatedly that he who believes John 3:16 must *live 1 Corinthians 13*. "By this shall all men know that ye are my disciples," says Jesus, "if ye have *love* one to another." It will be our purpose in the following meditations to dwell upon the beauties of Paul's great hymn of love. To that end we pray our Lord:

> Give us faith to trust Thee boldly,
> Hope, to stay our souls on Thee;
> But, oh! best of all Thy graces,
> Give us Thine own *charity!*

Love's Supremacy
(Over Lip Religion)

Though I speak with the tongues of men and of angels, and have not charity, I am become as sounding brass or a tinkling cymbal. *1 Corinthians 13:1*

There is an interesting connection between 1 Corinthians 13 and 1 Corinthians 12. In the 12th chapter Paul had cataloged the many and varied spiritual gifts which God has given to His church. In the 13th chapter he shows that *all* of these gifts—if not coupled with Christian love—are nothing. "Though I speak with the tongues of men and of angels, and have not charity, I am become as sounding brass or a tinkling cymbal."

There is an earnest warning in these words for every Christian. Though I be a church member all my life, though I be an officer in my congregation with a long and enviable record, though I have the highest degree of theological knowledge and occupy a place of highest prominence, yea, though I speak with angel eloquence about the Savior and His love—if in all these things I am not motivated by love to God and to my fellow man, then all of my "gifts" and all of my "accomplishments" have no value in the sight of God. To Him they are as the dull clank of dead brass and the offensive jangle of a clanging cymbal.

Let us beware of a loveless Christianity, one that can see a brother or sister in dire need and merely say: "God bless you." Rather let us come back again and again to Bethlehem, to Calvary, and melt our loveless hearts of stone in the warming rays of God's eternal love. If God so loved us, how can we withhold the full measure of our love even from the least of those for whom our Savior died? Well might we pray:

> Give me a faithful heart, Likeness to Thee,
> That each departing day Henceforth may see
> Some *work of love* begun, some deed of kindness done,
> Some wand'rer sought and won, Something for Thee. Amen.

Love's Supremacy
(Over Intellectual Attainments)

Though I . . . understand all knowledge . . . and have not charity, I am nothing.
1 Corinthians 13:2

Paul was one of the intellectual lights of his day, having enjoyed the best advantages afforded at Jerusalem. In the language of today, Paul was a college man. But it is not as a college man that Paul is remembered today. When the Lord by a miracle of His love transformed the proud and haughty Saul into the meek and humble Paul, Paul's diplomas and degrees took on an entirely new significance. They were but the measure of his talents which he now could dedicate to the loving service of his Lord and to the service of his fellow men.

Paul's intellectual attainments meant nothing—until they had been sanctified by the Savior's love, and consecrated to the unselfish service of the Savior's brethren.

We are living in a day of intellectual snobbishness. Wise men are glorying in their wisdom. The flames of intellectual pride and arrogance, in many instances, have dried up the cooling waters of sweet kindness. "This wisdom," however, says the Scripture, "descendeth not from above, but is earthly, sensual. But the wisdom that is from above is first pure, then peaceable, gentle, and easy to be entreated, *full of mercy and good fruits.*"

May God in His goodness grant us a wisdom that is surrendered to *love,* a knowledge which seeks no personal recognition or acclaim, but seeks only greater opportunities for the exercise of helpful, healing charity. Like the Savior, in whom dwelt all the wisdom of heaven, let us dedicate our intellectual attainments to humble service to all men.

It is at the foot of the cross that all knowledge finds its true perspective. That is why Isaac Watts could write:

When I survey the wondrous cross On which the Prince of Glory died,
My richest gain I count but loss And pour contempt on all my pride!

Love's Supremacy
(Over Mechanical Charity)

Though I bestow all my goods to feed the poor, and though I give my body to be burned, and have not charity, it profiteth me nothing. *1 Corinthians 13:3*

In these words Paul reaches the climax of his statements regarding the supremacy of love. At first reading we might say: "Surely, if a person bestows all of his goods to feed the poor and finally gives his body to be burned, that person has the gift of charity in the highest degree." "But no," says Paul, "it is possible for me to do all these things and still not have a heart of love."

Love is an attitude. It is a condition of the heart without which the activity of our hands can have no value. It is a comparatively simple matter to hand a hungry man a dime or stuff a dollar into a church envelope or contribute to the United Fund. It is an entirely different matter to have a heart which has been transformed by the Savior's love, a heart which daily thanks Him for His supreme sacrifice on Calvary's cross, and which then goes out in compassion to all who are in need of the Savior's love and ours.

We are living in a day of organized charity. Perhaps it would be well if first each of us would organize his *own* charity. Let us coordinate our heart and hands, our attitudes and actions. Let us make sure that every deed of love, every act of kindness is an expression of a heart which has been warmed by the love of Christ and which, like the heart of the Savior, bleeds with compassion for all mankind. "My little children," says John, "let us not love merely in word, neither in tongue, but in deed and in *truth.*" Let the deeds of our hands be the sincere expression of our heart, and let our heart be like the heart of Him who loved us and gave Himself for us. Our lips will then overflow in the prayer:

Take my *love*, my Lord, I pour At Thy feet its treasure-store;
Take myself, and I shall be Ever, only, all for Thee. Amen.

Love Suffereth Long and Is Kind

Charity suffereth long, and is kind; charity envieth not; charity vaunteth not itself, is not puffed up. *1 Corinthians 13:4*

Are things getting on your nerves? Do the countless little irritations of the day find you flying off the handle? Are you irritable, impatient, pouty? If you are, then thank God for the love and patience of near and dear ones for whom the chip on your shoulder has, indeed, become a painful cross.

Irritableness, impatience and bitterness are not the fruits of love. They are rather the evidences of a spirit that is hard and cold and selfish. *"Love suffereth long and is kind,"* says Paul. Love can absorb the shock of abuse, the impact of mistreatment, the stones of slander, the disappointments of false friendships, and still can maintain its peace and composure.

But love is not a mere sullen acceptance of an unfortunate circumstance. *"Love is kind,"* says Paul. Love is gracious, full of good will. In the midst of irritations, in the midst of trying circumstances, love is not only self-composed, but it is friendly, compassionate, and tender. In spite of irritations, trials, and vexations, love just goes on loving.

The source of such love, of course, lies beyond the walls of the human heart. It springs forever at the foot of Calvary's cross. There in an infinitely larger measure "love suffered long and was kind." That love, the love which drove the holy Son of God to die for sinful men, must enkindle in our hearts a similar affection, a similar patience, a similar kindliness.

The apostle Peter told the Christians of his day that Christ had left them an example which they were to follow. Although He was reviled, mocked, spat upon, and finally nailed to the cross, He never railed at His tormentors or answered them "in kind."

May we go back to that cross again and again. There let us pray for strength to bear up under our trials in quiet peace and gentle patience.

As Thou hast died for me, Oh, may my Love for Thee
Pure, warm, and changeless be. Lord, hear my prayer.

Love Envieth Not

Charity suffereth long, and is kind; charity envieth not; charity vaunteth not itself, is not puffed up. *1 Corinthians 13:4*

When the Savior was asked for a brief statement of the Law, He summed up the last seven commandments in the seven well-known words: "Thou shalt love thy neighbor as thyself." He knew that a man who loves his fellow men will not wish to do anything that would harm them. Love excludes disobedience, enmity, disloyalty, fraud, slander, jealousy. So Paul is merely repeating the thought of the Savior when he says: *"Love envieth not."* Love is not jealous. Love strives to keep the Ninth and Tenth Commandments.

Do we find it difficult to rejoice in the good fortune of another, to admire the excellences, the accomplishments, the virtues of our neighbor? Do we find it much simpler to belittle his achievements, to speak disparagingly of his attainments, to begrudge him whatever little degree of honor has come his way?

If so, we have need of growth in the grace of Christian love. True love will draw a family, or community of believers, so close to one another that the success of one is a cause of rejoicing for all. The well-known lines "We share our mutual woes, Our mutual burdens bear" apply equally as well to the joys, triumphs, successes, and good fortunes of our fellow Christians. The thrill of achievement which comes to *any* Christian should prove a source of joy to *every* Christian!

We are frequently so weak in this respect. Let us pray God to deliver us, for Jesus's sake, from the smallness of mind which lies at the root of envy. Only His love can cleanse our hearts of this besetting sin.

Create in me a clean heart, O God, and renew a right spirit within me. Grant me a full measure of Your love both for You and for my fellowman, so that I may rejoice in *his* good fortune. I ask this in the name of Jesus Christ, my Savior. Amen.

Love Vaunteth Not Itself

Charity suffereth long, and is kind; charity envieth not; charity vaunteth not itself, is not puffed up. *1 Corinthians 13:4*

When the Pharisee in the well-known parable thanked God that he was not as other people are "or even as this publican," he thereby showed not only that he was *proud,* but also that he had no love in his heart for the publican.

Pride, sinful pride, excludes love. They can never dwell together within a single heart. We cannot delight in reminding our brother of his inferiority if we truly love him; nor can we, if we have a true regard for him, parade before him our own superiority, either supposed or real.

We see so much pride today, because we see so little love. He whose heart goes out in true affection to those about him and who truly loves his brother will not indulge in self-display, or seek to "put on airs," or give way to sinful boasting.

Ostentation, or, as Paul puts it, "being puffed up," is not only the sign of a little mind, but it is the funeral wreath on the door of a heart in which Christian love has died.

Humility is the sweetest fruit of love, "the first daughter of Christian charity." The great church father St. Augustine once exclaimed: "Should you ask me, What is the first thing in religion? I should reply, The first, the second, the third thing—nay, all—is humility!"

Let us, then, be done with silly pride and shallow boasting. As we contemplate the unsearchable love of Him who humbled Himself for us, even to death on the cross, let us say with the poet: "When I survey the wondrous cross On which the Prince of Glory died, My richest gain I count but loss, *And pour contempt on all my pride!*" May we follow the example of the publican who prayed the thoughts of the Christian poet:

With broken heart and contrite sigh,
A trembling sinner, Lord, I cry;
Thy pard'ning grace is rich and free;
O God, be merciful to me. Amen.

Love Is Properly Behaved

Charity doth not behave itself unseemly. 1 Corinthians 13:5

Some years ago a best seller bore the title: *How to Win Friends and Influence People.* Whatever might be said about the contents of that book, we are sure that its readers would have won more lasting friends and would have influenced more people in the right direction, had they but read 1 Corinthians 13 and then prayed God, for Jesus' sake, to give them the crowning grace of Christian love.

"Charity doth not behave itself unseemly," says Paul. Literally, love does not deport itself *contrary to good form.* A heart that is filled with stubborn pride and loveless arrogance will find it difficult to behave within the limits of good manners. Not so with a heart that is filled with love.

Love is always forgetful of self and thoughtful of others. Love remembers its own place, is not rash, is not presumptuous. Love accords due respect and honor to friend and foe alike. Love is considerate, poised, and tactful. Love is the etiquette of heaven.

Someone has asked concerning the apostle Paul: "Who taught this tentmaker such noble and beautiful manners, such perfect tact in all his bearing, that even the great in this world were compelled to respect him?"

Paul's good manners were but the natural expression of a heart which had been transformed by the Savior's love, a heart that went out in tender compassion to every soul for whom his Savior had died. In Christ he loved them all. How could his behavior be otherwise than kind? God grant us an ever greater measure of His love and an ever greater readiness to *reflect* that love in our everyday behavior. We know His will. He will show us the way—and enable us to follow.

Love Keeps No Books

Charity taketh not account of evil. *1 Corinthians 13:5*

In Romans 4:8 and again in 2 Corinthians 5:19 Paul uses a striking verb to tell us that God *forgives* the sins of those who accept Jesus as their Substitute and Savior. We might reproduce the meaning of that word by saying: "God fails to make an entry into the books." He does not charge our sins to our account. He lets them sink into the sea of forgetfulness.

In 1 Corinthians 13 Paul uses the *same* verb to show what the Christian should do when *he* has been wronged, when *he* has suffered injury or injustice. Love takes no account of evil. It keeps no books. It has no ledger for the entry of wrongs on the debit side which are eventually to be balanced on the credit side with payments received in full—with interest. Love never owes anything but love.

Chrysostom once said: "As a spark falls into the sea and does not harm the sea, so harm may be done to a loving soul, but it is soon quenched, and the soul is not disturbed." Love is not enraged when it receives personal injury. It carries no grudge. It does not seek to get even.

If we have been keeping books, let us burn those books today. Let us destroy the record. Let us cancel old accounts. "Owe no man anything but to love one another." Difficult, you say? Yes, it is difficult for the "old Adam" each of us still carries within us. Even the apostle Paul had to admit that frequently he had to *struggle* to do what his enlightened conscience told him the Lord expected of him (see Romans 7:18-19).

But Paul knew where to go for strength in every circumstance of life—to Calvary's cross where hardened hearts are melted by the contemplation of the Savior's love. It was the apostle John who said: "If God so loved us, we ought also to love one another." We ought to "keep no books."

Lord, may the daily contemplation of Your love enable me to hold no grudge against my fellowman. Amen.

Love Believes What Love Dictates

Charity rejoiceth not in iniquity, . . . believeth all things, hopeth all things, endureth all things. 1 Corinthians 13:6-7

There is a peculiar perversity of the human heart which sometimes makes us wish that the very worst were true. We hear the slander of a careless tongue, the gossip of an idle mind, and seize upon the cruel revelation with relish and delight. We believe the worst because we hope the worst is true.

Such is not the way of love! Love is grieved by idle tongues that peddle hurtful rumors. Love thinks of him or her whose name is being harmed and goes forth to heal, to help the injured person. Love refuses to yield to dark suspicion, refuses to believe the wicked rumor. Love is always ready to find an excuse for the beloved, always ready to defend him, speak well of him, and put the best construction on everything.

Even though its simplicity and loyalty be abused again and again, even though the worst *is* true while he is hoping for the best, love still hopes on, trusting that the sweet persuasion of the Holy Spirit will change the erring brother's way. Love prays for the *best;* how, then, can it hope for the *worst?*

Let us search our ways. Do we really *love* the members of our family, the members of our congregation, our neighbors, our associates? Then we will not delight in the quiet whispers which are aimed like poisoned darts at their good name. In every case we will reach for the protecting mantle of Christian love, which "shall cover a multitude of sin." We will defend the absent brother or sister as far as we can in keeping with the truth. We will believe only what love demands that we believe. May the petition of the poet be our constant prayer:

> Oh, let me never speak What bounds of truth exceedeth;
> Grant that no idle word From out my mouth proceedeth;
> And then, when in my place, I must and ought to speak,
> My words grant power and grace, Nor let me wound the weak. Amen.

Love, the Badge of Discipleship

By this shall all men know that ye are My disciples, if ye have love one to another.
John 13:35

We have spoken much about love. In our devotions during the past days the word *love* has occurred much more frequently than the word *faith*. Have we perhaps attached undue importance to this single virtue? Not at all. In the life of the Christian love is indispensable. It is the inevitable manifestation of a heart which has been received into the family of God through faith in the Redeemer.

In His farewell address to His disciples that fateful night in the Upper Room, the Savior talked long and tenderly to His intimate friends about the urgency of love. In one of the most touching scenes of His life He singles out this queen of virtues as the badge of true discipleship: "By this shall all men know that ye are my disciples, if ye have love one to another."

Can love *still* be called the badge of the Christian? "Behold, how they love one another," the pagans exclaimed when they beheld the early church. "Behold, how they quarrel and argue and strive with one another," the world exclaims today as it observes many a Christian family and many a Christian congregation.

The world cannot see our faith, but it *could* see our love. Love is the public badge which is to give evidence of our calling. How are we wearing that badge? Let us pray God daily that ours might be a "faith which worketh by love," that the light of our love might so shine before men that they may glorify our Father which is in heaven. Let us keep ever burnished and shining the badge of true discipleship. To that end we invoke the presence and the power of God's Holy Spirit as we pray:

Spirit of Life, of Love, of Peace,
Unite our hearts, our *love* increase,
Thy gracious help supply.
To each of us the blessing give
In loving fellowship to live,
In joyful hope to die. Amen.

Love That Demands Surrender

Humble yourselves therefore under the mighty hand of God. *1 Peter 5:6*

Is it not a fact that some of us who are bearing crosses are doing so "under protest," in a spirit of suppressed rebellion against the gracious will of God? Such cross-bearing surely has no virtue and is displeasing in God's sight.

"*Humble* yourselves under the mighty hand of God," says Peter in the text above. In days of trial and trouble, when our human wisdom would dictate to God or would sit in judgment on His will, we are to silence our soul's complaints and surrender ourselves wholly, unreservedly, unconditionally, to His will.

We are to remember that it is the hand of our loving Father that is fashioning our lives. Our fate, our destiny is but as clay in the hand of the Master Potter, and since we know He *loves* us for Jesus' sake, we know that He will shape our lives according to the directions of His tender mercy. Whether for the present He sends us joy or sorrow, success or failure, health or sickness, we know that He *loves* us and that He never makes mistakes. His judgments may be unsearchable and His ways past finding out, yet we know that His thoughts toward us are thoughts of peace and love.

Complete surrender to His loving care is the only path to peace. In every sorrow there is a strengthening angel waiting to come to those who in humble faith have learned to say: "Father, not my will, but Thine be done." Let us, then, day by day, surrender ourselves ever more and more completely to the gentle leading and tender care of Him of whom we know: *He loves us!*

It was this kind of submission to the heavenly Father's will that moved the poet to write:

> Have thine own way, Lord; have Thine own way;
> Thou art the Potter, I am the clay.
> Mold me and make me after Thy will,
> While I am waiting, patient and still.

If Our Heart Condemn Us

If our heart condemn us, God is greater than our heart and knoweth all things.
1 John 3:20

There come moments, even in the life of a Christian, when the voice of conscience strikes terror into our soul. In the midst of a busy day or in the quiet hours of the night our heart is suddenly pierced by the sharp memory of sin—ugly sin, personal sin, *our* sin—and we experience the same agony of guilt which drove the apostle Paul to exclaim: "O wretched man that I am!"

David, the great sinner and great saint, knew the terrors of an accusing conscience: "When I kept silence," he says, "my bones waxed old through my roaring all the day long. For day and night Thy hand was heavy upon me." The burden of unforgiven sin was greater than he could bear.

But we Christians need bear no burden of unforgiven sin. That is what John means when he says: "If our heart condemn us, God is greater than our heart and knoweth all things." God looks at us through *Christ*. He knows that we are sinners, but He also knows that in Christ our guilt has been atoned, our sins have been forgiven, our accusing conscience has been silenced.

Afraid of your conscience? "Who shall lay *anything* to the charge of God's elect? It is God that justifieth. Who is he that condemneth? It is Christ that died, yea rather, that is risen again, who is even at the right hand of God, who also maketh intercession for us."

Let Satan, hell, and our own deceitful conscience shout endless accusations, let them tell us that our sins are too great or too many to be forgiven. It matters not. We can answer softly and serenely in the words of Horatio Bonar:

> I lay my sins on Jesus, The spotless Lamb of God;
> He bears them all and frees us From the accursed load.
> I bring my guilt to Jesus To wash my crimson stains
> White in His blood most precious Till not a spot remains.

Sun of My Soul

He that hath the Son hath life. *1 John 5:12*

It is said that Tennyson was walking one day in a beautiful garden where many flowers were blooming. A friend who accompanied him said: "Mr. Tennyson, you speak so often of Jesus. Will you tell me what Christ really means to you?" Tennyson stopped, thought a moment; then, pointing down to a beautiful flower, said: "What the sun is to that flower, Jesus Christ is to my soul."

Who of us must (or, at least, *should*) not say the same! What the sun is to the flower, Christ is to our souls. There is not a blessing in our life which, if we trace it back to the hand which gave it, does not lead us back to the creative power and the redeeming love of the Son of God.

No matter where we turn, no matter where we look—if there is anything good, anything true, anything that has brought lasting joy and gladness into our life—we recognize it ultimately as a gift which has come to us through faith in Jesus Christ, our Savior.

In days of gloom He is our *Light*. In days of *sorrow or despondency* it is the *warmth* of His love that buoys our drooping spirits. In days of temptation it is the *magnetism* of His cross which holds us from the paths of evil and draws us to His outstretched arms. Yes, in a sense unspeakably sublime, Jesus is to our souls what the sun is to the flowers. It was thoughts such as these that inspired the poet to write:

Sun of my soul, Thou Savior dear, It is not night if Thou be near;
O, may no earth-born cloud arise To hide Thee from my wondering eyes.

Truly, we can sing with the unknown poet: "Fair are the meadows, Fair are the woodlands, Robed in flowers of blooming spring: Jesus is fairer, Jesus is purer; He makes our sorr'wing spirit sing!"

A Room in Our Heart Called Mercy

Be ye therefore merciful, as your Father also is merciful. Luke 6:36

Over the beautiful arched doorway of a large hospital the following words are engraved in white stone so that all who enter may read and ponder: "Mercy is a room in our hearts for the misery of others."

Mercy is, as it were, a special room in our heart which is stored with genuine concern for others. In the Greek language both mercy and pity are synonymous. The same word is frequently used when describing the attitude of God toward fallen sinners. Paul writes to the Corinthians, for instance, "Blessed be God, even the Father of our Lord Jesus Christ, the Father of *mercies* and the God of all comfort."

Jesus uses the same word when He tells us in the text quoted above: "Be ye therefore merciful, as your Father in heaven is merciful." We are to follow the example of His Father.

While mercy can include a wide spectrum of meanings, in this particular instance the Savior is asking us to be slow to judge and quick to forgive. In this department of our Christian lives how difficult we frequently find it to locate that room marked "mercy"! How often we must fight the temptation to show spite, vindictiveness, bitterness, or anger! Ever and again we must pray for the Spirit-given graces included in the simple word mercy, namely, slowness to judge and readiness to forgive.

By nature we are *quick to judge* and *slow to forgive*. Jesus tells us that this is the very opposite of mercy. Hearts that have been warmed by the love of God, revealed to us through Jesus Christ, our Savior, are to reflect His love in their dealings with their fellowmen. He who took divine pity on us expects us to reach out to our fellowman in a love and kindness which reflects his own. How appropriate the prayer:

> Oh, let me never speak What bounds of truth exceedeth;
> Grant that no idle word From out my mouth proceedeth;
> And, then, when in my place I must and ought to speak,
> My words grant pow'r and grace, Lest I offend the weak.

A Debt That Was Canceled

Blotting out the handwriting . . . that was against us, . . . nailing it to His cross.
Colossians 2:14

It is said that at one time Henry Clay owed $10,000 to a bank in Kentucky. A number of sympathetic friends, knowing that Mr. Clay was troubled over his inability to pay, secretly raised the money and quietly paid off the debt. When Mr. Clay later came to the bank to discuss his large indebtedness, the cashier startled him with the statement: "Mr. Clay, you don't owe us anything!"

"Why, how am I to understand you?" "Well," said the cashier, "a number of your friends have contributed and paid off your debt for you—you don't owe this bank a dollar." Tears rushed into Mr. Clay's eyes, and, unable to speak, he walked away. His heart was overwhelmed by the joy of a great deliverance—deliverance from a crushing debt.

What a striking illustration of the central fact of the Christian faith! "And you, being dead in your sins," says Paul, "hath He quickened . . . having forgiven you all trespasses; blotting out the handwriting that was against us, . . . nailing it to His cross." That handwriting was the debt of unforgiven sin which stood against us in the court of heaven.

But that handwriting is now gone, destroyed, put aside, blotted out. Christ has paid the debt. At the foot of the cross on Calvary lies the handwriting that had been against us, its accusations forever covered by the redeeming blood of Christ. From heaven comes the divine acknowledgement: *"Paid in full! Forgiven through the Savior!"*

Contemplating this "heavenly transaction" which freed us forever from a debt we could not pay we confess and exult:

My soul looks back to see The burden Thou didst bear
When hanging on the cursed tree And knows her guilt was there.
Believing, we rejoice To see the curse remove;
We bless the Lamb with cheerful voice
And praise His bleeding love. Amen.

Is It Enough To Be "Religious"?

So Paul . . . said: "Men of Athens, I perceive that in every way you are very religious." *Acts 17:22 RSV*

Is it enough merely to be "religious"? We find a dramatic answer to that question in the Scripture reading suggested above. The apostle Paul was visiting the city of Athens, and as he walked along its streets he saw hundreds of statues of gods and goddesses and as many altars on which the "faithful" brought their sacrifices. All were symbols of pagan worship.

When he came to the part of the city where the students of art, literature and philosophy were wont to gather, he ascended Mars Hill, and began to speak: "Men of Athens, I perceive that in every way you are very religious. For as I passed along and observed the objects of your worship, I found also an altar with this inscription, 'To an *unknown* God.'"

With great skill and tact he then proceeded to tell them of the God whom they can *know,* namely, the God of "every nation" who had revealed Himself in the life and death and resurrection of His Son. He pointed them away from their gods of silver, gold, and precious metals to the God and Father of all men whose love embraces all. In other words, he preached the Gospel which God had commissioned him to proclaim.

That many understood what he was saying is evident from their reaction, for we are told that some laughed out loud. But Paul had been faithful to his trust. Merely being religious is not enough. The object of our worship must always be "the God and Father of our Lord and Savior, Jesus Christ" who has called us to be His children through the operation of His Holy Spirit.

How about us? Are we merely "religious"—going through the motions prescribed by rituals, living lives that merely measure up to the requirements of respectability? Or are we really the children of God, trusting daily in His mercy revealed to us by Jesus Christ, our Savior and Redeemer?

Lord, let me never be content with mere "religion." Rather, let my faith be rooted firmly in Jesus Christ, my Lord, and let it show itself in a truly Christian life. Amen.

The Christian and Moral Dilemmas

Who can understand his errors? Cleanse Thou me from secret faults. Psalm 19:12

Making a moral decision is not always a matter of choosing between black and white. Frequently it is a matter of choosing betwen two shades of gray and not being sure which is the darker. This is the thought which lies behind the words of King David quoted above. He admits that there were times when he had sinned without knowing it and prays the Lord to forgive all of his unintentional transgressions.

In the book *The Assisi Underground* a Franciscan priest admits that he had become "a cheat and a liar"—all in the name of God. What had he done? During the final months of World War II the Germans had occupied much of northern Italy and had begun rounding up all Italian Jews for transportation to the gas chambers in Germany. Almost daily frightened Jews knocked on the door of the Franciscan monastery seeking refuge. What was the priest to do? After earnest prayer, he took the hapless refugees in and kept them in secret quarters.

When German officers knocked at the door of the monastery, as they did at frequent intervals, asking if any Jews had been there, the priest had to make a moral decision. He could tell the truth and turn his secret "guests" over to their sworn enemies, thus insuring their death by becoming partners in a fracture of the Fifth Commandment, or he could tell a lie, thus sparing their lives, but breaking the Eighth Commandment. Truly, a moral decision.

What is the Christian to do when forced to make a decision for which he finds no clear guidance in Scripture? We are to turn to God in earnest prayer, and then we are to act both out of *awe* for His holy will and out of *love* for Him and for our fellow men and women. Being human, we will make mistakes. But we know that we have a gracious God who will forgive those mistakes for Jesus' sake. Each of us might well make David's prayer our own:

Who can understand his errors? Cleanse Thou me from secret faults. In Jesus' name. Amen.

Why Me, Lord?

I am not worthy of the least of all the steadfast love and all the faithfulness which Thou hast shown to Thy servant. *Genesis 32:10 RSV*

Ordinarily we hear the title of this meditation "Why me, Lord?" as a cry of desperation—as a cry of complaint against the Lord in the midst of calamity or adversity. "Lord, why *me?*"

In these few moments we propose to look upon these words not as an expression of *despair* but rather as a paean of *praise* and *thanksgiving.* Listen to Jacob on his way back to his father's house after spending many years with his Uncle Laban. He had left home with nothing but his staff and now he was returning, not only much wiser but also a very wealthy man.

What are his thoughts as he journeys homeward? His heart spills over with the well known words: "O God of my father Abraham, I am not worthy of the least of all the steadfast love and all the faithfulness which Thou has shown to Thy servant." He continues with a recital of all that God had done for him.

His words are permeated with a feeling of unworthiness. In effect, he is saying: *"Why me, Lord?* As I look back across the years, I must confess I did nothing to deserve Thy blessing. It was Thy steadfast love and faithfulness that did it all!"

Cannot the same be said of us who have been the recipients of God's grace and blessing through Jesus Christ our Lord? The next time disappointment or adversity strikes in our lives, let us recall the abundance of blessings God has already showered upon us from early childhood even until now—through no merit of our own. Even though the hurt be deep and the pain be real, the "why me?" of pain will be overshadowed by the "why me?" of His abundant, steadfast love and mercy—all unmerited, all undeserved. Even on his darkest day, the believer still says: "Why me? I am unworthy of all Thy kindnesses to me!"

When all Thy mercies, O my God, My grateful heart surveys,
Transported by the view, I'm lost In wonder, love, and praise.

The Quiet Understanding

Where two or three are gathered together in My name, there am I in the midst of them. Matthew 18:20

We have entitled this meditation "The Quiet Understanding," because it is based on a quiet promise the Savior made to His disciples— the full truth of which they did not understand until some years later; indeed, the full truth of which even we today are so prone to forget.

The "understanding" was that wherever two or three of His disciples would gather in His name, He would be in the midst of them. Is that still true today? Yes, it is. But what does it mean to "gather in His name"?

It means to come together, as believing Christians, to invoke His presence, to act in His spirit, in order to accomplish His purposes. Whether it be a Christian family or a Christian congregation, if we are gathered "in His name," we have the quiet understanding that He is with us—not as a spectator but as a participant, as both a guide and counselor, as the *Validator* of every action undertaken in His name.

How often must we admit that even though we have memorized the Savior's promise "where two or three are gathered together in My name ..." and have accepted its truth in theory, we have completely forgotten it when it came to practice?

In family groups, in committee or congregational meetings, or at church conventions, having invoked His presence, how often haven't we comported ourselves very much like Simon Peter outside the high priest's palace, saying in effect to the world about us: "I never knew the Man!" Yes, how often has Christ been present in our gathering—but only as a stranger? Lord, forgive us wherever we have sinned, and be with us always as our Savior and our Friend.

Abide, O dearest Jesus Among us with Thy grace;
Thy love protect and guide us Lest we to sin give place. Amen.

Life Must Be Altered

Not everyone that saith unto Me, Lord, Lord, shall enter into the kingdom of heaven. *Matthew 7:21*

Henry Melchior Muehlenberg, a pioneer of American Lutheranism in the 1700s, had a habit of speaking very frankly and forthrightly. Of a certain parishioner he said, she "sticks to the Unaltered Augsburg Confession with an unaltered heart and mind."

We can do very much the same with the Holy Scripture. We can praise it, quote it, defend it, and then live as though we had never heard its message. Our lives can be a complete contradiction of our profession. That is why the Savior warned: "Not everyone that saith unto Me, Lord, Lord, shall enter into the kingdom of heaven." Christianity is more than "saying"; it is believing and doing.

St. James was very outspoken on this subject throughout his epistle. A modern paraphrase of one of his passages would read: "If anyone hears the Word of God, no matter how devoutly, and then does nothing about it, he is as foolish as a man who looks into a clean glass mirror, sees a dirty smudge on his face, says 'Oh, my!' and then goes merrily on his way doing nothing to remove the smudge—in fact, dismissing the whole thing from his mind" (James 1:22-24). The mirror will have done its duty, but the man will still have a dirty face.

St. Paul wrote to the Christians in Corinth: "If any man be in Christ, he is a new creature [literally, a new 'creation,' wrought by the Spirit of God]; old things are passed away; behold, all things are become new." Or, as Martin Luther said, the baptized Christian should "daily come forth and arise a *new* man."

He who has put his faith in Christ cannot go on living with "an unaltered heart and mind." He has a *new* heart and a *new* mind which express themselves in a *new* life. How is our performance in this respect? Have we translated our faith into action day by day?

God grant that we may daily put our faith into action, for Jesus' sake. Amen.

Walking in Wisdom

Walk in wisdom toward them that are without, . . . Let your speech be always with grace. *Colossians 4:5-6*

Paul wrote the above admonition to his recent converts in Colossae, a city in Asia Minor. That he expected them to do their best at all times to behave as Christians goes without saying. But here he has a very special situation in mind.

How were they to comport themselves in the company of "outsiders"? In the larger context of the above passage he stresses particularly three points.

First, whenever they came into close contact with unbelievers, they were to "walk in wisdom." They were to "use their heads," as we would say today, being very careful lest by their behavior they make the Christian "way" seem unattractive.

Second, they were to "redeem the time." That means that they were to make full use of every opportunity, when in the company of the unconverted, for tactful but *effective,* clear-cut Christian witnessing, both by word and deed.

Third, their speech was always to be be flavored with grace, that is, they were to speak kindly, pleasantly, as a group of joyful people who were eager to share the good news of God's love which they had found in Jesus Christ, their Savior.

Suppose Paul's admonition were written to us (as, in a very definite sense, it *is*). Are our approaches to the unconverted always characterized by wisdom, by common sense, by seeking out the proper opportunity?

Above all, do we speak the good news as *good* news? As individuals, as congregations, as a church body, do we present our witness to the unbelieving world in a manner that is "flavored with grace," a manner that is pleasant, gracious, and winsome? We must resist the temptation to spread the Gospel with clenched fists and remember that it is the warm heart, the kindly voice, and the open hand that enables our "speech to be *endowed with grace.*"

Lord, grant me the grace always to speak Your Word in love. Amen.

Attuning Our Hearts to Lent

Take heed, therefore, how ye hear. *Luke 8:18*

Mr. Brown had just stepped from a crowded drugstore into a telephone booth. He had been told that an urgent message awaited him at home.

But try as hard as he would, he could not distinguish the voice at the other end of the line, and the message was lost in the clatter and the clamor of the crowded store.

Finally, he managed to catch one sentence. "John, dear," said the voice in the telephone, "please close the door behind you." He had forgotten to close the door to the booth, and the noises of the drugstore had drowned out the distant voice from home.

During these weeks, as we step from the busy, noisy world of everyday life into the hush and quiet of the Lenten season, let us make sure that we have closed the doors behind us. Let us close the door to all that would distract or disturb us in our solemn contemplation of the wondrous Lenten theme.

There is a message in the sacred Lenten season, a message from the Father's heart to ours. It is a message of peace and pardon, of courage and strength, of life and hope, through the wounds and death of Jesus Christ, our Savior.

It is up to us to make sure that we have *closed the doors* against the busy world that would deprive us of that message. It will be up to us to *open our hearts* to Him who went from Gethsemane to Golgotha so that we might go from earth to heaven. How appropriate the prayer:

Jesus, I will ponder now On Thy holy passion;
With Thy Spirit me endow For such meditation.
Grant that I in love and faith May the image cherish
Of Thy suff'ring, pain, and death That I may not perish.

Grant that I Thy Passion view With repentant grieving
Nor Thee crucify anew By unholy living.
How could I refuse to shun Every sinful pleasure
Since for me God's only Son Suffered without measure?

The Lenten Call

Come unto Me, all ye that labor and are heavy laden, and I will give you rest.
Matthew 11:28

What a gracious invitation, and what a priceless promise! Unfortunately, like other precious words of Christ, this invitation is in danger of becoming just another "Bible passage,"—"verse" number 539 on page 145 of our catechism.

But it is infinitely *more* than that. Let us during these Lenten days lift these words once more from the pages of our catechism and place them back upon the gracious lips of Him who spoke them.

But who was it that spoke them? Who was it that issued this incredible invitation and made this incredible promise? A grand offer from a penniless beggar means very little. A $1000 check on an overdrawn account means nothing. Did the One who made the offer have the power to fulfill it?

Thank God, He did! He still does. It was Jesus, the eternal Son of God, to whom was given "all power in heaven and in earth," who said: "Come unto Me, . . . and I will give you rest." It was the very God whom we had offended by our multiplied transgressions and who alone had the power to "forgive and forget" what we had done. It was *He* who called to us, and still calls to us across the years: "Come unto *Me* . . . and I will give you rest."

The word "rest" on the lips of the Savior is an all-encompassing word. It includes complete pardon for all our sins, a safe anchorage in all the storms of life, a quiet refuge from the tormenting anxieties of doubt and fear, and, at last, a quiet haven for weary souls when they reach their journey's end.

It was after he had accepted this invitation of the Savior that Horatius Bonar wrote:

I heard the voice of Jesus say, "Come unto Me and rest;
"Lay down, thou weary one, lay down, thy head upon My breast,"
I came to Jesus as I was, weary and worn and sad;
I found in Him a resting place, and He has made me glad.

Love Beyond Degree

Greater love hath no man than this, that a man lay down his life for his friends. John 15:13

The Bible has often been called God's love letter to man. Indeed, it is. But to recognize it as such one must be sure that he or she is reading it in proper perspective. Just what *is* that perspective?

Perhaps we can illustrate the true Biblical perspective by regarding the Bible as a large wheel with many different spokes, all of them revolving around one hub which holds them all together. That hub is the Gospel of the love of God in Christ Jesus. Do we really appreciate the divine love which permeates the Holy Scripture and which is the heart and center of God's revelation to you and me?

That love was manifested in the person and work of our divine Redeemer. Think for a moment of the immeasurable love that purchased our redemption. Christ surrendered the glories of heaven, endured the miseries of earth, and bore the pains of hell in order that He might bring His enemies to heaven. Was there ever greater love than this?

It was love, pure love, that brought Him from His heavenly throne. It was love, unsearchable love, that impelled Him to fulfill the Law's demands in the place of guilty sinners. It was love, supreme love, that drove Him to the altar of the cross, there to atone for the sins of a world that had spurned His every pleading.

It was this kind of love of which He spoke in His "farewell address" to His disciples on the eve of His crucifixion, when He said: "Greater love hath no man than this, that a man lay down His life for His friends." That love is our daily hope. That love contrived the way of our escape, closed the doors of hell behind us, and opened wide the gates of God's eternal paradise. In the presence of such love we can only bow our heads and pray:

> It was for crimes that I had done He groaned upon the tree;
> Amazing pity, grace unknown, And love beyond degree! Amen.

He Loved Them to the End

Jesus knew that His hour was come that He should depart this world; [and] having loved His own, He loved them to the end. *John 13:1*

A minister was boarding at a farmhouse. The farmer himself was not a Christian, but his wife was. For some time the minister had been waiting for an opportunity to make plain to this farmer the real meaning of Christ's sacrifice on Calvary.

Early one morning the farmer called the minister and said: "I want to show you something in the chicken house." As they entered the coop, they saw a hen sitting in her nest with a brood of little chicks peeping out from under her wings.

"Touch the hen," the farmer said. As the minister put forth his hand to touch the hen, he noticed that she was dead. She had been dead for hours. "Look at the wound in her head," said the farmer. "During the night a weasel came and drained her body of the last ounce of blood, but she never moved from the spot in her nest for fear her little ones might suffer harm."

The minister saw his opportunity to draw a perhaps homely comparison that would be meaningful to his friend. As they walked slowly and thoughtfully back to the farmhouse, the pastor surprised his friend by using the incident they had just witnessed as an illustration of the *love of Christ,* of whom the Scriptures tell us that having loved His own, He loved them to the very end.

On that first Good Friday Christ knew that at any moment He *could* very easily have come down from the cross, but He also knew that beneath the protection of His outstretched arms were the millions whom He had come to save. For them He was prepared to die. Praise God, that included you and me! Having loved His own, He loved us to the very end.

My soul to Thee alone, my Savior I commend.
Thou, Jesus, having loved Thine own, Wilt love me to the end.

Is It I, Lord?

And they were exceeding sorrowful and began every one of them to say unto Him, Lord, is it I? *Matthew 26:22*

Lent is a time of self-examination. It is not enough that, in a general way, we rehearse the account of the suffering and death of the Savior and that we be reminded that He is "the Lamb of God which taketh away the sin of the world."

It is so easy to slip unconsciously into the role of a mere spectator of the entire passion story, never really thinking of ourselves as participants. We accompany the Savior from the Upper Room to Gethsemane, to Pilate, to Herod, back to Pilate, along the Via Dolorosa, and out to Calvary, but we do so through a long-distance lens. We mislead ourselves into believing that the whole event is happening *there*—not *here*.

How important, then, that we bring the whole salvation event into a very close and intimate relationship with our own lives and that we see ourselves as participants in the unfolding, tragic drama. The question of the distraught disciples in the Upper Room will then become our own fear-filled question: *Is it I, Lord?*

We will hear our heart responding: Ah, yes, it is! I have caused Your sufferings in Gethsemane and Your agonies on Calvary. It was *my* sin that caused Your sorrow—*my* pride, *my* selfishness, *my* self-will, *my* disobedience.

I have betrayed You. I have denied You. I have forsaken You. I have mocked You. I have crucified You. O blessed Lord, it was my iniquity which nailed You to the cursed tree. O Lamb of God, You take away the sin of the world, have mercy on me!

> My burden in Thy Passion, Lord, Thou hast borne for me,
> For it was *my* transgression That brought this woe on Thee.
> I cast me down before Thee, Wrath were my rightful lot;
> Have mercy, I implore Thee; Redeemer spurn me not!

Pitfalls of Pride

Though I should die with Thee, yet will I not deny Thee. . . . [a few hours later:] I do not know the man. *Matthew 26:35, 72*

Simon Peter is our brother, and, sad to say, we all take after him very much. We all have a prideful and deceitful heart which is inclined to be just as over-confident and self-satisfied as was his. We all can wax bold and heroic when we are *among people of our own circles.* We all can so easily forget the wisdom of Solomon, who said: "Pride goeth before destruction, and a haughty spirit before a fall." We all can so quickly forget the advice of St. Paul: "Let him that thinketh he stand take heed lest he fall."

But let us profit from Simon Peter's disastrous example. Let us never enter there . . . where we know in advance we will have to deny our Savior. Let us never mingle intimately with the enemies of Christ.

Let us never make a practice, either in our business relationships or in our day-to-day social contacts, of mingling too intimately with those of whom we know in advance that they are the enemies of Christ. We may take every opportunity to witness to them, of course! But remembering the tragic experience of Simon Peter, let us never "risk our souls to warm our bodies."

Our Savior was at great pains to remind His disciples, especially on the night of His betrayal, that although they were *in* the world, they were not *of* the world. They were, in the essential aspects of their lives, *aliens* in a foreign land. They were children of God, citizens of heaven, people with a different life style from many with whom they would come in contact. *This* they could not deny. Of *this* they dare never be ashamed. Are we?

In the hour of trial, Jesus, plead for me,
Lest by base denial I depart from Thee.
When Thou see'st me waver, With a look recall,
Nor for fear or favor Suffer me to fall.

Victory in Surrender

Jesus kneeled down and prayed, saying, Father, if Thou be willing, remove this cup from Me; nevertheless not My will, but Thine, be done. Luke 22:41-42

When our blessed Lord entered the garden of Gethsemane, His soul was deeply troubled. He was "exceeding sorrowful, even unto death.' "And His sweat was, as it were, great drops of blood falling to the ground."

Yet when He leaves the garden only a short time later, we find Him calm and composed, His face resolutely set toward the inevitable death on the cross. The Man who had entered the garden "exceeding sorrowful" leaves it "exceeding strong," unperturbed, refreshed, determined. What had happened in the garden to make this striking difference?

He had reassured Himself of His Father's will. His Father's will was that He die for the sins of the world. To know, with the assurance of heaven, that He was carrying out His Father's will was all He needed to know. In that knowledge there was peace; in that knowledge there was strength.

So it is with us. Each of us has his own Gethsemane which we enter "exceeding sorrowful" and from which we emerge "exceeding strong." Many a mature Christian can attest that the greatest victories of the Christian life are to be found in complete surrender to the Father's will. We may not understand the reason for the cross—the sickness, the sorrow, the bereavement, the disappointment—but once we have recognized it as our *Father's will* and have learned to pray in humble, trusting faith: "Thy will be done," we have exchanged our exceeding sorrow for exceeding strength and joy.

How appropriate, our prayer:

Thy way, not mine, O Lord, However dark it be,
Lead me by Thine own hand; Choose Thou the path for me,
I dare not choose my lot; I would not if I might.
Choose Thou for me, my God; So shall I walk aright.

What Will Ye Give Me?

What will ye give me, and I will deliver Him unto you? Matthew 26:15

"What will ye give me?" This was not the first time in his life that Judas was tempted to ask that question. But it *was* perhaps the last. His greedy love of money had driven him to sell the best Friend he ever had—for 30 paltry pieces of silver.

"What will ye give me?" Must we not admit that we, too, find ourselves asking that question all too often? Looking for personal gain, personal profit, in everything we do? Never satisfied, always reaching out for more, always thinking, always asking the same old question: *"What will ye give me?"*

A young man once asked his grandfather: "When is a man rich enough, when he has $10,000?" "No," replied the elderly gentleman. "20,000?" asked the young man. "No," said the grandfather. "$100,000?" "No." "$500,000?" "No."

"Well," said the young man, "when *is* a man rich enough?" "When he has a little more than he has now, and that is *never*," replied the old man gravely.

Judas wanted to have a "little more" than he had then, and what a tremendous, tragic difference that little more made.

Even the best of Christians must beware of the insidious sin of covetousness, of the inordinate love of money. There is nothing wrong in wanting to get ahead, but there is very much wrong with succumbing to the lure of uncontrollable ambition. Unconsciously, we can find ourselves standing before the altar of the dollar sign instead of kneeling at the foot of the cross of Christ, our Savior. Well might we pray:

> Oh, let me with all men, As far as in me lieth,
> In peace and friendship live. And if Thy gift supplieth
> Great wealth and honor fair, Then this refuse me not,
> That naught be mingled there Of goods unjustly got.

Friend!

And Jesus said unto Judas: Friend, wherefore art thou come? Matthew 26:50

Did you catch the full force of that one-syllable word "friend"? If ever the full sweetness and tender yearning of the Savior's Gospel invitation was pressed into one little word, it was pressed into that little word "friend" that night in the garden of Gethsemane.

The holy, sinless Son of God speaks to one of the most despised characters ever to be named in Holy Scripture—and He calls him "friend." He knew full well that Judas had betrayed Him for 30 pieces of silver. He knew that the kiss He had just received from the betrayer's lips had delivered Him into the hands of His tormentors. He knew all this and more, and yet He calls him "friend"!

> Oh lovely attitude! He stands
> With melting heart and laden hands;
> O matchless kindness! And he shows
> This matchless kindness to His foes!

In this last fleeting moment He would let Judas know that in spite of his treachery, in spite of his black cruelty, Jesus is *still* his Friend, still eager to forgive him, if he will but return in penitence and faith.

Have *we* perhaps betrayed our Lord by behavior unworthy of our calling? Have we become guilty of some base sin, some wickedness which weighs heavily upon our conscience? Have we despaired of ever finding peace and pardon? Remember: Jesus, the *Friend of Judas,* is also our Friend!

> But will He prove a Friend indeed? He will; the very Friend you need;
> The Friend of sinners—yes, 'tis He With garments dyed on Calvary.

Whenever we have betrayed our Savior by sinful behavior, may we hear His loving voice still pleading: "Friend." Let us then return in penitence and faith.

Let These Go Their Way

If Ye seek Me, let these go their way. *John 18:8*

We have here a touching scene, indeed. The captive Savior, in one of the darkest moments of His life, stretching forth His protecting arm over His trembling disciples and saying to the band of ruffians: "If ye seek Me, *let these go their way."*

Our blessed Lord had come into the world to take His stand between us and our fiercest foes. Sin, death, and the power of the devil were the enemies which had come out against us "with lanterns and torches and weapons" to drag us into judgment. Against such an array of spiritual power we poor sinful mortals were helpless to prevail.

But in the Garden of Gethsemane, and especially on the cross on Calvary, our Savior stepped between us and the powers of darkness, received their arrows into His own body, and said: *"Let these go their way!"*

He still does the same today. When our guilty memories rise up to haunt us, when our conscience holds up our sin-stained record before us and threatens us with fearful judgment, our Savior steps between the piercing arrows of our conscience and our trembling heart and says: "Ye seek Me, let this man go his way!" What a soul-sustaining comfort! With such a loving Savior no evil can befall us.

Indeed, this is one of the primary functions the Bible ascribes to our Redeemer—He is our eternal Go-Between. He wards off the fierce attacks of our spiritual enemies or absorbs the fury of their fiery darts. Even of our final enemy, death, Paul exclaims: "Thanks be to God, who giveth us the victory *through our Lord Jesus Christ."* It is always Christ, our heaven-sent Go-Between, who protects us from the final enemy. Hence we pray:

> Lord Jesus, who dost love me, Oh, spread Thy wings above me
> And shield me from alarm! Though Satan would devour me,
> Let angel guards sing o'er me: "This child of God shall meet no harm."

One Man—for the People

And Caiaphas, the high priest, said unto them: it is expedient that one man should die for the people and that the whole nation perish not. *John 11:49-50*

These words were spoken by one of the greatest scoundrels ever to disgrace the pages of history—the high priest Caiaphas. Yet they were placed on those most unlikely lips by God Himself, for they contain a prophecy of the true purpose of the suffering and death of Jesus Christ, our Savior.

"One Man—for the people!" What an excellent summary of the earthly ministry of our Lord! What a clear statement of the purpose of His innocent death! Christ died for the people, in their stead, as their Substitute, the Righteous for the unrighteous.

The prophet Isaiah had written: "The Lord hath laid on Him the iniquity of us all." St. Paul writes: "God hath made Him to be sin for us who knew no sin, that we might be made the righteousness of God in Him." Again: "God commendeth His love toward us in that, while we were yet sinners, Christ died for us." And clearest of all: "Christ died for the *ungodly.*" These are clear and simple statements of the purpose of our Savior's suffering. "One Man—for the people."

Over and over again the Bible tells us that Christ died *for us,* in our place, as our ransom, our Redeemer. Let us find daily comfort in the remembrance of this blessed truth. He loved me and gave Himself *for me!*

> Alas! and did my Savior bleed, And did my Sovereign die?
> Would He devote that sacred head For such a worm as I?
>
> It was for crimes that I had done He groaned upon the tree;
> Amazing pity, grace unknown, And love beyond degree!

A Comfortable Christianity

But Peter followed Him afar off. Matthew 26:58

While his Lord was being led through the city streets, hooted and jeered and mocked, we read that Simon Peter "followed Him *afar off.*" Skipping from pillar to post, under the blanket of night, just far enough behind the procession to escape their notice, Peter managed to keep a safe distance between himself and the captors of his Master.

His love for the Savior demanded that he *follow,* but his love for himself, his comfort and convenience, demanded that his following be done "afar off." He would follow, but at a distance.

How often we have done the same. Dear Lord, of course I will follow You—but not now; my friends are looking. Dear Lord, of course I will follow You—but not too close. There are still some things which I must keep between You and me: my love of pleasure, my love of self, my love of ease, my desire for social gain and personal advancement. O Lord, let it never be said that I am not eager to follow You, but let me do it *comfortably.*

Let us be done with a purely comfortable Christianity. Let us be done with holding back, with lingering on the very edge of darkness, not quite ready for the light. With the Spirit's aid, we are to make our way to the *front* of the procession, to take our stand with Christ, and, in spite of scorn or ridicule or persecution, to say to friend and foe alike: I am this Man's disciple.

> Jesus, I my cross have taken, All to leave and follow Thee;
> Destitute, despised, forsaken, Thou from hence my All shalt be.
> Perish every fond ambition, All I've sought or hoped or known;
> Yet, how rich is my condition! God and heav'n are still my own.

The Recalling Look

And Peter [denying that he knew Christ] said: Man, I know not what thou sayest. And immediately . . . the cock crew. And the Lord turned and *looked* upon Peter. *Luke 22:60-61*

Scarcely had the curses fallen from Peter's lips when, as our text tells us, "the Lord turned and looked upon Peter." Oh, what a look that must have been! What crushing *Law* it must have preached to the wayward heart of Simon Peter. What bitter memories it must have brought to his wretched soul.

The sound of the cock crowing reminded him of the warning words of Christ, spoken to him earlier that evening: "This night, before the cock crow, thou shalt deny me three times." What a craven coward he had been, and what a despicable disciple!

But more! The look was also the sweetest *Gospel* ever told. It reassured Peter that the more miserable he was, the more he needed this Savior of his. It reassured him that Christ's loving invitation, "Come unto Me," still held good for him. The tender, loving eye of his familiar Friend promised mercy and forgiveness. There was light and love, tenderness and compassion in that look, even for the man who had so cowardly denied Him.

How often in the midst of some sinful act, or after an unkind or indecent word has fallen from our lips, have we felt that the Lord suddenly turned and *looked upon us!* How often have His accusing eyes burned deep wounds into our conscience! And how often have those same eyes reassured us of peace and pardon, of mercy and forgiveness through faith in His atoning blood!

There come times in the lives of all believers when we intentionally fall into sin, and our heart cries out for the assurance of forgiveness through Jesus Christ our Savior. In all such moments may we feel His loving look upon us and pray:

> In the hour of trial, Jesus, plead for me,
> Lest by base denial I depart from thee.
> When Thou see'st me waver, *With a look recall,*
> Nor from fear or favor Suffer me to fall.

His Blood Be on Us

Then answered all the people and said [to Pilate]: His blood be on us and our children. *Matthew 27:25*

There are two ways of understanding and applying the words quoted in our text above. On the lips of those who first spoke them, they were a call for God's punishment upon themselves and all future generations if the deed they were about to perpetrate was wrong.

But did you ever think of it? This horrid shriek of Christ's enemies could, without changing a word, be the fervent prayer of Christ's *friends*, especially of Christian parents who are eager about the spiritual welfare of their families: "His blood be upon *us* and on *our children!*"

The redeeming blood of Christ is the theme song of the Bible, the scarlet thread that runs throughout the Scriptures. John tells us: "The *blood* of Jesus Christ, His Son, cleanseth us from all sin." Peter says: "Ye were redeemed by the precious *blood* of Christ." Paul writes: "In whom we have redemption through His *blood.*" The Savior Himself says: "This is My *blood,* which is shed for the remission of sins."

We pray that this cleansing and forgiving power of the blood of Christ may be "upon us and on our children." We pray that His blood may avail for us before the judgment seat of God. "Abel's blood for vengeance Pleaded to the skies, But the blood of Jesus For our pardon cries."

In the blood of Christ lies our only hope. He died for us that we might live with Him. His death is the open door to heaven—for us and for our children.

> Dear dying Lamb, Thy precious blood
> Shall never lose its power
> Till all the ransomed Church of God
> Be saved to sin no more.

What Is Truth?

Pilate said unto him: What is truth? *John 18:38*

The world has found no satisfactory answer to Pilate's question: "What is truth?" In fact, with the emergence of modern mass advertising over radio, television, and the daily press, with each advertiser asserting the superiority of his own product over that of his competitor, even our children have learned to take all this talk about "truth" with a grain of salt. For them an "innocent skepticism" has become a way of life.

How infinitely more dangerous this latent skepticism becomes when we begin to transfer it to matters of the soul. In a world that has placed a question mark after almost everything our fathers and mothers believed in, have we been able to hold firmly to the Rock of our salvation and to say: *"This is the truth!"*?

There is the constant danger that we unconsciously drift into the frame of mind of Pontius Pilate and say that truth in matters of religion is merely a matter of opinion—a toss-up, a flip of a coin, a matter of choosing the right "parents." If you are born into one church, that church is true for you; if you are born into another, you may be sure its truth is "true enough."

What a tragic deception! Truth is still true, and error is still false, no matter where we find it. The Savior says: "If ye continue in *My* Word . . . ye shall *know* the truth." Again He says: "I am the Way, the Truth, and the Life." And again: "To this end was I born . . . That I should bear witness to the *truth.*"

Above all, let us never for a moment doubt this central truth of Scripture: Jesus Christ, the eternal Son of God, came down from heaven to suffer and die for us, that we may dwell with Him forever in the eternal mansions of His Father.

To Pilate's question: "What is truth?" our confident reply must always be: "Christ is truth. He is the Way, the Truth, and the Life, both now and forever."

Lord Jesus, whatever the world may say, may You always be the Way, the Truth, and the Life for me. Amen.

The Dying Thief

Verily I say unto thee, today shalt thou be with Me in paradise. Luke 23:43

Of the few persons whom the Scriptures specifically tell us are now in heaven, one was a *criminal!* It was to a man who had misspent his life in sin and shame but who in his dying moment had come to faith in the Redeemer that the Savior opened wide the doors to His Father's house and said: "Verily I say unto thee, today shalt thou be with Me in paradise." There was room, even for this dying thief, in the Father's house above.

Heaven *is* like that. Its mansions are peopled *not* with those who in this life paraded as models of piety and virtue while spurning the Savior's mercy, but with the vast unnumbered throng of converted dying thieves, penitent publicans, and those, both great and small, who have come "out of great tribulation and have washed their robes and made them white in the blood of the Lamb."

Beneath the cross on Calvary's hill there is mercy and pardon for all—even for the dying thief. What a comfort to know that *his* Savior is *our* Savior! What a blessed assurance to know that the same blood which availed for him will avail for us. "The blood of Jesus Christ, His Son, cleanseth *us* from all sin."

There are those who are offended by the hymnwriter's words, "There is a fountain filled with blood," but to us these graphic words are the poet's supreme endeavor to express the inexhaustible nature of our Lord's atoning love. Hence we sing:

> There is a fountain filled with blood Drawn from Immanuel's veins,
> And sinners plunged beneath that flood Lose all their guilty stains.
>
> The dying thief rejoiced to see That fountain in his day;
> And there have I as vile as he, Washed all my sins away!

Let us thank God that the same atoning blood that opened the doors of paradise for the penitent thief still avails for us, sinners though we are.

The Other Thief

And one of the malefactors railed on Him. Luke 23:39

A flippant young man who was leading a life of open sin had just been admonished by a Christian friend. Unimpressed, he shrugged his shoulder and answered with a smirk: "I've still got a lot of time for religion. Think of the thief on the cross!"

"Which one?" asked the friend most earnestly.

Yes, which one? There was another thief. For him the 11th hour was too late. Rejecting the Son of God with his dying breath, the other thief received no benediction from the Savior's lips. Out of the blackness of the eternity that was opening up before him there came, as it were, the frightful voice of doom: "Verily, I say unto thee, today shalt thou be with *me* in hell."

Yes, indeed! "Which one?" Which thief was the frivolous young man taking as his model when he gave his flippant reply, the one who was headed for paradise or the one who was headed for perdition? Too often the careless and unthinking sinner follows the example of the man who had turned his back on Christ and had set his face toward the regions of outer darkness.

As for us, let us follow the example of *neither*. While we rejoice in the mercy of God, which makes possible even a deathbed repentance, let us not trifle with God's mercy. "Now is the accepted time. Now is the day of salvation." Let us accept the dying Lamb on the cross as our Savior and Redeemer *now!*

May we never forget that for us our eternal salvation is always a matter of *today!*

> Today Thy mercy calls us To wash away our sin,
> However great our trespass, Whatever we have been.
> However long from mercy Our hearts have turned away,
> Thy precious blood can cleanse us And make us white today!

Lord, I pray, show me the mercy You showed the penitent thief. Amen.

Gambling on Golgotha

And for my vesture they did cast lots. John 19:24

What possible relevance can there be between a group of Roman soldiers playing a game of dice on Calvary that first Good Friday and the deepening of our devotional life today?

Perhaps we should first review the picture and etch it deeply in our hearts. With the divine plan of redemption reaching its climax only a few feet away, we see a gambling game going on within the very shadow of the cross. Utterly oblivious to what a tremendous event was transpiring on that cross at that very moment, a handful of soldiers went about their routine business of casting lots for what (for the moment) seemed a most important prize—the Savior's seamless vesture.

If only they had stopped their game just briefly—just long enough to look at the Man on the central cross and to try to relate to His unspeakable sorrow—and to ponder the question: Why? Why, O God, why? But, no, their eyes were fixed upon the ground and on the coveted garment.

When we look at the world today, preoccupied with growing national and international problems, or when we look at the life of the average person hurrying up and down the aisles of our department stores, don't we sometimes hope that they would look *up* and see Him who gives meaning to it all. If only, just for a moment, they would cease their meaningless "games" and look into the face of Him whose sorrow-filled eyes are fixed on them.

How about us? In the busyness of our workaday world, do we "Calvary's mournful mountain climb" only to "pass that cross unheeding"? Remember, it is possible to sing the hymns of Lent with our lips while our hearts are immersed in the preoccupations of our daily life. It is possible for us to kneel on the cushioned kneelers in our beautiful sanctuaries while never kneeling, in true repentance and faith, at the foot of the cross. Truly, this is a moment for introspection and self-examination.

Lord, let me never pass Your cross unheeding, forgetting Your tremendous sacrifice. Amen.

Father, Forgive Them!

Then said Jesus, Father, forgive them, for they know not what they do. Luke 23:34

Think for a moment. What do we see and hear? The Son of God, nailed to a cross, blood streaming down His cheeks and hands and feet, raising His voice above the tumult of His tormentors and praying to heaven: "Father, forgive them!" Here is a picture of compassion the likes of which the world has never seen.

But we have here far more than a picture. We have here an eternal fact of indescribably great significance. He who on Calvary's cross, while dying for the sins of all mankind, exclaimed: "Father, forgive them," still looks down in love upon His believing children and still pleads: "Father, forgive them!"

We are assured of this by the disciple whom Jesus loved. Many years later the beloved John tells the early Christians that as long as the earth stands Christ will always be their Advocate before His Father's throne, pleading "Father, forgive them." He will be their constant "Go-Between" until the day of His glorious return. We are told this in the Scripture reading indicated above.

Why should the Father forgive those who put their trust in Him who died on Calvary's cross? Because He died as their Redeemer, their Savior, their eternal Substitute, "who bore their own sins in His body on the cross" (1 Peter 2:24). The great Sin-Bearer is now the sinner's Spokesman before the majestic God of heaven!

What a marvelous comfort in days of darkness, in hours of doubt and despair, in moments when a heavy sense of guilt oppresses us, to know that we have a Mediator at the Father's throne who still is pleading: "Father, forgive them!"

> He lives to bless me with His love,
> He lives to plead for me above,
> He lives to calm my troubled heart,
> He lives all blessings to impart.

The Son of God

He made Himself the Son of God. John 19:7

Christ's enemies meant it as an accusation when they said: "He made Himself the Son of God." We repeat the same words, but in accents of joy and gladness. He whose sweat was, "as it were, great drops of blood" falling on the garden floor, He who bowed His bleeding head in death on Calvary's cross was, indeed, *the Son of God.*

That is the unsearchable and unspeakable wonder of the Lenten message. The Man on the center cross is the divine Creator, the omnipotent Sustainer, the supreme Controller of the universe. The hands on the cross are the hands of Him who set the sun and moon and stars in motion. Can these things be?

They *must* be! In order to redeem us it was necessary that our Savior be true God. The blood of no mortal could ever have paid the price. But "the blood of Jesus Christ, *God's Son,* cleanseth us from all sin." As the Son of God, the Savior was able to overcome sin, death, and the power of the devil *in our stead* and to bring a sacrifice which was sufficient to purchase our redemption.

His enemies may have shouted in derision: "He *made* Himself the Son of God," but the Roman centurion, standing at the foot of the cross, seeing the noonday darkness and feeling the earth quaking beneath his feet, smote his breast and (not sure of all the implications of the moment) whispered those words of dawning faith: "Truly, this *was* the Son of God!"

The object of our Lenten devotion, then, is no mere man. He is, in very truth, the omnipotent Son of the omnipotent God. Of Him we sing in humble adoration:

O sorrow dread! Our God is dead! But by His expiation
Of our guilt upon the cross Gained for us salvation.

Yes, it was, indeed, the Son of God who died on Calvary's cross, and through His death He rendered heaven's payment for human sin—yours and mine. For that we praise Him evermore!

According to the Scriptures

Christ died for our sins according to the Scriptures. *1 Corinthians 15:3*

When we read the above passage, we must remember that Paul is speaking—not of the completed Scriptures, as we have them in our Bible—but of the Old Testament Scriptures. Christ died for our sins, he says, in fulfillment of the Old Testament prophecies.

Isaiah, for instance, had written hundreds of years before Christ's crucifixion: "Surely, He hath borne our griefs and carried our sorrows; yet we did esteem Him stricken, smitten of God, and afflicted. But *He* was wounded for *our* transgressions, *He* was bruised for *our* iniquities; the chastisement [which brought about] *our peace* was upon *Him,* and with *His* stripes *we* are healed." (Read also Acts 8:26-35.)

Again and again in the story of our Savior's passion we read the recurring refrain: *that it might be fulfilled!* The great drama of Gethsemane and Golgotha was but the fulfillment of a pattern which had been decreed by the Holy Trinity in ages past.

On the first Easter Sunday we hear the risen Savior speaking to the disciples of Emmaus and showing them how according to the Scriptures it was necessary for Him to suffer and die for the sins of the world (cf. Luke 24:25-27). "According to the Scriptures."

What a comfort there lies for us in that thought! Our Savior's death was not a tragic accident, not the unfortunate end of an unfortunate life, but the glorious culmination of the Father's plan to ransom and redeem His wayward children. God had planned it that way. God had willed it that way. God had predicted it that way. Now God carries it out that way. That is what Paul means when he says: "Christ died for our sins *according to the Scriptures.*"

> How firm a foundation, ye saints of the Lord,
> Is laid for your faith in His excellent Word;
> What more can He say than to you He has said
> Who unto the Savior for refuge have fled.

Acquainted with Grief

A man of sorrows and acquainted with grief. *Isaiah 53:3*

A great writer who had lost his wife through death once wrote to a friend who had suffered a similar bereavement. "I have been through it all!" he said. "Nobody knows what it means but those who have been through it."

"Those who have been through it." There is One who has been through *every* sorrow, who has experienced *every* grief, who has felt the piercing pain of *every* agony. The sorrow of forsakenness, the grief of loneliness, the agony of rejected love, of bitter, cruel death—He knows them all, for He has been through them all. Truly, "a man of sorrows and *acquainted with grief.*"

As once more during this Lenten season we make our pilgrimage to Calvary's hill, let us take all of our sorrows, all of our heartaches, all of our dark fears and haunting worries and lay them at the foot of our Savior's cross. He is acquainted with our griefs. He has been through them all. But, thanks be to God, He has overcome them all by the saving, healing power of the miracle of Calvary.

That is what the inspired writer had in mind when he wrote: "Seeing, then, that we have a great High Priest, that is passed into the heavens, Jesus, the Son of God, let us hold fast our profession. For we have not a High Priest which cannot be touched with the feeling of our infirmities; but was in all points tempted like as we are, yet without sin. Let us therefore come boldly unto the Throne of grace, that we may obtain mercy and *find grace to help in time of need.*"

It is to this High Priest, who has already experienced all of our infirmities, who has already borne our griefs and understands our sorrows, that we sing:

Thou, ah! Thou, has taken on Thee Bonds and stripes, a cruel rod;
Pain and scorn were heaped upon Thee, O Thou sinless Son of God!
Thus didst Thou my soul deliver From the bonds of sin forever.
Thousand, thousand thanks shall be, Dearest Jesus, unto Thee.

He Loved Me

I am crucified with Christ; nevertheless I live; yet not I, but Christ liveth in me, and the life which I now live in the flesh I live by the faith of the Son of God who loved me and gave Himself for me. Galatians 2:20

Recently we read of a devoted mother who was so attached to her daughter that when the daughter died, the mother made a daily trip to her grave, regardless of wind and weather. On the 500th day, the mother's lifeless body was found lying across the daughter's grave. Her heart had broken under the constant remembrance of the death of her beloved.

How different is our remembrance of the death of *our* beloved, our Lord and Savior, Jesus Christ. As we take our place each Lenten season at the foot of Calvary's cross, we do so to drink deep of the hope and comfort and assurance which are ours in the death of our Redeemer.

> Come to Calvary's holy mountain,
> Sinners ruined by the Fall;
> Here a pure and healing fountain
> Flows to you, to me, to all,
> In a full perpetual tide,
> Opened when our Savior died.

As we go in spirit to the spot where Jesus died, we bow our heads in silent reverence, and we confess with Paul: "I am crucified with Christ. Nevertheless I live; yet not I, but Christ liveth in me. And the life which I now live in the flesh I live by the faith of the Son of God, *who loved me and gave Himself for me.*"

"He loved me!" O wondrous thought! "He gave Himself for me!" O precious comfort! Because He loved, and because He died, I shall live forever!

> Upon a life I did not live, Upon a death I did not die;
> Another's life, Another's death, I stake my whole eternity!

Lord Jesus, give me the faith to say with the apostle Paul: "The life I now live in the flesh I live by the faith of the Son of God who loved me and gave Himself for me." Amen.

Peace Through His Cross

Having made peace through the blood of His cross. *Colossians 1:20*

Have you perhaps been restless, fearful, guilty or haunted by the lingering sense of some specific sin? Has that sin built a wall of estrangement between you and your God?

If so, you may be sure you have a lot of company—some of it very good company. Think of King David, the "man after God's own heart," who in a weak moment had fallen into the double sin of murder and adultery. Just how utterly miserable he felt, he tells us in Psalm 51:1-15. Think of Simon Peter, the boastful braggart, who when he came to his senses "went out and sobbed bitterly." Or think of Martin Luther who in his earlier years brooded over his personal sins so constantly that at one time he despaired of ever finding a merciful God.

After true repentance and trusting faith in a God of grace, each of these men was soon to find out that their torturing fears were groundless. The forbidding wall of estrangement between them and their heavenly Father had been broken down. Their sins had been "nailed to the cross of Christ." The awesome wall of separation between them and their heavenly Father had been "done away with" in the atoning blood of Jesus Christ, their Savior and Redeemer. With the Christian hymnist they could sing; and we join them as they do:

> If my sins give me alarm And my conscience grieve me,
> Let Thy Cross my fear disarm, Peace of conscience give me.
> Grant that I may trust in Thee And Thy holy Passion;
> If His Son so loveth me, God must have compassion.

Lord Jesus, I thank You for having won forgiveness for me through the blood You shed on the cross. Grant that I may respond to Your love by living a life of Christian virtue. May I always give You love for love, and may I share Your love with all my fellowmen. Amen.

That I Might Be His Own

... Ye are not your own. ... Ye are bought with a price: therefore glorify God in your body, and in your spirit, which are God's. *1 Corinthians 6:19-20*

We are sometimes inclined to think of our religion purely as a negative thing. Christ has redeemed us from sin, death, and the power of the devil, we say. We are right, but that is not all there is to our religion. Christ has saved us not only *from* something, He has also saved us *for* something.

He has purchased us for *Himself.* Martin Luther describes this purchase most beautifully in his explanation of the Second Article of the Apostles' Creed, when he says:

> I believe that Jesus Christ, true God, begotton of the Father from eternity, and also true man, born of the Virgin Mary, is my Lord, who has redeemed me, a lost and condemned creature, purchased and won me from all sins, from death, and from the power of the devil, ... *that I may be His own,* and live under Him in His kingdom, and serve Him in everlasting righteousness, innocence, and blessedness, even as He is risen from the dead, lives and reigns to all eternity. This is most certainly true.

Are we always conscious of whose own we are? God tells us that we are not our own, but that we are *His,* by virtue of the price which His Son has paid for us. Do we live in the full awareness of that ownership? Do we think, speak, dress, and behave ourselves as people whom Christ has bought? Do we "bear in our bodies the marks of the Lord Jesus?" Do we reflect credit on our divine Owner? He expects us to.

Let us use this year's Lenten season to deepen our awareness of our *belonging* to the Lenten Lamb by the right of purchase, by the right of ownership. Let us pray:

> Thy life was given for me, Thy blood, O Lord, was shed,
> That I might ransomed be, And quickened from the dead.
> Thou gavest Thyself for me; I give myself to Thee

The Measure of His Love

As My Father hath loved Me, so have I loved you. *John 15:9*

There is nothing that the human heart craves more deeply than the comfort of understanding *love*. The child finds its assurance in the *love* of its mother. The mother finds her joy in the *love* of her children. The husband finds inspiration in the *love* of his wife, and the wife finds security in the *love* of her husband. All of us hunger and thirst for the deep and abiding satisfaction of knowing that we are *loved*.

How unspeakably comforting, then, to know that we are loved by the Son of God Himself! "As My Father hath loved Me, so have I loved you," He assures us. *"As My Father hath loved Me."* What a measure! The Father had loved His Son with a love beyond expression, a love that transcended human thought and speech. Now Jesus says, *"So have I loved you!"*

In an age which places so much emphasis on the development of self-esteem, self-worth, self-sufficiency, and self-reliance, we are in danger of applying these human attributes also to our personal relationship to God, as though, for some reason, we could stand in His presence on the basis of our own accomplishments.

Although not saying it in so many words, we often live our lives as though we were "the captains of our souls and the masters of our destinies." With such an attitude, we will never appreciate the full measure of God's love for us. With St. Paul, we must first learn to say out of the anguish of our heart: "O wretched man that I am!" Or with the poet we must learn to say: "False and full of sin I am."

Only then will we begin to appreciate the "immeasurable measure" of God's love for us in Christ. Only then will we be able to repeat the fervent prayer:

> Thy love to me, O God, Not mine, O Lord, to Thee,
> Can rid me of this dark unrest And set my spirit free.
> I trust Thy Son, O Lord; I rest on love divine,
> And with unfaltering lip and heart I call this Savior *mine*.

Love for the Unlovable

God commendeth His love toward us in that, while we were yet sinners, Christ died for us. Romans 5:8

"While we were yet sinners," God loved us. Have we ever thought of the wondrous love which those few words reveal? Before you and I love, we usually look for something lovable. We look for something worthy of our love. But God gave His Son to die *"for the ungodly"* (verse 6), "while we were yet sinners." God loved us in our ugliness. He loved us, says St. Paul, even when we were His "enemies." He loved us in our sin.

Yet His love was still righteous. His deep affection for His wayward children is not to be confused with that blindness which often makes earthly parents unconscious of their children's faults. No, His love was rigidly righteous. His love was just, and so the Savior died!

Sin was there! Sin was the gulf of separation between a loving Father and His sinning children. That sin had to be removed. The punishment must be paid, but the sinner must go free.

And so Christ died! He bore the guilt. He bridged the gap. And in view of His atonement the Father now can exercise His love in righteousness—His righteousness in love. Sin has not been merely overlooked, but it has been dealt with, and full payment has been made.

Christ's death is now a fact in history. But its *message* resounds throughout the corridors of time, radiating love and peace and reconciliation to all mankind. Indeed, we stand before that cross and say in humble faith "He died for *me*." It was this central fact of the Christian Gospel that inspired the moving lines of the penitent poet:

I do not come because my soul Is free from sin and pure and whole
And worthy of Thy grace; I do not speak to Thee because
I've ever justly kept Thy laws And dare to meet Thy face.

In Christ alone my trust I place, Come boldly to Thy throne of grace,
And there commune with Thee. Salvation sure, O Lord, is mine,
And, all unworthy, I am Thine, *For Jesus died for me!*

No Matter WHERE You Are

Come unto Me, all ye that labor and are heavy laden, and I will give you rest. *Matthew 11:28*

"Come," says the Savior. But what does He mean by that? How are we to "come"? How are we to find Him? How can we approach Him?

There is no tedious journey to be made. Christ is here, wherever His Word is being read, ready to bestow His peace and rest. Nor is there any long and laborious preparation required. The thief on the cross, within a few hours of his death, could still make effectual application and find admission into that "rest" which Christ had promised. He came to Christ, though fastened to a cross. He came just as he was—and just as he was, Christ accepted him. Remember, there are no exceptions to the gracious invitation of the outstretched arms:

"And *whosoever* cometh, I will not cast him out,"
O patient voice of Jesus, Which drives away all doubt,
Which, tho' we be unworthy Of love so great and free,
Invites us very sinners To come, dear Lord, to Thee.

When the Savior says, "Come," He meets us where we are. He lifts the burden from our shoulder, points us toward a land of glad tomorrows, places His nail-pierced hand in ours, and gently urges, "Come!"

No matter *where* you are—no matter *what* you are—the Savior wants you as you are. His invitation, particularly during this Lenten season, rings with the tenderness and the urgency of the eternal Lover of our souls: "Come unto Me, . . . and I will give you rest!" Therefore

Let not conscience make you linger Nor of fitness fondly dream,
All the fitness He requireth Is to feel your need of Him.

Just as I am, without one plea But that Thy blood was shed for me
And that Thou bidd'st me come to Thee, O Lamb of God, I come, I come. Amen.

Is Ours a "Blood Religion"?

In whom we have redemption through His blood [namely] the forgiveness of sins.
Ephesians 1:7

Some people dismiss the Christian faith as being a "blood religion." Properly understood, we thank God that it *is!* Throughout the Old Testament the shedding of blood (usually of a lamb) was associated symbolically with the salvation of God's people. The lamb died, and God's people went free. That was the significance of every observance of the Passover for some 1,500 years.

St. Paul tells us that, while the Old Testament lambs were symbols, the *substance* came in Jesus Christ. Writing to the Ephesians, he praises the love of God who gave us His only Son "in whom we have redemption through His blood [namely] the forgiveness of sins." He writes the *identical* words to the Colossians, praising God for having provided salvation for all men through the blood of His beloved Son.

Indeed, Paul explicitly relates the atoning significance of Christ's death to the Old Testament lambs when he tells his Corinthian Christians: "Christ, our Passover, is sacrificed for us."

In the New Testament we remind ourselves of this pivotal truth of our faith every time we celebrate the Lord's Supper and repeat the words of Christ Himself: "Drink ye all of it; for this is My blood of the New Testament, which is shed for many for the remission of sins."

The writer of the Letter to the Hebrews points his Jewish readers to the Old Testament rituals of sacrifice and then points them to the death of Christ as the final and complete fulfillment of these rituals. The Old Testament sacrifices merely forshadowed the once and for all saving act toward which they pointed. To paraphrase Hebrews 9:11-13, we hear the writer saying: "If sprinkling the blood of bulls and goats and heifers made the unclean clean, how much more will the blood of Christ cleanse our guilty consciences." In the Old Testament lambs were sacrificed as symbols—

But Christ, the *heavenly* Lamb, Takes all our sins away;
A sacrifice of nobler name And richer blood than they!

God's Love—and Christ's Death

But God commended His love toward us, in that, while we were yet sinners, Christ died for us. *Romans 5:8*

St. Paul tells us that God commended (demonstrated) His love toward us in that Christ died for us. There is a deep and unsearchable thought beneath those words. How can it be that God commended His love toward us in that Christ died? Should we not rather expect the apostle to have said: "Christ commended His love toward us in that Christ died?"

No, there is a glorious significance in the words just as they read. *God* showed His love in Christ's death. God was in that death. God had decreed it. God had planned it. And on Calvary's cross God carried out the decree of His eternal counsel.

The death of Christ in the sinner's stead was an act of free and loving choice on the part of the Father and the Son. God the Father loved us and gave His only Son into death for us. God the Son loved us and gave His life for us. O blessed miracle of divine compassion!

The Revised Standard Version of the Bible presents this miracle of redemption as follows: "While we were yet helpless, at the right time Christ died for the ungodly. Why, one will hardly die for a righteous man; though perhaps for a good man one will dare even to die. But *God* shows His love for us in that, while we were yet sinners, *Christ* died for us."

The death of Christ on Calvary's cross derives its saving power from the fact that He who died was no mere man, but, in deed and in truth, the only begotten Son of the Highest, "very God of very God," together with the Father and the Spirit. Hence St. John could write: "The blood of Jesus Christ, *God's Son*, cleanseth us from all sin." It took the death of the Son for God to atone for the sins of all mankind. That is why Isaac Watts, contemplating the noon-day darkness of Good Friday, wrote:

Well might the sun in darkness hide And shut his glories in
When GOD, THE MIGHTY MAKER, died For man, the creature's sin!

84

Epitaph—In a Word

In Him we have . . . forgiveness. Ephesians 1:7

Almost hidden in a secluded corner of a New York cemetery is a small gravestone polished smooth by the wind and weather of many years. The stone bears no name, nor is there any date inscribed on it.

Still legible on the face of the stone, however, in letters that neither wind nor weather has been able to erase, is one solitary word, "forgiven."

No monument, no obelisk, no vaulted mausoleum marks the final resting place of the anonymous person who lies buried there—only a simple stone—and the single word "forgiven."

Yet could any epitaph be more eloquent, more rich in meaning? The monuments that grace the graves of the great and mighty of this world frequently bear record in large letters of their heroic achievements in war or in peace, so that generations yet unborn may read of their brilliant accomplishments.

But a far greater glory was etched in the stone that marked the humble grave of that nameless person in the New York cemetery. To have found forgiveness at the hand of a merciful God—to have been welcomed home by a gracious Father who is willing to *forgive* because of Jesus Christ, His Son—could any life have ended in greater rapture?

May that epitaph await each of us at our journey's end—pardoned, cleansed, forgiven, redeemed by the precious blood of Jesus Christ who loved us and gave Himself for us.

Yea, Jesus' blood and righteousness
My jewels are, my glorious dress,
In these before my God I'll stand
When I shall reach the heavenly land.

Lord, may I live every day in the full assurance that You have forgiven all my sins through Jesus Christ, my Savior. May that assurance be mine, not only in life but also in death. Let me always find my highest joy in your unbounded grace and mercy. Amen.

The Great Cross-Sharer

I am crucified with Christ. Galatians 2:20

There are two crosses in every Christian's life. The first is the cross on which Christ died for us. The second is the cross on which we die for Christ. The first is a cross for us to *trust*. The second, a cross for us to *carry*.

Perhaps nowhere is the relationship between these two crosses more beautifully expressed than in the well-known words of one of the greatest Christian cross-bearers of all time, the apostle Paul himself: "I am *crucified* with Christ," he says, "nevertheless I live! Yet not I, but Christ liveth in me; and the life which I now live in the flesh I live by the faith of the Son of God, who loved me and gave Himself for me."

Yes, we are crucified with Christ. Not only must we execute a daily, painful crucifixion of our sinful selves, but we must also bear the chafing burden which a sinful world has always placed upon the backs of those who have sought to walk shoulder-to-shoulder with the Master.

But thanks be to God, beside every Christian cross-bearer there stands the omnipotent Cross-Sharer! Paul could bear up under every cross because the life which he now lived he lived "by the faith of the Son of God." In the power and presence of the Son of God he had found that no cross was so great but that he—and Christ—could bear it. "I can do *all* things through Christ who strengthens me," he said. It was no mere maudlin sentimentality that inspired the poet to write:

> Jesus, I my cross have taken, All to leave and follow Thee;
> Destitute, despised, forsaken, Thou from hence my All shalt be.
> Perish every fond ambition, All I've sought or hoped or known;
> Yet how rich is my condition! God and heaven are still mine own.

Have we learned to bear our crosses victoriously? Thank God, we have a Savior who shares our every burden. We can do "all things through Christ who strengthens us."

Repentance—What Is It?

[Jesus is speaking to His unbelieving countrymen and He says:] I tell you, . . . except ye repent, ye shall all likewise perish. *Luke 13:5*

The Greek word translated "repent" in our English Bibles has more than one meaning. In some instances it means merely "feeling sorry" that we have sinned, regretting this or that misdeed we have committed. When used in this sense repentance is more of an attitude or a feeling than it is an action: a feeling of sorrow over what we have done and a wish that we had not done it.

There are many passages, however, in which the very same word means much more. Literally, the word "repentance" means "a complete change of mind," a change so radical that it involves an about face, a turnaround, a total change of direction.

We find the word used in this sense in the Bible text quoted above. A group of His countrymen were trying to test Jesus. They reminded Him of the Galileans whom Pilate had slaughtered while they were worshiping in the temple and then asked: "Were these Galileans sinners above all others?"

Jesus recognized this as just another "catch question" and answered sharply: "I tell you, No! But except ye *repent,* ye shall all likewise perish." Here the word "repent" means more than merely feeling sorry; rather, it means a radical change of mind followed by a radical change of life. It is an urgent call to turn around and to head in the opposite direction.

The exact meaning of the word "repent" will always depend upon the individual context. To the hardened, impenitent sinner it will mean: "Stop! Turn around! Head in a new direction!" To the sensitive Christian it will mean: "Admit your sin and feel sorry that you have offended your God and Lord."

There is a sense in which the Christian life is one of *daily* repentance, daily sorrow for sin and daily assurance of God's grace through Jesus Christ, our Savior. Do we daily repent and reach out for the forgiving grace revealed on Calvary's cross?

Lord God, heavenly Father, I am sincerely sorry for all of my sins and iniquities. Forgive me, Lord, for Jesus' sake. Amen.

If God So Loved Us . . . !

If God so loved us, we ought also to love one another. 1 John 4:11

The world today is desperately in need of love. We cannot pick up a newspaper without reading headlines of strife and dissension, of pride and prejudice, cruel discrimination on the basis of class or color, and growing hostility between the nations of the world. Even in our own little circles how much spite and bitterness still remains.

But why? Why should we, for whom the Savior died, harbor ill will toward any man? The same Savior who loved us loved *him*—whether he is black or white or red or yellow. The same Savior who gave Himself for us gave Himself for *him*—no matter who he is or in what part of the world he lives, or how different his life and customs and language may be from ours. Can we hate any man whom our Savior loved and for whom He died?

The cross of Christ is the melting pot of the ages, where smouldering hatreds, blind prejudices, destructive strifes, and life-long enmities are melted in the all-embracing, warming love of Him who first loved us, and from whom come forth healing and refreshing streams of Christian charity. As the apostle Paul says: "The love of Christ leaves us no choice" (2 Corinthians 5:14 NEB). As John tells us in our text above: "If God so loved us, we ought also to love *one another.*"

Has the cross of Christ broken our proud hearts? Has His love put our bitterness to shame? Since we have found our peace with God in our precious Savior's wounds, have we learned to live at peace with all our brethren? He loved us! Do we love *Him*—and those for whom He died?

Lord of all nations, grant me grace To love all men of every race
And in each fellowman to see My brother, loved, redeemed by Thee.

With Thine own love may I be filled And by Thy Holy Spirit willed,
That all I touch, where'er I be, May be divinely touched by Thee.

A Day of Remembrance

His compassions fail not. They are new every morning. Lamentations 3:22-23

For many of us, especially those in the noonday or sunset of life, on these days when winter begins to lose its grip on nature and the flowers of spring begin to dot the landscape, our thoughts steal back (silently perhaps) to the days of our confirmation—to that solemn season when we pledged lifelong allegiance to the Savior and His church. What have the years done to that little boy in the proud new suit or to that little girl in the new white dress?

The passing years have brought their moments of pure and high devotion, moments when we walked the mountain tops of faith in the company of our blessed Savior. But, alas, they have also brought their moments of trial and temptation, moments when we have stumbled into the paths of sin far from the altars of our solemn promise.

By God's grace we have found forgiveness in the wounds of Christ for every base desertion. By God's grace we have been kept the children of His promise until this very day. By His grace we shall be kept secure unto the end. Let these days, then, be days of remembrance; let them be days of gratitude for His uncounted mercies, days of silent introspection in which, with the Spirit's aid, we strengthen the hallowed ties which bind our hearts to Him.

Surely, as we look back along the days that lie behind us and then look forward to those that lie ahead, we have every reason to pray:

> Thou on my head in early youth didst smile,
> And, though rebellious and perverse meanwhile,
> Thou hast not left me, oft as I left Thee.
> On to the close, O Lord, abide with me.

John Chapter Three, Verse Sixteen

For God so loved the world that He gave His only begotten Son that whosoever believeth in Him should not perish, but have everlasting life. *John 3:16*

There is an old legend that every time a sinner is converted, the angels of heaven enter his or her name in the margin of a large Bible, opposite the Bible passage which brought the individual to faith. It is only a legend, of course, but if it were true, how many millions of the redeemed of all ages would have their names inscribed opposite John chapter 3, verse 16!

Can we ever sufficiently thank God for the healing streams of comfort and hope which have come into our lives through the divine assurance of this jewel of the Scriptures? When trials beset us, when doubts assail us, when our faith would break beneath the burden of the strain, how often has our problem, our difficulty, our doubt, our anxiety dissolved and disappeared before the warmth of this divine assurance, like snow beneath the April sun?!

John 3:16 is God's love note addressed to you and me. It is the short but reassuring message that tells us that, come what may, He is the eternal lover of our souls. So dearly did He love us that He gave the most precious Gift He had, His only begotten Son, in order that we might not perish, but might live with Him in eternal bliss and glory.

In moments of doubt and despair, in moments of fear and anxiety, let our minds find rest in this comforting assurance of our blessed Redeemer. On His promise we can surely stake our all! With the Christian poet we can say:

God so loved the world that He gave His only Son the world to save
That all who would in Him believe Should everlasting life receive.

Be of good cheer, for God's own son Forgives all wrongs that we have done,
And washes us from sin's dread stain That we eternal life may gain. Amen.

Robed in White

And he said to me, These are they which came out of great tribulation, and have washed their robes, and made them *white* in the blood of the Lamb. Therefore are they before the throne of God, . . . and He that sitteth on the throne shall dwell among them. *Revelation 7:14-15*

A missionary to Japan who was in Nagasaki at the time the atomic bomb was dropped reports that "people wearing white were not hurt nearly as much as those who were wearing colors." White garments, it seems, offered an unexplainable protection against the terror which burned all else to a crisp!

God tells us in His Word that there will come a day far more terrible than the bombing of Nagasaki, when "the heavens shall pass away with a great noise, and the elements shall melt with fervent heat," and when "the earth also and the works that are therein shall be burned up."

Thank God that on that day we shall be clothed in white! We who have come to a penitent knowledge of our sins and to saving faith in Jesus Christ, our Savior, have washed our robes and made them *white* in the blood of the Lenten Lamb. We are safe in the arms of Him who "loved us and washed us from our sins in His own blood."

By God's unsearchable grace the spotted garment of our own righteousness has been covered over by the spotless robe of the righteousness of Christ. Through faith in Christ we are *robed in white!* How appropriate and how comforting that we can fold our hands each night and pray:

> Jesus, Thy blood and righteousness
> My beauty are, my glorious dress;
> Midst flaming worlds, in these arrayed,
> With joy shall I lift up my head.
>
> Bold shall I stand on that great Day,
> For who aught to my charge shall lay?
> Before Thy throne in robes of white
> I'll join fore'er the saints in light!

The Gospel According to God

I declare unto you the Gospel . . . how that Christ died for our sins according to the Scriptures; and that He was buried, and that He rose again the third day according to the Scriptures. *1 Corinthians 15:1-4*

There is always danger that a word, when used again and again, gradually loses its meaning. This can happen either unintentionally or by deliberate design. Such a word is the beloved word "Gospel," so dear to the believer's heart.

A professor, when asked for a precise definition of the Scriptural term "Gospel," replied: "The Biblical word 'Gospel' means good news for a bad situation." What a ghastly definition! An aspirin tablet may be good news for a person with a splitting headache, but it surely has nothing to do with the Christian Gospel.

One need not be a learned theologian to know what the Bible means by the word "Gospel." Listen to the apostle Paul as he writes to the Corinthians: "I declare unto you the *Gospel* which I preached unto you . . . how that *Christ died for our sins* according to the Scriptures; and that He rose again the third day according to the Scriptures." Or listen to the apostle Peter's clear words: "You were not redeemed with corruptible things, as silver and gold . . . but with the precious blood of Christ . . . and this is the Word by which the *Gospel* is preached to you."

Spelled out clearly and completely, the primary meaning of the word "Gospel" in Holy Scripture is the good news that our heavenly Father sent His only Son to earth to live, to suffer, to die, and rise again as our divine Redeemer so that, through faith in Him, our sins might be forgiven and we might dwell with Him in eternal bliss and glory. That, and that alone, is the "good news" on which we base our hope.

The Gospel shows the Father's grace, Who sent His Son to save our race,
Proclaims how Jesus lived and died That man might thus be justified. Amen.

Bought—for a Purpose

Ye are bought with a price; therefore glorify God in your body, and in your spirit, which are God's. 1 Corinthians 6:20

A visitor had attended the sessions of a large assembly of churchmen. At the conclusion of the sessions he was asked for his reaction. Weighing his words carefully, he said: "I will not believe in the Redeemer of these people until they have shown me that they have been redeemed."

We may not go all the way with him in his outspoken skepticism, but this reaction should cause us serious thought. It is possible for us to speak so much about redemption that we forget that we have been redeemed—redeemed to be God's own.

The word "redeem," literally, means to "buy back." The Lord who made us, and from whom we had strayed by reason of sin, has bought us back by paying the supreme price through the life, death, and resurrection of His Son—all in our behalf. That is why Peter tells us that we are a "purchased people"—purchased for a *purpose*, namely, to "show forth" the wonderful deeds of Him who bought us.

As a purchased people we belong to the Lord who paid the price of our redemption. Does this relationship become evident in our daily behavior, in our family life, at our church assemblies? Do we really *walk* as Christ's redeemed or do we merely *talk* about His great redemption?

It may pay us to read our text once more in its larger context. Paul tells us: "Know ye not that your body is the temple of the Holy Ghost which is in you, . . . and ye are not your own? For ye are *bought* with a price; therefore glorify God in your body and in your spirit, which are God's." Truly, we have been redeemed, but we have been redeemed for a purpose. May we say with the poet:

Lord of Glory who has bought us With Thy life-blood as the price,
Never grudging for the lost ones That tremendous sacrifice;
May our lives show forth Thy praises, May they tell Thy wondrous love,
May we live for Thee, Thee only Till we reach our home above.

Christ Defeated—

And when Joseph had taken the body, . . . he laid it into his own tomb. Matthew 27:59-60

There is an old story that, when the Battle of Waterloo was being fought, the people in England were dependent upon a system of semaphore signals to learn of the tide of battle which was being waged fiercely on the opposite side of the channel—against Napoleon Bonaparte. One of these signals was on the tower of Winchester Cathedral.

Late in the day it flashed the disheartening signal: "Wellington *defeated.*" Just at that moment one of those sudden English clouds of fog obscured the signal, and the whole countryside was plunged into deep despair. Suddenly the fog lifted, and the remainder of the message became clearly visible: "Wellington defeated . . . *the enemy!*" Within the space of a moment sorrow was turned into joy, and defeat was swallowed up in victory.

The analogy we are about to make may be imperfect, as analogies frequently are. But analogies do have a way of putting flesh and blood on what otherwise may be purely abstract concepts. If ever an inpenetrable fog of doubt and despair had clouded the eyes of Christ's disciples, surely it was the dense fog of disillusionment that settled on their world late Good Friday afternoon. All they could read during those dismal hours was "Christ defeated!"

O Sorrow dread! Our God is dead!

But on the third day, as the sun rose in the east, all traces of the fog were gone and the full message could be read across the channel: "Christ defeated . . . *the enemy!*" On the far horizon was a message, not of defeat but of victory.

Christ, the Lord, is ris'n today,
Sons of men and angels say!

What an unspeakable victory, not only for Him who issued triumphantly from the grave but also for all who, washed clean in His atoning blood, will follow in His celestial train!

Raise your joys and triumphs high:
Sing, ye heav'ns, and earth reply!

The Power of His Resurrection

That I may know Him and the power of His resurrection. *Philippians 3:10*

A noted communist, a teacher at the Free University of Berlin some years ago, stated his conviction that it was not the Sermon on the Mount but the resurrection of Christ that caused Christians to turn the world upside down.

How true! It was the miracle of the resurrection that not only boggled the minds but transformed the lives of the early believers. Remember, in point of time, they were "close up" to the first Easter. A tremendous event had happened, an event that not only shook the world but shook the lives of those who believed.

The apostle Paul was a different man after he saw the resurrected Christ. To the Roman Christians he wrote that Jesus of Nazareth was "declared to be the Son of God with *power* . . . by the resurrection from the dead." He electrified the Christians at Antioch with the astounding message that God had raised this Jesus from the dead, not 2000 years ago but only recently.

In fact, Paul is always and forever proclaiming the death and resurrection of Christ throughout all of his epistles. He devotes much of 1 Corinthians 15 to the resurrection theme, closing that chapter with the well-known doxology: "Death is swallowed up in victory. O death, where is thy sting? O grave, where is thy victory? . . . Thanks be to God, which *giveth us* the victory through our Lord Jesus Christ." To Paul, Christ's resurrection was the final seal of heaven assuring the validity of Christ's redeeming work.

The power of the risen Christ is still available to you and me today. He is still the object of our faith and the mainspring of our life. In Him our hope abides. This hope is founded on Christ's resurrection. With the poet we exult:

> Jesus lives! to Him the throne High o'er heaven and earth is given.
> I shall go where He has gone, Live and reign with Him in heaven.
> *God is faithful.* Doubtings, hence! This shall be my confidence.

Eternal Life Today

God hath given to us eternal life, and this life is in His Son. 1 John 5:11

Christian people sometimes make the mistake of thinking that eternal life is something which God will give them at some distant future date; something concerning which they and God have often spoken, but which has been placed in the "will call" for future delivery and future use.

The fact is, the believer has eternal life *today*. "These things have I written unto you," says John the apostle, "that ye may know that ye *have* eternal life" (1 John 5:13). John wanted his converts in Asia Minor to know that the eternal life of which he spoke was their possession right now.

The new life which God has created in the heart of a believer through faith in Christ is a life which will never die. Our intimate fellowship with the Savior, our life which is "hid with Christ in God," is a life which will continue beyond the doors of death out into the endless ages of God's eternity. That is very real, we have eternal life today!

What a difference that makes in our attitude toward the few short years which still lie between us and the valley of the shadow of death. There may be difficulties in our personal lives such as sorrow, sinning, and regret. There may be heartaches in the family circle: separation, disappointment, and bereavement. There may be world catastrophes still awaiting us, but these are all on *this* side, while the glorious life which God has already begun in us will continue and will enter into its greatest joys on *yonder* side.

> The saints on earth and those above But one communion make
> Joined to their Lord in bonds of love, All of His grace partake.
> Lord Jesus, be our constant Guide; Then, when the word is given,
> Bid death's cold flood its waves divide and land us safe in heaven.

"Very Much Alive and Well"

[Christ] is able to save them to the uttermost that come to God by Him, seeing He ever liveth to make intercession for them. *Hebrews 7:25*

Two men had been good friends for years, one an agnostic, the other a devout believer. Seated on the porch one evening, engaged in casual yet serious conversation, the agnostic responded to his friend's words of Christian witness by saying, "Yes, but you have to remember, Christ was only a man—He died!"

To which the believer responded, with no little animation: "Oh, no! He's very much *alive* and well!" You and I may not have said it that way, but could any words be more true? The writer to the Hebrews put it this way: "Christ is able to save them to the uttermost that come to God through Him, *seeing He ever liveth.*"

The writer of the Letter to the Hebrews had special reason for emphasizing the eternal deity of Christ, as he does in the very opening verses of his epistle. He was addressing his letter to Christians who were converted Jews. He knew that his readers were being influenced by their kinsmen who regarded Christ as an imposter at worst or just another prophet at best. Hence he takes every opportunity to remind them, to reassure them, that their Messiah is not dead but is seated at the right hand of God the Father, "making intercession" for all believers.

We are inclined to speak of Christ mostly in the past tense. That is very natural, since His birth, life, death, and resurrection did take place at points in time long past. But the Christ we worship is the One who is living in the *present,* the One who is "very much alive," who "lives and reigns to all eternity," still active on behalf of all who come to God through Him.

He lives, all glory to His name! He lives, my Jesus, still the same.
Oh, the sweet joy this sentence gives, "I know that my Redeemer lives!"

Lord Jesus, may I find daily strength and comfort from knowing that You are alive, speaking for me before Your Father in heaven. Amen.

The Great "I AM" Is with Us Still

Jesus said unto them, Verily, verily, I say unto you, Before Abraham was, I am.
John 8:58

There would be little comfort for us in the Christian Gospel if our Savior had been a mere man, confined to the limitations of time and space. The passage quoted above is therefore of great importance to us. When the people of His day accused Jesus of being an impostor who had recently appeared on the scene, He replied calmly: "Before Abraham was, I am."

Notice the present tense. Not, I *was,* but I *am!* We have here an echo of God's words to Moses in Exodus. The Lord was sending Moses to the children of Israel in Egypt and He instructed him to say: "I AM hath sent me." We have here also an instance of the many times Jesus asserted "I am" in the four Gospels such as "I am the Way," "I am the Door," and "I am the Light." There was always the clear implication that He not only always *was* but also *is* and always *will be* "Jesus Christ, the same yesterday, today, and forever."

The apostle Paul asserted the eternal nature of Christ again and again. He tells his Colossian Christians: "In Christ we have redemption through His blood . . . All things were created by Him, and for Him . . . He is *before* all things, and by Him all things consist." What a Savior!

And what a comfort for you and me! We worship not a distant Savior, distant neither in time nor space, but an *ever* living, *ever* loving, *ever* present Lord and Friend, One who can say in every age: "I AM!" In days of trouble and perplexity, when it seems that He is *not* (not present to hear our prayers, *not* present to help), His reassuring word still comes across the centuries, saying: "I AM!"

Even at the door of death, we shall sense His gracious presence and hear His gentle whisper: "I AM—HERE!" That is why you and I can pray:

Jesus, my Lord, be there, Welcome Thy wanderer home,
Clothed in Thy blood and righteousness, Trusting Thy grace alone.

Rest for the Restless Heart

Thou wilt keep him in perfect peace, whose mind is stayed on Thee. *Isaiah 26:3*

A young American Air Force captain came back from the war and found it impossible to settle down. Disagreeable at home, dissatisfied at work, and discouraged over his inability to "find himself," he finally went to a psychiatrist.

It took only a few sessions for the specialist to diagnose his trouble. "What you lack," said the doctor, "is a *center* around which your life can be integrated."

A friend directed the young man to a Christian pastor. Here he found the center around which he could build his life. For in the quiet of the pastor's study the young man met his Savior. Having seen Christ as his personal Savior and Lord, he saw *himself* in true perspective for the first time. Having seen Christ as the sure and immovable hub of his existence, he soon saw all the loose ends of his life being drawn together around a sure and steady center.

Have we found that Christ has given point and purpose to our lives? Have we found that Christ is the central Refuge of our lives to whom we flee for peace, for strength, for reassurance? The ancient church father St. Augustine once said: "Thou hast made us for Thyself, and our hearts are restless until they rest in Thee." Have we put our hearts to rest in Christ? Then He will keep our hearts in perfect peace.

Jesus, my Truth, my Way; My sure, unerring Light,
On Thee my feeble soul I stay, Which Thou wilt lead aright.

Give me to trust in Thee; Be Thou my sure abode;
My Help and Refuge in distress, My Savior and my God.

Does God Mean Me?

Him that cometh to Me I will in no wise cast out. John 6:37

Martin Luther once said that he was glad that God never mentioned him by name in any of the Gospel promises. If the Bible had ever said that Christ came into the world to save Martin Luther, he could not have been sure that *he* was the Martin Luther who was meant, for the world has had other Martin Luthers.

The great reformer found his greatest comfort in the fact that the Gospel promises are general, universal, and all-inclusive. "God so loved the *world* that He gave His only begotten Son, that *whosoever* believeth in Him should not perish but have everlasting life."

That "whosoever" was Luther's source of assurance. That, he was sure, included him. And likewise a host of other Gospel promises. "Him that cometh to Me I will in no wise cast out." "Him" included Martin Luther.

And that "him" includes you and me. In our weaker moments we may doubt that God's promises are really for *us.* We may think that our particular sins are too great, too numerous, to be included in the Gospel's offer of forgiveness, that we have strayed too far and sinned too often. We *cannot* be included!

But there stands that word—*"whosoever!"* "Whosoever believeth." "Him that cometh." Yes, that does include you and me. Though *my* sins be as scarlet, they shall be as white as snow. Though they be red like crimson, they shall be as wool. In days of doubt or spiritual uncertainity, we can always flee to the objective promises of Scripture. We can always find our comfort and assurance in its many all-inclusive whosoevers. These never change.

The poet translates the universal invitation of the Savior into these beautiful lines:

> "And *whosoever* cometh, I will not cast him out,"
> O blessed voice of Jesus, Which drives away all doubt,
> It tells of benediction, Of pardon, grace and peace,
> Of Joy that hath no ending, Of love that cannot cease.

Standing in His Grace

By whom also we have access by faith into this grace wherein we stand. Romans 5:2

We were visiting in the home of a Christian young couple. Suddenly their four-year-old daughter came running into the house crying. She had fallen and scraped her knee. With evident sympathy the father cleaned the abrasion, applied medication, and comforted his daughter by saying: "Don't worry, dear, God loves you."

In another home we may have dismissed this attempt at comfort as an empty, pious phrase. But here was a family which was living every day in the conscious awareness of God's grace in Jesus Christ. In the words of Paul, they knew not only that they had been "justified by faith" but that every day and every minute they were "standing in His grace." Even a bruised knee was an occasion to be reminded of God's love.

Or does this sound as though we are trivializing the Gospel—making it apply to the inconsequential happenings of life. Perhaps right here we should re-read the Scripture portion suggested above: Romans 5:1-5. Paul is in the midst of his great discussion of justification by faith alone. As a result of our justification in God's sight, he says, we are "standing in God's grace." He then goes on to explain what that means. As long as we are standing in a *relationship of grace* (that is, love and mercy), he says, there is nothing in life that can really harm us. Why? Because every minute we know God loves us.

Are *we* consciously "standing in God's grace"? Are our hurts, our pains, our disappointments, even our bereavements, made more bearable by the knowledge that in Christ God loves us? Remember! By faith in our Redeemer we have entered into a unique relationship by which we (in Paul's words) "have access, by faith, into this grace wherein we stand." Every minute, no matter what the circumstance, we know God loves us.

It is significant that the poet who starts his long hymn, "By grace I'm saved, grace free and boundless" ends his hymn seven stanzas later with: *"My heart is glad, all grief is flown,* Since I am saved by grace alone!"

Read Matthew 6:19-21

Thoughts of the Father's House

Where your treasure is, there will your heart be also. Matthew 6:21

The weary wanderer, as he rests at close of day, thinks fondly of his father's house. The familiar faces, the friendly voices, the tender recollections of distant loved ones, have inscribed their indelible pictures upon the album of his soul. And so when evening comes, he steals away from the busy world for quiet thoughts about his father's house. That is where his treasure is, and that is where his *heart* is also.

So, too, we Christians. We have a Father and a "Father's house," reserved for us in the land beyond the shadow. In that distant home lies the complete fulfillment of all our highest hopes. There dwells our Savior, who has prepared our home for us—and has prepared us for our home. There dwell those whom we "love most and best." And there we too some day shall dwell.

How natural, then, that ever and again we should find our thoughts stealing away to the inviting portals of our Father's house, to loved ones who have gone before, and to the eternal joys that await us there. That is where our *treasure* is; how could our heart be elsewhere?

It is several of these thoughts of our Father's house gathered from the pages of the Bible over which we shall linger each day in the following meditations. As we contemplate the beauties of the mansions which stand at our journey's end, we pray our heavenly Father that our hearts may be cheered, and our feet be guided ever more surely along our pilgrim path.

Each night, as we put another day behind us and look forward to our Father's house above, may we share the faith of the Christian poet:

> One sweetly solemn thought
> Comes to me o'er and o'er:
> Nearer my home today am I
> Than e'er I've been before.
>
> Nearer my Father's house,
> Where many mansions be,
> Where many loved ones gone before
> Mine eyes at last shall see.

My *Father's* House

In My Father's house are many mansions. John 14:2

There is something about the life beyond the grave that fills our hearts with dreadful awe and solemn wonder. Even the thought of heaven—with its unspeakable glory and grandeur—sometimes frightens us, and we ask: "Will I feel at home, will I be at ease in the celestial mansions?"

How wonderfully all of our fears and misgivings are silenced when, with the Savior, we can point to heaven and say: "My *Father's* house!" We first think *back* to our earthly father's house, to the days of our childhood. What sweet security, what freedom from responsibility, what complete assurance of abundant provision and daily protection were ours when we dwelt in our earthly father's house!

Then we look *forward.* Soon we shall be dwelling in our *heavenly* Father's house. There in an infinitely higher and nobler sense we shall dwell secure and free. There we shall enjoy in an indescribably fuller measure the bounty, provision, and protection of a loving Father's care. There we shall live in daily intimate communion with our *eternal* Father who will call us by our name.

What comfort, what strength, what joy are ours in the knowledge that beyond the portals of eternity there lies a *Father's* house. This Father's house is ours through Christ. It was through Him that we became "children of the heavenly Father" and heirs of eternal glory.

May we never cease to thank and praise Him for His matchless mercy which opened wide the doors to His celestial mansions. In days of sorrow, grief, or disappointment, may we find our deepest comfort and highest joy in the Savior's promise of a loving *Father's* house in heaven. That is where He was going. And so shall we.

My Father! Cheering name! O may I call Thee mine!
Give me with humble heart to claim A portion so divine.

There's Room Enough

In My Father's house are many mansions. *John 14:2*

In order to grasp the full significance of these words of the Savior, we must remind ourselves of His *purpose* in speaking them. He was taking leave of His disciples. Their hearts were in need of comfort and encouragement. And so He chooses words that will soothe their sorrow and silence all their fears. "Let not your heart be troubled," He says, " . . . in My Father's house are *many* mansions." In other words, there is ample room also for *you* in the place where I am going. And some day I'll come back again to bring *you* to the spacious mansions of My Father's house. There is room enough for all.

Yes, *there is room enough!* As the omniscient eye of the Savior looked out across the centuries and saw the countless throngs who would be brought to faith in Him, He thought it fitting to remind us that the expanse of His Father's house is limitless. There will be room for *all* who come to the Father through faith in Him. "In My Father's house are *many* mansions."

We may be sure: there will be room for you and me! He whose love has singled us out as objects of His all-redeeming mercy and has promised to preserve us unto the day of His heavenly kingdom has prepared and reserved a room for us. He has claimed and is holding our place in the eternal mansions. Therefore we can say with the confidence of Paul: "I know whom I have believed and am persuaded that He is able to keep that which I have committed unto Him against that day." What a glorious thought! There is *room* in the Father's house for all who trust the Savior; and through *Him* there is a place for us!

With that assurance in our heart we can rest our head upon our pillow each night with the spoken or unspoken conviction:

> Nearer my Father's house, Where many mansions be;
> Where, at my Savior's side, I know There's *room enough for me.*

The Purpose of the Gaps

In My Father's house are many mansions; if it were not so, I would have told you.
John 14:2

There come days, even in the life of the Christian, when we are tempted to wish that the Lord had revealed himself to us more fully. There are so many questions we cannot answer, so many mysteries we cannot explain, so many hurts and sorrows which we find it difficult to fit into our Father's gracious plan. If only He had told us more! If only He had told us this or that, it would appear to be so much simpler to believe.

In moments such as those let us catch the echo of the Savior's comforting words to His disciples: "If it were not so, *I would have told you.*" If there were anything about My Father's house—the way to it, the certainty of it, the glory of it—about which you lacked any information which is *needful* to you, you may be sure: "I would have told you."

It is true, our knowledge of the life to come and even of our life on earth is very incomplete. "Now we see through a glass, darkly," says Paul. There are gaps in God's revelation, but even the gaps have a purpose. They are the darkness in which we are to learn to hold His hand and walk by faith. Our Savior has told us all we need to know. He has told us of His Father's love, of salvation through His cross, of our assurance of eternal bliss and glory through faith in His redeeming work. If we had need to know more, he says, He would have told us.

How important, then, that when our future seems clouded with uncertainty, when there are great gaps in our knowledge of what lies in store for us, when even the thought of heaven seems punctuated with a question mark, we come back again and again to the clear and simple assurances of the Savior spelled out for us in Holy Scripture. The poet put it right when he said:

> *My knowledge of that life is small, The eye of faith is dim;*
> *But 'tis enough that Christ knows all; And I shall be with Him.*

As One Who Had Been There

In My Father's house are many mansions; if it were not so, I would have told you.
John 14:2

There is something remarkable about every reference of the Savior to His Father's house. He spoke as one who had been *there*. No one can read the account of His midnight interview with Nicodemus without being impressed with the authority with which the Savior spoke of the things of heaven. "We speak that we do *know* and testify that we have *seen*," He says.

No one could have witnessed that tender scene in the Upper Room when the Savior spoke fondly of His Father's house to His disciples without sensing the Savior's intimate and accurate knowledge of the house of which He spoke. Notice the assurance of His words: "If it were not so, I would have *told* you."

As one who stands on a mountain top—looking down into the valley beyond and telling his comrades behind him what he sees—so the Savior tells us about His Father's house and ours. The streets of the eternal city are familiar to Him, the mansions of the Father's house stand clear and bright before His all-seeing eye. He *knows* what lies beyond the valley, for He has *come* from there. That is why He can say with calm assurance: "If it were *not* so, I would have told you."

What a comfort to have as our dearest Friend Him who has already spent endless ages in the eternal Father's house, who knows the way, and who by His holy suffering and death for our sins upon the cross has opened that way for us. Into the hands of such an omniscient, *heavenly* Savior we can entrust our souls with utmost confidence. He will bring us to His Father's house.

> O sweet and blessed country, The Home of God's elect!
> O sweet and blessed country That eager hearts expect!
> Jesus, in mercy bring us To that dear land of rest,
> Who art, with God the Father and Spirit ever blest.

With that prayer within our heart, we can open each new day and go to bed each night, trusting in our Savior's promise.

"I Go To Prepare a Place for You"

I am going there on purpose to prepare a place for you. *John 14:2 NEB*

It was early that same day that Peter and John had gone ahead to Jerusalem to "prepare a place" for Jesus. In those days it was customary for travelers to send one or two of their company ahead to make the necessary provisions for food and shelter and to "prepare a place" for those who were soon to follow.

How beautifully the words of the Savior spoken that night in the Upper Room fit into the framework of this ancient custom. "*I* go to prepare a place for *you*," He says. "And if I go to prepare a place for you [notice the repetition of affection!], I will come again and receive you unto Myself." Christ, our fellow traveler on the highway of life who has tasted the hardships of our journey, has gone ahead to *prepare a place for us.*

We may not be able to picture all that is meant by these simple words of the Savior, but *this* we *do* know: His going ahead to the Father's house above was definitely for *our* benefit—"a place for *you*"—and His present activity in the heavenly mansions, His intercession before the Father's throne, His sovereign rule over heaven and earth, and His tender care for those who have come to God by Him are all a preparation for our eternal joy and glory. Our final, safe arrival in His Father's house is the purpose of His activity in heaven.

What a comfort when the journey becomes hard or the way dark to know that our Brother Christ, who has gone on ahead, is preparing a place for us in the celestial mansions. Through faith in Him we shall some day occupy our prepared place in the Father's house above.

But our Savior Christ is by no means to be considered an "absent landlord" constructing heavenly mansions for His loved ones. The same poet who wrote: "He lives my mansions to prepare, He lives to bring me safely there," also wrote:

He lives to silence all my fears, He lives to wipe away my tears,
He lives to calm my troubled heart, He lives all blessings to impart.

He who some day will receive us into eternal glory is the same Lord who is with us *now* in all His grace and mercy.

"I Will Come Again"

I will come again . . . that where I am, there ye may be also. John 14:3

"I will come again." As a mother soothes her weeping child, from whom she must be parted for a moment, with the whisper of assurance, "I will come again," so the Savior seeks to soothe the fears of His disciples with the comforting assurance of His imminent return. I must leave you now, He says, but "let not your heart be troubled . . . I will come again."

How effectively that simple promise of the Savior poured courage into their fainting hearts in later years is seen from Bible history. Trials and afflictions, pains and persecutions—all would have to be borne, to be sure—but only until *He* would come again, and then all would be supremely well. His coming, either at the death of the world or at the death of His disciples, cast a golden glow over all the road that stretched ahead. They were walking *toward the light* of His return. In that light all shadows fell behind them.

So, too, with us. All sorrows, all heartaches, all disappointments and bereavements, lose their bitterness in the comfort of the Savior's tender promise: "I will come again." I will come again to turn your sorrows into joy, your heartaches into gladness, your bereavements into heavenly reunions in My Father's home above.

He whose love brought Him to Calvary's cross, there to open the doors of His Father's house to a world which had spurned His *every* pleading, will come *again* to lead us across the threshold into the eternal mansions, prepared for all who love Him. What a glorious promise! What a heavenly prospect!

All who put their faith in the Savior's promise "I will come again" can face life triumphantly and repeat the lines of the Christian poet:

> I'll never cry again,
> Yes, I may weep today;
> But only while I'm still
> Upon my pilgrim way.
>
> Soon tears shall be no more
> Death's triumph shall be o'er,
> I'll see HIS FACE!—And then—
> I'll never cry again.

Open House in Heaven

I will come again, and receive you unto Myself; that where I am, there ye may be also. John 14:3

No one can trace the trend of the Savior's thoughts during the closing scenes of His earthly life without being deeply impressed by the one compelling force which lay behind His every word and deed: His affectionate attachment to His faithful few and His deep desire that His intimate and free companionship with them be continued in His Father's house above.

Thus, for instance, in His high-priestly prayer in the Upper Room that night, after imploring the Father's many blessings upon all Christians of all times, He climaxes this prayer of prayers with the jewel of all petitions: "Father, I will that they also whom Thou hast given Me *be with me where I am*; that they may behold My glory, which Thou hast given Me." He shares with His Father a desire which, when He repeats it to His disciples, becomes a promise: "I will come again and receive you unto Myself, that *where I am, there ye may be also.*"

Jesus has secured His Father's approval and permission to bring His friends into His Father's house. By His reconciling death He has unlocked the door of His Father's home. *Heaven is now an open house!* "Where I am, there ye"—ye who have come to the Father by Me—"may be also." What greater delight, what higher ecstasy can the sin-bound soul envision than to spend the endless ages in the Father's house with Jesus! Standing firmly on the Savior's promise that "where He is there we shall be also," we can sing and say with confidence:

Let us gladly live with Jesus; Since He's risen from the dead,
Death and grave must soon release us. Jesus, Thou art now our head,
We are truly Thine own members; Where Thou livest, there live we.
Take and own us constantly, Faithful Friend, as Thy dear brethren.
Jesus, here I live to Thee, Also there eternally. Amen.

The Road to the Father's House

And whither I go ye know, and the way ye know. *John 14:4*

Frequently during the Savior's intimate conversations with His disciples he had spoken to them concerning the *way* to His Father's house. Indeed, in a sense, that was the sum and substance of *all* of His discourses with them. The way back to the Father—to establish that way, to reveal it, to proclaim it—that was the supreme purpose of the Savior's coming. That is why on the eve of His departure He now can say to His disciples: "And whither I go ye know, and the *way* ye know."

As the Master Teacher he is encouraging them to recall to their minds everything that He had told them about His Father's house and the way by which we reach it. "Ye know the way," He says. In other words: "Think back! Recall all that I have told you about sin, faith, and forgiveness in My name, and about eternal life in My Father's house above. Surely, you *know* the way."

But there is also a deeper purpose in these compassionate words of Jesus. When you say to a friend: "You know the way to my home," you are inviting him to *come.* So Christ tells us, "Ye know the way," to remind us that we are *on* that way and to encourage us to continue on that way. He is reminding us that through faith in Him and His atonement for our sins we are daily making progress on the road from earth to heaven. Surely, we have every reason to rejoice. We know the way, and, by God's grace, we are on the road that leads us to our eternal Father's house. Knowing that, we can find strength, assurance, and direction at the dawning of each new day.

Thou art the Way; to Thee alone From sin and death we flee;
And he who would the Father seek Must seek Him, Lord, by Thee.

Thou art the Way, the Truth, the Life: Grant us that Way to know,
That Truth to keep, that Life to win, Whose joys eternal flow.

"My Father"

I go unto my Father. *John 14:12*

Few words were on the Savior's lips more frequently, and surely no thought was in His heart more constantly, than the thought of His *Father*. From His first recorded utterance, "Wist ye not that I must be about my *Father's* business?" to His dying gasp upon the cross, *"Father, into Thy hands I commend My Spirit,"* His life was a constant partnership with His Father. He had come *from* the Father, He was living *with* the Father, and He was going *to* the Father.

When speaking to His disciples in the Upper Room that night about the place where He was going, He did not speak about the tomb in Joseph's garden—that was not to be the end—but about "My Father," "My Father's house," and "I go to My Father." That was the point and purpose of His pilgrimage. From Bethlehem to Golgotha His life was a constant "going to the Father."

Can we say that about *our* lives? Despite the toil and trials of the day, do we feel each night the joy and satisfaction of the pilgrim who has come one day closer to his Father's house? Do we begin each day in the full consciousness that as each fleeting hour slips swiftly by "I am going to my Father"?

How often have we lived full days as though there were no Father at our journey's end—distrustful, discouraged, and despondent? How often have we trudged the steep hill upward as though our Father were far behind us in the valley and before us were nothing but bleak despair? No! With every passing day we are going forward to the Father, and, for Jesus' sake, we know our Father loves us.

> My Father! Cheering name! I joy to call Thee mine
> Both here on earth and there in heav'n I am forever Thine.
>
> Thy ways are little known To my weak, erring heart
> But 'tis enough for me to know That Thou my *Father* art.

Word from the Father's House

I will meditate in Thy statutes. . . . for Thy word quickened me. Psalm 119:48, 50

That letter from home! How it is looked for and longed for by the soldier overseas or by the lonely wanderer far from his father's house. Food or drink, health or wealth, friends or fortune, none of these will satisfy that aching hunger which craves just a *word* from home.

In a far higher sense, the psalmist tells us, the heart of the child of God yearns for word from his heavenly Father's house. From that Word He draws his spiritual refreshment, his courage for the way. Our heavenly Father has addressed a letter to each one of His children. It is a letter of admonition and instruction, of consolation and encouragement, of joy and triumph. This letter is to be found in the Holy Scripture.

Especially in those pages of the Bible which tell us of the birth, life, death, and resurrection of His Son (all in our behalf!) He has poured out His loving Father heart, telling us the good news about our elder Brother, who has won complete redemption for us and who is even now back in the Father's house preparing a place for us and awaiting our arrival there. Our Bible is our letter from the Father's house, our "word from home."

How we should turn to it again and again while absent from the homeland! How eager we should be to gather with fellow pilgrims every Sunday to hear another portion read and pondered and expounded. It is a *Word from the Father's house.* Let us hear it. Let us heed it. Let us love it!

> How precious is the Book Divine, By inspiration giv'n!
> Bright as a lamp its doctrines shine To guide our souls to heav'n.
>
> This lamp through all the tedious night Of life shall guide our way
> Till we behold the clearer light Of an eternal day.
>
> Lord, we thank You for Your Holy Word. May we always treasure it as a Word from our Father's house. May it guide and strengthen us on our homeward way. For Jesus's sake. Amen.

"Big Brothers" in the Father's House

For He shall give His angels charge over thee, to keep thee in all thy ways. *Psalm 91:11*

It is a familiar scene to see a carefree little two-year-old venturing boldly forth from the safety of his father's house and then, all unknown behind him, to see "big brother" who has been sent by a loving father to see that no harm befalls the little one.

Our Father's house is filled with legions of "big brothers"—His holy angels—whose constant duty it is to guard and keep us on our way. It is of these big brothers in the Father's home above of which the Scriptures say: "Are they not all ministering spirits, sent forth to minister for them who shall be heirs of salvation?" Again: "He shall give His angels charge over thee to *keep* thee in all thy ways. They shall bear thee up in their hands, lest thou dash thy foot against a stone."

How often in the midst of grave perils, when dangers threatened within and without, how often on the morning after a long night of anxious hours have we been able to say with Daniel: "My God hath sent His angel and hath shut the lions' mouths, that they have not hurt me!"

What comfort it should be to us, who are "the children of God by faith in Christ Jesus," to know that our heavenly Father has placed our stronger brothers as guardians to protect us on our way and to deliver us from every evil? Banishing doubt and fear, let us venture forth upon our daily tasks, confident of His loving and divine protection. With the hymn writer we can say:

> I walk with angels all the way, They shield me and befriend me;
> All Satan's power is held at bay When heavenly hosts attend me;
> They are my sure defense, All fear and sorrow, hence!
> Unharmed by foes, do what they may, I walk with angels all the way.

Food from the Father's House

Give us this day our daily bread. *Matthew 6:11*

Perhaps most of us are acquainted with Luther's classic explanation of the fourth petition of the Lord's Prayer: "God gives daily bread indeed without our prayer," he says, "also to all the wicked; but we pray in this petition that He would lead us to *know* it and to receive our daily bread with thanksgiving."

In other words, we are to recognize the *label of heaven* on every piece of food we eat. It has come to us from our Father's hand. If that hand would ever withhold its blessing, all the scientific knowledge and skill of man could not produce a single slice of bread to satisfy our gnawing hunger. The formula, the ingredients, the various processes which go to make our "daily bread" are the property of our heavenly Father, who in love is eager to share them with us, His children.

How beautifully David expresses this thought in the 145th Psalm. In his mind's eye he sees a farmer going out early in the morning with a large sack brimful with feed. Before he reaches the chicken coop, he sees dozens of eager and hungry chickens coming, running and clucking toward him, every eye firmly fastened on him and on his bag of feed.

In a similar manner, he says, "The eyes of all wait upon *Thee* O Lord; and *Thou* givest them their meat in due season. Thou openest Thine hand and satisfiest the desire of every living thing."

Do we accept our food as a gift from our heavenly Father? Or do we accept it merely as a matter of course, perhaps even habitually grumbling because it is not always exactly to our liking? If so, we have every reason to pray God, for Jesus' sake, to forgive our sins of ingratitude and to make us ever more grateful for the many blessings He has showered upon us.

Oh may we ne'er with thankless heart
Forget from whom our blessings flow:
Still, Lord, Thy heavenly grace impart;
Still teach us what to Thee we owe.

Read Psalm 121   **April 14**

Eyes Lifted Toward the Father's House

I will lift up mine eyes unto the hills, from whence cometh my help. My help cometh from the Lord. *Psalm 121:1-2*

The story is told of a young man who was tired of life. Surrounded by difficulties which to him seemed insurmountable he turned to his closest friend and said: "I have looked to the left, and I have looked to the right, but I can find no help." To which his friend replied: "Why don't you try the *upward look?*"

The upward look! How often we forget it. In days of trial and trouble we often find ourselves giving way to faithless worry, as though we had no Father in the Father's house above. Frantically we scan the *horizontal* horizons for help and forget that the first, pleading glance of the troubled Christian must always be a *vertical* look toward heaven.

Frequently it is in the school of affliction that the eyes of the Christian are trained heavenward. This was particularly true of King David, the man who wrote the words quoted at the top of this meditation. The life of David was filled with tragedy. The words of the hymnist "I walk in danger all the way" could be applied to David more than to the lives of most of us. On more than one occasion he had come within an inch of death. Only after long and bitter days in the dungeon of adversity did he learn to say with unwavering confidence: "I will lift up mine eyes unto the hills, from whence cometh my help. My help cometh from the Lord."

Have we learned to say and to *do* just that? In every day of trouble let us remember that we have a *Father* in the Father's house to whom we can go with every hurt, every fear, and every sorrow. We know that for Jesus' sake our Father *loves* us!

My Jesus, as Thou wilt. All shall be well for me;
Each changing future scene I gladly trust with Thee.
Thus to my home above I travel calmly on
And sing in life or death, My Lord, Thy will be done.

The Clocks of My Father's House

The Lord is not slack concerning His promise, as some men count slackness. *2 Peter 3:9*

Travelers to distant countries have been known to keep one timepiece set to the time of their native land so that, for reasons of sentiment, they might always know what time it is in the homeland. In a somewhat similar sense the Christian pilgrim keeps one clock, the clock of his faith and trust, in time with the clocks in his Father's house above.

The answer to my prayer, the lifting of my cross, the deliverance from a painful sorrow, or the granting of a long-sought pleasure are all scheduled for fulfillment, not according to the clocks and calendars on my kitchen wall, but according to the clocks of eternity, which are "telling time" on the walls of my Father's house.

God never comes too late with too little or too soon with too much. He is always on time—*His* time. His delays, when delays occur, are always the delays of love. His "little whiles" are always the preludes to greater revelations of His mercy. "For a small moment have I forsaken thee," He says, "but with great mercies will I gather thee." "Weeping may endure for the night, but joy cometh in the morning."

What a comfort to know that before the foundations of the world were laid all the clocks of heaven were set for the eternal welfare of those who would entrust themselves to the Savior's mercy through faith in His redeeming love. God's ways with us may indeed seem "past finding out," but in *Christ* we know that they are always the ways of love.

> Beloved, "It is well!" God's ways are always right;
> And perfect love is o'er them all, Though far above our sight.
>
> Beloved, "It is well!" Tho' sorrow clouds our way,
> 'Twill only make the joy more dear That ushers in the day.

A Friend in the Father's House

It is Christ that died, yea rather, that is risen again, who is even at the right hand of God, who also maketh [present tense!] intercession for us. *Romans 8:34*

Few memories of childhood are more vivid in later years than those melancholy moments when, having offended our father by some childish misdemeanor, we were "afraid to go home." What would Father say? What would Father do? Would there be any escaping the dreaded punishment? If only someone at home, perhaps Mother or Brother, would take our part, would "put in a word for us," and would incline our father to forgive us. If only we had a friend . . .

We *have* such a Friend—in the Father's house above! At this very moment He is "taking our part," is "putting in a word for us," is pleading with the Father to forgive us. That Friend is Jesus. "My little children," says John, "if any man sin, we have an Advocate [one who speaks for us] with the Father, Jesus Christ, the Righteous." Of this great Friend of sinners we are told in Hebrews 7:25: " . . . He is able also to save them to the uttermost that come unto God by Him, seeing *He ever liveth to make intercession for them.*"

Admittedly, our unaided human reason cannot grasp this Scriptural truth, but we have God's clear word for it. He who on Calvary's cross, while dying for the sins of all mankind, exclaimed: "Father, forgive them," still looks down in love upon His believing children and still is pleading: "Father, forgive them!" Oh, what a comfort, what a blessing beyond description to know that we have *such* a Friend in the Father's house above. Of Him we can sing with joy and confidence:

He lives to bless me with His love, He lives to plead for me above,
He lives my hungry soul to feed, He lives to help in time of need.

He lives to silence all my fears, He lives to wipe away my tears,
He lives to calm my troubled heart, He lives all blessings to impart.

Our Father's Thoughts Toward Us

How precious also are Thy thoughts unto me, O God! How great is the sum of them! If I should count them, they are more in number than the sand. *Psalm 139:17-18*

There is a deep beauty and sweet comfort in the truth that whatever comes into our lives as Christians had its first existence as a *thought* in the mind of God. Every success, every achievement, every sickbed, every sorrow, every changing scene of life through which we have passed and through which we *still* shall pass, all were but thoughts in the mind of our Father before they were permitted to find expression in our lives.

God's thoughts toward us who have become His children through faith in the Redeemer are always thoughts of love and mercy, of grace and tender kindness. As we trace the results of His thoughts toward us as they have found expression in our lives, we must exclaim with David: "How *precious* are Thy thoughts unto me, O God! How great is the sum of them!"

All that we are, all that we have, and all that we shall enjoy in the heavenly mansions of our Savior is the result of His gracious will toward us. Our puny reason may not grasp the mystery that lies behind this thought, but every good and every blessing that has come into our lives existed first in the heart of God.

How rich and how "precious" these blessings have been, how constant, how undeserved, and how well adapted to our needs. Surely, as we contemplate the unnumbered benefits which have come to us from our Father's love, we cannot but say in the words of the poet:

I praise and thank Thee, Lord, my God,
For Thine abundant blessing
Which heretofore Thou hast bestowed
And I am still possessing.
Inscribe this on my memory:
The Lord hath done great things for me
And graciously hath helped me.

Reunion in the Father's House

. . . and so we shall ever be with the Lord. 1 Thessalonians 4:17

Someone has said: "Death is not the end, it is the beginning . . . not a goal, but a gate . . . not a tragedy, but a triumph . . . not a going away, but a coming home . . . and the sorrow at the departure is more than compensated by the glad welcome on the other side. At the end of a long Christian life we have more friends and loved ones *there* than we have *here*."

Many Christians, particularly those who have already passed the noonday of life, have experienced the truth of that last sentence: "At the end of a long Christian life we have more friends and loved ones over *there* than we have *here*."

The mansions of the Father's house are peopled with the redeemed of all ages, those who have died in the holy faith by which we *live*. There dwell those whom we "love most and best," our pious fathers who have gone on before us, our believing mothers, our sisters and our brothers.

Oh, the glory of the day when we shall stand beside our loved ones in the Father's house above! What a thrice-happy reunion that will be. Through faith in their atoning Savior they have come "out of great tribulation and have washed their robes and made them white in the blood of the Lamb." Through faith in that same Savior we some day shall place our hand in theirs and join them in their eternal hymns of glory in the mansions of the Lord. Surely, the words of the poet are also ours:

Lord, while we pray, we lift our eyes To dear ones gone before us,
Safe home with Thee in Paradise, Whose peace descendeth o'er us;
And beg of Thee, when life is past,
To reunite us all at last With those who've gone before us.

Lord, at this moment we remember our dear ones who have already entered into glory. We pray, keep us firm in faith, that on that great day we may join them and worship You forevermore. Amen.

Homesick for the Father's House

For I am in a strait betwixt two, having a desire to depart, and to be with Christ; which is far better. *Philippians 1:23*

A noted theologian once said that if there had been one more Beatitude, it would have read: "Blessed are they that are homesick for heaven, for they shall be brought to the homeland." Doubtless, there is a kind of homesickness for heaven which is well pleasing to our Father. The Bible often tells us to direct our thoughts toward that "better country." So let us not think it unworthy of our Christian calling if, on occasion, we find ourselves saying with Paul: "I am in a strait betwixt two, having a desire to depart, and to be with Christ; which is far better."

But Paul knew that the Savior had a *purpose* in not taking His apostle to His Father's house at once. In the very next breath he says: "Nevertheless to abide in the flesh is more needful for *you*." The Savior had work for Paul to do. Souls were to be won. His kingdom was to be built. So Paul was to put his hand to the task before him, with vigor and with might, thus "shortening" the time which lay between him and that "great day" by active, free, and happy service.

What about us? Homesick for heaven? Yes, at times. But we are to occupy (to invest) the time that stretches out between us and our Father's house by constant, happy service in the Savior's kingdom. We are, like Paul, to keep our *hearts* "hid with Christ in God," but our *hands* are to be ever active in the service of the Savior's brethren. In that service we shall find joy. And in that joy we shall "hasten" the day of His appearing.

> Drawn to the Cross which Thou hast blest
> With healing gifts for souls distrest,
> To find in Thee my life, my rest,
> Christ crucified, I come.
>
> And then for *work* to do for Thee,
> Which shall so sweet a service be
> That angels well might envy me,
> Christ crucified, I come.

Joy in the Father's House

I say unto you, that likewise joy shall be in heaven over one sinner that repenteth.
Luke 15:7

What is it that makes the angels glad? Not the earthshaking headlines that shout from our daily newspapers. Not the news of victory on earth's great battlefields. Not even the cheering reports of mankind's most noteworthy achievements. But, rather, the thrilling news of "one sinner that repenteth": the joyful news that a wayward wanderer has been stopped short on the road to ruin and has been placed on the road that leads to the Father's house.

"One sinner that repenteth." That was you and I! There was joy among the family of heaven when through Holy Baptism or through the preaching of the Gospel we were born into the family of God. What a cheering comfort to know that we are not unwanted children in the Father's house, but that our birth into the heavenly family was an occasion for rejoicing among the company of heaven!

"One sinner that repenteth." That might also be that unbelieving friend with whom we come in daily contact. The man who works at the bench next to ours in the factory. The girlfriend with whom we eat lunch each day. The neighbor lady whom we meet in the grocery store several times each week and with whom we normally engage in conventional chitchat.

Have we done all in our power to bring these people into the circle of the Father's children through faith in the Redeemer? There will be joy in the Father's house the day we bring them in. There is room for all. There is *love* for all.

> Today our Father calls us, His Holy Spirit waits;
> His blessed angels gather Around the heavenly gates.
> No questions will be asked us, How often we have come;
> Although we oft have wandered, It is our FATHER'S home!

Lord, let me so live that my life may bring joy to the angels about Your throne. Amen.

The Glory of the Father's House

And the city had no need of the sun, . . . for the glory of God did lighten it.
Revelation 21:23

A little girl was walking with her father along a country road. The night was clear, and the child was enthralled by the splendor of the sky, all lit up with twinkling stars from one end to the other. After moments of reflection she suddenly looked up to her father and said: "Daddy, I was just thinking, if the *wrong* side of heaven is so beautiful, how wonderful the *right* side must be!"

In a sense, her remark merely reflected the logic of a child. In a higher sense, she was echoing the words of the psalmist who, when pondering the polka-dotted canopy of the midnight sky, exclaimed: "The heavens declare the glory of God; and the firmament showeth forth His handiwork."

No human tongue or pen has ever succeeded in describing the glory, the grandeur, and the magnficence of the Father's house above. That it is a place of entrancing beauty and matchless splendor the apostle John indicates in the Book of Revelation by interpreting heaven's glories in terms of costly jewels and precious gems and rarest metals.

How could heaven be anything else but beautiful? It is the habitation of our God, the royal palace of the King of kings! To that palace our Savior has gone to prepare a place *for us*. Through faith in His redeeming mercy we shall ascend some day to His beautiful home beyond the skies, more exquisite, more glorious, more wonderful than human speech can tell.

Jerusalem the golden, With milk and honey blest,
Beneath thy contemplation Sink heart and voice oppressed.
I know not, oh, I know not, What joys await us there,
What radiancy of glory, What bliss beyond compare.

My Father Is in the Father's House

. . . your Father knoweth that ye have need of these things. Luke 12:30

At one time in his life Martin Luther was much depressed and found it very difficult to conceal his melancholy mood. Soon he noticed that his usually cheerful wife had put on her mourning garments and had adopted an unaccustomed attitude of somber silence.

When he asked the reason for this sudden change, his pious Katie replied: "Why, I thought that God had died, the way that you've been acting; and so I thought it proper that I should go in mourning."

How often have *we* gone about our daily tasks as though there were a funeral wreath on our Father's house above, as though our heavenly Father had died and left us to fend for ourselves as best we could. How often have we plodded along our pilgrim path as though our Father's house were empty, as though there were no living, loving Father there to care for us, guide us, and shield us with His might and mercy.

In days of sorrow and adversity let us remember that "our God is in the heavens" and that with Him "nothing shall be impossible." He who gave us the choicest jewel of heaven, His only begotten Son, shall He not also give us those few temporal gifts which He deems necessary to support our earthly life? He who keeps the sun in its course and the stars in their paths, shall He not also find a way for *us?*

Paul Gerhardt was a man whose life was one tragedy after another. Yet he wrote some of our most beautiful hymns of faith and trust, trust in a heavenly Father whose Son he knew as Savior. Listen to his words of faith:

> Commit whatever grieves thee
> Into the gracious hands
> Of Him who never leaves thee,
> Who heav'n and earth commands,
> Who points the clouds their courses,
> Whom winds and waves obey,
> He will direct thy footsteps
> And find for thee a way.

Gifts from the Father's House

Every good gift and every perfect gift is from above, and cometh down from the Father of lights. *James 1:17*

From their earliest years children learn to look to their father's house as the one sure place from which their every need will be supplied. Food and shelter, warmth and clothing, tender care in days of sickness, and, above all, love and sympathetic understanding when big clouds of sorrow suddenly come upon their little lives, these are the priceless boons for which the little ones instinctively turn to their father's house.

These are also the priceless blessings for which we *older* "little ones" should constantly turn to our Father's house above. Surely, our *heavenly* Father is infinitely more able and willing to supply our needs, to heal our sicknesses, to lighten our burdens, and to soothe our sorrows than any earthly father. "If ye then, being evil, know how to give good gifts to your children," says Jesus, "how much more shall your Father which is in *heaven* give good things to them that ask Him?"

James emphasized the utter dependability of God when he says: "Every good gift . . . is from above and cometh down from the Father of lights, with whom there is *no variableness*, neither shadow of turning (1:17)." In other words, ours is a God who can be trusted, no matter what our lot in life may be.

In times of need let us remember that through Christ we are God's children, not God's orphans. He is our living Father, with ample gifts for all His children. "He that spared not His own Son, but delivered Him up for us all, how shall He not with Him also freely give us *all* things?"

> The Lord my Shepherd is, I shall be well supplied;
> Since He is mine and I am His, What can I want beside?

Lord, sometimes my faith in Your providence wavers and I am filled with doubts. May Your Holy Spirit fill my heart with faith in Your goodness, for You are truly my *Father*. Amen.

Inheriting the Father's House

To an inheritance incorruptible, and undefiled, and that fadeth not away, reserved in heaven for you. *1 Peter 1:4*

One of the most winning and appealing as well as one of the most significant aspects of Scripture is the homely way in which the entire story of salvation is woven within the framework of common everyday experiences in the family circle.

Our Father in heaven, in whose hands are all the destinies of man and in whose mountain heights and ocean depths are wealth and riches without measure, has prepared a "Father's house" for all His children. This heavenly mansion He has bequeathed to us, His adopted children through the Savior, without money and without price. It is ours as an *inheritance.*

Again and again when our Lord speaks of the eternal lot of the believer and the believer's relation to that lot He uses such expressions as "inheritance," "children of promise," "children of adoption," "heirs of God," "joint heirs with Christ," "inheritance of the saints in light," and "an inheritance reserved in heaven."

The apostle Paul had no doubt about his clear title to the heavenly mansions. A paraphrase of his words to Timothy would read: "I *know* in whom I have believed and am persuaded that He is able to keep what I have put into His charge until that day." He had no doubts about what lay in store for him beyond the sunset of this life.

Our Father's house is *ours!* Not because we have earned it or purchased it. That could never be. But because His love devised a way to make its blessings ours without any merit of our own. It is our *inheritance,* purchased by the Savior's love. What a blissful lot is ours! The title to our Father's house is written in *our* name, inscribed with the blood of Him who loved us.

> When from the dust of death I rise
> To claim my mansion in the skies,
> E'en then, this shall be all my plea:
> Jesus hath lived and died for me!

My Father's Love

And He said unto me, My grace is sufficient for thee; for My strength is made perfect in weakness. *2 Corinthians 12:9*

A traveler in Palestine was conversing with a Palestinian shepherd when he noticed that one of the sheep in the fold walked with some difficulty. On one of its legs he noticed an injury which had long since been healed. The shepherd, aware of the traveler's sudden interest, explained to him:

"You see, that sheep was born partially deaf. When it was a little lamb, it persisted in straying far from the fold, where it could not hear my voice. Time and again I was called upon to rescue it from the brink of disaster, until finally I had to inflict that injury on its leg myself. Ever since that day the sheep has limped, but it has also stayed much closer to me for guidance, safety, and protection."

The apostle Paul had a similar "injury." "A thorn in the flesh," he called it. We do not know exactly what this "thorn" was, but it is generally assumed that it was a physical affliction which caused him both pain and embarrassment. In his opinion it was a hindrance in his work, and so he called it "the messenger of Satan to buffet me, lest I should be exalted above measure. For this thing I besought the Lord three times, that it might depart from me. And He said unto me: My grace [my love] is sufficient for thee; for My strength is made perfect in weakness."

Our Father's love may have found it necessary to wound us, to visit us with some sorrow, some disappointment, some bodily affliction; but we can rest secure in the conviction that it was our Father's *love* that did it. His love always has a purpose, and His purposes are always right.

> Beloved, "It is well!" God's ways are always right,
> And perfect love is o'er them all Though far above our sight.
>
> Beloved, "It is well!" Though deep and sore the smart,
> The hand that wounds knows how to bind And heal the broken heart.

The Only Way to the Father's House

Jesus saith unto him, I am the Way, the Truth, and the Life; no man cometh to the Father but by Me. *John 14:6*

Jesus tells us that His Father's house is a broad and spacious dwelling "with many mansions," but He also tells us that the road that leads to it is narrow. In fact, he says that HE is the way, the only way. "Neither is there salvation in any other," says Peter, "for there is none other name under heaven given among men whereby we must be saved."

Christ is the sinner's only hope of heaven. Men have tried other ways. They have tried the road of culture. They have tried the road of character. They have tried the road of education. But each has been found to be a dead-end street, ending in darkness and despair. Only Christ is the *Way* to the happy home on high. That is why He says, "*I* am the Way, the Truth, and the Life; no man cometh to the Father but by *Me.*"

But, thanks be to God, this "narrow" way is as broad and as wide as the Savior's mercy. Even the most hardened sinner can find access to the Father's house through the mediation of the Son. At another time the Savior said: "I am the *Door*: [not a closed door, but an *open* door!] by Me if any man enter in, he shall be saved."

By His death on Calvary's cross for the sins of a fallen world Christ opened up a road that is broad enough to lead all men to the mansions of the Father—the road of salvation through trusting faith in His atoning blood. That is heaven's way. That is the *only* way. That is the high and holy way which, thank God, you and I are traveling to our Father's house above!

Men may rationalize. They may theologize. They may insist, as many do, that "*all* roads lead to heaven." But we who have staked our souls on Him who is both Lord and Savior will continue to confess:

Thou art the Way: To Thee alone From sin and death we flee,
And He who would the Father seek Must seek Him, Christ, by Thee.

Children of the Father

Ye are the light of the world. . . . Let your light so shine before men, that they may see your good works, and glorify your Father which is in heaven. Matthew 5:14, 16

A story is told of a boy who was leaving home for college. His father had included him in the morning prayer at the breakfast table, asking God to protect him and to grant him success in the career which he was undertaking. Rising from the table, the young man expected some final instructions and directions from his father. But all that his father said was: "Son, never forget whose son you are." Need he have said any more?

We Christian, too, are children of a Father away from our Father's house. "Behold, what manner of love the Father hath bestowed upon us, that we should be called the sons of God," exclaims the apostle John. How frequently in His "letters" to us—the Bible—has our heavenly Father admonished us to remember whose children we are. "Ye were sometimes darkness," He writes to the Ephesians, "but now are ye light in the Lord: *walk* as children of light!" Our Savior Himself has told us: "Let your light so shine before men that they may see your good works and glorify your *Father* which is in heaven."

How have we been behaving "away from home," away from the Father's house? Have we reflected credit upon our family name —*"children of God"*? Can our friends see our Father in *us*?

If we have failed in this respect, let us implore His divine forgiveness, for Jesus' sake, for whatever shame we have heaped upon His holy name by our waywardness and sin. Then, with the Spirit's help, may we put forth every effort to heed the admonition of the text above, to let our light so shine before men that they may see our good works and glorify our Father which is in heaven.

My Father! Cheering name! Oh, may I call Thee mine!
And may my life while here on earth Reflect the light of Thine!

My Father's Blessings

Bless the Lord, O my soul, and forget not all His benefits: who forgiveth all thine iniquities; who healeth all thy diseases; . . . who crowneth thee with loving-kindness and tender mercies. *Psalm 103:2-4*

How can I ever sufficiently thank my heavenly Father for all His kindnesses toward me? If I were to number His blessings, how could I ever find sufficient language to describe them? Surely, I, too, must say with the psalmist: "Bless the Lord, O my soul, and all that is within me, bless His holy name." Why? The psalmist answers this question in three relative clauses:

"*Who forgiveth all thine iniquities.*" That is the greatest of His benefits toward me. Nothing in life is more important, more comforting, or more encouraging to me than to know that, for Jesus' sake, my Father in heaven has forgiven me, has eternally thrown *all* my sins behind His back and will never remember them again. I am His forgiven child for time and for eternity.

"*Who healeth all thy diseases.*" He has given me a body that is "fearfully and wonderfully" made, He has given me health and strength, He has nursed me in sickness and sustained me in trials, so that today my hands are still able to do His will and my lips are still able to sing His praise.

"*Who crowneth thee with loving-kindness and tender mercies.*" The story of my life from early childhood to this present moment is a constant record of His love. My Christian parents, my church, my school, yes, *every* influence which brought me to the Savior's fold, not one of these was the fruit of *my* endeavors but all were the gracious leadings of His love.

As I stand today at the present milestone in my life and look back over the path by which the Lord has brought me to this moment, surely I have every reason to exclaim:

When all Thy mercies, O my God, My thankful heart surveys,
Transported with the view I'm lost In wonder, love, and praise!

Truly, the Christian life is one continuous doxology. Its theme? "Praise God from whom all blessings flow!"

Cries That Reach the Father's House

... and the cry of the city went up to heaven. *1 Samuel 5:12*

Someone has said that if only for one brief moment we could hear all of the prayers ascending to the Father's house from every corner of the world—the gasps of the wounded, the sick, and the dying; the cries of the forlorn, the forsaken, and the distressed—we could not bear the painful sorrow of it all. Only God, in His unsearchable attributes of love, mercy, justice, and wisdom, can both hear and bear that burden. But, praise His name! He can not only *hear*—He can also *help!* "The hand that wounds knows how to bind and *heal* the broken heart."

As the child cries out in the night for the soothing hand of Father or Mother, so we, the children of our Father, cry out to Him in the night of our uncertainty. We have His divine assurance that He will never leave us, that He will always be at our side with ready help and comfort: "He that keepeth thee will not slumber. Behold, He that keepeth Israel shall neither slumber nor sleep." "Call upon Me in the day of trouble; I will deliver thee." "Before they call, I will answer; and while they are yet speaking, I will hear."

As children of our Father, we will address our petitions to Him in our Redeemer's name. It is Christ who has *made* us the children of God and has won for us the priceless privilege of coming to our Father to "make our wants and wishes known." May we, then, come boldly, confidently, and humbly, knowing that in Christ our every prayer is acceptable to God our Father.

For this we have the example of the Savior Himself. Again and again, but especially in Gethsemane and on Calvary, His cry "went up to heaven"—His Father's house.

O Thou, by whom we come to God, The Life, the Truth, the Way,
The path of prayer Thyself hast trod—Lord, teach us how to pray!

Lord, may we come to You daily with our prayers and our petitions as dear children come to their dear father. In Jesus' name we ask it. Amen.

My Father's Chiding

The Lord is merciful and gracious, slow to anger, and plenteous in mercy. He will not always chide. *Psalm 103:8-9*

Are my crosses, my sicknesses, my disappointments, and reverses sent to me as *punishments* from the heavenly Father? Are they the cruel demonstrations of His anger? Frequently these questions rush in upon the troubled heart of a child of God when he is called upon to walk through the valley of adversity.

In moments like that we must always remember: *God never punishes His children!* He may visit them with chastening sorrow. He may correct them with the painful rod of bitter disappointment. But the rod is always in the hand of Him who loves us, and behind that hand is the heart which seeks our eternal bliss and glory. God *chastens* His children in love, he does not *punish* them in anger.

The punishment which satisfied God's wrath was borne for us *once and forever* by our Savior. We need endure *nothing* to appease His righteous anger. No penances, no sufferings, no sicknesses or disappointments, indeed, nothing that we could possibly endure could ever meet the demands of divine justice. Our Savior drank that cup for us. God's anger has been satisfied.

Whatever comes into our lives as Christians comes to us only from God's love. My illnesses, my losses, my disappointments, my misfortunes, are not the evidences of His righteous wrath toward me, but are the tokens of His mercy. What a *difference* this assurance makes when I am called upon to bear the burdens of this day! No matter what the burden, I can always share the comforting assurance of the hymn writer:

Judge not the Lord by feeble sense, But trust Him for His grace;
Behind a frowning providence He hides a smiling face.

O Lord, grant that, no matter what the circumstances, I may remember that You are my loving Father through Jesus Christ, my Lord. Amen.

In the Father's Hands

O Lord . . . Thou art my God. My times are in Thy hand. *Psalm 31:14-15*

A traveler in the Scottish highlands saw a cluster of beautiful flowers far down the mountainside. He promised a reward to a shepherd boy if he would pick them, offering to let him down by a rope. The boy eyed the stranger suspiciously and then, without a word, disappeared into the woods. In a moment he was back, but with him was his father. He was willing to be let down the mountainside, provided the rope was in his father's hands!

Our Father in heaven permits our feet to come upon steep and slippery places, far down the mountainside of human suffering; but no matter how deep the valley or how difficult the descent, we can always rest secure in the conviction that our times are in His hand. He holds the rope!

We shall go just so far down the hillside of adversity as His love would have us go. He knows our strength, He knows our weakness. He knows what we are to bring up with us from the valley—what lesson in humility, what lesson in trust, what lesson in Christian virtue—and He will bring us up again as soon as we have plucked these flowers for which His love has sent us.

What a comfort, when our cross seems heaviest, when it seems that our life has neither plan nor purpose, when it seems that we are being pushed about by a blind and merciless fate, to remember that in *every* valley of affliction *God holds the rope* and that our times are in His hands. He will guide us. He will hold us. Our faith is that of the poet who wrote:

> I am trusting Thee, Lord Jesus, Never let me fall.
> I am trusting Thee forever And for all.
>
> I am trusting Thee, Lord Jesus, Trusting only Thee;
> Trusting Thee for full salvation Great and free.

My Father's World

Are not two sparrows sold for a farthing? And one of them shall not fall on the ground without your Father. Matthew 10:29

Can the God who rules the vastness of the universe be concerned about *me* and my little problems and perplexities? Scientists tell us that the sun which gives us light and warmth, and whose size is many times that of our earth, is separated from us by some 93 million miles—and that the miles which separate the sun from the planet Neptune have been computed at 3,000 million.

Can the God who conceived such an inconceivable vastness, who brought these heavenly bodies into being, and who even today fills every mile between the planets with the power of His presence—can *he* be interested in *me*? Can He help, guide, and protect me?

Most assuredly, He can and will! He whose wisdom and omnipotence could create so great a universe to house the sun, the moon, and the stars surely will be able to raise protecting walls of love around our little lives.

This is our Father's world. No blind force, no blind fate, but our Father's love still guides and shapes the destiny of all His children in things both great and small. Again and again the Savior points us to the hand of His Father in the individual lives of His Christians. "Your Father knoweth what things ye have need of," He says. He who holds the planets in the hollow of His hand also holds the sparrows. And "*ye* are of more value than *many* sparrows." What a wondrous assurance! Through Christ the God of the trackless universe has become our Father. He is not only our Father who has made us and preserves us, but also our Father who has taken us into His family by the redeeming work of His beloved Son. Surely, in a very special sense the believer can say with joyful confidence: this is "my Father's world"!

Lord, may we never forget that this is our Father's world. In days of doubt or anxious fear, may we always remember that all things are in Your hands, and that all things work together for good to those who have committed their lives to You through Jesus Christ our Lord. In His name we ask it. Amen.

My Father Understands

He remembereth that we are dust. *Psalm 103:14*

Who understands us better than our father or our mother? Who is more intimately acquainted with our peculiarities, our faults and failings, our weaknesses and erors—than our father or our mother? And who is more ready to forgive us when we fail or to explain away and to cover our shortcomings with the mantle of sweet charity? The father heart remembers the limitations of the child—and in that remembance is moved to love and pity.

So, too, our *heavenly* Father.

He hath not dealt with us after our sins; nor rewarded us according to our iniquities. For as the heaven is high above the earth, so great is His mercy toward them that fear Him. As far as the east is from the west, so far hath He removed our transgressions from us. Like as a father pitieth his children, so the Lord pitieth them that fear Him. For He knoweth our frame; He remembereth that we are dust (Psalm 103:10-14).

He knoweth our frame—that we are so weak, so erring, and so sinful. That is why He offers us a salvation that is full and *free*, dependent upon no merit, no accomplishment, no worthiness of our own. In Christ and His atoning work we have everything that the loving Father heart of God could give: forgiveness of sins today and every day, and eternal life with God in the everlasting mansions. What peace, what joy, what confidence—to know that in heaven we have *such* a Father, a Father who knows us by our very names and who, knowing us, *forgives* us for Jesus' sake.

Surely, knowing ourselves for what we are, and knowing our Father for what He is, we have every reason to exclaim:

Amazing grace, how sweet the sound, That saved a wretch like me!
I once was lost, but now am found; Was blind, but now I see!

Through many dangers, toils, and snares, I have already come;
'Tis grace has brought me safe thus far, And grace will lead me home.

My Father's Business

Wist ye not that I must be about My Father's business? *Luke 2:49*

Jerusalem during the days of the Passover was just the place for a boy of twelve to have the time of his life! With soldiers stationed at prominent places, sights to be seen on every street, the marketplace humming with busy people, and children frolicking in holiday spirit throughout the city, Jerusalem afforded almost every attraction the heart of a boy could desire.

But for the 12-year-old boy Jesus there was *one* compelling attraction which drew stronger at His heartstrings than all the others— His Father's house, the temple, where He could be about His Father's business. And so His parents found Him "sitting in the midst of the doctors, both hearing them, and asking them questions." In the language of today, the boy Jesus had come in off the streets and, of His own accord, had gone to "catechism class." And He had done this because of a sense of "divine necessity." "*I must!*"

How greatly we need to develop a similar sense of "necessity" in *our* lives! We need to cultivate that still, small voice which says: "I must." In our morning and evening prayers, our prayers at the table, our attendance at public worship, our service and our contributions for the Kingdom, our personal, daily service to our fellowman—in all these things we need to cultivate that impelling sense of "divine necessity." Not that we are to do these things as the unwilling slaves of a cruel habit, but because "the love of Christ leaves us no choice." We *must*—because we *want* to!

Have you and I cultivated that God-given sense of "I must"? The Savior never lost it. It was not long before He died that He said: "I must work the works of Him that sent me, while it is day; the night cometh, when no man *can* work."

Lord, grant that I will always be about my Father's business! Whatever the call to selfless service (to You or to my fellowman), may I resist the temptation to say "I might." Rather may I say with an enlightened heart "I must." Amen.

Refuge in a World of Turmoil

Lead me to the Rock that is higher than I. *Psalm 61:2*

Few know better what it means to stand within the shelter of a rock than those who defended the island of Malta in 1941. From the safe ledges of their rock-built caverns they watched day after day, *unharmed,* as chaos and confusion swirled round about them. Outside the rock sure death would have been theirs. Inside the rock no danger could come near them.

What a striking illustration of that rock to which the Christian flees when the world seems to be toppling in pieces around him! That rock is the shelter of God's love. Round about us all may seem to be ruin; the storms of life may seem to be too much for us, too overpowering, too overwhelming. Our little faith may seem to be no match for the winds which seek to sweep us into the floodstream of destruction.

But there is a Rock! A Rock that is stronger than we. A Rock that is higher than we—a Rock that is above and below the shifting sands of all things temporal. It is this Rock of which the psalmist spoke so constantly when the foundations of his world seemed to be crumbling. "The Lord is my *Rock* and my Fortress." "The *rock* of my strength and my refuge is in God." "He only is my *Rock* and my Salvation."

Too often we think of our religion as something abstract. We think of it as a set of propositions to be memorized or as a set of fascinating doctrines to be debated. Nothing could be farther from the truth. At the center of our faith is a glorious *reality*—a reality which has meaning here and now.

In the midst of a world in turmoil *we have a rock!* It is the rock of our Savior's love and mercy: His assurance of unfailing guidance and protection. He is that rock which, in David's words, is "higher than I." He is the rock to which we *cling* and of which we *sing:* "Rock of ages, cleft for me, Let me hide myself in Thee."

In every circumstance of life may we find our deepest assurance, not in the shallow, shifting sands of earthly wisdom, but in the rock that is higher and stronger than we, our Lord and Savior Jesus Christ.

Walking "in the Light of the Lord"

Come ye, and let us walk in the light of the Lord. *Isaiah 2:5*

We've all heard the saying: "It is better to light a candle than to curse the darkness." Properly understood, there is much wisdom in this adage. It is so easy to fall into the habit of bewailing conditions in the world or in the church that some of us have become experts at condemning almost anything and everything of which we personally disapprove. In other words, our lips have become accustomed to *cursing the darkness.*

At times that may be called for. But more frequently we serve our Lord and our neighbor better by *lighting a candle.* Our text tells us that we are to "walk in the light of the Lord." If we walk in His light (the light of love and truth and wisdom), we will be lighting candles all along the way. And in doing so we will be bringing not only light but also help and healing to all whose lives touch ours.

We are reminded of a certain dedicated woman, a Red Cross volunteer, who spent two days a week for more than thirty consecutive years serving as a Gray Lady in a large city hospital. A recovered cancer patient, she spent much of her time radiating hope and cheer to others who were living through the same ordeal. So effective were her efforts that one of the staff surgeons, after visiting a depressed cancer patient, would write on the bedside chart: "Have Mrs. X spend some time with her." Why? Because he knew that her very presence would be sure to "light up candles."

Let each of us ask ourself frankly: What has been the greater emphasis in my life—cursing the darkness or lighting candles? Have I been "walking in the light of the Lord," sharing His love and joy with all whose lives touch mine? Surely, in this darkening world it is our Father's will that we hold high the light of His Gospel—and that we miss no opportunity to let it *shine.*

With Thine own love may I be filled And by Thy Holy Spirit willed,
That all I touch, where'er I be, May be divinely touched by Thee.

Prayers Must Have Hands and Feet

Pray ye therefore the Lord of the harvest, that He will send forth laborers into the harvest. *Matthew 9:38* Go ye therefore and teach all nations. *Matthew 28:19*

A missionary preacher once said: "Prayer must have hands and feet." How true! We find this thought implied in the two missionary imperatives quoted in the above texts, "pray" and "go."

On the one hand we are to *pray* to the Lord of the harvest that He will send laborers into His harvest—that is, send messengers out to proclaim His Gospel. And, on the other hand, we ourselves, who are His disciples, are to *go*—that is, we are to be active in harvesting the sheaves. Praying and going (being active) are essential parts in all missionary activity.

A noted churchman is said to have advised a friend: "Pray as if everything depended on God, and then work as if everything depended on you." That was good advice, not only for the man who received it but also for us. It is true, of course, that in the ultimate sense everything does depend on God; but it is also true that in a derived sense very much depends on us.

For instance, it will do no good for us to pray piously, "Thy will be done on earth as it is in heaven" and then to fold our hands in our lap and wait to see what happens. In a world of poverty and hunger, cruelty and injustice, we *know* what the will of our Lord is. Having prayed that His will be done, we are to do our very best to *do* it. As Martin Luther says, we are to be "little Christs," carrying out our Savior's will. In the words of the missionary preacher, we are to give hands and feet to our prayers. A well-known missionary hymn ends:

Raise up, O Lord, the Holy Ghost, From this broad land a mighty host,
Their war-cry "We will seek the lost, Where Thou, O Christ, wilt come."

Are we willing to be "raised up"? Willing to join the mighty host and go out to "seek the lost"? That would be giving hands and feet to our prayers. God grant it.

"Nevertheless"

And Simon, answering, said unto Him, Master, we have toiled all the night . . .
nevertheless at Thy word I will let down the net. Luke 5:5

One of the most significant words that characterize the Christian faith and life is (perhaps surprisingly) the word "nevertheless." We find a classic example of this in the Holy Scripture reading suggested above. As a professional fisherman, Simon Peter knew that the best time to catch fish in the Lake of Gennesaret was at night—and preferably in shallow waters. Yet in broad daylight Christ tells him to "launch out into the deep" and to let down his nets.

That was contrary to every instinct of the veteran fisherman. Yet we hear him say: "Master, we have toiled all the night, and have taken nothing, *nevertheless* at *Thy* word I will let down the net." What followed needs no retelling.

From a purely human point of view Peter knew the effort was sure to fail (he could have quoted a wealth of statistics against it), but at Christ's word he ventured forth. How often you and I must do the same, not only in our Christian faith but also in our Christian life!

Who, for instance, can understand the deep mysteries of Holy Scripture? For example, the Holy Trinity? The virgin birth? The substitutionary atonement? We can repeat the words but do we understand what lies behind them? No, not this side of heaven. Nevertheless, moved by the Holy Spirit, we *believe.*

And in our daily life, how often are we faced by situations beyond our power to fathom? We ask ourself: "Why must I bear this heavy cross? Why has my life suddenly become so meaningless, so pointless?" We may not know the answer, but *nevertheless* our Savior knows, and because He does, we'll trust His tender love.

There is a sense in which the Christian faith and life are one great "nevertheless." Our knowledge of God's ways with us is limited, but we know His love for us in Jesus Christ is boundless—and so we accept His will in humble faith and eager hope—*nevertheless.*

The "Trinity" of the Second Person

The grace of the Lord Jesus Christ and the love of God and the fellowship of the Holy Spirit be with you all. *2 Corinthians 13:14 RSV*

All evangelical Christians, of course, believe in the Holy Trinity as revealed in Scripture: in the Father who made us, in the Son who saved us, and in the Holy Spirit who, working through the Word and Sacraments, brought us to (and keeps us with) the Father and the Son.

But there is an ever present tendency, even among the best of believers, to make a sort of "Holy Trinity" out of the *Second* Person—to the neglect of the Father and the Spirit. From earliest childhood we are taught to sing: "Jesus Loves Me, This I Know," and over our folded hands at mealtime we are taught to pray: "Come, Lord Jesus, Be our Guest."

There is, of course, nothing wrong with either the hymn or the prayer. But, cumulatively, over the years, unless there is thorough and progressive instruction, this loving emphasis on "the Friend of little children" can result in an unintended "Holy Trinity of the Second Person." Or perhaps, better put, in a monotheism of the Christ whom Christians worship. It is possible that we end up praying to (and worshiping) "Jesus, Jesus, Jesus only"—to the exclusion of the eternal triune Godhead.

Notice, from the above text, how Paul words his final benediction to the Christians at Corinth: "The grace of our Lord Jesus Christ and the love of God [i.e., the Father] and the fellowship of the Holy Spirit be with you all." He had written to them about the Father (1 Corinthians 8:6), about the Son (1 Corinthians 2:2), and at length about the works of the Spirit (1 Corinthians 12:1, ff.). Now in the final sentence of his letter he commends them all to the Father, Son, and Holy Spirit whom he had proclaimed to them.

May we learn from Paul. While we love, worship, and adore the Second Person of the Trinity, we must never do so to the neglect of the total Trinity. Our prayers and praises must always echo the glad refrain:

"Praise Father, Son, and Holy Ghost." Amen.

A Bad Bargain

For what is a man profited, if he shall gain the whole world and lose his own soul?
Matthew 16:26

Unfortunately we frequently don't recognize a bad bargain until it is too late. We usually learn from such experiences, however, and become more wary in the future.

But wouldn't it be tragic beyond words to stand at the very portals of eternity and to learn at that crisis moment that our whole life had been a "bad bargain"—that we had made all of our investments in the wrong things? Jesus was referring to this ultimate "bad bargain" when He asked: "What is a man profited, if he shall gain the whole world and lose his own soul?"

Perhaps at no time in previous history has the world been so full of potentially "bad bargains." Ours is an age of materialism. Our lives are being cluttered with more and more "things": cars, television sets, radios, stereos, electrical gadgets, luxurious homes and furnishings, expensive and superfluous wardrobes, jewelry, and a hundred and one items that once were considered luxuries but now have become "necessities." What a daily challenge to keep our sense of values straight!

How about you and me? What do we consider our highest gain in life? Material possessions? Status? Popularity? Financial investments? There is nothing wrong in these things in themselves. But ultimately they will *all* prove bad bargains if we have not (above all else) invested in the *highest* good. Jesus tells us: "Seek ye *first* the kingdom of God [that is, our spiritual welfare] and His righteousness, and all these things shall be added to you." There is no higher good in all the world than to have Jesus Christ in our heart as our personal Savior and Lord. How eloquently the poet puts it:

What is the world to me With all its vaunted pleasure
When Thou and Thou alone, Lord Jesus, art my Treasure;
Thou only, dearest Lord, My soul's delight shall be;
Thou art my Peace, my Rest—What is the world to me!

141

"Lord, Help Me Love You Back"

God was in Christ, reconciling the world unto Himself, not imputing [charging] their trespasses unto them. *2 Corinthians 5:19*

The seminary professor had just finished expounding the above passage to his class. After a moment a student raised his hand and questioned: "Do you mean that Christ saved even a man like Adolf Hitler?" Without hesitation, the professor replied: "Yes, Christ saved even a man like Adolf Hitler—but Hitler never accepted Christ's salvation."

The professor was merely repeating what the Holy Scirptures say in the passage quoted above: "God was in Christ, *reconciling the world* unto Himself, not imputing [charging] their trespasses unto them." We are dealing here with what theologians call "objective justification"—that is, the *universal* amnesty which Christ won for the whole human race, without exception.

There is no sinner in this world for whom the Savior has *not* died—or for whom forgiveness has not been purchased. Christ died for both of the criminals who were crucified with Him—not just the one who accompanied Him to paradise. What a comforting thought for the believing Christian who, having fallen into sin, is terrorized by the magnitude of his transgression. He knows that in heaven he has a reconciled God who is eager to accept him back into the fold.

True, the penitent sinner must *believe* and *trust that* the offered reconciliation is for him. But the glorious fact is that it is already there— there by the grace of God—there for the vilest sinner. Before we were born, God said: "I love you." All that remains for us is to say: "Thank you, Lord! Because of the love of Jesus Christ, Your Son, who gave His life for me, I love You back!" Is that what you and I are saying—and doing? May the theme-thought of our life, expressed or unexpressed, always be:

Thee will I love, my Life, my Savior, Who art my best and truest Friend;
Thee will I love and praise forever, For never shall Thy kindness end;
Thee will I love With all my heart, Thou my Redeemer art.

The Ascension of Jesus

And it came to pass, while He blessed them, He was parted from them, and carried up into heaven. *Luke 24:51*

The above passage is taken from the closing verses of the Gospel according to St. Luke. Luke, also known as the beloved physician, was not one of the original 12 disciples of Christ, but was a close friend, companion, and coworker of St. Paul. He is the author both of the gospel which bears his name and of the Book of Acts.

In the opening verses of his gospel he tells us that it is his purpose to put in writing "those things which are most surely believed among us" and which have been attested by "eyewitnesses." Among those events "most surely believed" and reported by eyewitnesses was the miraculous ascension of Christ into heaven—recorded both in Luke's gospel and in the Book of Acts.

For our devotional purpose, let us linger on just four words in the text quoted above, namely the words "while He blessed them." In these few words we have the last picture of Christ to be seen by mortal men. The "last picture" of a departed loved one is frequently treasured as one of special significance. How fitting, then, that we dwell for just a moment on the last picture of our Savior which Luke has shared with us.

"*While He blessed them.*" His arms outstretched in loving benediction, Christ is gradually taken from this earth and "carried into heaven." No picture could be more appropriate or more expressive of the Savior's total mission here on earth. He had come to *bless!* He had come to "preach the Gospel to the poor, . . . to heal the broken hearted, to preach deliverance to the captives . . . to preach the acceptable year of the Lord" (Luke 4:18-19). By His suffering, death, and resurrection He had accomplished His mission and so, as if to leave a final signature, He departs with arms outstretched in benediction. As we contemplate the wonder of His glorious ascension, our prayer must be:

Draw us to Thee, For then shall we Walk in Thy steps forever
And hasten on Where Thou art gone To be with Thee, Dear Savior.

We Have a Representative

If any man sin, we have an Advocate with the Father, Jesus Christ the Righteous.
1 John 2:1

Does our conscience bother us? Are we afraid to face God? If so, would we welcome the opportunity of having someone talk to God for us?

There *is* someone who is willing and able to do that very thing! The Bible tells us in simple language: "If any man sin, we have an Advocate with the Father, Jesus Christ the Righteous. And He is the Propitiation [Reconciliation] for our sins; and not for ours only, but also for the sins of the whole world" (1 John 2:1-2).

An advocate is a representative, an attorney, one who talks to the judge for us. Our Lord and Savior, Jesus Christ, is our eternal Advocate before the eternal Judge on high. Of Him the Bible says: "He is able to save them to the uttermost that come unto God by Him, seeing He ever liveth to make intercession for them" (Hebrews 7:25).

He is the *only* Advocate, the *only* One who has been divinely empowered to represent the sinner before the court of heaven. St. Paul says: "There is one God and *one* Mediator between God and men, the Man Christ Jesus, who gave Himself a Ransom for all" (1 Timothy 2:5-6). Through Christ, and through Christ alone, we have free access to the Father heart of God.

What a comfort in days of sorrow, particularly when our heart is weighted down with the heavy burden of guilt or shame, to know that we have a Representative in heaven and to know that because He has died for us, He has won for us a place in the Father heart of God! He is indeed able to save us "to the uttermost."

> He lives to bless me with His love, He lives to *plead for me* above,
> He lives to calm my troubled heart, He lives all blessings to impart!

Grace—Free or Cheap?

[Jesus says:] If any man will come after Me, let him deny himself, and take up his cross and follow Me. *Matthew 16:24*

Dietrich Bonhoeffer was a German pastor who, in the late years of World War II, was locked up in a German concentration camp because of his outspoken Christian beliefs. While in prison he wrote many letters as well as a few books in which he expressed his unshakable faith in Christ as his personal Savior.

As he contemplated the state of Christianity, not only in his beloved Germany but also throughout the Western world, he came to the conclusion that one of the serious (if not fatal) illnesses of the contemporary church was its preoccupation with what he called "cheap grace."

What did he mean by that? He did not deny the Scriptural doctrine of "free grace," but he insisted that the modern church had made God's grace *cheap* instead of *free*. He lamented a religion which called for no sacrifice, no allegiance, no *commitment*. Or to use our traditional terms, he lamented a religion which preached *all* "justification" and almost *no* "sanctification."

One who accepts the grace of God also makes a personal commitment, he said. A commitment to be God's man or God's woman in all the varied situations of life. He pointed again and again to the word of Christ quoted above this meditation: "If any man will come after Me, let him deny himself, and *take up his cross and follow Me.*"

Christianity is no mere reading of a formal creed and then signing on the *dotted line*. Rather, it is taking a position with the redeeming Christ and then standing in the firing line. The *salvation* God has given us through Christ is free, but the price He sometimes puts on Christian *living* is very high. That price is symbolized by the cross which Christ asks you and me to bear. Listen as He speaks to us right now:

> I gave My life for thee, My precious blood I shed,
> That thou might'st ransomed be And quickened from the dead.
> I gave Myself for thee; *What hast thou giv'n for Me?*

"Only One of Each of Us"

I have redeemed thee; I have called thee by thy name; thou art Mine. Isaiah 43:1

After the Sunday school teacher had spoken to her class at great length about the love of God, especially about how He *showed* His love for us by sending Jesus to be our Savior, she decided to ask a probing question.

In her general review she asked the children: "Why do you think God loves us all so very much?" There was a long, unbroken silence as each child "thought hard" for the proper answer. Finally a timid little six-year-old raised her hand and ventured tentatively: "Because He has only one of each of us?"

What an answer—even though it ended with a question mark! Yes, among many other reasons, God loves us "because He has only one of each of us."

Or does that sound like a childish answer—the naive reply of a kindergartner? It may at first seem so, but beneath those words lies a theological truth, a truth which, the more we ponder it, the more it gives a deeper meaning to your life and mine. Suppose we repeat the little girl's reply: "God loves us all so very much 'because He has only one of each of us.' "

If that is true, and it *is* true, then in those inevitable moments when we feel so insignificant, so unimportant, so lost in the teeming mass of humanity, we can always remember that, in the eyes of our heavenly Father, we are something special, something unique. He does have "only one" of each of us. And, no matter who we are, rich or poor, black or white, red or yellow, famous or unknown, the great God of heaven speaks to our single, solitary self and says: "I have redeemed thee; I have called thee by thy name; thou art Mine." What an assurance! In moments of loneliness, depression, or seeming defeat—throughout the changing scenes of life we can speak these words of confident faith:

> The LORD my Shepherd is, I shall be well supplied.
> Since HE is mine and I am HIS, What can I want beside? Amen!

Amazing Grace

By grace are ye saved through faith; and that not of yourselves; it is the gift of God, not of works, lest any man should boast. Ephesians 2:8-9

It is said of John Wesley that one day he saw a drunken ne'er-do-well lying on a street in London. Looking at the man compassionately, he remarked: "There, but by the grace of God, am I."

How true—of all of us! Where would we be, were it not for the unmerited love and mercy of our God, showered upon us through Jesus Christ, His Son? We have been saved alone by His grace—His grace in Holy Baptism, in the Holy Supper, in the fellowship of the Christian congregation, in the influence of Christian parents and a Christian home.

Each of us, as we contemplate the redeeming and sustaining power of God's grace in our life, must confess with the poet, Horatius Bonar:

All that I was, my sin, my guilt, My death, was all my own;
All that I am I owe to Thee, My gracious God, alone.

Indeed, without His initiative—the initiative of divine compassion revealed on Calvary's cross—our spiritual condition at this moment would be most pitiable. We must confess with the apostle Paul that it was only God's grace, His undeserved mercy, that saved us and made us what we are—children of God and heirs of heaven. With the poet John Newton we sing:

Through many dangers, toils, and snares, I have already come;
'Tis grace has brought me safe thus far, And grace will lead me home.

Praise God for His abundant mercy!

O Lord, I thank You for Your amazing grace that saved a wretch like me. May Your grace attend my every day until my journey's end. Amen.

Afraid To Confess Christ?

Whosoever therefore shall confess Me before men, him will I confess also before My Father which is in heaven. *Matthew 10:32*

The story is told of a Christian young man who went to spend several months in a lumber camp. The camp was notorious for its rough and lawless characters. When the young man returned, one of his friends asked him how he had fared in that kind of company. "Oh, fine," he said, "they never caught on."

Several months in the company of godless men—and they had never "caught on" to the fact that he was a Christian. What a perfect record—*of shameful denial!* He had been afraid to confess Christ in the midst of godless men because he was afraid of the consequences.

But what of our own record in the presence of Christ's enemies? Is it really so much better? What hiding of our colors, what dodging of the issue, what shaving of the truth, what flagrant, base denial of the Savior does our record show? Of John the Baptist we read: "He confessed and denied not." Too often we have denied and confessed not!

There is a species of church members that might be called "chameleon Christians." A chameleon is a lizard that is able to change the color of its skin. As a result, it is frequenlty indistinguishable from the grass in which it slinks and slithers. God forbid that we make our way through this sinful world as chameleons, always changing our colors, always concealing our true identity as Christians.

Let us pray Him to forgive us our sins of cowardice. Like Simon Peter, after he had been forgiven and restored by the Lord whom he denied, let us confess our Savior before friend and foe. Like the early disciples, let us act on the conviction that "we cannot but speak the things which we have seen and heard"—the things that pertain to our salvation. Surely, He who shed His lifeblood that we might live has the right to expect no less!

Ashamed of Jesus, that dear Friend On whom my hopes of heav'n depend?
No, when I blush, be this my shame, That I no more revere His name!

The Assurance of His Face

The Lord your God is gracious and merciful, and will not turn away His face from you. *2 Chronicles 30:9*

It was well past midnight. Little, four-year-old Tommy had been asleep for hours. Suddenly he awoke from a bad dream. Not knowing whether he was alone in the large, dark bedroom, he whispered into the darkness: "Daddy are you there?"

From the other side of the room came the comforting voice: "Yes, Tommy, Daddy's here." For a moment Tommy lay silent, still not quite sure his bad dream was imagined. Once more he whispered: "Daddy, is your face toward me?"

And once more the kind voice of his father assured him: "Yes, Tommy, my face is toward your bed." With that assurance the little fellow turned over, closed his eyes, and drifted back to peaceful slumber.

How much like little Tommy you and I are when the thick, impenetrable darkness of fear settles upon our little lives. Is our heavenly Father near us? Is He really watching over us? Does He see our plight? How comforting in such moments to know that "the eyes of the Lord are over the righteous, and His ears are open unto their prayers."

On Calvary's cross God showed His face to us: a face of love, of tenderness, and divine compassion. Or, as St. John writes: "In this was manifested the love of God toward us, because that God sent His only begotten Son into the world, that we might live through Him."

Because of Calvary we can know with an assurance that will not waver that "the Lord our God is gracious and merciful and will not turn His face away from us." Like little Tommy we can rest assured as long as we know that our Father is with us and that His eyes will be upon us throughout all the changing scenes of life. We have His Word for that!

In Thee I place my trust, On Thee I calmly rest;
I know Thee good; I know Thee just; and count Thy will the best.
Let good or ill befall, It must be good for me;
Secure of having Thee in all, Of having all in Thee. Amen.

Waters of Refreshment

As the hart panteth after the water brooks, so panteth my soul after Thee, O God.
Psalm 42:1

David was well acquainted with the terrain of a semi-arid country. He had often seen a hart (a deer) almost consumed by thirst, "panting after the water brooks" which still lay beyond the far horizon. Would the struggling animal make it to the trickling brook and be refreshed?

The psalmist likens himself to the fainting deer. His troubled heart is in desperate need of the refreshment only God can give him. And so he cries out: "As the hart panteth after the water brooks, so panteth my soul after Thee, O God!"

The life of David, from his early youth until his declining years as King of Israel, can very well be described by the words of the poet: "I live in danger all the way." Much of his personal tragedy was the result of his own sinning, of which he repented with heaving sobs of sorrow. We need only to read his Fifty-first Psalm in which he pours out his broken heart to God. Indeed, we find this great man of God "panting for the waters of refreshment" which he could find only in the heart of God.

Has life ever brought *us* to that pass where our soul panted after God "as the hart panteth after the water brooks"? If so, thank God, our Lord, that He was always there—right beside us. All we need do is throw ourselves upon His unending love and mercy, which is revealed to us in the Gospel of our Redeemer. Every life has its arid stretches where the horizon seems bleak and burning, where there seems to be no promise of refreshing, healing waters. But our gracious Lord has assured us that the water brooks are there, waiting for us to stoop and drink. There we will find pardon, peace, and strength for the stretch that lies ahead. On more than one occasion the Savior spoke of the "water of life" (John 4:10) which was His to give, freely and without price, to all who would put their trust in Him.

Lord God, heavenly Father, may I find daily refreshment in the Gospel of Jesus Christ, my Savior. Amen.

Take God's Word for It

It is better to trust in the Lord than to put confidence in princes. *Psalm 118:9*

We all can learn a lesson from the newly converted Christians in Berea. We are told in Acts 17:11 that they not only believed the Gospel which Paul and Silas had preached to them, but that they also "searched the Scriptures daily, whether those things were so." They wanted to be sure that the things Paul had told them were, in deed and in truth, the Word of God!

We will do well to follow their example. Although we are to honor those in authority in the church (our pastors, our teachers, our church leaders), we are to rest our hope of eternal life not on the word of any man but only on the Word of God.

It is comparatively easy in our everyday life simply to follow the leader and ask no questions. That is not the way the Lord expects us to operate in matters spiritual. We are to make sure that our Leader is *Christ* and that the Word on which we base our hope is *His.* That means going back to the Scriptures again and again to see "whether or not these things are so." Do we believe the Gospel merely because we take some person's word for it or because we take *God's* Word for it?

When was the last time we opened our Bible for serious study? When was the last time we sat in on a Bible class and took an active part in the discussion? Christ told the religious leaders of His day not to get hung up on traditions handed down by men but (literally) to "ransack the Scriptures" to make sure they had found God's eternal truth.

Speaking to those who had come to faith in Him, He later said: "If ye continue in *My* Word, . . . ye shall know the truth, and the truth shall make you free" (John 8:31-32).

Notice, it is *His* Word in which His beloved must abide—not in the speculations nor in the pious traditions of men. Therefore let us abide in the truths which *He* has spoken and which His inspired apostles later preserved in written words.

Lord, may I always rest my faith only in You and Your Word, and not in the traditions of men. Amen.

Make All the Good People Nice

Adorn the doctrine of God, our Savior, in all things. *Titus 2:10*

A young mother was helping her five-year-old with her evening prayers. After concluding her formal prayers, the little girl paused for a moment, then added: "Dear God, make all the bad people good and all the good people nice."

Exactly what she meant by this unusual prayer, we are not sure, but we do have a clue to the meaning of the second half of it. If only all the good people in the world were—nice! If only all who profess the Christian faith, who attend church, who work on committees and commissions, who represent the church to the world were as pleasant, and winsome as Christ's followers ought to be!

Occasionally those who profess to be doing the Lord's work display a brusqueness, a lovelessness, even a nastiness that ill becomes His disciples. Their very attitude belies their profession. In the language of our little girl, they are the "good people" who aren't "nice."

The apostle asks us to "adorn the doctrine of God." Another translation of this passge reads: "Add luster to the doctrine of God our Savior." We are to be pleasant, gentle, kind, always displaying the fruits of the doctrine we profess. Are we among the "good people" who are "nice"? Pray God we are.

And having prayed, let us strive for continued growth in those Christian graces which will be attractive to those with whom we have daily contact—both inside and outside the church. Let our lives sparkle as they "adorn the doctrine of God," drawing the attention and, with the Spirit's help, winning the approval of our fellowmen. To that end we repeat the poet's words:

Make me to walk in Thy commands,—'Tis a delightful road,—
Nor let my head or heart or hands Offend against my God.
Assist my soul, too apt to stray, A stricter watch to keep;
And should I e'er forget Thy way, Restore Thy wand'ring sheep.

The Miracle of Pentecost

And there appeared unto them cloven tongues like as of fire and it sat upon each of them. And they were all filled with the Holy Ghost. *Acts 2:3-4*

The story of the first Pentecost need hardly be repeated here. Its details can be recalled by reading the Scripture portion suggested above. The importance of this festival for the faith and life of the Christian can hardly be overemphasized.

To appreciate this significance, we must go back a little more than seven weeks before the miraculous event took place. It was the night before His crucifixion and the mood was somber as Christ spoke to His disciples in what might be called His farewell address. Their hearts were heavy as they sensed the direction of the Savior's thoughts. Again and again He referred to the Comforter whom He would send them from the Father.

He said, for instance, "I will pray the Father, and He shall send you *another* Comforter . . . even the Spirit of truth." A few moments later He confided: "The Comforter, which is the Holy Ghost . . . shall teach you all things." And a few moments later: "The Comforter . . . shall testify of Me."

The Greek word for "comforter" can be translated variously. Literally it means a person who has been called to one's side to be of help—as an advocate, a spokesman, or prompter. It was only moments before His ascension into heaven that Christ told His disciples not to leave Jerusalem until this promise of the Comforter (namely, the Holy Spirit whom He would send from the Father) had been fulfilled.

The miracle of the first Pentecost is the fulfillment of that promise. Of the assembled group we read: "They were all filled with the Holy Ghost." And the rest is history. Empowered by the Spirit of God, the disciples went out into all the world, heralds of the King, proclaimers of the Kingdom. You and I have been enlightened and empowered by the same Holy Spirit. In a very real sense, today and every day is Pentecost. God is giving us His Holy Spirit through His Word. It is for *us* to proclaim that Word to the nations. God grant it for Jesus' sake. Amen.

The Holy Ghost

No man can say that Jesus is the Lord, but by the Holy Ghost. *1 Corinthians 12:3*

There is the ever-present danger that in our constant emphasis on Jesus Christ as our Savior and Lord we (without intending to do so) overlook the importance of the Holy Spirit in our Christian lives. Martin Luther has given us an eloquent description of the Holy Spirit's work in his explanation of the Third Article of the Apostles' Creed. Let us read his words slowly and thoughtfully. He says:

> I believe that I cannot by my own reason or strength believe in Jesus Christ, my Lord, or come to Him; but the *Holy Ghost* has called me by the Gospel, enlightened me with His gifts, sanctified and kept me in the true faith; even as he calls, gathers, enlightens, and sanctifies the whole Christian Church on earth, and keeps it with Jesus Christ in the one true faith; in which Christian Church He daily and richly forgives all sins to me and all believers, and will at the Last Day raise up me and all the dead, and give unto me and all believers in Christ eternal life. This is most certainly true.

What a beautiful statement of faith! While it is true that Christ has won for us complete salvation through His substitutionary atonement on the cross, it is also true that we have come into personal possession of that salvation only through the operation of the Holy Spirit. Paul tells us in the text quoted above: "No man can say that Jesus is the Lord, but by the Holy Ghost."

Working through the means of grace (the Gospel and the sacraments) the Holy Spirit has enlightened and continues to enlighten our hearts so that we can see Christ as our personal Redeemer and can put our trust in Him. And having enlightened us, He continues to enrich our lives with the abundance of spiritual gifts that Christ has won for us. Well might we pray:

> Holy Ghost, with light divine, Shine upon this heart of mine;
> Cast down every idol throne, Reign supreme, and reign alone.

Love

The fruit of the Spirit is love, joy, peace, longsuffering, gentleness . . . Galatians 5:22

Jesus told His disciples: "By their fruits ye shall know them." In that instance He was speaking of false prophets, whose daily lives would expose the falseness of their teaching. But it is also true of Christians that "by their fruits ye shall know them." The genuineness of our faith will be revealed by the kind of lives we lead; by our *fruits* our fellowmen will know us.

In the passage quoted above Paul is encouraging his converts in Galatia to demonstrate their faith by "showing forth" *the fruits of the Spirit.* In this and the following devotions we will meditate on a few of the "fruits" that Paul mentions. The first in his list is love. Once a person has truly grasped the miracle of God's love in Christ, he is bound to reflect that love in his attitude toward others. Of the early Christians it was said: "Behold how they love one another!"

Can the same be said of us? In many cases (praise God!) the answer is yes. Yet when one looks at the church today, one is often saddened by the evident absence of brotherly and sisterly love. The petty faultfinding, the bickering, the peevishness, the back-biting, the open feuding that have frequently soured the lives of Christian families, Christian congregations (sometimes, even Christian churchbodies)—surely, these are not a "fruit of the Spirit." They are rather "the works of the flesh," against which the Scriptures warn us.

Love, true Christian love, cannot be added to our lives as an ornament is added to a Christmas tree. Genuine Christian love must be a *fruit.* It must be a part of the tree. It must be a natural outgrowth of something that is alive within us. It must be an inevitable fruit of the *Spirit*—the Spirit implanted into our heart at Holy Baptism and nourished daily by the Gospel. That Spirit must find utterance not only through our lips but also through our lives. What is our record in this respect? Do we *love* as much as we say we do?

Lord, grant us a greater measure of Your Spirit, so that we may love even as You have loved us. Amen.

Joy

The fruit of the Spirit is . . . joy. Galatians 5:22

JOY was a dominant note in the lives of Christ's apostles. This does not mean that the lives of His followers were cushioned by beds of roses. No, there were hardships to be endured. But they found joy in the *midst* of hardship, gladness in the *midst* of pain. "As sorrowful, yet always rejoicing" is the way the apostle Paul put it.

No one in all the world has a better right to joy and gladness than has the trusting child of God. The Christian alone knows beyond the shadow of a doubt that all his sins have been forgiven and that, through Christ, he has a clear title to a mansion in the Father's house above.

He alone has the divine assurance of comfort in sorrow, strength in sickness, solace in bereavement, help in distress, and ultimate triumph in the midst of dire calamity. And this assurance is signed and sealed in the blood of the Son of God Himself! He lived and died and rose again that our "joy might be full."

Small wonder that the apostle Peter could write of the Christians who were scattered throughout Asia Minor that they "rejoice[d] with joy unspeakable and full of glory" (1 Peter 1:8). Could he write that of us today?

There is the danger of settling for a sort of "cosmetic joy"—the joy of the forced smile, the perfunctory glad hand, and the professional glad word. All entirely superficial. The joy of which Paul is speaking in the text above goes far deeper. It permeates all of our thinking, speaking, and doing. It brightens both our inner and outer life. It radiates wherever we are or wherever we go. Thank God for this precious "fruit of the Spirit," which is *joy*, and let us cultivate it more and more.

O Lord, restore unto me the JOY of Your salvation! Amen.

Peace

The fruit of the Spirit is . . . peace. *Galatians 5:22*

Among the various "fruits of the Spirit" which Paul mentions, the third is peace. Let us mark well: he does not say that our peace is the fruit of our *circumstances*. We are all tempted to look at our circumstances and to find in them the reason for our peace of mind. Our children are well, our finances are sound, our friends are kind, and so we are "at peace."

But when things suddenly change, we discover to our dismay that our peace was drawn from our circumstances and not from the *Lord* of our circumstances. Such a peace is not the fruit of the Spirit. It is the fruit of our environment, and our environment changes like the weather.

The Bible tells us: "thou wilt keep him in perfect peace whose mind is *stayed on Thee*" (Isaiah 26:3). Those who have experienced the love of God in Christ have learned to throw their entire weight on God, trusting that "underneath are the everlasting arms" (Deuteronomy 33:27).

Into His hands they commit all of their *yesterdays*, knowing that for Jesus' sake He will forgive them; into His hands they commit *today*, knowing that it is another day of grace; and into His hands they commit all of their *tomorrows*, knowing that all of His mercies, which have been "new unto us every morning," will be just as new, just as sure, and just as all-sufficing tomorrow as they are today. That is the peace and assurance which is "the fruit of the Spirit."

How about the peace that you and I enjoy today? Is it merely the result of our comfortable circumstances? Or is it the peace that has its roots in the Gospel of Jesus Christ, our Savior?

Bane and blessing, pain and pleasure, By the cross are sanctified;
PEACE is there that knows no measure, Joys that through all time abide.

Long-suffering

The fruit of the Spirit is . . . long-suffering. *Galatians 5:22*

We have been meditating on a few gifts of the Spirit which Paul mentions in his letter to the Galatians. Today we examine the gift which he calls long-suffering. Perhaps we can start by showing what long-suffering is *Not*.

Are things getting on our nerves? Do the countless little irritations of the day find us flying off the handle? Are we touchy, grouchy, impatient, pouty? Then remember, irritableness, impatience, and bitterness are not "the fruit of the Spirit." They are rather "the works of the flesh." They are the very opposite of long-suffering!

In another place, Paul reminds us that "Charity suffereth long and is kind" (1 Corinthians 13:4). Love can absorb the shock of abuse, the impact of mistreatment, the stones of slander, the disappointments of false friendships—and can still maintain its peace and composure.

Love is always gracious and full of good will. In the midst of irritations, in the midst of trying circumstances, love is not only self-composed, but it is friendly, compassionate, and tender. In spite of trials, and vexations, love just goes on loving.

The source of such loving patience, of course, lies beyond the walls of the human heart. It springs forever at the foot of Calvary's cross. There in an infinitely larger measure love suffered long and was kind. That love, the love which drove the Son of God Himself to die for sinful men, must enkindle in our hearts a similar affection, a similar patience, a similar kindliness.

Godly patience is a "fruit of the Spirit." Let us pray daily for a greater measure of this priceless virtue.

Give us faith to trust Thee boldly, Hope to stay our souls on Thee;
But oh! BEST of all Thy graces, Give us Thine own charity!

Kindness

The fruit of the Spirit is . . . gentleness. Galatians 5:22

The word which our English Bible translates "gentleness" in the above passage could perhaps better be translated "kindness." And still more specifically, it is a sort of *active* kindness that the apostle had in mind; not only a kindness which refrains from doing evil to one's neighbor, but a kindness which is always on the alert, looking for ways to *help* him and to be of service to him.

How desperately the world today needs that sort of kindness, that attitude which is willing not only to look upon every human being as our friend, as a fit subject for the full measure of our love, but which is willing also to translate itself into *deeds* of kindness to every person whose life touches ours.

We all are in danger of restricting our kindness to our thoughts or to our words. We think kindly thoughts. We speak generous words. Perhaps we even find ourselves breathing a silent "God, bless you!" when we see people who are in need. But the fruit of the Spirit is an outgoing, *active* kindness—a kindness which DOES something about the needs of our neighbor.

It is quite possible that the priest and the Levite in the parable thought kindly about the poor man who fell among the thieves. But the Good Samaritan did more than think—*he acted*. It is this kind of action in the Christian life which is "the fruit of the Spirit."

Such kindness is but the natural expression of a heart which has been transformed by the Savior's love. When we find ourselves becoming cold, callous, or indifferent to the needs of those around us, or perhaps even openly rude, uncharitable, or unkind, let us flee again and again to *His* love for pardon and for strength.

> Give me a faithful heart, likeness to Thee;
> That each departing day henceforth may see
> Some work of love begun, Some deed of kindness done,
> Some wand'rer sought and won, Something for Thee.

The Holy Trinity

Go ye, therefore, and teach all nations, baptizing them in the name of the Father, and of the Son, and of the Holy Ghost. Matthew 28:19

The doctrine of the Holy Trinity will always be a mystery to our finite minds. It is said that one day the great church father St. Augustine, in deep meditation on the doctrine of the Trinity, was walking along the seashore. Suddenly his attention focused on a small girl carrying one shell of water after another from the sea to a little hole which she had dug in the sand.

"What are you doing, little girl?" he asked. In all innocence she replied: "Oh, I'm going to empty the sea into this little hole." Augustine smiled, but as he walked along, he said to himself: "That is exactly what I have been trying to do. I have been trying to encompass the doctrine of the Holy Trinity with this little mind of mine."

But while the doctrine of the Holy Trinity cannot be grasped by the human mind, there can be no doubt that it is clearly taught in Scripture. Matthew tells us that when Jesus stepped out of the Jordan after having been baptized, the Holy Spirit, in the form of a dove, descended upon Him and a voice from heaven (the Father's) said: "This is My beloved Son." This incident recorded the presence of all three persons of the Trinity.

Then, too, the Savior on several occasions spoke of the Spirit whom He would send from the Father—again indicating the activity of three persons. Perhaps clearest of all is Christ's final command to His disciples, namely, that they should baptize "in the name of the Father, and of the Son, and of the Holy Ghost." That is, in the name of the Holy Trinity.

This doctrine may be unsearchable, but it means very much to the believer. We have a Father who created and preserves us. We have His Son, our Savior, who became one of us in order to redeem us. And we have an ever-present Comforter, the Holy Spirit, who proceeds from both, who preserves us unto life eternal. Oh, ever blessed Trinity!

Faithfulness

The fruit of the Spirit is . . . faith. Galatians 5:22

The word "faith" in the above text is better translated faithfulness—around which cluster all such attributes as dependability, trustworthiness, loyalty, and fidelity. These qualities, says Paul, are further "fruits of the Spirit."

The true believer is a man of his word. He is a man who can be trusted to do his *best* under any circumstances. He is a man who has won the confidence of those with whom he lives and works from day to day. He is a man who gives a day's wage for a day's work, or, if he happens to be the worker, he is a man who gives a day's work for a day's wage. In short, he can be *counted* on to do his duty.

The story is told of a young man who, seeking employment came from the country to the city. With suitcase in hand, he entered the office of a successful employer and asked whether there was any opening. "No, my young man, I'm afraid there is not. Try again in a week or so," was the answer of the man at the desk. As the young man turned to leave, the lock on his suitcase came loose, and the contents of the case fell to the floor.

Among the items which fell helter-skelter to the floor was a worn copy of the Bible. When the employer's eye fastened on the Bible, he suddenly changed his mind and said: "Just a minute, young man, on second thought I believe we *do* have an opening."

The employer had lived long enough to know that one of the fruits of the Spirit is faithfulness, trustworthiness, reliability.

He who has found forgiveness for his sins at the foot of the cross cannot be anything but faithful. Let us pray for an ever greater measure of this splendid Christian virtue.

> Oh, grant me, Lord, to do, With ready heart and willing,
> Whate'er Thou shalt command, My calling here fulfilling. Amen.

Meekness

The fruit of the Spirit is . . . meekness. Galatians 5:23

Let's admit it. There are times when we feel that we cannot afford to be meek—cannot afford to be humble and of a lowly spirit. After all, we have so many things to boast about, so many accomplishments to our credit. How will our friends ever know about them if we don't at least *whisper them from the housetops?*

Yes, there are times when like the lonely desert flower in Gray's "Elegy in a Country Churchyard," we feel that we have been "born to blush unseen And waste our fragrance on the desert air." The fear of being unnoticed, unheralded, and unsung is a universal human trait—but definitely not a "fruit of the Spirit."

Simon Peter had such fears. And every time he tried to overcome them by asserting his own virtues, he made a sorry mess of things. But Simon Peter learned his lesson. It was an altogether different Simon who in later years wrote: "Be clothed with *humility*; for God resisteth the proud and giveth grace to the humble."

Robert Louis Stevenson once said to a friend: "The most dangerous height I ever climbed was Mount *Ego*." The great church father St. Augustine once exclaimed: "Should you ask me, What is the first thing in religion? I should reply, The first, the second, the third thing—nay, all—is humility!"

Let us, then, be done with silly pride and shallow boasting. As we contemplate the unsearchable love of Him who *humbled* Himself for us, even to the death of the cross, let us say with the poet:

> When I survey the wondrous Cross
> On which the Prince of Glory died,
> My richest gain I count but loss
> *And pour contempt* on all my pride.

God be merciful to me, a sinner, for Jesus' sake. Amen.

Self-Control

The fruit of the Spirit is . . . temperance. Galatians 5:22-23

Few scenes are more pathetic, more tragic, than that of a man who has lost his temper. He is like a car careening down a dangerous hill with a madman at the steering wheel. He has lost *control*—lost control of his thoughts, his words, and his actions. And woe to that man, woman, or child who happens to get into his way!

A lost temper is not a "fruit of the Spirit." It is a work of the flesh. It is a surrendering of the controls to Satan. And the devil, as Scripture pictures him, is always "lying at the door," eager to take over at less than a moment's notice. Indeed, a lost temper has been called "the devil's open door."

What heartache, what havoc, what pain and misery have followed in the wake of those moments when men or women have lost their tempers! And, on the other hand, what heartache, what havoc, and what pain have been *avoided* by those who have learned, with the Spirit's help, to *curb* their passions!

"They that are Christ's," the apostle tells us in the verse following our text, "have crucified the flesh with the affections and lusts." Through faith in Christ, who by His death has atoned also for their sins of wrath, Christians have tapped that power which enables them to resist all temptations to fly off the handle. Through faith in Christ they have learned to "live in the Spirit," and produce "the fruit of the Spirit"— temperance, even-mindedness, self-control.

May God grant us a greater measure of His Holy Spirit that we may cultivate the grace of Christian temperance.

O God, forsake me not! Take not Thy Holy Spirit from me
And suffer not the might Of sin to overcome me. Amen.

Living in the Spirit

If we live in the Spirit, let us also walk in the Spirit. Galatians 5:25

We know that certain climates are more conducive to good health than others. For persons who are afflicted with lung diseases, for instance, the high altitude of Colorado or the warm, dry air of Arizona are the climates most likely to bring recovery.

There is also such a thing as a *spiritual* climate—a climate which will insure the health of our souls and the vigor of our spiritual lives. The Bible tells us that we are to "live in the Spirit." We are to live and move and have our being in the things of God—His Word, His Sacraments, His Church. We are to cultivate and to maintain a *close* association with those established ordinances through which His Holy Spirit can operate within our lives. *There* we shall find the most healthful climate for our souls.

But this health of soul is to show itself in vigorous, energetic action. "If we *live* in the Spirit," says St. Paul, "let us also *walk* in the Spirit." And walking in the Spirit means spiritual exercise—the exercise of "love, joy, peace, long-suffering, gentleness, goodness, faith, meekness, temperance," the very virtues of which we have spoken in our previous meditations.

Have we been living in the Spirit? Have we devoted ourselves to daily prayer and meditation on His Word? And, if so, have we also been *walking* in the Spirit—by deeds of daily Christian virtue?

Remember, our friends cannot *see* the Spirit who occupies our hearts. They will recognize His presence only as we permit His presence to become visible in our attitudes and behavior. Are we permitting His inner presence to become evident in our lives?

O Holy Spirit, enter in, And in our hearts Thy work begin! Amen.

Take a "Beautiful Savior" into a "Beautiful Summer"

The heavens declare the glory of God; and the firmament showeth His handiwork.
Psalm 19:1

Summer is the time of vacations, the time for trips into the great outdoors. As we make our travel plans, perhaps we can learn a valuable lesson from the following little story. A family was on its way to a Sunday outing in the mountains. It was midmorning when they drove by a church. Worshipers, dressed in their Sunday best, were seen gathered at the front entrance.

From the back seat of the car came the voice of five-year-old Karen: "Daddy, aren't *we* going to church today?" In the front seat both father and mother exchanged embarrassed glances. Since the question had been addressed to him, the father felt obliged to answer.

"We can worship God in the mountains," was his short reply. There was a brief moment of silence. Then from the back seat came the sage observation of which only a five-year-old is capable: "But we *won't,* Daddy, *will* we?"

The father had sought refuge behind an evasion all too popular today, even among church members. It is true that our Lord can be worshiped in the mountains. He can be worshiped in the plains, in the valleys, and along a thousand streams. But in her five short years Karen had learned that while God *can* be worshiped from hills or dales or mountaintops, He usually *isn't.*

It will call for a conscious effort on our part to include God in our vacation plans. The majestic mountains may tell us of His might, the gorgeous beauty of a summer landscape may tell us of His wisdom, but only the Gospel of our Savior's tender mercy can tell us of God's love. And it is this love that we are to recall and celebrate in conscious acts of Christian worship—not only in the hushed silence of the sanctuary, but also in God's great out-of-doors. On mountaintops, in plains and valleys, beside the bubbling brooks the Christian heart can sing:

Fair are the meadows, Fair are the woodlands,
Robed in flow'rs of blooming spring; Jesus is fairer, Jesus is purer;
He makes our sorr'wing spirit sing. . . .

Oh, come, let us worship the Lord!

This Is the Life!

This is life eternal, that they might know Thee, the only true God, and Jesus Christ, whom Thou hast sent. *John 17:3*

"This is the life!" How often have we heard people give vent to their exuberant feelings in those four short words. Stretched out on the sun-baked sands of a breeze-swept shore, or relaxing in the cooling shade of a spreading tree, they breathe deeply of the bracing air and sigh: "Ah, this is the life!" This is the life that refreshes and rebuilds.

In a similar, yet completely different, sense the trusting child of God relaxes upon the sure foundation of his Savior's promises and says to all the world: "*This* is the life!" He has found a life—in the very midst of life—which refreshes and sustains his soul in every changing circumstance.

That life he has found in Jesus Christ, his Savior. Jesus says: "This is life eternal, that they may know Thee, the only true God, and Jesus Christ, whom Thou hast sent." He who has God as his Father and Jesus as his Savior has stepped from death to life; and the life into which he has entered is a glorious life that will never end. It is a "life eternal."

Have we found the secret of this spiritually invigorating life in Christ? It is the secret of a penitent heart turned upward to God for daily mercy, for forgiveness in Jesus' name, for strength to carry the burden just another day. It is also the secret of a life that is constantly reaching out to others, bringing help and hope and healing in the name of Him who loved us.

That is the life which is ours through faith in the precious Gospel promise—the life of which Horatius Bonar wrote those immortal lines:

> Thy Word first made me feel my sin, It taught me to believe;
> Then, in believing, peace I found, And now, I live! I LIVE!

May that be the joy and rejoicing of each of us. Having found our life in Christ—we live, we live!

Knowing God

This is life eternal, that they might know Thee, the only true God, and Jesus Christ, whom Thou hast sent. John 17:3

One of the most priceless privileges of the Christian is to *know God.* To know Him (as He has revealed Himself through Jesus Christ, His Son) is to have new life—a life of victory over sin and sorrow here on earth and a life of eternal joy in the Father's house above.

But to know God means more than merely to know *about* Him. Many know what the Bible has to say about the mighty Maker and Ruler of our universe. They may know, for instance, that He is a Spirit, that He is omnipotent, omnipresent, holy, just, and righteous.

But a person can know all this, and much more, and still not know God! That kind of knowledge is not *life.* It is still death. The words of Jesus quoted above might be expanded to read: "This is life eternal, that they might in their hearts know Me as their Savior and thus *experience* Thee, that they might have *fellowship* with Thee, that they might have Thee as their personal, loving Father, the only true God, and Jesus Christ, whom Thou hast sent."

By faith in Jesus Christ, our Redeemer, we Christians have come to know God personally. We have entered into intimate fellowship with Him. We have walked with Him and have talked with Him. Or, as the patriarch Job once put it: "I have heard of Thee by the hearing of the ear, but now mine *eye seeth* Thee." He knew God as his kind and loving Father. Thank God that, through Christ, we have learned to know Him thus. In that knowledge we have *life*—both now and forever.

To God the Father, God the Son, And God the Spirit, Three in One
Shall glory, praise, and honor be Now and throughout eternity!

O blessed Holy Trinity, I thank You for having revealed Yourself to me—for letting me know the loving God You are!

167

Having Jesus

This is life eternal, that they might know Thee, the only true God, and Jesus Christ, whom Thou hast sent. *John 17:3*

To get the full force, the full strength and comfort of these words, we must remember that it was Christ Himself who spoke them. It was on the night before His crucifixion, while speaking to His Father, that Jesus said these words to Him: "This is life eternal, that they might know Thee, the only true God, and [ME] Jesus Christ, whom Thou hast sent."

To have Jesus is to have eternal life. Why? Because Jesus Himself has told us: "God so loved the world that He gave His only begotten Son, that whosoever believeth in Him should not perish, but have everlasting *life*" (John 3:16). "My sheep hear My voice," says Jesus, "and I know them, and they follow Me; and I give unto them eternal *life*" (John 10:27-28).

Jesus can give eternal life to His followers because He has *earned* it for them. It is His to give. By His spotless life He has perfectly fulfilled God's Law for all mankind, and by His innocent suffering and death He has paid the entire debt of human guilt. That is why the Bible can say of Him that he has "abolished death and hath brought *Life* and immortality to light" (2 Timothy 1:10).

The important thing is that we actually *have* Jesus. We possess Him as our own. For in that possession we have *life*—life now and life forever. "This is the record," John tells us, "that God hath given us eternal life, and this life is in His Son. He that hath the Son hath life" (1 John 5:11-12). Remember who spoke almost all the words quoted in this meditation. Could any words be more clear—more sure?

Thou art the Way, the Truth, the LIFE: Grant us that way to know,
That Truth to keep, that LIFE to win, Whose joys eternal flow.

Lord Jesus, having You in my heart by faith, I know the Way, I have the Truth, and I enjoy the Life. How can I ever thank You? Amen.

The Abundant Life

I am come that they might have life, and that they might have it more abundantly.
John 10:10

These words are taken from the well-known "Good Shepherd" chapter of St. John's gospel. Speaking in a parable, the Savior had just pointed out that he who is *not* the shepherd, but a *thief*, breaks into the flock to kill, to steal, and to destroy.

In contrast to the pillage and death which are wreaked by the intruder who comes "to steal, and to kill, and to destroy," the Savior speaks those familiar words: "*I* am come that they might have LIFE, and that they might have it more abundantly," literally, "that they might have life, and have a *surplus* of it."

A surplus of life! What a thought! And yet that is exactly what the Christian has. Added to the life which is his by nature and which is being lived by all men around him, the believer has the life "which is hid with Christ in God" (Colossians 3:3). He has the life which is his by faith in the death of Jesus Christ, his Savior.

And what a life that is! It is a life of full assurance of pardon for all his sins; a life of peace with God, that "peace which passeth understanding"; a life of love and hope and "joy in the holy Spirit"; a life of strength and power and victory "through Christ, which strengthens" him; a life of willing, happy service to his fellowman, a service not out of constraint but out of love.

It was this kind of life of which the Savior frequently spoke throughout His ministry (John 6:33). In His long discourses on the Bread of Life He refers to Himself as *being* that Bread. And He says that those who eat of that Bread (who believe) will have life—true life, spiritual life, the kind of inner life which He will give to each believer "as a surplus." Do you and I have such life within us—new life created by the Gospel through the Holy Spirit? Pray God that we do.

> Lord, give us such a life as this; And then, whate'er may come,
> We'll taste e'en here the hallowed bliss Of an eternal home.

The Purchased Life

Ye are not your own, for ye are bought with a price. 1 Corinthians 6:19-20

One of the greatest sources of strength for the believer is the knowledge that he belongs to Christ. We are His possession, given to Him by His Father. In His high-priestly prayer the Savior places petition after petition before His heavenly Father. But for whom is He praying? *"For them which Thou hast given Me."*

We are His by right of purchase. This is what St. Paul means when he says: "Ye are bought with a price." This is what St. Peter means when he says: "Ye are a chosen generation . . . a people of His *purchasing.*" This is what Martin Luther means when he says: "I believe that Jesus Christ . . . has redeemed me, a lost and condemned creature, purchased, and won me . . . that I may be *His own.*"

Because of that divine transaction—the purchase of all mankind by the death of God's beloved Son—I am His, His for time and for eternity. Notice the strong claim of possession in the following well-known words of Christ:

"My sheep hear My voice, and I know them, and they follow Me. And I give unto them eternal life. And they shall never perish, neither shall any man pluck them out of My hand. My Father, which *gave* them Me, is greater than all; and no man is able to pluck them out of My Father's hand" (John 10:27-29).

How different life becomes with *every* remembrance that we are Christ's, the purchase of His love, and that we are therefore precious in His sight! Let that remembrance go with us throughout the day, granting fresh courage, new strength, and greater victory. Praise God: through Christ we are *His,* now and forever!

The Lord my Shepherd is, I shall be well supplied.
Since He is mine and *I am His,* What can I want beside?

The Rooted Life

He shall be like a tree planted by the rivers of water, that bringeth forth his fruit in his season; his leaf also shall not wither; and whatsoever he doeth shall prosper. Psalm 1:3

Have you ever walked down a city street which was lined with stately elms? Rising high on each side, like pillars in a huge cathedral, they extend their leafy arms across the street so that they form a beautiful canopy of green, affording shade throughout the summer months.

In years gone by, at regular intervals among the elms, one would see a shabby wooden telephone pole, splintered, and weather beaten. Although it stood as erect as the elms, it sprouted neither branches, nor leaves, and contributed nothing to the symphony of green and yellow which thrilled the heart of every passer-by.

Why the difference? The answer, of course, is simple. The elms had roots, and the telephone poles had none. The elms had tapped an unseen source below the ground from which they drew their daily sustenance, while the telephone pole was merely a piece of lifeless wood sunk into the earth.

The heart which is "hid with Christ in God" has found a secret source of daily nourishment. The person who has found his soul's redemption in the life and death of Christ, his Savior, is "like a tree planted by the rivers of water, that bringeth forth his fruit in his season; his leaf also shall not wither; and whatsoever he doeth shall prosper" (Psalm 1:3).

The Christian life is the *rooted* life, rooted deeply and firmly in the promises of God. In those promises there is strength, assurance, and final victory.

Remember the illustration above—the picture of the shabby telephone poles and the luxuriant elm trees? Perhaps we should take a moment and ask ourselves: which do we resemble most?

Lord, keep me firmly rooted in Your Word. Amen.

The Expectant Life

We . . . are citizens of heaven, and from heaven we expect our Deliverer to come, the Lord Jesus Christ. Philippians 3:20 NEB

The great preacher G. Campbell Morgan once said:

> To me the second coming of Christ is the perpetual light on the path which makes the present bearable. I never lay my head on my pillow without thinking that, maybe, before the morning breaks, the final morning may have dawned. I never begin my work without thinking that perhaps He may interrupt my work and begin His own. Until He comes, I am not looking for death, I am looking for *Him*.

Looking for Him! What a difference that makes in our outlook on life and in our attitude toward life's problems and perplexities. Of the early Christians we read that they spent every day in the expectation of Christ's imminent return. He had promised, "I will come again," and His followers found daily strength and courage in that promise. We may be sure, that promise still stands!

His coming, either at the death of the world or at the death of His followers, cast a golden glow over all the road that lay ahead. They were walking *toward the light* of His return. And in that light all shadows fell behind them.

So, too, with us. All sorrows, all heartaches, all disappointments and bereavements lose their bitterness in the sweetness of the Savior's tender promise: "I will come again." He whose love brought Him to Calvary's cross, there to open the doors of His Father's house, will come *again* to lead us across the threshold into the eternal mansions, prepared for all who love Him.

What a wonderful prospect! As we approach our journey's end, our eyes are not upon death, but upon *Him* who has promised to return—to take us to that land beyond the far horizon where we "shall obtain joy and gladness; and sorrow and sighing shall flee away."

Even so, COME, Lord Jesus! Amen.

The Triumphant Life

Nay, in all these things we are more than conquerors through Him that loved us. *Romans 8:37*

How often, when someone has asked us how we are faring or how we are feeling, have we answered: "Oh, all right—*under the circumstances.*" Perhaps there was a reason for such an answer, but strictly speaking, the Christian need never live "*under his circumstances,*" for God has enabled him to live *above* them.

The Scripture passage quoted above follows a listing of some terrible circumstances—tribulation, distress, persecution, famine, nakedness, peril, sword. But what does the apostle say about all these circumstances? Does he say that these are the inevitable vexations of life which are bound to get us down?

"Nay, in all these things we are more than conquerors through Him that loved us!" We are more than conquerors. We have surmounted these circumstances. We have risen *above* them. And how did we get there? "Through Him that *loved* us."

Only through Christ can our lives become victorious—in the highest and fullest sense of that word. For only he who has found full forgiveness for all his sins through faith in the Redeemer can truly say (what Paul said just before he wrote these words): "If God be for us, who can be against us? He that spared not His own Son, but delivered Him up for us all, how shall He not with Him also freely give us *all* things?"

The only circumstance *under* which the child of God must live is the circumstance of God's love and mercy. That "circumstance" will never change. For we have our Lord's assurance: "I have loved thee with an everlasting love; therefore with loving-kindness have I drawn thee." Living under that "circumstance," we can live above all others.

Lord, let me walk in the full assurance of Your love. I ask it in the name, and for the sake, of Jesus Christ, my Savior. Amen.

The Grateful Life

Bless the Lord, O my soul, and forget not all His benefits. Psalm 103:2

How can I ever sufficiently thank my heavenly Father for all His kindnesses toward me? When I consider the unnumbered blessings which He has strewn upon my path since early childhood, I must exclaim with the psalmist: "Bless the Lord, O my soul, and all that is within me, bless His holy name!"

"*Who forgiveth all thine iniquities.*" That is the greatest of all His benefits toward me. Nothing in life is more important than to know that for Jesus' sake God has forgiven me, has thrown all my sins behind His back and will remember them again no more forever. Through Christ I am His child for time and for eternity.

"*Who healeth all thy diseases.*" He has given me a body that is "fearfully and wonderfully made." He has given me health and strength to lead a productive life. He has nursed me and all my loved ones in days of critical illness and has, in mercy, granted returning health. He has nourished and sustained the members of my body so that today my hands are still able to do His will and my lips are still able to sing His praise.

"*Who crowneth thee with loving-kindness and tender mercies.*" The story of my life from early childhood to this present moment is a constant record of His love. My Christian parents, my Christian home, my church, my school, yes *every* influence which brought me to, or has kept me in, the Savior's fold—all were not the fruits of *my* endeavors, but were the gracious leadings of His love.

Surely, I have every reason to rejoice with the psalmist and to join the chorus of all believers in the hymn of praise:

When all Thy mercies, O my God, My rising soul surveys,
Transported with the view, I'm lost In wonder, love, and praise!

174

The Profitable Life

Godliness is profitable unto all things, having promise of the life that now is and of that which is to come. 1 Timothy 4:8

An unbelieving soldier was making fun of his buddy who was a sincere believer. "The trouble with you," said the scoffer, "is that you think you are better than the rest of us."

"Not better," replied the Christian young man, "just better *off.*"

How true! The person (he or she) who has come to God through faith in Christ is *indeed* better off than the one who has not. The person who, out of gratitude and love for the Savior, leads a Christian life, who deals honestly with his neighbors, who lives at peace with his fellows, who tries, with the Spirit's help, to obey the laws of God and man, is much better off than the man who turns his back on Christ and leads a life of sin.

The point that our text is making is that not all of the rewards of the Christian faith lie on the other side of the grave. We have many of these rewards both here and now—in "the life that now is." True, many of them are intangible, but, oh, how precious! Among them are peace, contentment, love, joy, daily fellowship with Christ, the assurance of ultimate victory. With these in our heart, surely we are "better off" than the person who has never experienced them.

In addition, our Lord, according to His gracious will and unfailing wisdom, also blesses His faithful with earthly blessings too numerous to mention. Martin Luther lists them in his explanation of the fourth petition. Indeed the believer in Christ is "better off"—both "in this world and the next."

Lord, how can I ever thank You for all Your goodness to me? Amen.

The Empowered Life

I can do all things through Christ, which strengtheneth me. Philippians 4:13

An elderly pastor was asked how he had managed to change so much since the days of his youth. In his younger years, especially those following immediately upon his graduation from the seminary, he had been a proud, self-reliant, and impetuous man. But as the years wore on, he had become a man of endless patience and deep humility.

"It was this way," he answered. "Many years ago, when I was on the verge of losing my temper one day, I stopped in my tracks and uttered the prayer: 'Lord Jesus, give me Thy patience.' Well, I caught myself in time, and Jesus *did* give me patience.

"From that time on, I made it a practice of going right to Jesus whenever I saw temptation coming. If it was a temptation to impurity, I cried within myself: 'Thy *purity*, O Lord!' If it was a temptation to pride, self-righteousness, or arrogance, I cried within myself: 'Thy *humility*, O Lord!' No matter what the temptation, I always turned to Christ and pleaded for the grace which would lead me in the opposite direction from that in which the devil was trying to lead me."

St. Paul had found a similar power in his own life. From the first dramatic "turn around" on the Damascus Road (Acts 9) throughout the rest of his life he did "*all things* through Christ" who strengthened him. In Christ he had found power to resist temptation, to endure affliction, and to live a victorious Christian life. In Christ that power is available to you and me today. In His power alone we, too, shall conquer.

> Thou seest my feebleness; Jesus, be Thou my Power,
> My Help and Refuge in distress, My Fortress and my Tower. Amen.

The Life of Adornment

Adorn the doctrine of God, our Savior, in all things. Titus 2:10

A jewelry salesman had spent an autumn evening painting storm windows. The following morning, as he took his place behind a counter of sparkling necklaces, he became painfully aware of his soiled hands.

"Of all people," he thought to himself, "I should have hands that are immaculately clean. There is nothing more unfitting than to offer a string of pearls for sale when one's fingers look soiled and stained. Hands like mine make a poor background for precious jewelry."

The jeweler was right. Stained hands were not meant to sell dazzling jewelry. And neither were blemished lives meant to sell the pearl of great price. The man whose life has become soiled and stained by all manner of bad habits will not be an effective salesman for the Gospel of our Lord.

Christ does not expect us to make His Gospel *unattractive* to the unchurched and to the unbelieving by our careless speech and conduct. On the contrary, He expects us to make His Gospel *attractive* by our lives of love and consistent Christian virtues. This applies both to our lives as individuals and to our life as a Christian congregation.

The Bible tells us that we are to "*adorn* the doctrine of God, our Savior, in all things." Our lives are to be proper settings for the pearl of great price which the Christian Gospel offers. Our lives are to be adornments for the Gospel. What a precious privilege! What a tremendous responsibility!

Are our hands clean? Are we fit salesmen for the Savior? If not, let us plead for pardon, and strength to think, and live in a manner that *adorns* His precious Gospel message.

Lord, may I adorn Your precious Gospel with a Christian life. Amen.

The Pardoned Life

In love . . . Thou hast cast all my sins behind Thy back. Isaiah 38:17

The deepest hunger of the human heart is the hunger for God's love. When the psalmist exclaimed: "As the hart panteth after the water brooks, so panteth my soul after Thee, O God," he gave expression to his longing for the assurance of God's love.

The God who has made Himself known to man in the Holy Scriptures is the God of infinite compassion and pity, of everlasting mercy and grace. It is such a God as this for whom the human heart (despite all protestations to the contrary) is searching: a God who in love will reach down to man; a God who in love will quiet the haunting accusations of a guilty conscience; a God who in love will find a way to temper justice with mercy; a God who in love will come out to meet His prodigal sons and daughters with a message of pardon and peace.

Such a God is revealed to us *only* in the Scriptures. It was He, and He alone, who conceived a plan of salvation which made such pardon possible. God's pardoning love was made possible in Christ.

St. John devotes much of his first letter to the revelation of God's love and to the purpose of this revelation. He says: "In this was manifested the love of God toward us, because that God sent His only begotten Son into the world, that we might live through Him. Herein is love, not that *we* loved *God,* but that HE loved US and sent His Son to be the propitiation [reconciliation] for our sins."

It was in Christ that justice and mercy met. He died to atone for the guilt of all mankind. By His death He paid the penalty of justice and opened up the gates of mercy. In Him, and in Him alone, we have Heaven's pledge of full and free forgiveness.

Lord, how can I ever thank You for Your wondrous love and mercy!

The Contented Life

I have learned, in whatsoever state I am, therewith to be content. Philippians 4:11

All of us are tempted, at times, to become dissatisfied with our lot in life. We find it difficult to be happy because someone, perhaps "less worthy" than we, has been elevated to a position of prominence, while we have been left to struggle on unnoticed and "unappreciated."

The eminent John Newton once said: "If two angels came down from heaven to execute a divine command, and one was appointed to sweep the streets, they would feel no inclination to change employments." And why not? Because each would have the sure conviction that he was doing what his Lord had asked him to do and that by his service, great or humble, he was glorifying God.

No matter what pathway of life God has chosen for us, we may find joy in *His* choice, for it is the path along which He has chosen to lead us to glory. The writer of the 84th Psalm had learned to evaluate the various pathways of life when he said: "I had rather be a doorkeeper in the house of my God than to dwell in the tents of wickedness."

The secret of real, Christian contentment is to be in the place where God wants us to be and to be doing the things He bids us do. Paul knew that he was leading his life on pathways of God's own choosing. And knowing that, he could say: "I have learned, in whatsoever state I am, therewith to be content." Have we learned to say the same? Can we say with the poet:

> Thy way, not mine, O Lord,
> However dark it be.
> Lead me by Thine own hand;
> Choose out the path for me.
>
> I dare not choose my lot;
> I would not if I might.
> Choose THOU for me, my God;
> So shall I walk aright.

He who can pray that prayer from his heart will know the secret of true contentment. He will be able to say with Paul: "I have learned, in whatsoever state I am, therewith to be content."

The Patterned Life

We know that all things work together for good to them that love God. *Romans 8:28*

Our lives are in the hands of God as an unfinished carpet is in the hands of a weaver. All the smaller threads which to us seem very unimportant are being gathered together by the busy hand of God and woven into place. Though the color of an individual thread may seem unpleasant to us, we know that later it will appear as a beautiful strand in the carefully planned design which God is weaving.

Luther once said: "The ways of God are like a Hebrew book, which can only be read backward." God's ways cannot be understood by those who demand an explanation of His purpose as He deals with us from day to day. Rather we must wait patiently until His purposes have been accomplished and then, beginning at the end, look back down the years to see His gracious will unfolding. Only then are His Fatherly leadings revealed clearly before our eyes.

But what a comfort to know that, through Christ, the pattern He is weaving is the pattern of infinite compassion! What a comfort to know that throughout our lives there is a heavenly harmony and that the Author of this harmony is the Lord of love and mercy!

What a source of faith and courage to know that everything that comes our way—be it calamity or success, pain or pleasure, joy or sorrow, health or sickness, poverty or wealth—everything has its place in the orderly pattern of God's providence and therefore *must* work together for our good!

Knowing this, let us walk with God by faith until He permits us to walk with Him by sight. We have His Word that *all* things are working together for our good.

> Lord, give us such a faith as this, And then, whate'er may come,
> We'll taste e'en here the hallowed bliss Of an eternal home.

The Life That Counts

Ye are the light of the world. *Matthew 5:14*

A little clock in a jeweler's window stopped one day for only half an hour. The hands stood still at 8:20 a.m. School children on their way to school, noticing the time, stopped to play; people on their way to work, when they saw the clock, slowed their pace; and a man, hurrying by to catch a train, slackened his gait when he saw that he still had plenty of time.

But all were *late* because one little clock had stopped! Never had these people realized how much they had depended on that little clock in the jeweler's window until for the first time in their lives it had led them astray.

In a sense, everyone who professes to lead the Christian life is very much like that little clock. People all around us are, consciously or unconsciously, being influenced by what we say and do. If we permit our Christianity to "stop" for just a little while, if by careless speech or improper conduct we set a bad example, we are likely to lead our fellowmen astray—just as surely as did that little clock.

It is wrong to assume, even for a moment, that our lives, just because they are "little," do not count; that our actions are unimportant; that our influence is insignificant. Christ tells *every* Christian, even the humblest, "You are the light of the world." And then He adds pointedly: "Let your light so *shine* before men, that they may see your good works and glorify your Father which is in heaven." By our very lives we are to point the way for others.

Your life is an instrument in the hands of Christ to bring others to Him and to heaven. How important, then, that each of us make his life count to the fullest! Each of us is a light in the world.

Lord, I pray You in Jesus' name: may my life be an influence for good and not for evil. May Your Holy Spirit guide me so that I may truly be a *light* which leads my fellowmen to You. Amen.

Make Every Sunday a Milestone

Oh, worship the Lord in the beauty of holiness! Psalm 96:9

Sunday! From early childhood and throughout our life the word "Sunday" has a special charm for the heart of the believer. To the Christian pilgrim perhaps no day is more rich with blessed memory, or more bright with golden promise! Sundays are to him the cool and green oases which separate the hot and sandy trails of life. Sundays are the milestones on the way to his Father's house where he pauses to receive tidings from the homeland and to revive his strength and courage for that part of the journey which lies ahead.

Sunday is his day of public worship. All of the hurts, the bruises, the disappointments, the failures, the sorrows, and the sins of the week are taken to God, in humble prayer, pleading for pardon because of the Savior's mercy. And with forgiveness assured once more and sealed forever by the Gospel's promise, we sing hymns of praise and adoration to the Lord of our salvation.

Does each Sunday find us, as families and as individuals, thus worshiping the Savior? In the statistics of heaven does each Sunday really find us numbered among the *worshipers* or merely among those *present*? Surely we have every reason to make sure that in each service our presence will feel the touch of *His* presence and that our worship will be a worship in spirit and in truth!

Let us so order our lives and so discipline our minds that each day of the week will be a preparation for a truly spiritual happening next Sunday. We have an appointment, an audience, with the King of Heaven. "Oh, come, let us worship and bow down; let us kneel before the Lord, our Maker!" Let us prepare our hearts to *worship*—this Sunday and every Sunday.

Lord Jesus Christ, to us attend, Thy Holy Spirit to us send,
With grace to rule us day by day, And lead us in true wisdom's way.

Teach Thou our lips to sing Thy praise, Our hearts in true devotion raise,
Our faith increase, and grant us light, That we may know Thy name aright!

The Greatest Martyr

Lord, teach us to pray. *Luke 11:1*

The scene is familiar to every Bible student. The disciples had come upon Jesus while He was engaged in solitary prayer. When He had finished, they asked: "Lord, teach *us* to pray."

In response, Jesus taught them what has become known as the Lord's Prayer or the "Our Father," a prayer which has been prayed in Christian homes and churches ever since; a prayer which has invoked and has been rewarded with divine blessings down through the centuries.

There is a danger, however, that we recite the Lord's Prayer merely as a ritual, as a mechanical Pater Noster. Martin Luther said that the Lord's Prayer "is the greatest martyr on earth, tortured and abused by everyone." He meant: The Lord's Prayer is so often prayed unthinkingly, mechanically, with our lips and not with our hearts.

A good way to overcome the tendency to pray the Lord's Prayer simply as a matter of rote is to review Martin Luther's explanation of each of the seven petitions as we have them in our Small Catechism—and to do this at regular intervals. Once we have refreshed our memory on exactly what it means to pray: "Hallowed be Thy name" or "Give us this day our daily bread," we will not be inclined to repeat these words unthinkingly.

Indeed, the more we become acquainted with the deeper (and broader) meaning of each of the seven petitions of the Lord's Prayer, the more we will be inclined to approach this prayer in the spirit of David who said: "Let the words of my mouth and the meditation of my heart be acceptable in Thy sight, O Lord, my Strength and my Redeemer." We will need the Spirit's guidance to keep our hearts and minds on the words that we are saying. Well might we assume the attitude expressed below:

> Holy Spirit, Lord divine, Breathe into this prayer of mine;
> Grant that all I say may be Prompted only, Lord, by Thee.

Planned Joy

Rejoice in the Lord alway; and again I say, Rejoice. Philippians 4:4

Ten-year-old Kristin wrote to her grandparents: "I am going to be helping in vacation Bible school this year. I am *planning to enjoy it.*"

Some people, even Christians, are constantly planning to be miserable. They insist on looking at tomorrow through dark-colored glasses. If it's a picnic, they're "just *sure* it's going to rain." If it's a party, they're "just *sure* the whole thing will be a flop." If it's a new venture for church or family, they're "just *sure* it'll never work out." In a sense, their whole life is one of planned misery.

God tells us that the life of the Christian should be one of planned joy. "Rejoice in the Lord alway, and again I say, Rejoice." We are to rejoice, above all, because the most rapturous moment of our life still lies ahead. "The Lord is coming soon," the apostle says in the very next verse. And because our Lord is coming, our prevailing mood should be one of gladness. There will still be thorns and crosses, to be sure, but in the distance shines the crown.

Some will say: "Yes, but that's all too theological. I still have to live in *this* world. I believe that the Lord is coming soon, but I have a child, critically ill, in the hospital. I need help—*now!*"

As Christians, we know that *all* of life is "theological," involving, as it does, our personal relationship with God through Christ. We know that in the life of the believer, every tragedy is but a prelude to another triumph. Read Paul's great hymn of praise (Romans 8:35-39). Yes, even death, in its Christian perspective, is a cause for deep down, inner joy. It brings us into the presence of Him whom to know "is pleasure forevermore."

Indeed, the redeemed of Christ, when speaking of the ultimate issues of life, have every right to say: *I am planning to enjoy it!*

Undertake Big Things for Christ

Go ye therefore and teach all nations . . . and, lo, I am with you alway, even unto the end of the world. *Matthew 28:19-20*

Before World War II a certain brand of cigarettes was advertised in every city and town in Japan. It was the most popular brand in the country, not because of its superior quality, but because it was backed by American interests who believed in doing "big things in a big way."

A Japanese Christian statesman one day pointed to one of these advertisements and remarked: "If Americans would put as much money into advertising Christianity as they put into advertising that cigarette, they would have the Gospel of Christ in every hamlet of this empire within five years."

We know that proclaiming the Gospel of salvation dare never be put into the category of mere advertising. But, properly understood, might not the words of the Savior find application here: "The children of this world are in their generation wiser than the children of light"? Are we, as individuals and as a Church, afraid to do "big things in a big way" for the sake of Jesus Christ, our Savior?

Let there be no mistake: He *expects* us to undertake great things for Him. "Go ye into all the world and preach the Gospel to every creature." "Ye shall be witnesses unto Me . . . unto the uttermost part of the earth." Surely, His—and ours—is a global program. Dare we shrink from our tremendous task because of its very bigness?

Surely not! Someone has said: "Undertake great things *for* God. And expect great things *from* God." Notice, the Savior's great commission to all believers contains not only a command but also a promise: The command is: "Go!" The promise is: "I'll be with you." He has promised to be right at our side as we carry out His worldwide program. With Him at our side and with the world as our field, let us put courageous hands to the task of winning men, women, and children for heaven.

Redeemed by Grace

Things which are despised hath God chosen. *1 Corinthians 1:28*

Can it really be possible that God loves ME! So often I have failed Him! So often I have sinned! So often I have had to say with Paul: "O wretched man that I am . . . I know that in me . . . dwelleth no good thing." Is it possible that God could consider ME a *saint*, poor, miserable sinner that I am?

Macaulay tells of a poor apprentice who made a cathedral window entirely out of the pieces of glass which his master had condemned and thrown away. Upon completion, it won the admiration and acclaim of all who saw it. His master's boasted work, made of exquisite panels of beautiful glass, was rejected; but the window made of condemned materials by the hand of the unknown artist was given a place of honor in the great cathedral.

So our Savior's kingdom is made up of rejected materials. He has taken the fallen sons of men and has set them, like diamonds, to sparkle forever in the diadem of His glory. "The base things of the world and things which are despised [the humble, those of little worth] hath God chosen."

What a blessed thought! The base things of the world—that means ME—hath God chosen, and by His unsearchable mercy in Christ He has drawn me into the company of those whom He will come to gather "in the day when He makes up His jewels." Yes, I can be sure God loves me *as I am*. And, loving me through Jesus Christ my Savior, He will guide, protect, and keep me to the end. With the poet we can marvel:

> By grace! None dare claim any merit;
> Our works and conduct have no worth.
> God in His love sent our Redeemer,
> Christ Jesus, to this sinful earth;
> His death did for our sins atone,
> And we are saved by grace alone.

Lord, I thank You that, unworthy though I am, You have chosen me to be Your child through Jesus Christ, my Savior. Amen.

Read Philippians 3:7-14

Eyes Toward the Lord

Mine eyes are ever toward the Lord. *Psalm 25:15*

A group of boys were trying to see who could make the straightest track across a snowy field. Only one of them succeeded in making a path which was almost perfectly straight. When asked how he managed to do it, he said: "It was easy. I just kept my eyes fixed on the lightning rod on top of the barn at the end of the field—while the rest of you kept looking at your feet."

"*Mine eyes are ever toward the Lord*," says the child of God. In the workaday world in which we live, there may be heartaches and disappointments, irritations and vexations, trials and temptations, but, in the midst of it all, our eyes are ever toward our Lord. Our Lord and we share every trial, and in that very act of sharing, our burdens lose their weight, and our trials lose their sting.

How often throughout the day and in the dark hours of the night do our eyes meet the eyes of our Savior. And in that mutual glance there is hope and strength. For "the eyes of the Lord are upon the righteous, and His ears are open unto their cry. . . . The righteous cry, and the Lord heareth and delivereth them out of all their troubles" (Psalm 34:15, 17).

Are we keeping our eyes "*toward the Lord*"? Or are we, like Peter on the Sea of Galilee, keeping our eyes on the stormy waves which would draw us down into despair? Let us press courageously forward, "looking unto Jesus, the Author and Finisher of our faith; who for the joy that was set before Him endured the cross, despising the shame, and is set down at the right hand of the throne of God" (Hebrews 12:2).

In the above passage the Christian life is compared to a race. But notice how we are to run: "*looking unto Jesus,* the Author and Finisher of our faith." In Him we have not only our goal but also our source of strength. Is our daily life thus focused? Are we always keeping our eyes "toward the Lord"?

Lord, in the midst of the world's distractions, grant that the eyes of my faith may always be directed toward You. Amen.

187

Next Sunday—Will We Really Pray?

Let the words of my mouth and the meditation of my heart be acceptable in Thy sight, O Lord, my Strength, and my Redeemer. Psalm 19:14

Presumably, we shall occupy our accustomed pew in church next Sunday. Together with our fellow pilgrims we shall rest from the burdens of the week and shall seek communion with our Father. Whatever may have been our differences during the week—in wealth or health or fortune—we shall be as one when we kneel before the Throne of mercy.

> Before our Father's throne
> We pour our ardent prayers;
> Our fears, our hopes, our aims are one,
> Our comforts and our cares.

But will we really *pray*? There is always a danger, especially when set liturgical forms are used, that public prayer becomes a matter merely of the lips and not a matter of the heart. How often, when we have stood in church joining in the prayers of the congregation, have we had to admit that "the words of our mouth" had very little in common with "the meditation of our heart"?

Prayer, *true* prayer, is more than the mere repetition of set phrases. It is more than the chanting of a beautiful liturgical response. It is the sinner's intimate, personal pleading directed straight to the Father heart of God. True prayer is *always* heart to heart—*our* heart to *God's* heart. And it is always in the Savior's spirit and in the Savior's name.

Surely, in public worship, as we prepare to approach our Father with our petitions, we have every reason to repeat the prayer of David: "Let the words of my mouth and the meditation of my heart be acceptable in Thy sight, O Lord, my Strength and my Redeemer." Or we may wish to turn to our hymnal and offer the silent prayer:

> Lord Jesus Christ, be present now,
> Our hearts in true devotion bow,
> Thy Spirit send with grace divine,
> And let Thy truth within us shine. Amen.

The Believer's Zest for Life

Finally, my brethren, rejoice in the Lord! Philippians 3:1

"Ho hum. Another day at the same old grind!" How often haven't we greeted the dawn of a new day with a listless yawn and a depressing sense of boredom? And then how often haven't we reached for our robe as though we were about to don a funeral garment?

Admittedly, there are days when we will feel like that. But this attitude of "ho hum" is not God's will for us. The apostle Paul was constantly encouraging the early Christians to rejoice! In fact, a modern paraphrase of the above Scripture passage would read: "Always be cheerful in the Lord. I never get tired of saying this, because I know it's good for your souls." Only a few verses later he comes back to this recurring theme: "Rejoice in the Lord always, and *again* I say, Rejoice!"

The believer in Jesus Christ is to develop and exhibit a zest for life. Knowing that each new day is a day of divine grace, he is to sweep away the cobwebs of "ho hum" and to breathe deeply and joyfully of the clean, refreshing air of God's abundant love and mercy. Then, in the words of Martin Luther, he is to "go joyfully" to his daily task. Do we do that?

Catherine Winkworth, the famous English poetess of the past century, knew the true and abiding joys of the Christian life. It is she who translated these jubilant lines:

Oh, rejoice, ye Christians loudly, For our JOY hath now begun,
Wondrous things our God hath done. Tell abroad His goodness proudly
Who our race hath honored thus That He deigns to dwell with us.
Joy, O joy, beyond all gladness, Christ hath done away with sadness.
Hence all sorrow and repining, For the Sun of Grace is shining!

Speak Up! Speak Out for Christ!

We cannot but speak the things which we have seen and heard. Acts 4:20

Have we ever spoken to that unchurched friend about Christ? It is a comparatively simple matter to speak to him about our pastor, about the choir, or about what is going on at church this week—*but do we ever speak to him about Christ?*

Of Peter and John we read that they could not but speak the things which they had seen and heard. Those things were the life and death, the resurrection and ascension of their Savior. In the light of those stupendous facts all other topics of the day faded into insignificance. How could they talk about anything else when their heart was fairly bursting with the good news that *Christ had come* and that by His death and resurrection He had redeemed the world!

Should we not feel a similar sense of urgency? True, times have changed. What was current news in the days of John and Peter has become ancient history now. It is frequently difficult to broach the subject of religion in today's society. But have we "heard" or "seen" anything more precious than the Gospel of complete redemption through the Savior? And is there anything which our unchurched friend needs more desperately to be told?

What is it that so often ties our tongue when our Lord becomes the subject of our conversation? Are we afraid to mention His name lest our friends consider us too pious? Afraid to tell what Jesus means to us lest we be accused of carrying our religion on our sleeve? True, we must exercise tact and wisdom in these matters, but too frequently we hide behind the word "tact," when the *real* word is "timidity."

Let us be done with groundless fear, timid silence, and false politeness which forbids the mention of our Savior's name. The world is in dire need to hear the very things we have to say. Let's say them!

Lord Jesus Christ, grant me the joy of sharing the riches of Your grace with others. Amen.

The Whole World in His Hands

In Him [Jesus Christ] all things hold together. *Colossians 1:17 RSV*

We all have heard the nursery rhyme: "Humpty Dumpty sat on a wall; Humpty Dumpty had a great fall. All the king's horses and all the king's men Couldn't put Humpty Dumpty together again." A Christian mother had just repeated this rhyme to her four-year-old son. The boy thought for a moment, then, as if having suddenly come up with a solution, he said with bright-eyed confidence: "Jesus could have done it!" Yes, Jesus could have put Humpty Dumpty together again!

How true—in a much higher sense! Paul tells us that Jesus Christ not only put all things together in the beginning, but that He still *holds* them together. As the omnipotent Son, together with the Father and the Spirit, He is the unifying force that holds both the physical universe and all human history together.

In fact, throughout his epistles Paul presents Christ not only as our Savior and Redeemer but also as our omnipotent Creator and Sustainer. He tells the Ephesians, for instance, that the Father has put Christ "above all principality, and power . . . and dominion . . . and hath put *all* things under His feet." He does, indeed, "hold all things together."

Most important for you and me, Jesus Christ holds our little lives together. In a world that seems to be flying apart, not only does He "hold the whole world in His hands," but He holds also you and me. When things seem at their very worst, we can rest assured: He holds all the pieces and He knows where every piece belongs. With the poet we can sing:

> In Thee all fulness dwelleth, All grace and power divine;
> The glory that excelleth, O Son of God is Thine.
> We worship Thee, we bless Thee, To Thee, O Christ, we sing;
> We praise Thee and confess Thee, Our gracious Lord and King!

Love Seeks To WIN the Erring Brother

Go and tell him his fault between thee and him alone. Matthew 18:15

The above is taken from the well-known words of Christ regarding fraternal admonition. He outlines three steps for admonishing an erring Christian. First, we are to speak to him privately, our aim being to *win him back*. If we fail, we are to take one or two witnesses with us, our aim again being *to win the brother back*. If we fail again, we are to enlist the loving aid of the Christian congregation, always with the same objective: *To win our brother back*.

If, despite all our efforts, our brother fails to repent, we are to love him as "an heathen man and publican"—with the same inexhaustible love our Savior showed to the heathen and the publicans of His day. They were on the outside of the church but on the inside of His heart.

The question has frequently been debated: if a member has committed a public sin (one that is public knowledge), is it necessary for the individual Christian to take the first step and speak to him privately? In such cases let the law of love and sanctified Christian judgment prevail. Which approach is most likely to do the most good to the erring brother or sister? Remember, Paul tells us: "Now abideth faith, hope, charity . . . But the greatest of these is charity."

We profess our faith in the supremacy of charity (loving kindness) in the following words from a well-known hymn:

> Give us faith to trust Thee boldly,
> Hope, to stay our souls on Thee;
> But, oh! *best* of all Thy graces,
> Give us Thine own charity.

Let charity, then, be the final arbiter of all of our behavior—of all our attitudes and actions toward the erring brother or sister. In the absence of valid reasons to the contrary, let us speak to the public sinner privately—in all kindness, tenderness, and understanding. But for the grace of God we ourselves would be going the erring sinner's way.

It Takes Two To Make a Sermon

Take heed therefore how ye hear. *Luke 8:18*

During these days our pastor is busy, preparing for next Sunday's sermon. He is devoting many hours to prayer and study in order that he may bring us some important message from God's Word. He devotes much time to the preparation of each sermon, because he considers this one of the most important functions of his ministry.

But has it ever occurred to us that we, too, have a share in the responsibilities of this preparation? That we can prepare ourselves to *hear* a sermon just as the pastor prepares himself to *preach* it? As someone has well said, it takes *two* to make a sermon—the one who preaches it and the one who hears it! Whether or not a specific sermon will accomplish its God-intended purpose will depend, at least in part, on how well the worshiper has prepared him-or-herself to hear it.

Whether or not you and I will be fruitful hearers this coming Sunday will depend very much upon our frame of mind—yes, our "frame of heart"—today, tomorrow, and throughout the week. Keeping late hours on Saturday, or engaging in family quarrels and bickerings until just before leaving the house in anger five minutes late for church, will surely *not* prepare our hearts for a fruitful sowing of the Word.

We shall take to church in our hearts next Sunday what we put into them today. How important, then, that already today, by prayer and meditation, we prepare the soil of our hearts so that the precious seed might enter! "Take heed therefore how ye hear!"

Well might we pray, not only each time we open this book for personal or family meditation, but also each Sunday as we enter our accustomed pew:

Lord, open Thou my heart to hear, And through Thy Word to me draw near;
Let me Thy Word e'er pure retain, Let me Thy child and heir remain.

Reconciliation or Vindication?

First be reconciled! *Matthew 5:24*

We hear so much about reconciliation today. We hear the *word* so often and see the *deed* so seldom that we begin to wonder whether or not there really is such a thing as "reconciliation."

Could it be that what we really mean by that word is *vindication?* Has reconciliation come to mean proving ourselves to be right? Or, still worse, proving our brother or sister to be wrong? When we ask our brother to be reconciled, are we (despite our pious allegations to the contrary) asking him to admit that he was wrong—so that we can live at peace with him again?

This can happen in families, in congregations, in whole denominations. In effect we say: "Come on, let's get together and admit that *you* were wrong." That is NOT what the Holy Scriptures mean by reconciliation.

The Greek word that is translated "reconciliation" or "reconcile" in this passage involves a changing of disposition—not only our brother's but also ours. How frequently attempts at reconciliation fail because we bring to each successive attempt the same hostility, the same stubbornness, the same prejudices with which we closed our last conversation. Rather, with the Holy Spirit's help, let us cleanse our hearts and minds and approach our brother in love and understanding.

If our attitude in the past was hateful, it should become friendly. If it was cold or distant, it should become warm and loving. If there is to be genuine reconciliation, we must be sure the change begins in *us*. Frequently that will mean getting down from our high horse and apologizing for whatever we have done to cause the unhappy relationship. Are you and I up to that?

"Comfort? Who Needs It?" "You Do!"

Comfort ye, comfort ye My people, saith your God. Isaiah 40:1

We shall never forget the incident even though it happened more than fifty years ago. We were eating dinner with relatives when a young lady at the table (she was in her late teens) observed with animation: "I *like* our new pastor, but why is he always talking about *comfort?*"

We tucked the remark away in our subconscious, but with the passing years it has taken on more and more significance. What millions of bruised and broken lives need today, perhaps more than ever, is the message God commanded the prophet Isaiah to proclaim: "Comfort ye, comfort ye My people, saith your God."

Isaiah was to bring the Good News to God's chosen people, God's message of peace to Jerusalem. It is noteworthy that the word "comfort" appears more than a hundred times in our Bible, frequently as an imperative to God's messengers. They were to bring *His* comfort to *His* people. In the language of today, they were to proclaim the Gospel with all its comforting assurances.

But is God's message of comfort all that important? And must it be repeated again and again? The answer, of course, is yes. Into every life there come days when our heart cries out for the solace which only God can give. Who can count the hours of loneliness, sickness, and pain that must be borne by millions in every section of the world—or the heartbreaking feeling of being unnoticed, unneeded, or unwanted?

All of us have wrestled beneath the gnarled trees of our own Gethsemanes—tortured by life and death decisions. Thank God that in moments like that He has a strong eternal Word of *comfort* for you and me. In our heart of hearts we can hear Him saying: "Lo, I am with you! I, who died for you, who rose again, who am now at the right hand of My Father, pleading for you. I know your hurts, your pain, your sorrow. Just put your hand in mine. I will uphold you until your journey's end."

Lord, grant me Your comfort in the trials of life. Amen.

Christian Citizenship

Ye are the salt of the earth. *Matthew 5:13*

Today the citizens of the United States are celebrating its birthday. What should be our distinctive role in this celebration? As grateful children of our heavenly Father we will, of course, want to thank Him for the uncounted blessings He has showered on our land. Truly, He has blessed us beyond measure.

But we will want to do more than merely give thanks. Our Lord, who gave His life for us, has told us that we are to be "the salt of the earth." That applies not only to our private lives as individual Christians but also to our civic lives as Christian citizens. As salt, we are to help preserve the health of our nation; we are to help prevent the spread of corruption.

Many sincere believers feel uncomfortable when it comes to taking part in governmental affairs. This is due, in many cases, to a lifelong misconception of the idea of "separation of Church and state." The Christian is not only a practicing member of his church, he is (or should be) a practicing member of his community, his city, his state, and his nation. Having rendered unto God the things that are God's, he must also discharge his rightful obligations to the community in which he lives.

How desperately our nation needs the salt of Christian witness and action! Dishonesty, greed, profanity, divorce, and sins of sexual impurity are all about us. In concert with other God-fearing citizens we are to do all within our power to stay the spread of moral decay which threatens our land. Salt that is not applied is worthless. We are to pray, to speak, to work for the welfare of the land we love. Are we doing that?

> Lord, while for all mankind we pray, Of every clime and coast,
> Oh, hear us for our native land, The land we love the most. Amen.

The Road to Hell Is Paved . . .

As a man thinketh in his heart, so is he. Proverbs 23:7

The road to hell is paved with euphemisms. The word "euphemism" may be defined as the use of a pleasant-sounding word for an ugly, frequently sinful thought. In our day it has become popular to use euphemisms especially when referring to gross sins against God's ordinance, which calls for chastity. There was a time when such sins were called by names which in themselves were offensive to Christian sensibilities.

For instance, in a nationally televised show, with an audience of millions, the master of ceremonies and his guests discussed the most sordid of sins most entertainingly and at great length (evoking hilarious laughter) without the use of a single offensive word! In fact, during the past few decades the world has created a whole new vocabulary, all in delightful pastel shades, that covers the transgression of each of God's commandments.

Have we been beguiled by these euphemisms? Do we think of certain sins more lightly because the world has given them more attractive names? Remember, "As a man thinketh in his heart, so is he." Call sin whatever you will, it is still sin. It is still arrogant rebellion against a holy God. Thank God that we have a Savior who died for the ugly sins to which we give pretty names.

Having been assured of His forgiveness, let us pray for spiritual wisdom so that we may always *recognize* sin to be sin when we see it or hear it, and let us pray for the Spirit's power to *resist* the stratagems of Satan, no matter how cleverly he may disguise them. To that end we pray:

Create in me a new heart, Lord,
That gladly I obey Thy Word
And naught but what Thou wilt, desire;
With such new life my soul inspire.

Are You Afraid?

There is no fear in love, but perfect love casteth out fear. 1 John 4:18

Are you afraid? Afraid of your conscience? Afraid of tomorrow? Afraid of the long uncertain road which lies ahead? *In the next few meditations we will speak of some of the basic fears that haunt the human race, including Christians in their weaker moments,* and we will view these fears in the light of God's Word.

A noted newspaper columnist, when writing his final column, stated that after having read more than 90,000 letters from his readers, he was convinced that "Fear is private enemy No. 1." The great and the lowly, the rich and the poor, the cultured and the unlettered—it made no difference—through every level of society there ran, like a poisoned stream, the paralyzing disease of fear.

But God does not want His children to be afraid. *"Fear not"* is the divine overture which might well be prefixed to every Bible promise. "Fear not," thy sins are forgiven thee. "Fear not," there shall no evil befall thee. "Fear not," your heavenly Father knoweth that ye have need of these things. "Fear not," I have redeemed thee, I have called thee by thy name. Thou art Mine.

We who have experienced the love of God in Christ need never be afraid of anything that our loving Father might have in store for us. "If God be for us, who can be against us? He that spared not His own Son, but delivered Him up for us all, how shall He not with Him also freely give us *all* things?"—also the needed strength and courage to bear the burdens of each day?

In every cross, in every trial, in every problem or perplexity we can feel our Savior's loving hand upon our shoulder and hear His reassuring voice: "FEAR NOT!"

Oh, Lord, remind me daily of Your tender love for me. And let the remembrance of Your love cleanse my heart of every fear. In Your mercy grant my prayer. Amen.

Afraid There Is No Forgiveness for You?

Him that cometh to Me I will in no wise cast out. *John 6:37*

A distressed mother came to her pastor with the excited confession: "Pastor, I have committed the unpardonable sin!" The kind and wise clergyman gave no sign of surprise or alarm but simply asked her: "And are you sorry for it?"

"Yes, Pastor, *dreadfully* sorry!" was her anguished reply. "Then you have committed nothing that cannot be forgiven. No sin, no matter how great, cannot be completely pardoned through sincere repentance and trusting faith in Jesus, our Redeemer."

That is the supreme glory and comfort of the Christian Gospel! The disease cannot spread farther than the cure. "Where sin abounded, grace did much more abound." There was sufficient grace for Peter, who "went out and wept bitterly;" for Paul, who cried out: "Oh, wretched man that I am;" and for the penitent publican, who smote upon his breast and said: "God, be merciful to me, a sinner."

And there is sufficient grace for *us!* That is what the Bible means when it assures us: "If any man sin, we have an Advocate [One who speaks for us] with the Father, Jesus Christ, the Righteous: and He is the Propitiation [the Payment] for our sins and not for ours only, but also for the sins of the whole world."

Believers in the sin-atoning Savior need never be afraid that a particular sin is beyond forgiveness. All who have learned to look with pleading faith toward Calvary's cross for their assurance of forgiveness have experienced the blessed truth of the Savior's promise: "Him that cometh to Me *I will in no wise cast out.*"

I heard the voice of Jesus say, "Come unto me and rest;
Lay down, thou weary one, lay down, Thy head upon my breast."
I came to Jesus as I was, Weary and worn and sad;
I found in Him a resting place, And He has made me glad!

Afraid To Take God at His Word?

Underneath are the everlasting arms. *Deuteronomy 33:27*

In the early days of our country a weary traveler came to the banks of the Mississippi for the first time. There was no bridge. It was in the midst of winter, and the surface of the mighty stream was covered with ice. Could he *dare* cross over? Would the uncertain ice be able to bear his weight?

Night was falling, and it was urgent that he reach the other side. Finally, after much hesitation and with many fears, he began to creep cautiously across the surface of the ice on his hands and knees. About halfway over he heard the sound of singing behind him. Out of the dusk came another man, driving a four-horse load of coal across the ice and singing merrily as he went his way!

Here he was—on his hands and knees, trembling lest the ice be not strong enough to bear him up! And there, as if whisked away by the winter's wind, went the other man, his horses, his sleigh, and his load of coal—upheld by the ice on which *he*, the weary traveler, was creeping!

Some of us have learned only to *creep* upon the promises of God. Cautiously we venture forth upon His promises, as though our light step might make His promises more secure. Let us dismiss such fears! Our faith is founded upon the unchangeable and unbreakable promises of God. "I will strengthen thee; yea, I will help thee." Yea, "*underneath are the everlasting arms!*"

In days of peril or perplexity, when our faltering faith seems no match for the gathering storm, may we hold fast to the faith of the Christian poet:

> Now I have found the firm foundation
> Which holds mine anchor ever sure;
> 'Twas laid before the world's creation
> In Christ my Savior's wounds secure;
> Foundation which *unmoved* shall stay
> When heaven and earth will pass away.

Afraid for the Safety of Loved Ones?

Fear not; for God hath heard the voice of the lad where he is. Genesis 21:17

Are you worried over the safety of absent loved ones? Afraid that the hand of the Lord may be shortened so that He will be unable to protect them and preserve them? Afraid that the temptations of the world, of Christless and wicked companionship, will be too much for them and they will be overcome by sin and unbelief?

Hagar, the mother of Ishmael, once felt that way. She had despaired completely of God's ability to preserve her only son. But into the depths of her despair came the clear and reassuring voice from heaven: "Fear not; for God hath heard the voice of the lad where he is."

Similarly, we may be sure that God has heard the voice of our absent loved ones where *they* are. Our Savior is *their* Savior. His promise "Lo, I am with you alway," embraces both them and us. To them He says, as He does to us, "I have called thee by thy name; for thou art Mine."

It goes without saying that we ourselves are to pray for our absent loved ones. The Scriptures urge us to "pray for one another" and assure us that "the effectual, fervent prayer of the righteous man availeth much." We are to "pray without ceasing"—not that we are to spend our entire life on our knees but that the line of communication between us and our Lord is to be kept open constantly.

Our absent loved ones who have been placed into the Savior's arms in Holy Baptism may be absent from *us*, but they are never absent from the watchful eye and loving care of Him who assures both them and us: "I will not forget thee. Behold, I have graven thee upon the palms of My hands." Let us, then, with firmest confidence commit our loved ones into the Savior's keeping.

> Holy Father, in Thy mercy Hear our anxious prayer;
> Keep our loved ones who are absent 'Neath Thy care.

Afraid To Let God's Will Be Done?

Thy will be done. *Matthew 6:10*

Yes, we must admit it, there are times when we are afraid to let God's will be done! Like Simon Peter, we can so easily see the pleasant detour *around* the cross, while our Lord directs us to take the straight hard road that leads to our own little Gethsemane and to our own little Calvary.

Why *must* this happen to me? Why this string of sudden reverses, painful disappointments, and bitter disillusionments? Why must I struggle on day after day with these "fightings and fears within, without"? Why? Why?

It takes real faith to stand up under the burden of our cross and say to our God:

> Thy way, not mine, O Lord, however dark it be.
> Lead me by Thine own hand; Choose Thou my path for me.
> I dare not choose my lot; I would not if I might.
> Choose Thou for me, my God; So shall I walk aright.

And yet it is only in that complete surrender and submission to our Father's will that the burden of our cross is lightened. When we see our Father's hand in our cross, we will see His hand on the *underside,* helping us to bear it.

We may not be able to understand or to explain the reason for one particular cross, but we will not *need* to understand it or explain it if we know that our gracious Father has placed it there and that, through Christ, His thoughts toward us are thoughts of kindness and of mercy. Praise God, for His thoughts are infinitely *better* than our thoughts, and His ways are infinitely better and higher and wiser than our own.

If, at times, we are afraid to submit to what evidently is God's will for us, let us remember the poet's words:

> Beloved, it is well! God's ways are always right,
> And perfect love is o'er them all, Though far above our sight.

Afraid of Loneliness?

Fear thou not; for I am with thee. Isaiah 41:10

There come moments into the life of everyone of us when the world seems to pass us by and we are left to eat the bread of loneliness. The rich and the poor, the mighty and the weak, the dweller in the palace and the tenant in the shack—all have felt at some time or another the piercing pang which comes with the knowledge of being unnoticed, unneeded, or unwanted.

For the child of God, however, the lonely hour need not be filled with gloom and sadness. Our Lord has given us His promise that He will hallow all our lonely hours with the comfort of His presence: "I will never leave thee nor forsake thee."

And our Savior has given us a beautiful example of using our lonely hours to cultivate the companionship of Heaven. Again and again we are told that He was "alone," in order that He might be with His Father. On the mountain, in the desert, in the early morning hours, and beneath the olive trees in Gethsemane's garden we see Him welcoming and cherishing that solitude which enabled Him to speak more intimately and more earnestly with His Father.

Let our hours of solitude be precious hours, spent in the company of Heaven. Let them be hours of quiet communion with our God. Let them be the green oases in the desert of life, where we pause for the journey which still lies before us.

To insure the most profitable use of our lonely hours, we may wish to have uplifting Christian literature lying handy—a New Testament, a book of devotions, or any inspirational book of our choice. These will help us cultivate and maintain an awareness of the nearness of the Savior in our hours of quiet solitude.

> Jesus, the very thought of Thee With sweetness fills the breast;
> But sweeter far Thy face to see And in Thy presence rest.
> Nor voice can sing, nor heart can frame, Nor can the memory find
> A sweeter sound than Thy blest name, O Savior of mankind.

Afraid of God's Justice?

There is one God and one Mediator between God and men, the Man Christ Jesus.
1 Timothy 2:5

During the First World War a French officer fell wounded in front of the French trenches. The enemy's shrapnel was bursting all around him where he lay, entirely unprotected. Seeing his danger, a private crawled out of the trench, dressed the officer's wounds as best he could, and, lying down beside him, whispered in his ear: "Don't worry, I'm between you and the shells. They must touch me first."

What a beautiful picture of Him who, on Calvary's cross, placed Himself between us and the thunderbolts of God's justice and then assured us: "Do not fear! I am between you and the strokes of God's wrath. They must touch Me first."

Jesus is the eternal Go-Between. He is the Mediator between God and men. By His sinless life and by His holy, innocent suffering and death in the sinner's stead He has taken His place between me and the stern demands of God's consuming justice.

And now I need not fear. As the prophet Isaiah foretold: *He* was wounded for *my* transgressions, *He* was bruised for *my* iniquities, the chastisement that brought about *my* peace was upon *Him,* and by *His* stripes *I* am healed.

To each of us the Savior says: "Do not fear! I have stood between you and the avenging wrath of a just and holy God. I have absorbed the pain and anguish of your punishment when I died for you on Calvary's cross. You need do nothing—but put your hand in Mine." What a wonderful Redeemer!

With such a Savior there is nothing in life or in death that can harm us. With the Christian poet we can say:

> Thy wounds, not mine, O Christ, Have cleansed my guilty soul;
> Thy stripes, not mine, O Christ, Have made my spirit whole.
> Thy death, not mine, O Lord, Has paid the ransom due;
> Ten thousand deaths like mine Would have been all too few.

Afraid of Serious Illness?

When I awake, I am still with Thee. Psalm 139:18

A distressed patient in a hospital was being prepared for her operation. A Christian attendant took her hand and whispered: "Madam, you have nothing to fear. Only one of two things could possibly happen and both of them are good. If you should die, you will be with Jesus. If you should live, Jesus will be with you. In either case, both of you will be together."

What a precious thought! In health or in sickness, in joy or in sorrow, in life or in death *both of us* (Jesus and I) will always be together.

"When I awake, I am still with Thee," says David. That is the comfort of every Christian sickbed. The night may be long and trying, the sleep feverish and fitful, the body faint, and the heart anxious, but no matter what the trials of the night may be—"when I awake, I am still with Thee!" And to be with *Christ*—what greater comfort could there be!

Even after the night of "life's little day" is over, when the curtains of eternity are lifted and the Sun of Righteousness beams forth in all His healing brilliance—even *in death*, "when I awake, I am still with Thee!" Can we ever sufficiently thank our heavenly Father for this glorious assurance?

There is nothing in sickness which can harm us if through faith in Christ we have placed ourselves, for time and for eternity, securely into the Father's hands. His presence will go with us in sickness or in health—and in His presence no evil dare come nigh us!

It was this sure conviction of the Savior's healing presence in every scene of life and of His saving presence at the very door of death that inspired Horatius Bonar to write:

> I lay my wants on Jesus, All fullness dwells in Him;
> He healeth my diseases, He doth my soul redeem.
> I lay my griefs on Jesus, My burdens and my cares;
> He from them all releases, He all my sorrows shares.

Afraid To Launch Out?

I can do all things through Christ which strengtheneth me. *Philippians 4:13*

We are told that at the top of every music manuscript of the great Johann Sebastian Bach appear the two Latin words: "Iesu, iuva!"— "Jesus, help!" The world's mightiest master of music did not dare place his fingers on the organ or compose a single melody without first calling on his Lord for help.

In Luther's Small Catechism we are instructed to begin every day with a prayer to God for guidance and protection and then "go joyfully to our work, singing a hymn," trusting that God will grant success to all that we undertake in His name.

The secret of successful living, of progress and achievement, lies not in mastering the techniques of applied psychology or in the bold venturesomeness which comes from "knowing all the angles"—but in remaining close to the Savior, who is the Source of all our strength.

"I am the Vine, ye are the branches," says Jesus, "he that abideth in Me, and I in Him, the same bringeth forth much fruit, for without Me ye can do nothing." Paul had experienced the truth of this assertion. That is why he could say: "I can do all things *through Christ, who strengthens me.*"

Let us make sure that in every task we undertake, be it great or small, we are undertaking it *with* Christ and *for* Christ; then let us be confident that we will prevail *through* Christ! Having committed our endeavor to Him in prayer, let us launch forth cheerfully, boldly, confidently—knowing that in all things He will guide and bless us. Whatever the outcome, be it success or seeming failure, we will know that our labors have been performed in His name and the results will be in accord with His good and gracious purpose.

> With the Lord begin thy task, Jesus will direct it;
> For His aid and counsel ask, Jesus will perfect it.
> Every morn with Jesus rise, And when day is ended,
> In His name then close thine eyes; Be to Him commended.

Sermons That Never Get In

And it came to pass, as he sowed, some fell by the wayside, and the fowls of the air came and devoured it. *Mark 4:4*

In the parable of the sower we are told that the seed which fell upon the trodden footpath remained *outside* the soil. The ground had been so hardened by the constant tread of many feet that the grain never got beneath the crusted surface, and it remained exposed until the birds of the air devoured it.

So, too, the *hearts* which we take to services of public worship on Sunday mornings. It is possible for a heart to be so hardened by the constant tread of evil habits that the precious Gospel seed can find no entrance. One of these evil habits, strange to say, may be the constant hearing of the truth itself in a mere mechanical manner. The soul may be sermon-hardened as well as sin-hardened. One may get so in the habit of having Gospel truths preached to him, without ever coming to any new decisions or without ever showing the least reaction, that by and by one takes no notice *at all* of what is being said, and the sermon falls *outside* of him—like snow upon a roof or rain upon a rock.

Let us take heed! We must beware of the sermon that gets no farther than our eardrum: it leaves us weaker than it finds us. For we *imagine* that we have received the seed, but the birds of the field will soon devour it. Let us implore God's Holy Spirit, for Jesus' sake, to prepare our hardened hearts for a fruitful sowing of the seed. He alone can make them ready. And when we enter His courts to hear His Word, let us pray with meaning and with purpose:

Thy presence, gracious Lord, afford,
Prepare us to receive Thy Word;
Now let Thy voice engage our ear,
And faith be mixed with what we hear.

Afraid of Misfortune?

Fear not . . . . when thou passest through the waters, I will be with thee. Isaiah 43:1-2

Man is instinctively afraid of misfortune. The millions upon millions of dollars in the vaults of insurance companies are a symbol of man's unspoken dread of an evil day and of his efforts to soften the blow of calamity whenever it might fall.

The child of God, however, has an assurance which is greater than all the props which men have built to hold back the waters of adversity. No matter how great the misfortune, how stark the tragedy, he has his God, the God revealed in Holy Scripture, and he knows that *his God is there*—right in the midst of calamity!

"Fear not, for I have redeemed thee; I have called thee by thy name. Thou art mine. When thou passest through the waters, I will be with thee; and through the rivers, they shall not overflow thee. When thou walkest through the fire, thou shalt not be burned; neither shall the flame kindle upon thee. For I am the Lord, thy God!"

A believing Christian who had just been informed of the death of his son remarked: "Whenever my tragedy becomes baffling, I lay it against Calvary." *There* is the real insurance against despair in the midst of misfortune. If God so loved us from eternity that He decreed to give His only begotten Son into the "calamity" of Calvary—so that we might be His own and live under Him in His kingdom—then surely He will not allow any tragedy to rob us of the ultimate enjoyment of that blessed promise. No matter what our circumstance, our inmost prayer can always be:

> My Spirit on Thy care, Blest Savior, I recline.
> Thou wilt not leave me to despair, For Thou are Love divine.
> Let good or ill befall, It must be good for me;
> Secure of having Thee in all, Of having all in Thee.

The believer in "that great Shepherd of the sheep" who has died for him need have no fear of the day of misfortune, for he has the guarantee: his Shepherd will be with him.

Afraid To Pray?

For ye have not received the spirit of bondage again to fear; but ye have received the Spirit of adoption, whereby we cry, Abba, Father. *Romans 8:15*

Afraid to pray?! Yes, there come moments in the lives of all of us when our guilty conscience is struck with terror at the very thought of stepping into the presence of our just and holy God—"false and full of sin" as we are. But those are the dark moments when Satan has blinded us to the glorious, sin-atoning work of Jesus Christ, our Savior.

Through Christ, through His redeeming sacrifice on Calvary's cross for sinners such as we, the mighty God of heaven has become our loving Father. And that makes all the difference in the world when we prepare to step into His presence. That is why the Savior, when His disciples asked Him, "Lord, teach us to pray," began His model prayer with the words *"Our Father."*

Luther, in commenting on this introduction to the Lord's Prayer, says: "God would by these words tenderly invite us to believe that He is our true Father and that we are His true children, so that we may with all boldness and confidence ask Him as dear children ask their dear father."

Afraid to pray? Will a loving child be filled with fear at the thought of sharing his hurts and sorrows, his troubles and heartaches—yes, even his guilt—with him whom he has learned to know as his understanding, sympathetic father?

St. Paul told the Christians in Rome that, having been accepted into the family of God by grace through faith, they could now address God with the intimate, childlike term of affection, "Abba! Father!" And the writer to the Hebrews, reminding them that Christ was now their Spokesman in heaven, urged them to "come *boldly* unto the Throne of grace, that they might obtain mercy and find grace in time of need." That is why the believing heart can pray:

Just as I am Thou wilt receive, Wilt welcome, pardon, cleanse, relieve;
Because Thy promise I believe, O Lamb of God, I come. I *come!*

Afraid of the Daily Task?

And I said, Oh, that I had wings like a dove! For then would I fly away and be at rest. Psalm 55:6

Did you ever feel like running away—away from the burdensome tasks of the day, away from the monotonous grind of a drab routine, away from the heavy responsibilities which seem to hang like threatening clouds across the dawn of each new day?

King David felt that way. When he saw great and vexing problems piling up like thunderclouds on the horizon, he exclaimed: "Oh, that I had wings like a dove! For then I would fly away and be at rest." He wanted to run away from everything. But David soon found that he could not run away from *anything!* He could not run away from *himself,* his *conscience,* or his *God.*

David could not find rest by running away. Neither can we. We must find our happiness where we are. That is God's will. No matter what our particular task—be it that of a mother wearing herself out for her children or of a father who works from early morning till late at night to earn a livelihood for his family—we must remember it is the task which *God* has given us. And that is all we need to know.

He has promised to give His angels charge over us to keep us in *all our ways.* Let us then "stay on our way" and keep our rendezvous with His angels. They will be with us in every path of duty. Whatever we do, let us do it heartily, as to the Lord, and not to men. In such service there is joy and great reward.

There will still be problems to be faced—crosses to be borne. Our Lord has promised us no exemption from the burdens of this life. But He *has* told us what to do with every burden we must bear. We are to run to Him! The Christian poet has put it well:

Whither, oh whither should I fly But to my loving Savior's breast?
Secure within Thine arms to lie And safe beneath Thy wings to rest.

On the wings of prayer we can take all of our troubles to our Lord and Savior whose heart is always open to our pleas.

Afraid Your Faith Is Too Weak?

A bruised reed shall He not break, and the smoking flax shall He not quench. Isaiah 42:3

Are you afraid that your faith is too weak? Afraid that God could not possibly accept a faith such as yours—so weak, so wavering, so full of doubtings and misgivings?

Then dismiss your fears. God's salvation is not dependent upon the quality of the faith that receives it. A million dollar check is worth a million dollars whether it is held in the uncertain hand of a child, in the wavering hand of an invalid, or in the strong, firm grasp of a robust and healthy man.

We are not saved because our faith is *strong*, nor are we lost because our faith is *weak*. Else we would never know if our faith is strong enough, if we believed deeply enough, or if we trusted firmly enough. No, we are saved because God in His mercy chose us to be His own; we are saved because God in His mercy gave His only begotten Son into death to redeem us.

Upon that fact, and upon that fact alone, we rely. Not upon the strength or weakness of our faith. We ask not: How strong is my faith, but how great is God's love? Not, how strong is my faith, but how great is Christ's redemption? God's love and Christ's redemption are great enough and strong enough to save to the uttermost even those of weakest faith.

In the text above Isaiah assures us: "A bruised reed He will not break and a dimly burning wick He will not quench." (RSV). Or more plainly: a bruised stem He will not break off but will rather support and strengthen it; a flickering, sputtering lamp He will not put out but will rather nurse it back to full-flame. The prophet is speaking of the coming Savior who in His mercy will keep even the faintest faith alive.

Let us, then, get rid of all doubts and misgivings. Let us thank God that in His mercy He has assured us that even a weak faith saves.

May we pray the fervent prayer of the man in the Gospel (Mark 9:24): *"Lord, I believe! Help Thou mine unbelief!"*

Afraid You Are Too Late?

Now is the accepted time; behold, now is the day of salvation. *2 Corinthians 6:2*

A man who had spent a wicked life lay critically ill. Turning to his pastor, he asked: "Do you think that a deathbed repentance does away with a whole life of sin?" "No," answered the pastor quietly and reassuringly, "but Calvary does!"

Calvary does away with every sin. "The blood of Jesus Christ, His Son, cleanseth us from *all* sin," says St. John. "Though your sins be as scarlet, they shall be as white as snow; though they be red like crimson, they shall be as wool."

It is not a question of being late or being early, of being *more* guilty or *less* guilty, of being old or young—it is merely a question of accepting NOW the abundant pardon which is ours through the limitless love of Jesus Christ, our Savior. There is love, mercy, and pardon for *all alike.*

Do you feel that you have been harboring some secret sin too long to be forgiven, that you have trampled upon God's grace too long to ask for pardon? Take heart! Where sin abounded, God's love did much more abound. If you are still able to read (or hear) these words, it is *not too late!* "Now is the accepted time. Now is the day of salvation."

The penitent thief on the cross was very late but not *too* late. The hour was late in the life of Zacchaeus, but not *too* late. He still was privileged to hear from the lips of the Savior: "*This day* is salvation come to this house!" This day! Have we recognized this day as a day of grace? Whatever our present circumstance, let each of us lift our heart to the Throne of grace and say with the Christian poet:

> *Today* Thy mercy calls us To wash away our sin.
> However great our trespass, Whatever we have been,
> However long from mercy Our hearts have turned away,
> Thy precious blood can cleanse us And make us white *today.*

Afraid of Adversity?

Every branch that beareth fruit, He purgeth it, that it may bring forth more fruit.
John 15:2

We are told that in the botanical gardens at Oxford, England, a fine pomegranate was cut down almost to the root because it bore nothing but leaves. Sometime later the keeper was able to report that a marvelous transformation had taken place and that the tree was now bearing fruit in abundance. All that it had needed was to be cut back and to be cut back severely.

Our heavenly Father sometimes finds it necessary to cut back the trees that are growing in *His* garden. "Every branch that beareth fruit, He purgeth it [He prunes it], that it may bring forth more fruit." Notice! This pruning is done on the branch that *is* bearing fruit so that it may bring forth *more* fruit. The heavy growth of brittle brush and useless twigs must constantly be cut away to safeguard, assure, and multiply the yield.

Has our heavenly Father perhaps found it necessary to cut back drastically some branch in our life on which we had pinned our highest hopes? The loss of health? The loss of wealth? The loss of a loved one? The painful emptiness of bitter disillusionment? These are drastic cut backs, to be sure. But they are cut backs with a gracious purpose. God is not cutting down the tree, He is improving one of its promising branches.

We who have come to God through Christ have learned to know a Father's love. Could His love send us any sorrow which, in His wisdom, was not intended for our good? If ever we doubt His gracious plan for us, we will do well to remember the beautiful hymn of reassurance:

Beloved, "It is well!" God's ways are always right,
And perfect love is o'er them all, Tho' far above our sight.

Beloved, "It is well!" Tho' deep and sore the smart,
The hand that wounds knows how to bind And heal the broken heart.

Stubble-Filled Hearts

And some fell among thorns. Matthew 13:7

The thorny ground of which the Savior speaks in the parable of the sower is not to be pictured as ground in which thorns and briar bushes had grown large and strong, but rather as soil which had not been properly *cleaned* and in which the roots and seeds of thorns and weeds were still present in abundance. These seeds and roots and stubble, which should have been removed before the sowing of the good seed, grew rapidly, the Savior says, and soon choked the tender blade of grain. And so it died and bore no fruit.

God willing, next Sunday our hearts will again be the field for the sowing of the Gospel message. During the week much stubble and worthless seed have been strewn across the sowing field: the constant press of worldly cares, the faithless worries, the frequent sinning, the preoccupation with selfish interests, the overfeeding of our selfish egos.

These are the briars and the stubble which threaten to infest (and take root in) our heart with every passing day. The Savior calls them "the cares of this world and the deceitfulness of riches." Unless we are aware of their presence and invoke the Holy Spirit's aid in dealing with them promply and effectively, the seed which is sown in church next Sunday will "fall among thorns" and will soon be choked.

Effective sermon hearing calls for consistent Christian living. The challenge comes to us throughout the week. Are we filling our lives with *competing* influences which threaten to choke out the precious Gospel seed? Only two persons know for sure—God and you. Therefore let us pray:

> Holy Ghost, with power divine, Cleanse this guilty heart of mine;
> In Thy mercy pity me; From sin's bondage set me free.
>
> Holy Spirit, all divine, Dwell within this heart of mine;
> Cast down every idol throne; Reign supreme, and reign alone.

Afraid To Sin?

Shall we continue in sin . . . ? God forbid. . . . For the wages of sin is death, but the gift of God is eternal life through Jesus Christ our Lord. *Romans 6:1, 23*

Chrysostom, the eloquent church father, had incurred the anger of Emperor Arcadius. Enraged, the emperor consulted with his counselors as to the best method of punishing the powerful preacher.

"Confiscate his property!" said one. "Whom will that harm?" asked his majesty. "Not Chrysostom, but only the poor, to whom he gives all he has."—"Cast him into prison!" said a second. "What would be the use? He would glory in his chains."—"Well, then kill him!" said another. "How would that help? It would only open the gates of heaven to him."

Finally, one wiser than the rest proposed: "There is only one thing in the world that Chrysostom fears. He is afraid to sin. *We must make him sin!*"

Can the same be said of us? Afraid to sin? Or have we tamed the ugly monster of sin to the point where we can live fairly comfortably with it? Let us remember the words with which Martin Luther begins his explanation of each of the Ten Commandments: "We should *fear* and *love* God . . . ."

We should stand in awe of God because of His holiness and righteousness. We should love Him because of his immeasurable compassion freely bestowed on us through Jesus Christ, His Son. We should learn to recoil instinctively from the dreadful consequences of sin, and be drawn to ever higher degrees of holiness by the wondrous love poured out for us on Calvary's cross.

We dare never forget that it was *our* sin which caused our blessed Lord to die for our redemption. Out of love for Him, may we take our stand with St. Chrysostom and not be ashamed if the world mockingly says of us: "He is afraid to sin."

Oh, Lord, teach me to walk in Your ways, to hate sin, and to love You more and more. Amen.

Afraid To Be Humble?

Be clothed with humility, for God resisteth the proud and giveth grace to the humble. *1 Peter 5:5*

Yes, we might as well admit it. There are times when we are afraid to be humble, afraid that if we don't sing our own praises, the song will never be sung! Afraid that our own virtues and accomplishments will go unnoticed. Afraid, lest, like the desert flower, we be born to blush unseen and waste our fragrance on the desert air.

Simon Peter once had those fears. Whenever he tried to overcome them by asserting his own virtues, he made a sorry mess of things. But Simon Peter learned his lesson, and it was an altogether different Simon who in the late years of his life wrote to his Christian friends: "Be clothed with humility, for God resisteth the proud and giveth grace to the humble."

Robert Louis Stevenson once said to a friend: "The most dangerous height which I ever climbed was Mount *Ego.*" Pride, and not humility, is the thing to be feared! The great church father St. Augustine once exclaimed: "Should you ask me, What is the first thing in religion? I should reply, The first, the second, the third thing—nay, all—is humility."

The apostle Paul points to our Savior as the perfect example of humility which we should follow. A paraphrase of Paul's words would be: "Let this mind be in you which was also in Christ, who, although He was true God, stepped down to the status of a mere man, and then willingly humbled Himself, becoming a servant, obedient until death, yes, even death on a cross" (Philippians 2:5-8). What an example to keep before us!

As we contemplate the unsearchable love of Him who humbled Himself for us, even to death on a cross, let us say with the poet:

> When I survey the wondrous cross
> On which the Prince of Glory died,
> My richest gain I count but loss,
> *And pour contempt on all my pride.*

God, be merciful to me, a sinner. For Jesus' sake. Amen.

216

Afraid To Make Trial of God's Love?

Oh, taste and see that the Lord is good. *Psalm 34:8*

We can well imagine the thoughts which must have surged through the mind of the prodigal son as he trudged along the road that led back to his father's house. Would the door be open—the door to the familiar home of his childhood, and the door to his father's heart? Or would those doors be closed to him forever? How did his father feel? What did he think? What would he say? What would he do?

The young man would never know unless, despairing of all else, he would throw himself completely on his father's mercy. And so he did *just that.* He decided to make trial of his father's love. And "when he was yet a great way off, his father saw him, and had compassion, and ran, and fell on his neck and kissed him." There was love aplenty—even for the prodigal—in the tender father heart.

And there is also love aplenty in the Father heart of our *heavenly* Father. "Oh, taste and see that the Lord is good," He pleads with us. "Where sin abounded, grace [love and mercy] did much more abound," says Paul. Or, as John says: "In this was manifested the love of God toward us, because that God sent His only begotten Son into the world, that we might live through Him. Herein is love, not that we loved God, but that *He loved us,* and sent His Son to be the propitiation for our sins."

After we have wandered down the path of sin far from God, how comforting it is to know that, if we return to Him in penitence and faith, He is not a stern Judge determined to mete out justice, but rather, a loving *Father,* waiting with outstretched arms, eager to receive us, eager to forgive us. In view of the Gospel message, could we ever doubt the fullness, the tenderness, the all-sufficiency of the love of God in Jesus Christ, our Lord!

Just as I am, Thy love unknown Has broken every barrier down;
Now to be Thine, yea, Thine alone, O Lamb of God, I come, I come.

Afraid God Cannot Help?

Fear not! Believe only! *Luke 8:50*

Have you ever felt that the situation was so far out of control that it would be futile to call upon God for help? The friends of Jairus in the above Gospel reading felt that way. That is why they sent to him and said: "Thy daughter is dead; trouble not the Master." The case is now beyond His power to help.

But the Bible tells us that Jesus felt differently. He recognized no limit to His power to relieve the distess of those who came to Him. And so He says: *"Fear not; believe only,* and she shall be made whole." The situation had gotten beyond the control of Jairus, but not beyond the power of Jesus.

We are reminded of the desperate plight of the Israelites in their flight from Egypt. With the Red Sea before them and the chariots of Pharaoh behind them, we read that "they were sore afraid and cried unto the Lord." Even divine help at that moment seemed out of the question. But what did Moses tell them? "Fear ye not! Stand still and see the salvation of the Lord!"—They stood still. And the Lord did send His salvation.

Have we learned to *stand still* and to let the Lord take over? The drowning man, gasping for his last breath, cannot be saved as long as he keeps struggling to support *himself* above the water. It is when we surrender ourselves, body, mind, and soul, to the redeeming love and protecting care of Christ that we learn to stand still and see God's abundant power to help. The Christian poetess, Catharina von Schlegel, had learned the art of placing her problems into the hands of the Lord and then "standing still." Who can match the beauty of her words:

Be still, my soul, thy God doth undertake
To guide the future as He hath the past.
Thy hope, thy confidence, let nothing shake;
All now mysterious shall be bright at last.
Be still, my soul; the waves and winds still know
His voice who ruled them while He dwelt below!

Afraid of Death?

My desire is to depart and be with Christ, for that is far better. Philippians 1:23 RSV

It is said of a great theologian that every night before he retired, he would go to the window, draw the curtain aside, look up into the starry heavens, and say: "Perhaps *tonight*, Lord?" And in the morning as he arose, his first movement would be to raise the blind and, looking out upon the graying dawn, to inquire: "Perhaps *today*, Lord?"

So, too, we Christians. From the early years in which we learned to fold our hands and say, "If I should die before I wake, I pray Thee, Lord, my soul to take," until that final hour in which we will pray, "Father, into Thy hands I commend my spirit," we know that it is "perhaps today" or "perhaps tomorrow" that our Father will call from heaven and take His weary child home. With David we are always conscious of the fact that "there is but a step between me and death."

But death holds no terror for the Christian. We know that our Savior's death upon the cross has guaranteed that our death will be but the opening of the gates of paradise.

That is why the apostle Paul could speak of Christians as those that *love* the Lord's appearing, those that long for final, sweet communion with their Savior. And that is why he, personally, could write in the evening hours of life: "I have a desire to depart and to be with Christ, which is far better." Yes, that is why every Christian can join in the confident assurance of the psalmist and say: "Yea, though I walk through the valley of the shadow of death, I will fear no evil, for THOU art with me!" With the Christian poet we can sing:

> O sweet and blessed country, The home of God's elect!
> O sweet and blessed country That eager hearts expect!
> Jesus, in mercy bring us To that dear land of rest,
> Who art, with God the Father and Spirit, ever blest. Amen.

Afraid God Has Passed You By?

Are not two sparrows sold for a farthing? And one of them shall not fall on the ground without your Father. Matthew 10:29

Does it seem at times that God has passed us by, that we are the one person for whom He has failed to plan or to make provision? Our heavenly Father does not *want* us to feel that way.

Again and again the Savior points to the hand of His Father in the *individual* lives of His believers. "Your Father knoweth what things ye have need of," He says. He who holds the planets in the hollow of His hand also holds the sparrows. "Fear ye not, therefore; ye are of more value than *many* sparrows."

Think for a moment of what God has *already* done for us! Today we are feeding upon the green pastures of His Word and are being led beside the still waters of His comforting assurances—ONLY because God from eternity saw us out in the desert of sin and decreed that we should be brought into the shelter of His fold. We were lost and would have remained forever lost had not His mercy found us.

But His mercy *did* find us. His love *did* bring us into the safety of the fold. Dare we doubt that He who went the bitter path of Calvary in order that He might seek and save His wandering sheep—dare we doubt that He will care for us and keep us now that He has gathered us among His own?

In moments of loneliness or depression, when our faith in God's surrounding presence and His providing love begins to waver, let us recall the reassuring words of Christ: "Are not two sparrows sold for a farthing? And one of *them* shall not fall on the ground without your Father?" Surely, He who remembers the tiniest sparrow will not forget those for whom He bled and died. The Christian poetess, Mrs. C. D. Martin, caught the significance of this comparison when she wrote those memorable lines:

> His eye is on the sparrow, And I know He watches me.
> I sing because He loves me; I sing because I'm free.
> For His eye is on the sparrow, And I know He watches me.

Fair Weather Christians

Some fell upon stony places, where they had not much earth. Matthew 13:5

As the sower went forth to sow his seed, we are told that some fell upon "stony places." We can best picture these "stony places" as solid beds of rock above which lay only a thin layer of soil. This seed, we are told, sprouted immediately. In fact, it is probable that at first it grew faster than the others because the underlying rock reflected the warmth of the spring sunshine and helped the seed to germinate. But soon it withered and died, for it could strike no *roots*. Or, as the Savior says, there was "not much earth."

What a striking picture of the fair-weather Christian—the Christian who indeed has a certain emotional experience every time he hears a sermon, but who is seldom gripped by any *deep* and *abiding* conviction! When the hot summer sun beats down upon him—in the form of trial and tribulation and temptation—the tender blade of his faith begins to wilt and shrivel and soon blows away. It cannot stand the heat of adversity or the strong winds of temptation, because it has "not much earth."

Let us ask ourself in all seriousness: what sort of soil do we normally bring to our Sunday morning worship? Do we bring only the shallow top layer of our heart, beneath which lies a solid rock of worldly interests, or do we bring the impenetrable stones of indifference, impenitence, perhaps even unbelief?

If so *now* is the time to implore the Holy Spirit to remove any hardness from our hearts—any "stony places"—and to prepare them for a fruitful hearing of the Word. It is He, and He alone, who can convert a stony heart into a fertile field, ready for a fruitful sowing. With the poet let us pray:

See, to Thee I yield my heart, Shed Thy life through every part;
A pure temple I would be, Wholly dedicate to Thee. Amen.

Only the Holy Spirit can prepare our hearts for a fruitful hearing of the Word. Let us pray Him for His aid and blessing.

Afraid Your Talents Are Too Small?

Therefore I take pleasure in infirmities . . . for when I am weak, then am I strong.
2 Corinthians 12:10

Mr. Moon, the man who did so much to bring the Gospel to the blind, once addressed a large audience of blind people in England. He said: "When I became blind as a young boy, people tried to comfort my mother because of the heavy cross with which I was afflicted. But they were wrong. God gave me blindness as *a talent* to be used for His glory. Without blindness I should never have been able to see the needs of the blind."

Mr. Moon consecrated his *talent of blindness* to the Lord—and published the Gospel in raised type in nearly 200 languages and dialects!

Can we say, then, that we have no talents or that our talents are too small? All of God's dispensations to us are talents which we are to dedicate to His glory—our health, our sickness, our wealth, our poverty, our time, our social position, our daily contacts. All are talents which a merciful Father has placed into our hands for use in His service.

We gain nothing by wasting our time in idle dreaming about the talents we do *not* have. Rather, we are to do our very best with the talents we *do* have. If blindness can be accepted as a talent and dedicated to the service of the Savior, surely there will be no want of talents in our lives if we will but recognize them. Out of love to the Redeemer, who gave Himself that we might live, let us consecrate our every thought, our every talent, our every moment, to the greater glory of His name.

At this very moment may the eyes of our faith see the Savior standing in our midst and may we hear Him saying:

> I gave My life for thee, My precious blood I shed,
> That thou might'st ransomed be And quickened from the dead.
> *Great gifts* I brought to thee; What hast thou brought to Me?

May the sincere answer of our heart be: "Thou gave'st Thyself for me; I give *myself* to Thee."

Afraid of the World's Enmity?

Greater is He that is in you than he that is in the world. *1 John 4:4*

The aged John wrote to his "little children." "Marvel not, my brethren, if the world hates you." They were not to be surprised if their loyalty to Christ and His Gospel would incur the hatred of the unbelieving world. They were to remember that as long as they would remain in this world, they would be in enemy territory. The world would oppose them, even hate them.

But they should not be afraid. And why not? "Because greater is He that is in you than he that is in the world." John never forgot the words which His Savior had spoken in the Upper Room: "If the world hate you, ye know that it hated Me before it hated you. . . . In the world ye shall have tribulation, but be of good cheer, *I have overcome the world!*"

With this victorious, world-conquering Savior in his heart, the balance of power was always in John's favor—no matter how mighty the opposition! "Greater is He that is in you than he that is in the world."

Paul uttered a similar thought when he said: "Who shall separate us from the love of Christ? *Shall . . . persecution? . . .* Nay, in all these things we are more than conquerors through Him that loved us" (Romans 8:35-37). We need have no fear of the world's enmity as long as we have the Savior's friendship.

Do we *have* that friendship? Do we live in daily close communion with Him whom we profess to carry in our heart? Do we come to Him in daily prayer "making all our wants and wishes known"—asking for pardon, for strength, for guidance? Do we associate with Him through Word and Sacrament—through regular church attendance, through frequent participation in His Holy Supper? Do we make sure that He is not only in our Bible but also in our heart? God grant that we do.

Oh, Lord, I pray You, dwell within my heart so that I may overcome the temptations of the world. For Jesus' sake. Amen.

The Monogrammed Gospel

[Jesus said:] This is My body which is given for you . . . . This cup is the new testament in My blood, which is shed for you. *Luke 22:19-20*

The purpose of a monogram is to individualize—to indicate that a certain item is *one's own*. It is in this sense that we call the Lord's Supper "The Monogrammed Gospel."

There is, of course, much comfort in the spoken Gospel as we hear it from the pulpit each Sunday. We rejoice in all the Gospel proclamations, particularly the repeated assurances which are couched in the almost constant refrain of "whosoever." As Martin Luther put it, he found great consolation in every Gospel "whosoever," because he was sure that, unworthy though he was, he was included in the universal promise that "whosoever believeth in Him [Christ] should not perish, but have everlasting life."

But in the Holy Sacrament this universal becomes particular, this general becomes personal. Both in action and in Word the offer and the assurance are addressed to the individual believer. To you, singly, Christ says: "This is My body which is given for *you*, Mary Smith." "This is the cup of the new testament in My blood, which is shed for *you*, Peter Martin." In other words, by His very choice of pronouns the Savior singles each of us out and deals with us individually as we stand before His altar.

The apostle Paul realized this very personal aspect of Holy Communion. He encouraged his converts to avail themselves of this particularized blessing frequently. Of the early Christians we read that "they continued steadfastly in the apostles' doctrine and fellowship, and in breaking of bread and in prayers."

Are we as zealous, as eager, to partake of the Lord's Supper as they were? Are the words "given for you" and "shed for you" as precious to us today as they were on the day of our first Communion? Holy Communion is a communion in many senses but, we dare not forget, it is a communion between us and Him who died for us that we might live. Therefore let us heed His urgent plea, *"This do!"*

Cry Arson!

The tongue is a small thing, but what enormous damage it can do! James 3:5 LB

In the above passage St. James describes the devastating potential of the human tongue. He says, in part: "The tongue is a flame of fire. . . . [It] is set on fire by hell itself, and can turn our whole lives into a blazing flame of destruction and disaster." For a graphic description of the dreadful potential of the tongue it will pay to read the entire passage (James 3:1-12 LB).

We know, of course, that it is not the physical organ known as tongue that is responsible for all the havoc. It is the human heart! The Savior tells us: "Out of the *heart* proceed . . ." Then He lists a shocking catalog of wickedness. The tongue merely relays what the heart dictates. "As a man thinketh in his heart, so is he"—so he thinks and speaks and writes.

In his epistle James makes a number of striking comparisons. He says that we can place a small bit into the mouth of a horse and make his whole body subservient to our will. We can attach a small rudder to a large ship and, despite wind and wave, the rudder will determine the ship's direction. We can light a small match in a large forest, and soon the entire forest will be ablaze. Even so, says James, is the human tongue. Though small in size, its potential for good or evil is almost immeasurable.

What sins of the heart, of the tongue, of the pen call for sincere repentance in this our day? Our tongues and our pens have, indeed, set our world aflame! God forgive us wherever our careless speech has contributed to the spreading holocaust. Even in a world aflame, there is still healing and forgiveness in Jesus Christ, our only Savior.

Lord, remove all hatred from my heart and fill it with Your love so that I may speak no evil. In Jesus' name. Amen.

The Hem of His Garment

If I may but touch [the hem of] His garment, I shall be made whole. Matthew 9:21

There come times, even in the life of the believer, when every door seems to be closed, when there seems to be no escape from the troubles that beset us: a loved one lying on a sickbed for years, a broken marriage which has resulted in untold grief and pain, a wayward child for whom we had such rosy hopes.

Where do we turn when every door seems closed, when there seems to be no God in heaven who is conscious of our need, or who, if He is there, seems to turn a deaf ear to our every plea?

The unnamed woman in our text provides us with an excellent example of what to do in such a circumstance. Jostled by a milling crowd, she approached Jesus from the rear, *saying to herself:* "If I may but touch the hem of His garment!" There was no spoken prayer; in fact, there was no prayer at all. It was merely a sigh of faith, an unspoken confession of trust in the love and omnipotence of the Son of God to whom she had drawn so close.

"If I may but touch the hem of His garment!" You and I can do just that. His omnipotence, wisdom, and love are that close to us. Let us reach out with the hand of faith, no matter how weak, and claim the promise of His Word. It will never fail us.

In his touching hymn "Jesus, Lover of My Soul" Charles Wesley, the English hymnist, reaches out for the helping hand of Christ—in words that you and I might well repeat:

> Other refuge have I none; Hangs my helpless soul on Thee.
> Leave, ah, leave me not alone. Still support and comfort me!
> All my trust on Thee is stayed, All my help from Thee I bring;
> Cover my defenseless head With the shadow of Thy wing.

Let us always remember that Jesus is, indeed, the Lover of our soul, eager to help in time of need. We have His Word. May we always trust it.

Live Up to Your Name!

Ye are all the children of God by faith in Christ Jesus. Galatians 3:26

There is a legend about Alexander the Great which makes a point that all of us well might ponder. Apparently, one of his generals had behaved in a manner unbefitting his rank. At the next meeting of his staff Alexander upbraided the general severely, ending his rebuke with the stern command: "Change your conduct or change your name!"

What a challenge—not only for the guilty general but also, for you and me! The Holy Scriptures have given us many noble names: children of God, children of light, salt of the earth, royal priests, ambassadors for Christ, and many others.

Peter gives the Christians in Asia Minor a most unusual name—a name that is difficult to reproduce in modern English. He calls them "a people for a possession." To his original readers that meant: "Ye are a purchased people." They no longer belonged to the world; they belonged to the Christ who "bought" them. In his explanation of the Second Article of The Apostles' Creed Luther says that Christ has "*purchased* and won" us, that we might be Christ's own and "live under Him in His Kingdom."

But why these extraordinary names? St. Peter tells us why: "That you may declare the wonderful deeds of Him who called you out of darkness into His marvelous light" (1 Peter 2:9 RSV)—the light of His love and mercy through Jesus Christ, His Son and our Savior.

Are we living up to our name as "children of the Father?" If not, let us heed the words of Alexander as they apply to our faith and life: "Change your conduct or change your name!"

Lord, I am Your child through Jesus Christ, my Savior. May my life always reflect credit on Your name. Amen.

Read Matthew 7:24-27 **August 5**

Fruitful Hearers

Keep thy foot when thou goest to the house of God, and be more ready to hear.
Ecclesiastes 5:1

In the parable of the sower the Savior gives us three characteristics of the fruitful hearer of the Word when He says: "[Those] on the good ground are they, which in an honest and good heart, having heard the Word, keep it and bring forth fruit with patience" (Luke 8:15). First, then, there is attention: they *"hear."* Second, there is meditation: they *"keep."* And finally, there is obedience: *"they bring forth fruit."*

The good hearer goes to church to *hear!* He knows that in the providence of God there is something in the morning's lessons and sermon especially for him. His opportunity to hear the Word is precious, and he is determined not to squander it.

The good hearer furthermore listens to *"keep."* For him the sermon is not a meal to be swallowed hurriedly on Sunday morning and then forgotten, but it is a table that is to remain spread throughout the week. He intends to come back to it again and again for nourishment and strength.

And finally the good hearer listens to *obey.* He "brings forth fruit." He is a doer of the Word and not a hearer only.

Might we not very well measure our hearing according to these three standards of the Savior? Do we really go to church to hear? And do we really hear to keep? And do we listen to obey? What does our record say?

As we take our seat in our accustomed pew each Sunday, may our heart turn heavenward as we breathe the thoughts of the poet:

Here Thy praise is gladly chanted,
Here Thy seed is duly sown;
Let my soul, where it is planted,
Bring forth precious sheaves alone.
So that all I hear may be
Fruitful unto life in me. Amen.

228

Be Careful of the Company You Keep

Be not deceived; evil communications corrupt good manners. *1 Corinthians 15:33*

Another translation of the above passage would be: "Don't fool yourself; evil company corrupts good morals." For our meditation, let us restrict the application of this admonition to the books we read, the movies we see, and the television programs we follow. These are the company we keep for many hours each day.

What kind of company are we keeping? A recent survey revealed that the book market (especially paperbacks) has been glutted with a shocking amount of filth, illicit sex, profanity, and blasphemy. The same is true of current box-office-hit movies. And even television, that ever-present companion in most homes, has an increasing number of programs and commercials that reflect the language and the morals of a decadent society.

Never in all of human history has it been more true that "the world is so much *with* us." The old adage "a man's home is his castle" is becoming less and less true. The world has invaded our living rooms, our bedrooms, and our kitchens by means of the television screen, the omnipresent radio, and the printed page. Invited or uninvited, the world has become a constant guest in millions of Christian households.

How are we coping with this company we keep? Are we becoming a part of the crowd? Do we think more lightly of the steady stream of sins we see and hear? If so, God forgive us for Jesus' sake. And may He grant us His sanctifying Spirit so that we may resist the powerful allurements that surround us. It is to His Holy Spirit that we now pray:

Lord, to Thee I yield my heart, Shed Thy life through every part;
A pure temple I would be, Wholly dedicate to Thee.

Rejoice, Young Man, Young Woman!

Rejoice, O young man, in your youth, and let your heart cheer you . . . . But know that for all these things God will bring you into judgment. *Ecclesiastes 11:9 RSV*

There is a false notion among many young people, especially among teenagers, that Christianity and fun are mutually exclusive—that a consistent Christian life rules out all the joy and merriment which one usually associates with youth. In many instances this is a misconception that has been handed down from the age of Pietism and is still to be found among some Protestant groups.

But nothing could be farther from the truth. It is the will of God that young people everywhere enjoy themselves. Their youthful vigor, their natural optimism, their relative freedom from the responsibilities which are yet to come—all are gifts of God which they are to enjoy and to celebrate with "cheer."

But they are to do so responsibly. No matter what they do—in the natural exuberance of youth—they are to remember that they are accountable to God for their every thought, word, and deed. Does this sound like smothering the word "rejoice" with a wet blanket?

By no means! All redeemed children of God, whether they be 7, 17, or 70, should live their entire life in the conscious presence of the Lord. They are to *rejoice* in God's presence, knowing that, through Christ, God has become their loving Father and they His loving children.

One of the theme words of Paul was "joy." Again and again he reminded his converts of the precious blessing of their salvation and exhorted them to rejoice. Let all young people experience this "joy in the Lord" and express it in their daily lives. With Martin Luther let them say:

My heart for very JOY doth leap, My lips no more can silence keep!

God Opens Windows

God will not allow you to be tested above your powers, but when the test comes He will at the same time provide a way out, by enabling you to sustain [bear] it. *1 Corinthians 10:13 NEB*

In the popular musical "Sound of Music" Sister Maria, when confronted by a momentous decision which was to change the entire course of her life, spoke the well-known line of assurance: "When God closes a door, somewhere He opens a window." Millions of Christians who have faced many "closed doors" (heartaches, trials, and disappointments) in their lives will rise up to say a hearty Amen to her confident expression of faith.

In fact, many of the world's great have achieved their most heroic accomplishments in the face of "closed doors." John Milton wrote *Paradise Lost* and *Paradise Regained* after having been afflicted with total blindness. Beethoven wrote some of his greatest music, including his Ninth Symphony, after he was almost completely deaf. By no means would the writer of this page put himself into the class of Milton or Beethoven, but he would be remiss, were he not to add his own personal witness. After this writer's eight years in the preaching ministry the Lord, in His unsearchable wisdom, permitted him to lose his preaching voice but led him into a literary ministry which has reached around the world.

Sister Maria was right when she said: "When God closes a door, somewhere He opens a window." She was right because she was merely echoing the words of our text above: God may permit trials to come our way, but with every trial He will also provide "a way out." Does this sound like a sentimental "greeting card" assurance? Not to the *believer* who takes his stand at the foot of the cross of Christ! There in the darkness which shrouds the noonday sun we see the shining light of God's eternal love—a love from which no "closed doors" can ever shut us out.

> Judge not the Lord by feeble sense,
> But trust Him for His grace;
> Behind a frowning providence
> He hides a smiling face.
>
> Blind unbelief is sure to err
> And scan His works in vain;
> God is His own Interpreter,
> And *HE* will make it plain.

Mum's the Word?

Come and hear, all you who fear God, and I will tell you what He has done for me.
Psalm 66:16 RSV

There is a tendency among some church-goers to consider their religion a "private matter"—something strictly between themselves and God. They pray privately at home, and even their public worship in church is, in a sense, private—they speak to God and God speaks to them, but that is where it stops. Although they may deny it, their attitude toward their relationship to God and His relationship to them is "Mum's the word!"

How different from the attitude of the psalmist in the short text quoted above. He wanted everyone to "come and hear" what God had done for him: how God had shown him mercy, how God had answered his prayers, how God had forgiven all his sins. Is this also true of us? Are we really eager to share with others what God has done for us through Jesus Christ our Savior?

Admittedly, it is much easier to *talk* about such sharing of the good news with others than actually to do it. We are living in a culture where unsolicited religious conversation is frowned upon or, at best, considered awkward and embarrassing. In polite society today, when it comes to meaningful religious conversation, there seems to be an almost universal understanding: "You keep your mouth shut, and I'll keep my mouth shut."

How are we to break this conspiracy of silence? First, by following the example of the psalmist in our personal prayer life. David felt perfectly at home when speaking to God. Do we? The more we speak to God in personal, intimate prayer, the more we'll feel inclined to speak to our fellowman about our relationship with Him. The more we'll feel inclined, also, to speak freely of our faith within the family circle and with those whose lives daily touch ours.

Let us strive more and more to "witness" winsomely to one and all of the wonderful salvation we have found in Jesus Christ, our Savior. May God's Holy Spirit attend our faithful witness.

Lord, may I be a constant witness to Your wondrous love. Amen.

When the Christian Says, "Shut Up!"

Who will be the accuser of God's chosen ones? Romans 8:33 NEB

Yes, there is a time when the Christian can say: "Shut up!" That time is when Satan accuses him of sin—when his accusing conscience tries to convince him that there is no hope.

At that moment the penitent believer in Christ can fling the Holy Scriptures at "his majesty the devil" and say with St. Paul:

> If God is on our side, who is against us? He did not spare His own Son, but gave Him up for us all. . . . *Who will be the accuser of God's chosen ones?* It is God who pronounces acquittal; then who can condemn? It is Christ . . . who died, and more than that, was raised from the dead, who is at God's right hand, and indeed pleads our cause. . . . Nothing in all creation . . . can separate us from the love of God in Christ Jesus our Lord. NEB

What Paul is saying in the above words is simply this: no one, not even the devil, can effectively *condemn* the repentant sinner who has fled to the Savior for refuge. Let the devil rant and rave and hurl his endless accusations, the believer in Christ can calmly say: "Shut up! You have nothing to say to me. I have a Savior who is not only my Redeemer but also my Advocate. He has, once and for all, settled my accounts in heaven, and He still represents me before the throne of His heavenly Father. Be silent, Evil One. Begone!"

This does not mean that every time our conscience accuses us we must repeat the above explicit dialog. No, it means that, as long as we are "standing in God's grace" through faith in Jesus, our Redeemer, we need have no fear of the accusations of the Evil One. Standing at our side is He who has not only washed us clean in the blood of His cross but also continues to be our eternal Advocate and never-failing Defender.

> Lord Jesus, I confess that I have often yielded to the temptations of the Evil One and have sinned against You and Your Word. Thank You for assuring me of Your love and forgiveness. Amen.

233

The Power to Cope

Take therefore no thought for the morrow; for the morrow shall take thought for the things of itself. Matthew 6:34

Any honest appraisal of the years that lie immediately ahead is bound to include a large amount of foreboding. The entire human family seems to be in ferment—economically, socially, politically, morally, and militarily. Indeed, many a believer wonders if we are perhaps living in that period of world upheaval which the Savior described in Luke 21:25-26 when he said that the nations would be "in perplexity" and men's hearts would be "failing them for fear, and for looking after those things which are coming on the earth."

In the midst of what might be termed a "cosmic anxiety," (an almost universal fear of the future) many are finding that the mounting pressures are just too much for them. Their inability to cope with life has resulted in the rise of cults of all descriptions, in the increase of alcoholism, drug addiction, divorce, mental illness, and a host of other social problems.

How does the believer in Christ cope with all the pressures of our trying times? There is no pat answer—no aspirin that will make all of the pressures of life go away. But there *is* an attitude (both a mind-set and a heart-set) which enables the true believer to "cope." The Savior encourages this attitude when He says: "Seek ye *first* the kingdom of God and His righteousness; and all these things shall be added unto you."

Jesus dealt with the problems at hand by encouraging His followers to give God, who already knows their needs, the central place in their lives. They should fix their eyes on *Him,* and not on the storms which loom on the horizon. Our Father in heaven is the Lord not only of our lives but also of the storms that threaten. In His omnipotence *He* will "cope." And in His love, revealed through His beloved Son, *He* will see us through.

Lord, in Your love, enable us to cope—no matter what. May we find daily strength in Your mercy and Your might, through Jesus Christ, our Savior. Amen.

Does My Life Really Have a Purpose?

Through faith we understand . . . . Hebrews 11:3

A few years ago an extraordinary paper, written by two London scientists, slipped almost unnoticed into modern scientific literature. Marshalling a list of fantastic "facts," they had come up with a "new" theory explaining the origin of the universe.

Perhaps the most significant statement of the book, especially for the Christian believer, comes in the final chapter. It reads: "The more the universe seems comprehensible, the more it also seems pointless." What a depressing thought for the person who is struggling with the vexing problems of life and the inevitable approach of death. If the entire universe is pointless, what is the point of continuing the daily struggle?

The believer's outlook on life, however, is not based on the speculations of fallible men. The Scriptures tell us: "Through *faith* we understand that the worlds were framed by the Word of God." What is more, we are told that the world continues to exist for a *purpose.* Paraphrasing the words of Paul (Romans 8:18-25), the entire creation continues to exist for the ultimate demonstration of the complete redemption of all who are in Christ. Or, in simpler terms, the world continues to exist (and we continue to live) in the sure hope of the triumphant return of God's eternal Son. Then "the ransomed of the Lord shall return . . . with songs and everlasting joy upon their heads; they shall obtain joy and gladness, and sorrow and sighing shall flee away" (Isaiah 35:10).

But while we wait and hope, we must also work, for that is part of God's purpose for our lives. We are to be "co-workers together with God," helping to achieve His purposes. As the Savior, so also we must say: "I must work the works of Him that sent me." For, indeed, we have been "sent" and, having been sent, we are to contribute to the final attainment of His purpose. Each morning as we face the duties of another day, we well might pray:

Dear Lord, I *know* You have a purpose for me today. Grant me a willing heart so that I may serve You faithfully. Amen.

Open Doors for the Gospel

A wide door for effective work has opened to me, and there are many adversaries.
1 Corinthians 16:9 RSV

The apostle Paul was in the city of Ephesus when he wrote the above remarkable statement to the Christians in Corinth. He was planning to come to Corinth but had decided to stay in Ephesus a little longer because a wide open door for effective work had opened up for him there—"and there are many adversaries."

To Paul, it would seem, the many adversaries were part of the wide open door for his Gospel ministry. They were a part of the *challenge.* Far from discouraging him (and giving him an excuse to leave the city) they merely deepened his determination to stay and preach the Gospel. He *knew* that his Gospel was "the power of God," and so any opportunity to expose more people to that "power" was a wide open door, regardless of attendant circumstances.

How about us and our attitude toward our unbelieving friends and neighbors, our community, our nation, and our world? Have we perhaps developed a "closed door" complex—permitting our difficulties to obscure our opportunities? Do we see nothing but closed doors for our personal witness—closed doors for our church's worldwide mission outreach?

How different from the attitude of Paul. He considered obstacles part of the "wide open door" God had placed before him! Perhaps, if we are honest with ourselves, the greatest obstacle to our personal witness to the Christian Gospel lies within our own heart. In our secular society speaking about Christ and matters of salvation "just isn't the thing to do." Perhaps! But we do have a message, and the message must be delivered—with tact, to be sure. But delivered it must be. Pray God for more and more open doors and for the courage to enter them. Remember:

> If you cannot speak like angels, If you cannot preach like Paul,
> You can tell the love of Jesus, You can say He died for all.
> If you cannot rouse the wicked With the Judgment's dread alarms
> You can lead the little children To the Savior's waiting arms.

To Each—a Special Gift

Each one of us has been given a special gift in proportion to what Christ has given.
Ephesians 4:7 TEV

Many of us excuse ourselves from direct involvement in Christ's mission and ministry (frequently misnamed church work) because we "don't have the necessary gifts." Perhaps unconsciously we limit God's spiritual gifts to such passages as Ephesians 4:11 where we are told "He gave some, apostles . . . some, pastors and teachers"—as if these were the only "spiritually gifted" members of His church.

A careful reading of the above passage, however, plus a reading of 1 Corinthians 12 and 13, will convince us that the Lord has given a particular spiritual gift to each believer, no matter what his or her station in life may be.

But how are we to determine what our particular gift or *gifts* are? Not by sitting and waiting for some spectacular revelation. True, we are to spend time in prayer and Bible study. But ordinarily our particular gifts find expression in the fellowship of the Christian congregation or in our exposure to the world about us or both.

It is in our contact with others that we see the many needs for loving, helpful Christian service. Here we find the challenge to match our Spirit-given gifts to the pressing needs of our fellowman and to *use* our gifts as God directs.

It may be the need for comforting companionship for a lonely soul, for intercessory prayer, for spoken witness, for a patient, understanding heart and a sympathetic ear. Or it may be the need for a leadership role in the Christian congregation or in the community or in an organized charitable endeavor.

No matter. None of us has all of God's gifts. But all of us have some. It is up to us to recognize them as gifts of God and to employ them generously in the Savior's service. Daily we must hear Him whispering softly to our conscience:

I gave My life for thee: Give thou thyself for Me.

Happiness Is . . .

Happy are those whose wrongs are forgiven, whose sins are pardoned. *Romans 4:7 TEV*

What really *is* happiness? If we were to judge by the smiling faces, the exuberance, and the bubbling zest for life of those who appear in our television commercials, we would have to conclude that happiness is primarily a matter of getting and having *things.*

If, on the other hand, we were to judge by the daily news that fills those same television screens, we might be inclined to believe that there is no such thing as happiness. Almost all is tragedy.

The Word of God tells us that there *is* such a thing as true happiness, but it is not a product to be sought or bought. It is rather a *by-product* of a gift that God has already given us. He has given us His love, His mercy and His pardon—all through Jesus Christ, our Savior. Along with these precious gifts He gives us happiness: genuine, deep-down happiness which abides forever.

Happiness, Paul tells us in Romans Five, consists ultimately in "standing in God's grace." That means living everyday in the constant awareness of God's forgiving love—knowing, beyond all doubt, that we are His and He is ours and that nothing (not even Satan, death, or hell) can ever separate us.

Even in moments of deepest sorrow the Christian knows a joy that can never be erased. It is the joy he has found in Jesus Christ his wonderful Redeemer. It was a man who was living in God's grace (God's love) who wrote the lines:

> Joy, O joy, beyond all gladness, Christ has done away with sadness!
> Hence, all sorrow and repining, For the Sun of Grace is shining!

Happy is the man who is living in that "Sun"—the Sun of God's unchanging grace and mercy. Storms may come and clouds may gather, earthly treasures may fly away, but nothing can rob the believer of his joy. He knows that for him the Sun of Grace is shining! And in that Sun there is joy forevermore!

Read Isaiah 55:8-11

God's Ways Are Not Always Our Ways

Who hath known the mind of the Lord? Or who hath been His Counselor? . . . How unsearchable are His judgments, and His ways past finding out! Romans 11:33-34

In the face of personal tragedy, are we always justified in saying: "It was God's will"? When an infant dies on the operating table as the result of professional negligence, is it right to say that God *willed* the infant's death? When a marriage breaks up because of the brutality of an incurably alcoholic husband, is it right to blame God? Was it really *His* will?

Surely, not! Admittedly, the ways of God are "past finding out," and it will do us no good to philosophize learnedly about what is "in the mind of the Lord." We *do* know that the God revealed to us in the message of the Gospel is preeminently a God of love. Indeed, St. John tells us that "God *is* love." True, He is also righteous, just and holy, but in His dealings with His believing children He merges all of His divine attributes into the primary attribute of love. "God showed His *love* toward us in that, while we were yet sinners, Christ died for us."

But we are still living in a world that is out of joint—out of harmony with God because of sin. And sin has brought with it, its curse: sorrow, suffering, and death to all mankind. Christ told His followers that, as long as they were in this world, they could expect tribulation—but in Him they could find peace. Tragedy, trial, and tribulation entered the world not because of God's will but because of man's disobedience.

Consequently, we dare not say that each specific misfortune that befalls the Christian is the result of a specific act of God's will. That would be a denial of God's assurance: "There is therefore no condemnation [no divine judgment] to them which are in Christ Jesus." No matter what the difficulty, we know that we are under the over-ruling providence of Him who loves us and that His ultimate will for us is always good.

Lord, let me live every day in the assurance of Your grace. Amen.

Getting Ready

And they that were ready went in with Him to the marriage. *Matthew 25:10*

A little girl came home from Sunday school and said to her mother: "Mama, teacher told us today that God puts people in this world so that they can get ready for heaven." "Yes, dear, that is right," said the mother. "But why don't we see anybody getting ready?" asked the child.

A childlike question! And yet, in some respects, how true! "Why don't we see anybody getting ready?" In the hurry and hubbub of our busy world men have become so preoccupied with the affairs of the day that many of them seem to have forgotten all about "getting ready."

And yet the psalmist tells us: "Thou carriest them away as with a flood . . . they are like grass. . . . In the morning it flourisheth and groweth up; in the evening it is cut down and withereth." Surely, we have every reason to continue with the psalmist and pray: "So teach us to number our days, that we may apply our hearts unto wisdom" (Psalm 90:5-6, 12).

In other words, teach us to "get ready." In the parable of the ten virgins we read: "They that were *ready* went in with Him to the marriage." Those who were not ready stayed outside. To them the doors were forever closed.

Are we "getting ready"? Do we daily confess our sins to God, our Father, and pray Him in Jesus' name for forgiveness? Have we rested our case, for time and for eternity, in the hands of Jesus, who is mightily able to save to the uttermost them that come to God by Him?

And do we translate our faith into a daily life that reflects credit on our divine Redeemer—a life of love, of kindness, of personal concern for "the least" of our Savior's brethren? Then we are ready. Then we are abundantly prepared.

> Lord, grant me Your Holy Spirit so that I may always be ready for Your coming. May I be "kept by the power of God, through faith, unto salvation." Amen.

Comforted—So That We May Comfort Others

Blessed be God . . . who comforteth us . . . that we may be able to comfort them which are in any trouble. *2 Corinthians 1:3-4*

In the Revised Standard Version the above passage reads:

Blessed be the God and Father of our Lord Jesus Christ, the Father of mercies and God of all comfort, who comforts us in all our affliction, so that we may be able to comfort those who are in any affliction, with the comfort with which we ourselves are comforted by God.

In other words, Christians have been comforted by "the Father of mercies" so that they, in turn, may comfort others with the *same* comfort with which they themselves have been comforted by God. Do we really do that?

When we visit the sick, the lonely, the bereaved, the disheartened, do we content ourselves with the usual "Chin up! Cheer up! Things'll turn out all right!"?

Or do we comfort them with the same comfort with which we ourselves have been comforted? We have been comforted by a loving God who has taken us to His bosom through the redeeming work of Jesus Christ, His Son. We have been comforted by the Scriptural assurance, not only that we have a loving Father in heaven, but also that "all things work together for good to them that love God, to them who are the called according to His purpose."

We are to share *that* comfort with all who are in distress—either by reason of painful illness or by any other kind of misfortune. In short, we are to share Christ with them: the Christ who has seen us through our own adversities; the Christ who, ultimately, is the only Source of lasting consolation, the only Dayspring of our hope. Have we cultivated both the art and the practice of "comforting others with the comfort with which we ourselves have been comforted"? Let us remember the poet's words:

To comfort and to bless, To find a balm for woe,
To tend the lone and fatherless, Is angels' work below.

Lord, may I comfort others, as You have comforted me. Amen.

Who Is in Charge?

The Lord reigneth. *Psalm 93:1*

There are times when even the most faithful of believers finds it difficult to accept the truth of the above statement of King David. In a day when it seems that the good and gracious will of God is being thwarted on every hand, when it seems that "the principalities and powers, and the rulers of the darkness of this world" have gained the upper hand, how can we say (and really believe) that "the Lord reigneth"?

Or, to come closer to home: when a loved one lingers on a bed of pain year after year, eagerly awaiting the angel of death, or when the weight of some sorrow has brought us to the very brink of despair, how can we say (and really believe) that "the Lord reigneth"? Wouldn't it seem more reasonable, more believable, to say that things had gotten even beyond *His* power to control?

We must confess frankly: there is no ready, no rational, explanation for every adversity that befalls the believer. David, the man who was inspired to say "the Lord reigneth" experienced many a heartache and many a heartbreak in his life. Indeed, he "lived in danger all the way."

But he had learned, when treading the deepest, darkest valley, to say with utmost confidence: "The Lord is my Shepherd." No matter how steep the descent or how painful the terrain, he knew the watchful eye of his Shepherd-King was upon him—and that His was the eye of love.

The Lord Jesus is our Good Shepherd and, even though we may not understand His leading it is enough to know that it is *He* who is in charge. With our hand securely in His, we can say with David: "Surely goodness and mercy shall follow me all the days of my life; and I will dwell in the house of the Lord forever." Of the reigning Christ we can confidently sing:

> Blessings abound where'er He reigns;
> The prisoner leaps, unloosed his chains;
> The weary find eternal rest,
> And all the sons of want are blest.

True Wisdom—What Is It?

The fear of the Lord is the beginning of wisdom. Psalm 111:10

We are living in a day in which the field of human knowledge is expanding at a faster rate than ever before. During the past few decades we have witnessed a veritable knowledge explosion in almost every field of human endeavor with the result that the average eighth grader of today has knowledge of facts which were unknown to all previous generations.

There is a great difference, however, between knowledge and wisdom. Perhaps no one knows this with greater conviction than the humble, trusting, believing child of God—the Christian who is living in a state of grace through faith in Jesus Christ, his Savior and Redeemer.

It is possible for a man or woman to be a scientific genius and, at the same time, to be a spiritual ignoramus. The psalmist tells us in the psalm quoted above that "the fear of the Lord is the beginning of wisdom." (Fear here means humble awe of the Almighty and His Word of revelation.) David starts another psalm with the sweeping statement: "The *fool* [no matter how well educated] hath said in his heart, There is no God!"

Paul devoted much of the opening chapter of his first letter to the Corinthians to the relative roles of human wisdom and divine revelation. Paraphrased, his words would read: "Since the world in all its wisdom could not know God, it pleased God [through the preaching of what seems foolishness, namely, the Gospel] to save them who would believe" (1 Corinthians 1:20-21).

The revelation of God's love is not to be found in the splitting of the atom nor in the far reaches of the telescope. No, the source of our highest wisdom is supra-natural. Thank God, He has *revealed* Himself in Jesus Christ on the sacred pages of Holy Scripture! The person who has come into the right relationship with God through His beloved Son has, indeed, been made "wise unto salvation." There *is* no higher wisdom.

> Thou art the Truth; Thy Word alone
> True wisdom can impart;
> Thou only canst inform the mind
> And purify the heart. Amen.

Character—Tried and True

Suffering produces endurance, and endurance produces character. Romans 5:3-4 RSV

We've often heard it said: "He's a character." Usually, this is said in ridicule or disparagement. Properly understood, however, it can also be said of the true believer in Christ that "he's a character"—a very *distinctive,* remarkable, character.

To get the full force of this statement one must read the above passage in its total context, Romans 5:1-8. Here we are told that he who believes in Jesus Christ as his Savior is not only justified (declared righteous) in God's sight, but that he is also frequently led through a series of experiences (trials and tribulations) that result in a certain quality of life that expresses itself in a certain kind of character. The Greek word means a "character that is *tried* and *true.*"

The believing Christian is, indeed, a man or woman of such character. Having trusted Christ not only as his Savior but also as his Lord, and having borne the cross of true discipleship, he has the *character* to stand up for what is right and to oppose that which is wrong. Are you and I known in our community, in our place of work, in our social circle, as persons of Christian character—tried and true?

It was a man of Christian faith and noble character who, in the face of approaching death, wrote these words of unswerving confidence:

> Go, then, earthly fame and treasure; Come, disaster scorn and pain!
> In Thy service pain is pleasure; With Thy favor, loss is gain.
> I have called Thee Abba Father! I have stayed my heart on Thee.
> Storms may howl and clouds may gather, All must work for good to me.

The man who wrote those lines had a "character" that was tried and true. With Christ in his heart, he was ready for anything that might come his way. Do *we* have a character that has stood the test? God grant it. Amen.

Not Everything Is Black Or White

As a Christian, I *may* do anything, but that does not mean that everything is good for me [to do]. *1 Corinthians 6:12 Phillips*

For some of us, it is difficult to remember that not everything in life is either black or white. As a result, we are quick to sit in judgment on our fellow Christian when, in fact, he is not deserving of such judgment.

The mature Christian recognizes that there are many, many aspects of human behavior which God has neither commanded nor forbidden. By way of example we mention such things as the growing of a beard, the choice of clergy vestments, the choice of a specific order for public worship, the moderate use of alcoholic beverages, or the eating or the abstaining from certain foods.

In each of the above instances, the apostle Paul would have said: "Go ahead—do as you like. You are a free man, a free woman, under the Gospel of Jesus Christ. Let no one judge you or condemn you."

But he would have *added:* "Be careful how you *use* your freedom. If by your action, you cause your weaker brother to act against his conscience by following your example, *don't do it.*"

We have a good example of what Paul means in Romans, chapter 14. The question was: "Is it wrong to eat certain kinds of meat?" Paul's answer was: "No, it is not wrong, but if I am in the presence of a brother whose conscience tells him it is wrong, I will refrain from eating the meat. Why? Lest by my example I cause my brother to act against his conscience and thereby commit a sin." In other words, Paul himself was free, but Christian love placed limits on the freedom which was his.

This is a very important teaching of the Scriptures. How many a weak Christian has been led to go against his conscience because a stronger Christian has made careless use of his Christian freedom. Paul warns us emphatically (Romans 14:14 ff.) not to use our freedom as a "stumbling block" for the weaker brother or sister who does not as yet share our degree of Christian knowledge. We must use our freedom carefully, wisely, and lovingly.

The Apple of His Eye

Christ also loved the church and gave Himself for it. *Ephesians 5:25*

In his letter to the Ephesians Paul has much to say about the Church. This is true especially of his eloquent description in chapter 2:19-22, where he likens the Church on earth to a beautiful temple, made up of "living stones"—that is, of all those who truly believe in Christ as Lord and Savior.

On several occasions Paul goes out of his way to assure us that Christ loved the Church—in fact, loved it so much that He gave His life for it! That means that we who have come to faith are, in a real sense, living every day of our lives as objects of His love. What a reason for reassurance, for joy and thanksgiving!

True, the Bible also tells us that Christ loved the whole world. And He still does! But when we read the Ephesians passage quoted above in its fuller context, we see that, when speaking of the Church, the family of His redeemed, His love takes on an utterly unique dimension. Listen! Paul tells us that Christ loved the Church so much that He "gave Himself for it; that He might sanctify and cleanse it with the washing of water by the word; that He might present it to Himself a glorious Church, not having spot or wrinkle . . . but that it should be holy and without blemish."

In other words, when St. Paul speaks of the Church in this chapter, he is not speaking of any human organization. The Church on which Christ lavishes His affection, for which He lived and bled and died, is that vast unnumbered throng from many lands and many races who have come to love Him as their Savior and Redeemer and serve Him as their Lord and Master. *That* Church He loved (past tense) and still loves (present tense) and will continue to love throughout the ages (future tense).

That Church is "the apple of His eye," something glorious, something precious, "holy and without blemish." Why? Because, in His unlimited grace, He has *declared* it so!

I love Thy Church, O God, Redeemed in every land,
Dear as the apple of Thine eye And graven on Thy hand.

Faith and Life

Thou believest that there is one God . . . the devils also believe and tremble. James 2:19

The above is taken from a remarkable chapter of the epistle of St. James. The point that he is making is that there is more to "believing" than merely saying so. Faith has many dimensions, and one of them is "works" which are the natural *fruits* of Christian faith.

There is the ever-present danger that we identify saving faith with personal acceptance of a series of intellectual propositions. Putting our signature, as it were, to a carefully formulated creed. But saving faith is much more than agreement with doctrines. Our Catechism divides faith into three parts: knowledge, assent, and confidence.

First, we must *know* what the Bible teaches about salvation and the Christian life. We must *know* that "God so loved the world that He gave His only begotten Son that whosoever believeth in Him should not perish, but have everlasting life" (John 3:16). Then we must *assent* (that is, agree) to the Gospel message of redemption through Jesus Christ His Son. We must accept it as the truth. Finally, we must put our full *confidence,* our complete trust, in the Christ who is presented to us in Scripture—the Christ of Bethlehem, of Calvary, of the empty tomb, the Christ now enthroned in glory.

Such a faith simply cannot remain passive or inactive. As Martin Luther frequently points out, it is a dynamic, active thing, constantly praising God and serving those whose lives touch ours.

Do you and I have such a faith—a faith that knows, accepts, and trusts Jesus Christ as our personal Lord and Savior and then finds joy in carrying out God's will? May God's Holy Spirit grant each of us such a faith.

> Lord, give us such a faith as this; And then, whate'er may come,
> We'll taste e'en now the hallowed bliss Of an eternal home.

God's Word—to Christian Families

Let the Word of Christ dwell in you richly. *Colossians 3:16*

The above words are significant in themselves. But they take on added significance when we remember that they form the introduction to Paul's detailed instruction to Christian *families*. The Scripture regards "the Word of Christ" as the most important link in the Christian family circle.

In the hectic hubbub of our modern world, how easy it is to forget this. In a day of rampant secularism, when even the *name* of Christ is considered almost exclusively as part of a theological vocabulary, a word irrelevant to daily life, how difficult it is for some of us to let His Word dwell among us richly! A thousand other words, yes! The name of Christ—how awkward in the context of daily family living!

Our Lord tells us that it ought not so to be. Christian families should live on a *rich* diet of His Word—in daily prayers, daily devotions, the frequent use of "hymns and spiritual songs," and regular attendance at church. Nor should these become a mere ritual. They should find expression in a common bond of love and Christian fellowship.

How is it with us? Does the Word of Christ dwell among us *richly* or, for the most part, does it dwell among us *poorly*—perhaps in a long neglected catechism or in a dust covered Bible in our basement? Does Christ enter frequently into our family conversation? Does a day go by without His name on our lips? Do we lift our hearts to Him in "hymns and spiritual songs"—not only in formal worship but also at the ironing board and kitchen sink—even if only in worshipful humming? May each of us learn more and more to pray:

Jesus, Thy words alone impart Eternal life; on these I live;
Here sweeter comforts cheer my heart Than all the powers of nature give.

Oh, Lord Jesus Christ, let the good news of Your Gospel dwell among us richly in our hearts and in our homes. Amen.

God's Word—to Christian Parents

Ye fathers, provoke not your children to wrath, but bring them up in the nurture and admonition of the Lord. *Ephesians 6:4*

The Bible speaks clearly of the primary duties of Christian parents. They are, of course, to provide for the physical needs of their children—such as food, clothing, and shelter. But more important, the Lord holds them responsible for the spiritual *"nurture and admonition"* of each child He gives them.

For the word "nurture" we might substitute the word "feed" as it is used in Christ's command to Peter: "Feed My lambs." Christian parents are to lead their children to the green pastures of God's Word where they will learn of the love of their Savior and also learn to "love Him back." In this important task Christian parents will enlist the aid of others, such as pastors and church school teachers.

The Greek word for "admonition" may be translated "disipline" or "correction." While Christian parents will love their children, they will also discipline and correct them. They will not be *soft* in the face of repeated, stubborn misbehavior.

As the Lord's representatives, theirs is the sometimes difficult duty to discipline—not in anger, but in love; not to show who's boss but to show what the will of the Lord is. Let the love of Christ motivate both father and mother in everything they say or do.

We are living in an age of growing permissiveness. To the extent that this is a reaction to some of the harsh and loveless authoritarianism of the past, it may claim a degree of justification. But this does not alter the divine command. Our Lord does not say *"let them go";* He says, *"bring them up."* And this requires both loving nurture and loving admonition.

Oh, blest the parents who give heed Unto their children's foremost need
And worry not of care or cost! May none to them and heaven be lost.

God's Word—to Christian Children

Children, obey your parents in the Lord; for this is right. *Ephesians 6:1*

To the above words Paul immediately adds: *"Honor* thy father and mother; which is the first commandment with promise, that it may be well with thee, and thou mayest live long on the earth."

According to the divine plan children are to look upon their parents not only as their superiors in a biological sense but as the representatives of God who are responsible for their welfare both physically and spiritually. Because of this relationship children are to *look up* to their parents.

And, looking up, they are to obey. Paul says that they are to obey them "in the Lord," that is, because of the Lord's clear command and gracious promise. Children are to obey their parents out of both love and respect, their ultimate loyalty, of course, always being to the Lord who bought them (Acts 5:29) and whose will they seek to follow.

How is it in *our* family? Do children "look up" to father and mother as those who are taking God's place—especially during their childhood and youth? And, looking up, do they willingly obey? If so, we have God's first foundation for family happiness.

If so, then parents and children can join hearts and lips in the beautiful lines of the poet:

Blest such a house, it prospers well, In peace and joy the parents dwell, And in their children's lot is shown How richly God can bless His own.

God grant it, for Jesus' sake. And may He grant that the Holy Spirit, given to our children in Holy Baptism, continue to enlighten them with His gifts, sanctify them, and keep them in the true faith unto the end. Amen.

A Model Prayer of Intercession

Lord, behold, he whom Thou lovest is sick. *John 11:3*

The above passage is quoted from the well-known story of Lazarus and his two sisters, Mary and Martha. Because Lazarus lay seriously ill, his sisters sent a message to Jesus, who at that time was some distance away, in a neighboring village. The message informed Jesus of the illness of their brother.

We have in their brief message an excellent example of intercessory prayer. Notice, first, the brevity of their message: "Lord, behold he whom Thou lovest is sick." A simple informative sentence. No specific request. No telling Jesus what to do. It would be enough merely to share their problem with Him. He would know best what to do.

Then, notice the exact wording of their brief message. Not *"he* who loves *You"* but *"he* whom *You* love" is sick! They are appealing to the Savior's love which He had demonstrated so many times before. His love, not any special merit of their brother, was the only basis of their hope.

What an example of truly Christian intercessory prayer: sharing with our heavenly Father the needs of our brothers and sisters in Christ, and leaving all decisions to His love which He has shown us in Jesus Christ, our Savior.

As we fold our hands in sleep each night, do we share with our Father in heaven the needs of particular relatives and friends, mentioning them by name? Do we lay their personal hurts, their particular wants, their particular anxieties before Him? It may seem to be an exercise in futility to inform an omniscient God of the personal needs of others, but we have His express command "pray for one another." And His command is coupled with His promise. He will hear! How appropriate, then, that *all* the members of God's family sing:

> Before our Father's throne We pour our ardent prayers;
> Our fears, our hopes, our aims are one, Our comforts and our cares.

Blessed Assurance

The Lord will preserve me unto His heavenly Kingdom. *2 Timothy 4:18*

Can I really be sure that I am saved? Can I know beyond the shadow of a doubt that someday I shall be with Christ in heaven?—Yes, indeed, I can be sure.

The salvation which Christ has won for me and every sinner is free, *complete,* and final. Having found forgiveness for all my sins at the foot of Calvary's cross, I can have the assurance of the apostle Paul, who said: "Nothing shall be able to separate us from the love of God, which is in Christ Jesus, our Lord."

Such an assurance would, indeed, be out of the question if my final salvation were due, even in the slightest measure, to my own cooperation or my own achievement. But salvation is a free gift of God—*all the way.*

Paul painstakingly employs the clearest of language to emphasize that "all that we are and all that we ever hope to be" (both here on earth and in heaven) are undeserved *gifts* of God. He uses different Greek words to make this point. In Romans 3:24 he says that we are "justified freely [literally, *gift-wise*] by His grace." In Romans 6:23 he tells us that eternal life is an undeserved *gift* (literally, *free* gift) through Jesus Christ our Lord.

Not only my coming to faith, but also my remaining in faith and my dying in faith are a part of that perfect gift which God has given me through His beloved Son.

"Ye are kept by the power of God through faith unto salvation," says Peter. It is not we, but God who does the keeping. In His care the believer in Christ is safe—safe now and safe forever.

> Thy works, not mine, O Christ, Speak gladness to this heart;
> They tell me all is done, They bid my fear depart.
> Thy death, not mine, O Christ, Has paid the ransom due;
> Ten thousand deaths like mine Would have been all too few!

Soul Company

Now therefore ye are no more strangers and foreigners, but fellow citizens with the saints and of the household of God. *Ephesians 2:19*

One of the fundamental cravings of the human heart is the deep-seated desire to "belong." Left to ourselves, we feel lonely, unhappy, and incomplete. Our soul cries out for company. And not until we find true companionship for our souls, do we find that happiness for which our inmost heart is hungering.

Through Christ the Christian has found "soul company" which has enriched his life beyond all measure. Through Christ he is walking through the world hand-in-hand with those people who are doing the best, the finest, and the loveliest things in all the world today. *What glorious companionship!* Through Christ he has become a part of that family to which the world owes everything that it has received from 2,000 years of Christian influence. *What splendid fellowship!* Through Christ he has joined hands with those people of whom the Savior says: "Ye are the salt of the earth . . . . Ye are the light of the world." *What a sublime association!*

Do we always place this valuation on our membership in Christ's Church? Do we always fully realize that *without* Christ we were "strangers and foreigners," but that *with* Christ we have become "fellow citizens with the saints" and members of "the household of God"? Let us treasure this fellowship, and let us cultivate it more and more. John Fawcett said it well in his familiar hymn:

Blest be the tie that binds Our hearts in Christian love;
The fellowship of kindred minds Is like to that above.
Before our Father's throne We pour our ardent prayers;
Our fears, our hopes, our aims, are one, Our comforts and our cares.

Who Am I

I have redeemed thee . . . thou art Mine. Isaiah 43:1

A distressed young man had just poured out his heart to his pastor. "If only I could *find* myself! Sometimes I actually wonder who I am or where I fit in!" The pastor thought a moment, then reached for an old worn catechism. While doing so, he said: "John, there are times when I feel the same way, wondering who I am and how I could possibly fit into God's scheme of things. When I begin feeling that way, I always reach for my catechism and read Martin Luther's explanation of the three articles of the Apostles' Creed."

And then he began to read slowly:

I believe that God has made *me*. . . . I believe that Jesus Christ . . . has redeemed *me* . . . that I may be His *own* . . . and serve Him . . . . I believe that . . . the Holy Ghost has called *me* by the Gospel . . . and will at the Last Day raise up *me* . . . and give unto *me* . . . eternal life. This is most certainly true.

As they continued to converse, the young man began to see himself not as a lonely speck floating in the universe, but as a unique creation of God, a God who was interested in him, who knew him, who loved him, who had sent His Son into the world to make him one of His very own. He became aware of a definite relationship between himself and the Lord who was not only his Creator but also his personal Redeemer and Comforter. More and more, he saw who he *was*—God's own! God's own—with a purpose!

It may seem the height of naïveté to point a person who is undergoing an identity crisis to the Apostles' Creed for mental and spiritual therapy. But is it really? A careful, prayerful study of the creed will tell us who we are, what we are here for, and where we are going. Try it!

Lord, You have made me, redeemed me, called and sanctified me. You have told me who I am—Your child, through Jesus Christ my Lord. Use me to the glory of Your name and to the welfare of my fellowmen. May I be forever Yours, and may You be forever mine. In Jesus' name. Amen.

The Joy of the Gospel

Thy Word was unto me the joy and rejoicing of mine heart. *Jeremiah 15:16*

From the above passage we see that the *Word of God* is meant to be a source of "joy and rejoicing" to the heart of the believer. While this is most certainly true, we must be careful not to oversimplify this profound truth. It will not do simply to tell our non-church-going neighbor to read the Bible, assuming that he will find "joy and rejoicing" in his reading. Many Bibles contain more than 1,000 pages, a large portion of which makes most *depressing* reading.

Over the years this writer, in his radio and television ministry, has received hundreds of letters from sincere seekers after truth who say: "I've tried to read the Bible but I get nothing out of it." How, then, is it that the *believer* can find "joy and rejoicing" in the message of the Holy Scriptures?

Primarily, because he has learned to put God's word of judgment and God's word of grace in proper perspective. It is in God's revelation, recorded in the pages of Holy Writ, that he has found not only pardon for his sins but also peace and love and joy as the permanent tenants of his soul.

How do *we* read our Bible? Do we find in it "joy and rejoicing for our hearts"? We will, if we relate all that we read to the central message of God's Word to us—the revelation of His tender mercy unveiled before our believing eyes in the life, death, and resurrection of His Son, in our behalf.

But joy in our *heart* should never be an end in itself. It should rather be the source of joy in our *lives*—a joy that becomes visible in the kind of life we lead. With Luther we must say: "My heart for very joy doth leap; my lips no more can silence keep." The joy of the Gospel, which we have found in "the Word," must spill over into a life of Christian love and *action*.

Lord, may I always show the joy of my heart in the joy of my life. And may my inner joy enable me to bear winsome witness to those who do not yet believe in You. Amen.

Wiser Than Our Prayers

[God] is able to do exceeding abundantly above all that we ask or think. Ephesians 3:20

God sometimes answers our prayers by withholding from us the very things for which we ask. That should not surprise us. He who is the allwise God and who is "able to do exceeding abundantly above all that we ask or think" will surely know best how to answer our petitions.

In His divine providence He may find it necessary to overrule our ignorance and to give us not what we *ask* for, but what we *need*. Of a certain man it was said:

> He asked for *strength* that he might achieve;
> he was made *weak* that he might obey.
>
> He asked for *health* that he might do great things;
> he was given *infirmity* that he might do better things. . . .
>
> He asked for *all things* that he might enjoy life;
> he was given *life* that he might enjoy all things.

How vividly the above quotation describes much of the prayer life of both the apostle Paul and many a Christian!

Does it seem sometimes that *our* prayers have gone unanswered? If we prayed in faith, trusting in the merits of the Savior, we may be sure that God is answering them. Perhaps not in the way we desired, but He *is* answering them—in His own way and in His own time and in a way which is designed for our eternal good.

Paraphrasing the words of Christ in Luke 11:9-13, "If we have asked Him for a scorpion, shall we complain if He has given us a fish? If we have asked him for a stone, shall we complain if He has given us a loaf of bread?" Let us always remember: His answers are wiser than our prayers.

> I leave all things to God's direction,
> He loveth me in weal and woe;
> His will is good, true His affection,
> With tender love His heart doth glow.
> My Fortress and my Rock is He:
> What pleaseth God, that pleaseth me.

What Are We Working For?

Do not labor for the food which perishes, but for the food which endures to eternal life. *John 6:27 RSV*

Frequently when a person is depressed or at loose ends, his friends will tell him to lose himself in his work. "Get busy and you'll forget your troubles." There is, of course, a sense in which that is true, for idleness is the devil's workbench.

But there is also a sense in which such advice is dangerous. It is possible for us to get so wrapped up in our work that we neglect our spiritual needs—with the result that our personal faith in Christ as Lord and Savior gradually shrivels up and dies.

That is what Christ means when He says to you and me: "Do not labor for the food which perishes, but for the food which endures to eternal life, which the Son of Man will give to you."

A few verses later Jesus makes the remarkable statement: "I am the bread of life." In other words *He* is to be the highest goal of all our striving—the prize for which we labor. Even more, *He* is to be the source of our most needed sustenance, the true food on which we live.

In our Christian life we are to cultivate and to maintain a proper scale of priorities. We must work, to be sure. But in all that we do we must never lose our sense of relative values. Our paycheck, our car, our home, our bank account dare never become ends in themselves. Important as they are, we have found something of greater value. The poet puts this all in marvelous perspective when he says:

What is the world to me! My Jesus is my Treasure,
My Life, my Health, my Wealth, My Friend, my Love, my Pleasure,
My Joy, my Crown, my All, My Bliss eternally.
Once more, then, I declare: What is the world to me!

Lord, in all that I do, may I never let anything come between You and me. You are my greatest Treasure. Amen.

257

Speaking the Truth in Love

But speaking the truth in love . . . grow up into Him in all things, who is the Head, even Christ. *Ephesians 4:15*

We frequently hear the statement that considerations of truth must take precedence over considerations of love. Like many other valid abstract propositions, these words have often been grossly misunderstood or misapplied or both.

They have been understood to mean that there are times when truth and love are mutually exclusive. They have been understood (alas!) as giving the believer the right to abdicate the requirements of love in order to defend the truth.

Some have thought (erroneously, of course) that if truth is the supreme end to be achieved, then it makes little difference what means are used to achieve it, even if these means include bitterness, vindictiveness, and hatefulness.

The history of the Christian church includes many tragic chapters recording the cruel deeds of otherwise pious men who sought to defend the truth, not in a spirit of love, but by violence and bloodshed. Even so saintly a man as John Calvin (in 1553) was instrumental in having a man by the name of Servetus burned alive because he could not subscribe to the doctrine of the Holy Trinity!

The Scriptures indeed exhort us to speak the truth, but to do so "in love." If a brother has erred, we should show him his error. Even if we fail, we should still love him. Indeed, his very need for correction should make us love him more. How often we have failed to extend our erring brother (or sister) the love he so sorely needed! *Had he seen our love, he might have seen the truth.*

How important, therefore, that in our attempts to deal with matters of truth and error, we deliberately and prayerfully adopt a strategy of love. We can count on our old Adam to vote "no" to such an attitude. But we can also pray the Holy Spirit for a special measure of His grace so that our new man may maintain the upper hand, enabling us both to speak the *Truth* and to speak it in *Love.*

Saints by God's Grace

The good that I would I do not, but the evil that I would not, that I do. Romans 7:19

"If he had been a real Christian, he wouldn't have had a nervous breakdown." Have you ever heard that remark? Besides being unkind, the remark is untrue. Good Christians *do* have nervous breakdowns— not because they are Christians, but because they are still human, subject to all the ills to which our human flesh is heir.

Perhaps the greatest illustration of this truth is the apostle Paul himself. Here was a man of heroic stature, bold, courageous, confident, not afraid to have his say in the presence of kings and princes. Yet this tremendous man admitted that he had feet of clay. He was a *chronic* sinner, yes, the "chief of sinners." Although he knew what was right, he frequently found himself failing to do it. And although he knew what was wrong, that was the very thing he often did. He was, as Luther put it, simultaneously a saint (by God's grace) and a sinner (because of his human weakness).

Isn't this the very situation in which you and I find ourselves again and again? How frequently we find our list of good *intentions* so much longer than our list of good accomplishments! And how often our list of determined "no-no's" (those things we know we should *not* do) turns out to be our day's agenda!

Surely, our conscience, like that of Paul, tells us that we, indeed, sin daily. And we participate in the human tragedy that follows in the wake of sin—including such things as breakdowns. But thanks be to God! He *still* gives us the victory through Jesus Christ our Lord.

He still declares us righteous because of Jesus Christ, His Son. Sinners though we are, God looks at us through Christ and all He sees are saints. Praise God we still can sing:

> Jesus, Thy blood and righteousness
> My beauty are, my glorious dress,
> Wherein before my God I'll stand
> When I shall reach the heavenly land.

Thou Art the Potter

We are the clay, and Thou our potter. Isaiah 64:8

Perhaps all of us are acquainted with the beautiful hymn:

"Have Thine own way, Lord; have Thine own way.
Thou art the Potter; I am the clay.
Mold me and make me after Thy will,
While I am waiting, yielded and still."

What a beautiful prayer to pray each morning—or any hour of the day! When things go wrong, when everything in our life seems topsy-turvy, when there seems to be no rhyme or reason to the pattern of our life, how comforting to know: "*Thou* art the Potter, I am the *clay*." The Potter knows what He is doing, even though the clay does not.

Our constant prayer must be: "Mold me and make me after Thy will." The Potter has a plan in mind. His skillful hands are at work to bring a thing of beauty out of formless clay. It is for us to wait, to yield, and to be still until we see the will of our Lord as He has planned it.

While He fashions our life, and while we wait uncomprehendingly, we can recall His words to the prophet Isaiah: "My thoughts are not your thoughts, neither are your ways My ways . . . . For as the heavens are higher than the earth, so are My ways higher than your ways, and My thoughts than your thoughts" (Isaiah 55:8-9). Indeed, there may be long stretches in our life during which the Lord is molding our destiny "while we are waiting, patient and still."

Have we been discouraged, depressed, despondent, ready to throw up our hands and "chuck it all"? If so, let us throw those hands up to Him who is shaping our lives according to His gracious will. Let us deliberately throw ourselves into His care. He has promised that, even though we cannot see it now, He is working for our good. Let us follow the example of the prophet Isaiah who, in one of Israel's darkest days, cried out: "O Lord, Thou art our FATHER; we are the clay, and Thou our Potter." What a comfort to know that, in the life of the Christian, both the clay and the trowel are in our Father's hands!

Love Looks the Other Way

Charity [love] shall cover the multitude of sins. *1 Peter 4:8*

Two young boys were eating dinner at the home of their wealthy aunt. The table was covered with the finest linen and set with expensive china and gleaming silver.

Unnoticed by others at the table, the younger boy accidentally spilled some gravy on the immaculate tablecloth. The older boy, eager to spare his younger brother unnecessary embarrassment, quickly took his own napkin and spread it over the offending spot.

We have in this incident an excellent parable of what St. Peter meant when he said: "Love shall cover the multitude of sins." Love's primary object is not to *expose* the erring brother, but to *help* him. The older boy could have exclaimed: "Aha! Look what Johnny did!" Instead, he kept silent and did his best to rectify the situation.

How desperately we all need to learn this lesson! How different our world (and our church) would be if each of us would learn to overlook our brother's frailties, to bear with him, to exercise Christian patience and forbearance! True, there is a time for corrective action, but there is also a time for healing silence, a time when love can "cover the multitude of sins."

What has our personal record been in this respect? We must confess that there have been times when our sinful heart has found almost ghoulish glee in "pouncing" upon a hidden fault or moral failure of a brother or a sister and then spreading it with a loud whisper throughout the neighborhood—or throughout the congregation. That is the very *opposite* of love! Rather, let each of us speak the heartfelt prayer:

Lord of all nations, grant me grace To love all men of every race
And in each fellowman to see My brother, loved, redeemed by Thee.

"Take Thou My Hands and Lead Me"

He calleth His own sheep by name and leadeth them. *John 10:3*

Have you ever stood alone at a crossroad in life, fearful and trembling lest you make the wrong decision? Or have you ever stood in the midst of one of those proverbial moments that "try men's souls," perhaps at the deathbed of a loved one, perhaps in the midst of a personal tragedy you had tried so desperately to avoid? In moments like that have you experienced the piercing pang of "lostness"—the pain which cries out: What of tomorrow? and tomorrow? and tomorrow?

It is at *those* moments that there comes to the believing heart the silent whisper: "Fear not, I am the Lord who *leads* you. Take My hand and hold it. I have gone this way before. My cross is the assurance of My love, the assurance of your comfort, the assurance of a better day."

It is the familiar voice of our Good Shepherd whom David describes so beautifully in Psalm 23—the Shepherd who leads us not only in the paths of righteousness but also through the valley of the shadow, where our feet have never gone.

In every day of doubt, despondency, or dark despair our fervent prayer must be:

"Take *Thou* my hands and lead me O'er life's rough way;
Toward heavenly mansions lead me From day to day.
Alone my footsteps falter Or wander wide;
Lord who my life canst alter, Be Thou my Guide."

Notice, the writer of those beautiful lines used the plural: "Take Thou my *hands* and lead me." He could have used the singular. But he wanted to express his complete submission to (and his complete dependence on) his Savior-Shepherd. All ultimate decisions at the difficult crossroads of life were to be made with the counsel of Him who was both His Savior and Lord. Do we share such a faith in our Savior Christ? Then we can sing:

He leadeth me. O blessed thought!
O words with heavenly comfort fraught!
Whate'er I do, where'er I be,
Still 'tis God's hand that leadeth me!

The Gospel Needs No Teeth

I declare unto you the Gospel . . . that Christ died for our sins according to the Scriptures. 1 Corinthians 15:1-3

A militant defender of the faith was overheard to say with no small amount of indignation: "What we need is to put more teeth into the Gospel!" We may attribute his remark either to an imprecise form of speech or to a complete ignorance of what the Gospel really is.

The Gospel needs no teeth. In fact, it would not know where to put them. The Gospel is rather a pair of extended arms (God's arms) and a pair of inviting hands (God's hands), inviting the sinner to come home—home to the Father's house.

In its strictest sense the Gospel is a simple declarative sentence which can be summed up in five short words: "Christ died for our sins." Even in those few instances where the Scripture uses the imperative, e.g., "Believe on the Lord Jesus Christ," it is using what the theologians call the "evangelical imperative," that is, inviting the unbeliever to believe the good news about Jesus Christ and His substitutionary death for sinners.

There is the ever-present danger of "snarling" the Gospel as if it were a legal summons—an extension of the Law—a stern command. A preacher who was noted for his legalism more than for his evangelical approach was known to clench his fists and to wear a forbidding frown as he dramatized the Gospel invitation: "Come unto Me, all ye that labor and are heavy laden; and I will give you rest." His very tone of voice and manner belied his message.

No, the Gospel never needs "more teeth." It needs more outstretched arms, and more kindly voices to speak its message. It needs more and more believers who, in love, will extend Christ's gracious invitation to a sin-laden world:

"Come unto Me, ye weary, And I will give you rest,"
O blessed voice of Jesus, Which comes to hearts opprest!
It tells of benediction, Of pardon, grace, and peace,
Of joy that hath no ending, Of love which cannot cease.

Freed to Serve

Though I be free from all men, yet have I made myself servant to all, that I might gain the more. *1 Corinthians 9:19*

During the early days of the 19th century a wealthy plantation owner was attracted by the heartbreaking sobs of a slave girl who was about to step up to the auction block to be sold. Moved by a momentary impulse of compassion, he bought her at a very high price and then disappeared into the crowd.

When the auction was over, the clerk came to the sobbing girl and handed her, her bill of sale. To her astonishment, the unknown plantation owner had written "Free" over the paper that should have delivered her to him as his possession. She stood speechless, as one by one the other slaves were claimed by their owners and dragged away.

Suddenly, she threw herself at the feet of the clerk and exclaimed: "Where is the man who bought me? I must find him! He has set me *free!* I must *serve* him as long as I live!"

What an apt confession of the believing Christian: "He has set me *free!* I must *serve* Him as long as I live!" Martin Luther understood this fact of Christian life. In his Small Catechism he writes: "I believe that Jesus Christ . . . has redeemed me, a lost and condemned creature, *purchased* and won me . . . that I may be His own, and live under Him in His kingdom and *serve* Him . . . ." Luther knew, as few men in his time, that Christ had, indeed, purchased him, and that through that purchase he had been made free forever. But free to serve the Lord who bought him! The hymn writer Genevieve Irons devoted the first three stanzas of her hymn "Drawn to the Cross" to the worship of the crucified Christ. But listen to her fourth and final stanza:

And then for *work* to do for Thee,
Which shall so sweet a *service* be
That angels well might envy me,
Christ Crucified, I come. Amen.

Lord, I am Yours. May I serve You all my life. Amen.

When Actions Speak Louder Than Words

Be ready always to give an answer to every man that asketh you a reason of the hope that is in you. 1 Peter 3:15

The above words can best be understood in their total context, namely, verses 8 to 16. Here Peter tells the early Christians that their lives are to be so totally different from the world that many will be prompted to ask: "What *is* it about you? What is it that makes you so—'different'?"

In other words, our Christian *lives* are to be an inseparable part of our Christian *witness*. Peter did not advocate a "coat lapel" evangelism which asks the stranger imperiously, "Are you saved?" Rather he urged, along with our words of witness, a "Christian life" evangelism which makes the stranger ask "Are you for real?"

Simon Peter, the man who wrote the text quoted above, bore this kind of witness. We read in Acts 4 that both by *word and deed* he made a tremendous impression on the leaders of the temple. Of them we read: "When they saw the complete assurance of Peter and John, who were obviously uneducated and untrained men, they were staggered, recognizing them as *men who had been with Jesus*" (Acts 4:13, Phillips). There are occasions when we bear most eloquent testimony to our faith by revealing, perhaps unconsciously, that "we have been with Jesus."

Is there anything about our daily conduct that would brand us as being close friends of Jesus and therefore "different"? Peter clearly expected his believers to lead such lives. That is why he urged: "Be ready always to give an answer to every man that *asketh* you a reason of the hope that is in you." When was the last time our Christian life evoked such a question from an unbelieving friend or neighbor? Well might we repeat the poet's prayer:

Take us, O Lord, and use us Thy messengers to be:
Our prayers, our gifts, our service We offer here to Thee—
That every man and nation May hear what we have heard
And in our *Lives* shall witness The power of Thy Word.

"You Can't Go Home Again"

Thou carriest them away as with a flood. Psalm 90:5

The novelist Thomas Wolfe wrote the line so full of insight: "You can't go home again." Do what we may, we can never reconstruct the past. A visit home, after a long absence, is never a visit home, because the world has moved on and the people, the places, the streets so familiar to our childhood are no longer there—except in the pictures, the sounds, and the fragrance of our memories. As philosophers have said, you can never put your finger into a rushing stream or bubbling brook twice at the same place. The second time it will be a different stream, made up of waters never felt before.

How true of life—of yours and mine! In a somewhat modified metaphor, the psalmist says: "Thou carriest them away as with a flood." There is something inexorable, irreversible about a flood. We go where the surging waters take us. We can never "go back."

How fortunate that, though we can never go home again, our Savior has assured us that we still are headed home—to His home. In His Father's house are many mansions, and that is where His grace is drawing us. Let the past be the past! It has been forgiven—covered by the love and mercy of Him who died that we might live. The future is ours; we are truly going home!

That is why, with our hand securely fastened in that of our Savior who is not only our divine Redeemer but also our Guardian and our Guide, we can pray with all confidence:

Oh, Christ, our Lord, in years to come,
Whatever may betide us.
Right onward through our journey home
Be Thou at hand to guide us;
Nor leave us till at close of life,
Safe from all perils, toil, and strife,
Heaven shall enfold and hide us.

'Tis the Inward Eye That Sees

I have heard of Thee by the hearing of the ear, but now mine eye seeth Thee. Job 42:5

These words are taken from the final chapter of the book of Job. At the height of his prosperity, when everything was running smoothly, Job had indeed *"heard* of the Lord by the hearing of the ear"—but now, after having been disciplined in the school of adversity, after having been tried and tested in the crucible of life, he could say: *"but now mine EYE seeth Thee!"*

That is the blessed experience of every believing child of God. For him life is a constant and progressive revelation of the love and providence of a gracious Father in heaven.

Many of the precious Gospel promises which in his childhood he has learned "by the hearing of the ear" take on added meaning with every passing year, until with tried and tested Job he can exclaim: "But now mine *eye seeth!"* Contrary to the laws of our physical life, the eyes of our faith grow brighter and clearer as the darkening shadows lengthen.

We believers in Christ can never sufficiently thank God for the gift of eyes that see—eyes that see the burden of our sin, to be sure, but eyes that see beyond that burden to Bethlehem's manger, to Calvary's cross, and to the mansions in the Father's house, assured to us through Jesus Christ, our Lord.

We can take no credit for our spiritual sight. In fact, we cannot explain it to the full satisfaction of those who do not believe. Our feelings are somewhat like those of the blind man who was healed by Jesus. To the unbelievers who cross-examined him, he replied: "Whether He [Jesus] is a sinner, I do not know; one thing I know, that though I was blind, now I *see!"* (John 9:25 RSV).

How many of us must confess the same. By the mysterious working of His Holy Spirit God has given us "inner eyes" that see the wonders of His redemption. With John Newton we must confess:

> Amazing grace! How sweet the sound That saved a wretch like me!
> I once was lost, but now am found. Was blind, *but now I see!*

Exploration of Inner Space

Keep thy heart with all diligence, for out of it are the issues of life. Proverbs 4:23

Our modern world is greatly preoccupied with the exploration of outer space. Nor is there anything inherently wrong with that. But we, as Christians, should be even *more* preoccupied with the exploration of *inner* space. Again and again the Lord exhorts His people to search their *hearts* and see what they might find in them.

There is a sense in which the heart, as the seat of human emotion, is the center of the universe for *every* human being. In the text quoted above we are urged to be diligent in our daily "heart searching"—that is, in taking a regular inner look to make sure that all is in order.

And why? Because "out of the heart are the issues of life." The Savior Himself left no doubt as to the source of sin and wickedness when He said: "Out of the *heart* proceed evil thoughts, murders, adulteries, fornications, thefts, false witness, blasphemies." In other words, sin is no mere skin disease; it is a heart disease that threatens our destruction. Our outward behavior will normally reflect the spiritual condition of our inner selves.

How important, then, that not only our lips, but also our heart be filled with faith, hope and love for Jesus Christ our Savior and for our fellowman. Yes, how important that the "inner space" of our lives be and remain the throne-room of Him who loves us and gave Himself for us.

Frequently throughout the day, but especially upon arising each morning and upon closing our eyes each night, it will pay us to take a conscious *inward* look and to "check" the throne-room of our heart to make sure that *HE,* our Lord, is dwelling there.

Well might we paraphrase the words of the Christian poet:

"Oh, blest the *heart,* what-e'er befall,
Where Jesus Christ is all in all!
Yea, if He were not dwelling there,
How dark and poor and void it were!"

When Stress Comes to the Believer

Cast all your anxieties on Him, for He cares about you. 1 Peter 5:7 RSV

A noted psychiatrist recently wrote: "Stress never depends on what happens to you, but on how you take it." He may not have been writing from a Christian perspective, but he was expressing a general Christian truth.

In the above passage Peter is speaking primarily of the stresses which the early Christians were experiencing because of their faith, but he certainly does not exclude the common stresses of everyday life. He says: "Cast *all* your anxieties on Him."

But how can one do that? Peter's answer (drawn from his *entire* epistle) is that we do this by living constantly in the awareness of the Cross. Christ lived and died not only as our Redeemer, but also as our *Example*. Peter exhorts the early Christians to bear their cares and crosses not only bravely but also triumphantly, adding "for even hereunto were ye called; because Christ also suffered for us, leaving us an example, that we should follow in His steps."

None of us can duplicate the perfect example of Christ, of course. But we are admonished, with the Spirit's help, to *try*—to try to imitate the "mind of Christ." Our Lord lived His entire life and walked into the very jaws of death, basking in the light of a glorious eternity. Even His darkest and most trying hours (including Gethsemane and Calvary) were illumined by that light. He knew that no matter what the pain or anxiety of the moment, His Father "was in there with Him."

We have the same assurance. No matter what the stress, no matter what the anxiety, we can consciously and deliberately cast our entire burden on Him, for we know He cares for us. In fact, we have this permanent invitation:

"Come, ye disconsolate, where'er ye languish;
Come to the Mercy-seat, fervently kneel.
Here bring your wounded hearts, here tell your anguish;
Earth has no sorrow that heaven cannot heal.

We Have a "More Sure Word"

We have also a more sure Word . . . a light that shineth in a dark place, until the day dawn, and the day star arise in your hearts. *2 Peter 1:19*

Recently a new *Encyclopedia of American Religions* was published, listing 1,200 different religions, denominations, cults, and sects—each propagating its own beliefs.

To some this proliferation of religious beliefs may be confusing. This need not be. In the epistle from which the text above is taken St. Peter assures his new converts that he and the other apostles were "eye witnesses" of everything they preached and wrote.

Indeed, he makes special reference to the miraculous revelation on the mount when the Father spoke from heaven saying: "This is my beloved Son, in whom I am well pleased," adding (according to Luke) *"hear ye Him!"* More precisely, "listen to Him!"

Jesus Himself said: "My sheep hear My voice . . . and they follow Me." We hear His voice in Holy Scripture. In all matters pertaining to our personal salvation, His words are crystal clear. They tell us of His Father's love and of His (Christ's) redeeming work. In the midst of all the din and clamor, of claims and counterclaims, we know our Shepherd's voice. Indeed, we do have a "more sure Word."

But we would make a mistake if we merely *boasted* of our possession of the Word—or if we merely used it for purposes of discussion, debate, or even controversy. Christ tells us that we are to hear His Word and to *follow* it! We are to rejoice in the glad news of the Gospel, and we are to lead lives which reflect our inner joy. His Word is to be believed and to be lived. Thank God, we have His Word. The question is, Are we really living it?

Lord, grant me Your Holy Spirit so that, in a world of doubt and confusion, I may always hear and *Heed* the "more sure Word" of my Savior's voice. Amen.

Stop the World!

The field is the world. *Matthew 13:38*

Some years ago the refrain of a popular song ran "Stop the World! *I Want to Get Off!*" It may seem like a foolish question at first, but isn't that what many a Christian has done—or, at least, would like to do? Stop the world and get off?

Especially is this true of many who have reached middle age or beyond. Somewhere, somehow, they have managed to "stop their world" at a certain point in the past. They are still working on the problems of 20 or 30 years ago and find the world of today an alien, perhaps even hostile, place in which to live. They disapprove of almost every change in lifestyle that has occurred since "the good old days." Finding life almost impossible to cope with, they cry out (at least, in effect): "Stop the World! I Want to Get Off!"

That is not the will of our Lord. He has put us into the world of *today* and expects us to proclaim His Gospel to the world as we *find* it—not as we remember it. The world of *today* is our field. The world that confronts us *now* is in desperate need of you and me and millions of other believers who are stewards of the precious Gospel. Rather than "getting off," let us "get on" with the task which He has given us.

The Savior frequently stressed the "today-ness" of our task as workers in the Kingdom. We hear Him exhorting His disciples: "Lift up your eyes, and look on the fields, for they are white *already* to harvest!" There is no time to lose.

The apostle Paul also expressed a certain urgency in his epistles, using such words as "now," "today," and "high time." He wanted his converts not only to make sure of their own salvation *now* but also to get involved in the challenge of the church as it confronted them in their day.

We too must guard against dwelling unduly on the past. Our challenge is the present. We must heed our Savior's call *today!*

Hark the voice of Jesus crying, "Who will go and work TODAY?
Fields are white and harvests waiting, Who will bear the sheaves away?"

The Quest for the Best

I count all things but loss for the excellency *of the knowledge of Christ Jesus, my Lord. Philippians 3:8.*

To the apostle Paul there was no higher goal in life than to know Christ and to bask in the light of His daily presence. To him such knowledge and such a life were the *"supreme worth"* of human existence—another way of translating the Greek word for "excellency" in the text above.

Nor did he consider the achievement of such knowledge and such a life a static, one-time experience. He tells us that, although he had learned to know Christ as his personal Savior and Lord, he continued to strive toward greater excellence in Christian faith and life—and he implies that he will continue such striving until his journey's end.

Listen to what he tells his Philippian Christians: "I have not yet reached perfection, but I press on, hoping to take hold of that for which Christ once took hold of me. . . . All I can say is this: forgetting what is behind me, and reaching out for that which lies ahead, I press toward the goal to win the prize which is God's call to the life above in Christ Jesus" (Philippians 3:12-14 NEB). To Paul his continued growth in Christian faith and life was like a race (1 Corinthians 9:26-27) into which he was determined to put *every* ounce of effort, always keeping his eyes on the goal.

How about us? Did we "finish the course" on the day of our confirmation? Or have we sought to deepen our Christian knowledge? And how about our Christian life? Are we continuing the struggle, with the Spirit's help, for constant improvement? Paul never gave up the struggle, and neither dare we. Consciously, unswervingly our Christian life must continue to be—*a quest for the best.* May none of us ever give up that quest!

O Lord, grant me Your grace that I may deepen my faith and improve my Christian life from day to day. In Jesus' name. Amen.

Consuming and Conserving

[Jesus said:] Gather up the fragments that remain, that nothing be lost. *John 6:12*

An English diplomat, visiting America for the first time, was interviewed at the Washington airport just before his return to London. After a few routine questions, he was asked: "What was it about America that impressed you most?"

He reflected for a moment, then replied, to the surprise of everyone: "*Kleenex.*" Commenting both on the marvelous usefulness of the product and on its "practical omnipresence" in American life, he went on to say that he also saw in Kleenex a symbol of American wastefulness of its natural resources, quoting statistics on the amount of wood pulp we Americans thoughtlessly "*throw away*" each year.

Agree with him or not, we must admit that we as a people have become wasteful of God's material blessings. Against this backgroud, the words of Christ take on added meaning. "Go out and gather the crumbs, that nothing be lost." We are not to waste God's gifts, particularly His "natural resources." Rather, we are to treasure, guard, and preserve them for future generations. We are to *conserve*—not only to *consume!*

What does this have to say to us today about our wasteful use of such natural resources as gasoline, oil, and electricity, as well as our rape of the forests and our careless use of the fertile soil of our farmlands—all of which have been entrusted to our stewardship and for whose proper care and preservation our gracious Lord holds *us* responsible?

It is significant that He whose omnipotent hand had fed 5,000 instructed His disciples to go out and "gather up the fragments that remain, *that nothing be lost.*" Conservation was just as important to Him as was consumption. Can the same be said of us?

Lord, grant us the grace to be conscientious stewards of *all* that You have entrusted to our care. In Jesus' name. Amen.

Letters from God

You are a letter from Christ, written . . . by the Spirit of the living God.
2 Corinthians 3:3 LB

To get the full impact of the striking sentence quoted above, we must remember the historical and cultural context in which it was written. The city of Corinth was the sin capital of ancient Greece. Wickedness of every description ran rampant, not only in private places but even in its pagan temples.

The small group of Christians living there were a pitiable minority— a handful of "misfits" in a society that had become a cesspool of iniquity. And what does Paul write to this small group? We shall paraphrase his message as follows: "Never mind your small number. Each of you is a personal letter to everyone you meet; a letter that can easily be read. And remember! Each of you is a letter, written not by us, but by the Spirit of the living God."

Letters from God, addressed to a godless world! That's what the Corinthians were. And that's what God intends you and me to be— letters from Him—for all the world to read. By our attitude, our speech, our daily conduct, as well as by our spoken witness, we are to reflect the love of God in Christ to all the world about us.

Since each of us, by virtue of the Spirit's calling, is a "letter from God" to those with whom we come in daily contact, we might well ask: "Just how am I being read?" Is my life different from that of my unbelieving friends? or have I become a blank letter with no message for my fellowman to read—a silent witness with no message from *Him* who dwells within my heart? If so, then let me pray this heartfelt prayer:

Dear Lord, grant me the faith, the love, the courage to speak Your Word to those who do not know You. Grant me Your Holy Spirit that I may truly be Your messenger to straying souls, both near and far. In Jesus' name. Amen.

"I" Trouble

[John the Baptist said:] Ye yourselves bear me witness that I said, I am not the Christ, but that I am sent before Him. . . . He must increase, but I must decrease. *John 3:28-30*

There is a peculiar type of idolatry to which we all are prone. That is the worship of the unholy trinity of "me, myself, and I." It seems that whenever we begin to arrange our priorities, we are inclined to place a capital "I" at the head of the list. In the jargon of our day, we make a practice of always looking out for "Number One"—meaning *Me!*

How different from the example of John the Baptist in the text quoted above! When the friends of John came to him, complaining about the growing popularity of Christ (inferring that John should *do* something about it), he merely answered: "He must increase, but I must decrease."

If only we could emulate the example of John in everything we do! If only *we* could find genuine satisfaction in keeping our egos backstage and rejoice in seeing our Savior upstage. It is *He* who must always and forever occupy the center of our Christian life and witness—not we. It is *He* who must always remain "Number One."

Many a family, yes, many a Christian congregation, has come to grief because of a member who was afflicted with "I" trouble. The person who must always occupy the limelight, whose opinions must always prevail if harmony is to be maintained, is sure to be an irritant in any group. His ill-concealed ego honors niether himself nor the Lord whom he professes to serve.

To unseat an inflated or autocratic ego from the throne room of our heart is one of the most difficult of Christian graces. It is by no means easy for our old Adam to agree with the words of John the Baptist: "Christ must increase, but I must decrease." Let each of us ask himself in all honesty: can I repeat those words of John and really *mean* them? May God give each of us grace so that we can.

Lord, may all I think, say, or do glorify Your holy name. Amen.

Omniscient Love

If our heart condemns us, God is greater than our heart and knoweth all things.
1 John 3:20

There are moments in our lives when we look into the secret chambers of our heart for evidence that we are God's children but fail to find that evidence. Searching our souls for assurance of salvation, we find assurance only of our sin. Our very heart condemns us, accuses and convinces us of innumerable transgressions, and finally confronts us with the crushing judgment: You are lost!

It is at moments like these that the divine assurance of the text above falls like sweetest music on the soul. Though our heart condemn us a thousand times, though its inner precincts roar and thunder endless accusations, "God is greater than our heart and knoweth all things."

But what is it that God knows—that our heart has failed to tell us? What is it that God knows—that can reverse the terrible judgment of our heart?

God looks at us through Christ! He knows that we are sinners, but He also knows that in Christ our guilt has been atoned, and our sin-stained lives have been accounted righteous in His sight. He knows that He has accepted us as permanent members of His family, not because of the fickle feelings of our deceitful heart, but because of the unchanging Christ who is our eternal Friend and Savior.

Therefore let heart, soul, mind, or whatever other faculty we may have, tell us that we are *lost*. It matters not! Our source of assurance rests in His all-knowing love. The anchor of our soul has found its hold in the eternal Rock of Ages. He is "greater than our heart." He knows all things. And He tells us that we are saved! In moments of spiritual uncertainty or doubt you and I can say with unshakable assurance:

I cling to what my Savior taught, And trust it, *whether felt or not!*

The King of Love, My Shepherd Is

Yea, though I walk through the valley of the shadow of death, I will fear no evil, for Thou art with me. *Psalm 23:4*

Death is the hour no one can evade. Death is the hour toward which all religion looks. But only he who by faith has placed his hand into the hand of Christ can truthfully repeat the words: "Yea, though I walk through the valley of the shadow of death, I will fear no evil; for *Thou* art with me."

Christ is the Christian's eternal Shepherd in the valley of the shadow. Christ is the individual believer's last and truest Friend in that final, solemn hour which by nature every mortal dreads—the hour when "the silver cord is broken, and the pitcher shattered at the well, and the immortal spirit must quit its earthly tabernacle and return to the God who gave it."

Jesus has tasted the bitterness of that fate-filled hour for all of us. He has entered the dark unknown which lies ahead of you and me and has filled its frightening gloom with the brightness of His presence. He has cleared the valley of our foes.

When in God's kind providence we are called upon to place our feet upon the road which leads into the valley, we shall see our Shepherd beckoning and shall hear His reassuring voice of invitation: "Be not afraid, it is I. I have passed this way before. This valley is engraved with My eternal footprints. Only trust Me. Only follow!" It is this blissful assurance of his Shepherd's loving presence which enables the Christian to say with David: "Though I walk through the valley of the shadow of death, I will fear no evil; for *Thou* art with me."

It is because we know "the King of love our Shepherd is," that we can sing:

> "Goodness and mercy, all my life,
> Shall surely follow me;
> And in God's house forevermore
> My dwelling-place shall be."

May this bright prospect shed light upon our path until we reach our journey's end. For Jesus' sake. Amen.

Law and Gospel

[Christ died and rose again] that repentance and remission of sins should be preached in His name. *Luke 24:47*

It was John Wesley, the founder of Methodism, who once said that the Word of God "must be preached not only to comfort the afflicted but also to afflict the comfortable."

This is just another way of saying that the church, especially its pastors, must distinguish properly between Law and Gospel. There are those whose primary need is to hear the Law, and there are others whose primary need is to hear the Gospel. In the words of our catechism, "The Law must be preached to . . . impenitent sinners, the Gospel to sinners who are troubled in their minds because of their sins."

The Law (as summarized in the Ten Commandments) exposes our sin and terrifies our conscience. The Gospel (as summarized, for example, in John 3:16) reveals to us our Savior and brings comfort and pardon and peace. Both Law and Gospel are necessary in the life of the believer and in the life of the church. We are to preach "repentance and forgiveness" in Christ's name. But the dominant theme of our life is to be God's marvelous forgiveness. We are to rejoice in the love of Him who, despite our sins, has shown us mercy without measure through Jesus Christ our Savior.

The "old evil foe" would like nothing better than to have the individual Christian *confuse* Law and Gospel. He would have us make the Gospel into a new Law—as if our faith in the Gospel were a "good work" which God is obliged to reward with salvation. No, there is no Law in the Gospel! The Gospel is first, last, and always good news; and even our faith (which trusts the Gospel) is a free gift of the Spirit. The poet knew the great difference between the Law and the Gospel when he wrote:

> All that I was, my sin, my guilt, My death were all my own;
> All that I am I owe to Thee, My gracious God alone.

"Living Above"

If ye, then, be risen with Christ, seek those things which are above. *Colossians 3:1*

Over the door of a little cabinet maker's shop there hangs a sign which reads: "Living Above." It is a notice to his customers that, whenever the shop is locked, he can be found in the room above.

What a blessing it is for a man to be *"living above"* his work—to have his heart and mind far above the level of the humdrum of his daily toil. He may not be able to escape the boredoms and frustrations that have become a part of the daily grind, but his life—his *real* life—can be lived above them.

Does this perhaps sound like merely an "escape" from the realities of life—a flight from the difficult and sometimes irksome duties which are part of making a daily living? It *could* be if we failed to understand the apostle's real meaning. But listen to what he says: "If ye, then, be risen with Christ, seek those things which are above, where Christ sitteth on the right hand of God. Set your affection on things above . . . . For . . . your life is hid with Christ in God."

Paul is asking us not to desert our work but to live *above* it. For the devout child of God this means that he will cultivate the habit of periodically throughout the day stealing to the "room above" for a moment's communion with his Savior. Not to get away *from* our work but to be strengthened *for* it. We are, indeed, to live many moments of our lives on the "upper floor" with Christ, and from our association with Him we are to derive the strength and joy and inspiration to perform the duties that confront us while occupied on the "lower floor."

That is what Paul means by "living above." Let us cultivate this blessed habit. Let us spend more hours with our Lord.

> Savior, I long to walk Closer with Thee.
> Led by Thy guiding hand, Ever to be
> Constantly near Thy side, Quickened and purified,
> Living for Him who died Freely for me.

The Hidden Arsenal

Thy Word have I hid in my heart, that I might not sin against Thee. Psalm 119:11

We are living in a day of stockpiling secret weapons. In fact, a great portion of our material resources is going into such stockpiling just in case, either by accident or by design, some enemy might launch a worldwide holocaust.

The Holy Scriptures give us a good example of a different kind of stockpiling: the stockpiling of God's Word. We are to fill our hearts with readily usable references to His Word. David says: "Thy Word have I hid in my heart, that I might not sin against Thee." God's Word, hidden in our heart, is to be our sword and shield in our daily battle with Satan, sin and evil.

The Savior Himself has given us a good example of using the "secret weapon" of God's Word to overcome the devil's wiles. He parried each of the devil's insidious temptations with a direct quotation from Deuteronomy. He had "hid them in His heart."

When the devil tempted Him in the wilderness to command stones to be turned into bread, Christ simply answered: "*It is written,* man shall not live by bread alone." When the devil suggested that Christ jump from the pinnacle of the temple, Christ replied calmly: "*It is written* again, Thou shalt not tempt the Lord thy God." And when the devil offered Him all the "kingdoms of the world," if He would only "fall down and worship him," the Savior was quick to reply: "*It is written,* Thou shalt worship the Lord Thy God, and Him only shalt thou serve." In each case He reached into the arsenal of His heart where He had "stored" the appropriate Word of God.

The Bible often calls the Christian life a "warfare"—a struggle against powerful spiritual enemies. And it is quick to recommend the most effective weapon in this warfare: "the sword of the Spirit, which is the *Word of God.*" What about our own spiritual defense program? Have we stored God's Word within our heart?

Where Reason Stops and Revelation Starts

Consider your call, brethren; not many of you were wise according to worldly standards. *1 Corinthians 1:26 RSV*

Is Paul implying in the above words that the congregation at Corinth was made up of a "bunch of ignoramuses'"—dropouts who had failed to make the grade? By no means! The point that he is making in this entire chapter is that salvation comes *not* through worldly wisdom but only through the revelation that God has given us in Christ.

In fact, mere worldly wisdom, unenlightened by God's Holy Spirit, leads people *away* from the cross of Christ. That is why Paul says, a few verses later, that God chose to redeem us through the death of His Son "so that no human being might boast in the presence of God. He is the Source of your life in Christ Jesus, whom God made *our wisdom* . . . and redemption. Therefore . . . let him who boasts boast of the Lord."

Paul goes to great pains throughout his epistles to make it abundantly clear that it is God's Holy Spirit and not our superior intellect that converts our mind from unbelief to faith. Each of us is tempted from time to time to "prove" the validity of the Christian faith by the application of human reason, by logic, or by historical or geographical evidence. In that direction lies disaster. In that direction lies uncertainty, doubt, and ultimate despair.

There is an important lesson for all of us here, a lesson we dare never forget. We are members of Christ's family today not because we can "prove" our faith by charts and diagrams, but because we have a gracious God in heaven who planned our salvation from eternity, who sent His Son to redeem our race, and who called us to be His own by the operation of His Holy Spirit. 'Twas not our logic, but His love! It is only such a Spirit-wrought faith that can say:

"My hope is built on nothing less Than Jesus' blood and righteousness;
I dare not trust the sweetest frame, But wholly lean on Jesus' name.
On CHRIST, the solid Rock, I stand; All other ground is sinking sand."

The Downward Drag of Sin

Blessed is the man that *walketh* not in the counsel of the ungodly, nor *standeth* in the way of sinners, nor *sitteth* in the seat of the scornful. *Psalm 1:1*

Did you notice the three verbs that are italicized in the above text? They denote a progression—a progression in the wrong direction. First we *walk* in a direction we should not be going. Then we stop walking and *stand* in places where we should not be standing. Finally we *sit*, indicating that we intend to stay for a while, having become comfortable in our new environment.

Such is the downward progression of sin—crafty, cunning, insidious, and, perhaps worst of all, imperceptible. None of us is immune to sin's deceptions. How often have we first walked, then stood, and then sat in the midst of worldly influences until we felt perfectly at home there?

Consider, for instance, the gradual change of attitude of many a church member toward the Scriptural teaching on sex, marriage, and divorce—or the quality of the everyday vocabulary of many a "believer." Well might we take the time to ask ourselves: are we walking with the Lord or sitting with the world?

Many a nominal Christian who in years past was in his accustomed pew every Sunday seldom sees the inside of a church today. When did the change take place? Or how many a church-goer who in times past would have been shocked while looking at an immoral movie can now sit through a whole show with an attitude of "ho-hum"? Have we *walked,* then *stood,* and then *sat down*—comfortable in the presence of sin and wickedness? How fitting are the poet's words:

Sin is a monster of so frightful mien
That to be hated needs but to be seen;
Yet seen too oft; familiar with her face,
We first *endure,* then *pity,* then *embrace.*

From this deliver us, heavenly Father, for Jesus' sake. Amen.

Whose House Is This?

Here we have no lasting city, but we seek the city which is to come. *Hebrews 13:14 RSV*

The fable is told of a weary wanderer in the Middle Ages who, trudging all day long with all of his earthly possessions on his back, came to a gleaming white castle silhouetted against a gold and purple sunset.

With night approaching, he rapped at the door of the castle and soon the door was opened, presenting a princely figure. The wanderer hesitated a moment, then inquired: "Is this thy house, Sir? And could I have lodging for the night?" In poetic Medieval English this prince replied:

> This house is mine, and yet *not* mine!
> Nor can tomorrow's owner say "'Tis mine."
> And he who follows him they'll bear away.
> Whose IS this house? Oh, pilgrim say!

Within a few generations the gleaming castle would still be there, but where would its present occupants be? The Christian hymnist dwells on this theme in the well-known lines: "Time, like an ever-rolling stream, Bears all its sons away; They fly forgotten as a dream Dies at the opening day."

How important that we in our "busy, busy" lives, preoccupied with the necessity of making a living, take time out each day for a brief but solemn reflection on the transitoriness of all things temporal. The writer of the Letter to the Hebrews reminds us that "here we have no continuing city, but we seek the city which is to come."

While we walk through the world that is temporal, our eyes must always be fixed on things that are eternal—on "the Word of God which liveth and abideth forever." That Word reminds us that our ultimate destination is "Jerusalem the golden With milk and honey blessed, . . . O sweet and blessed country, The home of God's elect." That is the "lasting city" for which we seek and for which we yearn. And for which we live from day to day.

Jesus, in mercy bring us To that dear land of rest. Amen.

Do We Coddle Evil?

Make not provision for the flesh, to fulfill the lusts thereof. Romans 13:14

Our dictionaries tell us that the word "coddle" means "to treat tenderly or indulgently, to pamper." If the whole truth were told, there are besetting sins in the life of *every* Christian which he would like "to treat tenderly or indulgently or to pamper." These are the sins we are warned against in the above text.

They are the sins we find most appealing: the sins toward which we look forward and for which we even frequently make preparation. They are the sins against which the Scriptures expressly caution: "Make no provision for the flesh, to fulfill the lusts thereof."

In a day like ours there are so many opportunities for participating in sins of the flesh, especially sins of impurity—in thought, in word, or in deed! Christian historians have called ours a decadent civilization. Much of the so-called entertainment that is offered on the stage, in movie theaters, and on the television screen is an insidious invitation to join the world in its culture of immorality. At best, it makes a mockery of God's commandments.

Are there sins in your life and mine toward which we actually look forward and for which we actually *make plans?* Sins of unkindness, strife, dishonesty, drunkenness, reveling, yes, even gross sins of sexual impurity? Our Lord says: "Make no provision for these! Never include them in your plans!"

But the same Lord speaks tenderly to the repentant sinner who has fallen prey to Satan's wiles: "Though your sins be as scarlet, they shall be as white as snow; though they be red like crimson, they shall be as wool." And why? Because you have a Savior—Jesus Christ—who died for you. That is the Gospel truth!

Whenever tempted to coddle evil, we well might pray:

> In the hour of trial, Jesus, plead for me
> Lest by base denial I depart from Thee.
> When Thou see'st me waver, With a look recall
> Nor for fear or favor Suffer me to fall.

"Safe in His Arms"

And God shall wipe away all tears from their eyes; and there shall be no more death. *Revelation 21:4*

Having tucked her four-year-old into bed, a mother bent over the child as she listened to her prayers: "Now I lay me down to sleep. I pray Thee, Lord, my soul to keep. If I should die before I wake, I pray Thee, Lord, my soul to take. And this I ask for Jesus' sake. Amen."

As the mother emerged from the bedroom, an elderly aunt who had overheard the prayer said indignantly: "How *dare* you put such maudlin thoughts of death into the head of a child!"

The aunt could hardly have been more wrong. Little Sandy was being raised in a Christian home. Any mention of death merely conjured up in her childlike mind beautiful thoughts of the many mansions in her Father's house where some day she would live in unending joy with Jesus, who was as *real* to her as the pillow beneath her head!

She had learned to sing the stanza of the favorite children's hymn: "When I am playing, Jesus takes care. When I am sleeping, Jesus is there; And when I die, my Jesus will come, And *safe in His arms He'll carry me Home.*" Not only did she sing the hymn, she believed it with all her little heart! The Jesus who some day would come for her was the Jesus who loved her. There was nothing maudlin about that.

Christian parents know that death is a part of life and that they dare not gloss over it in silence. A sad part? Yes, in many ways. Maudlin? Not if the child's faith has been grounded in the Friend of children who has invited all children to come to Him, and who some day will welcome them into the Father's heavenly home.

Christian parents will therefore make it a point to teach their little ones their bed-time prayers, starting perhaps with the simple, single word "Abba" and progressing to the beloved:

> "Lord Jesus, who doest love me, Oh, spread Thy wings above me
> And shield me from alarm! Though evil would assail me,
> Thy mercy will not fail me; I rest in Thy protecting arm."

Healing Love

I am the Lord that healeth thee. *Exodus 15:26*

Someone once said: "In sickness let me not so much ask, Am I getting better *from* my pain, as, Am I getting better *for* it?" One of the purposes of our heavenly Father in allowing sickness to come to His children is that they might be the "better for it."

It is true that some people never look *up* until God lays them on their back. Even we Christians sometimes need the loving chastenings of our heavenly Father to redirect our eyes from earth to heaven. But do we always let our sicknesses, our sorrows and reverses, serve the purpose which God would have them serve?

Do we use these visitations to purify our faith, to bring us closer to "the Lord who healeth us?" Do we permit these manifestations of the weakness of our mortal bodies to remind us "how near our end might be" and to teach us to number our days that we may apply our hearts unto wisdom?

To be sick and not to be brought thereby closer to God is to be doubly sick. But to be sick and in that sickness to find ourselves being drawn closer to our Savior is to be blessed in the midst of our affliction.

Let us invite the Savior's cheering, healing presence to hallow every hour of sickness which comes into our home. He is "the Lord that healeth thee." His love has saved our souls; His love will share our sorrows; His love will help us bear the pain; His love can heal our bodies.

How fortunate, indeed, is he who in days of serious illness can lay his feverish head upon his pillow and breathe the simple, faith-filled prayer:

> I lay my wants on Jesus, All fullness dwells in Him;
> He healeth my diseases, He doth my soul redeem.
> I lay my griefs on Jesus, My burdens and my cares;
> He from them all releases, He all my sorrows shares. Amen!

We Need No "Voices in the Night"

Faith cometh by hearing, and hearing by the Word of God. *Romans 10:17*

What do we say to the person who writes a book and says: "I was sitting there in my prison cell and suddenly, like a flash, I heard a voice and I knew that I was 'born again'?" We simply say: "With God nothing is impossible, but that is not the way He ordinarily works the miracle of rebirth. That is not the way He has promised us in Holy Scripture.

The only way that holds His sure promise is through His "means of grace," the Word and the Sacraments. The apostle Peter reminds the early Christians that they were "born again . . . by the Word of God, which liveth and abideth forever." Not by a flash that came out of nowhere! And Paul reminds his Roman Christians that "faith cometh by hearing, and hearing by the Word of God." Not by mysterious "voices" that merely echo our emotions!

It is through the Word, the written or spoken message of the love of God in Christ Jesus, that we are born again. And it is through the Word that we are "kept by the power of God, through faith, unto salvation." We need no voices in the night. Our God has spoken, once for all. In Christ He has told us that He loves us. That, and that alone, is our assurance.

But there is also a wider application of this truth to the Christian life. Some church members absent themselves from God's appointed "means of grace" for more than a year—and still want to be "members in good standing." It would be unwise to make a blanket judgment in all such cases. But such persons, at best, are living in spiritual danger. They have cut themselves off from the one "spiritual life support" that God has expressly offered us—*His Word and Sacrament.* They may be following "voices," but not God's voice. How important that our hearts remain forever attuned to His Word!

Lord, may my faith rest ever only on Your Word. Amen.

"Our Fathers Said . . ."

Put not your faith in princes, nor in the son of man, in whom there is no help. Psalm 146:3

Lest this meditation be misunderstood, let it be stated clearly: we are, indeed, to honor and respect the opinions and traditions of our forefathers. It is in their accumulated wisdom and experience that much of the stability of our present civilized society rests.

But there is a lurking danger when we apply this principle indiscriminately to matters of Christian faith and life. In these matters it will not do simply to rehearse the old refrain "our fathers said." That was the refrain of Christ's enemies. It was also the refrain of many of the opponents of Martin Luther.

While we are to accord our fathers in Christ all due honor and respect (no matter in which century they may have lived), we must be careful lest we elevate them to an implicit sainthood—or even to the level of infallibility. We must remember that they were subject to the same human limitations as both we and the dedicated fathers of our church today are.

In matters of faith and life there is, ultimately, only *one* authority for the believer, and that authority is the Holy Scripture. Paul calls this authority "the foundation of the apostles and prophets, *Jesus Christ* Himself being the chief cornerstone." It is to the apostles and prophets, but especially to Jesus Christ, the very "Word made flesh," that we are to turn for spiritual guidance and strength, for comfort and reassurance, in the daily struggles of life. Well might we heed the poet's words:

> Trust not in princes, they are but mortal;
> Earth-born they are and soon decay.
> Naught are their counsels at life's last portal,
> When the dark grave doth claim its prey.
> Since, then, no man can help afford,
> Trust thou in CHRIST, our God and Lord.
> Hallelujah! Hallelujah!

Lord, may I always put my trust in You. May Your Word always be a lamp unto my feet. Amen.

How Near the Cross?

By means of the cross He united both races [Jews and Gentiles] into one body and brought them back to God. *Ephesians 2:16* TEV

A noted theologian observed: "The nearer we get to the cross, the nearer we get to each other." And how right he was! In fact, that was the whole point of a major section of Paul's letter to the Ephesians, particularly in the suggested reading at the top of this page.

Writing to former Gentiles, he reminds them that it was the cross of Christ (His sacrificial death for the sins of all races and all people) that had brought both Jews and Gentiles into one spiritual family. They who had been strangers and enemies were now *one*—one in Christ. They were one through the redeeming cross of Christ, whose blessings they now shared.

How true the opening lines of this devotion are also for us today. "The nearer we get to the cross, the nearer we get to each other." The cross of Christ has not only saving but also healing, sanctifying powers. The closer we get to it, the more our hearts will soften, the more readily the chips will fall from our shoulders, the more we will be inclined to extend the hand of loving friendship to those who stand close to the cross with us, no matter what their race or color.

Are we living near the cross? Not only at home and at church, but also in our daily lives as we associate with others? Pray God that we are and that "the nearer we get to the cross, the nearer we will get to each other."

Lord of all nations, grant me grace To love all men of every race
And in each fellowman to see My brother, loved, redeemed by Thee.

Break down the wall that would divide Thy children, Lord, on every side.
Let me seek first my neighbor's good In bonds of Christian brotherhood.

Sympathy and Empathy

We have not an high priest which cannot be touched with the feeling of our infirmities, but was in all points tempted like as we are, yet without sin. *Hebrews 4:15*

Jesus demonstrated (and still demonstrates) two characteristics which every believer might well strive to emulate: sympathy and empathy. Both words have Greek origins. The former means to feel *with* someone, the latter to feel *in* someone—in the sense of looking at the world through *his* eyes, or of walking in his shoes.

We are told in the gospels that Jesus had "compassion" on the multitudes, meaning that He felt *with* them and *for* them. That is sympathy. In the Scripture reading suggested above we are told that Jesus can put Himself in our place, even today, because He has "walked in our shoes," fighting the daily battle with the forces of evil—but without sin. That is empathy.

Perhaps we will understand this concept better if we take it in its total context. The writer to the Hebrews is telling his Jewish readers that they now have a High Priest (a Go-Between) *in heaven.* He tells them that this heavenly high priest is unique in that He has lived through all of our heartaches and sorrows. He knows them all first hand. He "has a heart" for us, because He has been through it all. He has true *empathy.*

If we are to be "little Christs" in the world today, perhaps we should ask ourselves: What is *our* score in the exercise of sympathy and empathy? Can we really feel with and for our neighbor, and can we really experience his hurt and sorrow by "walking in his shoes?" Can we identify with him so closely that, by word and deed, we can be a "little Christ" to him? More important than "can we?" is "do we?"

Lord, grant me a sympathetic heart—and gentle lips and ready hands that I might help my neighbor in his need. Amen.

The Debt of Love

Owe no man anything, but to love one another. *Romans 13:8*

We are living in an age when almost everyone is insisting on his "rights." There are certain areas of life, of course, in which there is nothing wrong with that. But there are also certain areas of daily Christian living in which *obligations* and *responsibilities* take precedence over *"rights"*—either real or so-called.

Paul puts this thought very simply (some say too simply) when he says, "Owe no man anything, but to love one another." He, of course, was not using the word "owe" in its usual sense. He knew that the vendor down the street was not going to accept "love" in payment for the sandals he was selling.

No, Paul was using the word "owe" in a much higher sense. He was speaking of the relationship of "debt" we have all incurred as a result of Christ's death for us on Calvary—our debt to Him and to all mankind. The inexhaustible debt of love! That is the supreme obligation of every follower of Christ.

Instead of harping and carping incessantly about our "rights," how much more becoming it is for a child of God to seek earnestly to pay his honest "debt"—the debt of love and kindness and helpfulness he *owes* his fellowman!

Love is not optional in the Christian's life. It is a *debt,* a debt we owe, a debt we have to pay if we will bear the name of Christ. It may be that we have to sacrifice some of our presumed "rights" in order to pay our debt of love. Then let us sacrifice and pay it!

Let us always seek to emulate the poet who stood in spirit at Calvary's cross and exclaimed:

But drops of grief can ne'er repay The debt of Love I owe;
Here, Lord, I give myself away, 'Tis all that I can do. Amen.

A Religion of Joy

Rejoice evermore! *1 Thessalonians 5:16*

It is a caricature to picture the Christian as a man with a long face, a heavy book, and a black umbrella. Christianity is not the religion of the killjoy.

The life of Christ itself is a living contradiction of the claim that to be a consistent Christian one must be an apostle of gloom. The Savior mingled freely with the common people of His day, took part in their innocent pleasures, and hallowed their homely joys with the benediction of His presence.

If Christ was no killjoy, neither are His followers. In fact, no one on earth has a better right to be happy than the Christian. He alone knows beyond the shadow of a doubt that his sins are all forgiven and that through Christ the Father's house is his assured inheritance.

He alone has the divine assurance of enduring comfort in sorrow, strength in sickness, solace in bereavement, help in distress, and ultimate triumph in the midst of calamity. And this assurance of the Christian is no mere "whistling in the dark." It is an assurance based upon the eternal promises of God, vindicated by the death and resurrection of His Son!

Have we made full use of our birthright of joy and gladness? Even in those dark moments when there seems to be no reason for rejoicing, have we learned to look *beyond* the dark moment to the bright firmament of God's Gospel promises? Paul Gerhardt, a hymnist who had few peers, and who during The Thirty Years War experienced a series of heartbreaking personal and family tragedies, wrote the hymn: "Rejoice, my heart, be glad and sing, A cheerful trust maintain; For God, the Source of everything, Thy Portion shall remain." His faith in Christ was his inexhaustible source of joy.

Lord, grant us a faith that can rejoice in Your love and goodness despite surrounding circumstances. In Jesus' name. Amen.

The Open Mind

Grow in grace and in the knowledge of our Lord and Savior Jesus Christ. *2 Peter 3:18*

It is a sign of the growing and maturing Christian that he keeps his mind open to the further instruction and guidance of the Holy Spirit as He speaks to us through His written Word.

When we have memorized the last page of our catechism we have not learned everything. There is much, much more that our gracious Lord is eager to reveal to us if we will continue to approach His Word humbly and with an open mind.

Yes, there may even be some childish preconceptions that we will have to discard. For this writer the process began when he gave up the childish notion, at age four or five, that the Holy Spirit lived in a creaky closet in the church attic, the directon in which the pastor always pointed when referring to the Holy Spirit.

Growth frequently involves both subtraction and addition—the giving up of the old (if it was wrong) and the adding of the new (if it is right). We are to maintain an open mind—open to the enlightening Spirit of God as He speaks to us through Holy Scripture.

Notice, Peter is encouraging continued growth particularly on two levels—in knowledge and in grace. The former is largely a matter of our intellectual grasp of the basics of our Christian faith. As excellent as Martin Luther's Small Catechism is, there is much in it that calls for that maturer understanding that comes from additional study in later years.

Then, too, we are to grow "in grace," that is, in our personal awareness and conviction of God's redeeming love. The Lord loves not only the world in general, He loves you and me in particular. We are to grow in that love! Our text does not call for static Christians; it calls for ever-growing Christians—people, both young and old, who are growing daily "in grace and in the knowledge of our Lord and Savior Jesus Christ."

Lord, keep my heart and mind open to Your Spirit's leading. Amen.

Grace to the Humble

God giveth grace unto the humble. *James 4:6*

It is a principle of Christian life that the man who grows in the grace of Christian humility is given *other* graces also. It is the humble man to whom the Holy Spirit adds the grace of sympathy, of kindliness, of tenderheartedess. It is the humble man to whom the Lord gives the understanding heart and the grace of Christian charity.

Sympathy, kindliness, tenderheartedness, patience, charity—these are gifts of the Spirit which the proud man finds most difficult to receive and to put into daily practice. These are the graces which God pours most easily into *humble* hearts.

A noted theologian once said: "I used to think that God's gifts were on shelves, one *above* the other; and that the taller we grew in Christian knowledge, the more easily we could reach them. I now find that God's gifts are on shelves, one *beneath* the other; and that it is not so much a matter of growing taller in knowledge as it is a matter of stooping lower in spirit; and that we have to go *down,* always *down,* to get His best gifts."

If only we could learn that all-important lesson! The Savior was not merely uttering beautiful words when He said: "Blessed are the poor in spirit, for theirs is the kingdom of heaven. . . . Blessed are the meek, for they shall inherit the earth." Blessedness, *true* blessedness, can come only to the heart that will stoop low enough to reach it. "God giveth grace to the *humble.*"

O God, for Jesus' sake, forgive our sins of foolish pride. Cleanse our hearts of arrogance, conceit, and selfishness. Make us empty cups, O Lord, that You may pour Your fullness into our empty lives. Grant, O Lord, that we may be compassionate, tenderhearted, and kind to others, even as You have been to us. This we ask in Jesus' name.

Give me a faithful heart, Likeness to Thee,
That each departing day Henceforth may see
Some work of love begun, Some deed of kindness done,
Some wanderer sought and won, Something for Thee.

Our Love-Hungry World

Bear ye one another's burdens, and so fulfill the law of Christ. *Galatians 6:2*

Doctors and psychologists have recently discovered that thousands of babies die from a lack of love. Numerous cases are on record to show that babies who were wasting away have been quickly restored to health when given "proxy mothers" who did no more than love them and caress them.

The reason these "proxy mothers" saved the babies lives, we are told, is that they gave the babies something absolutely necessary for health and a sound personality—a feeling of being loved and wanted, a feeling of security.

It is not only *babies* who suffer from a lack of love. Untold numbers of men and women the world over are suffering mentally and emotionally, some even physically, because "nobody cares."

What a challenge to everyone who calls himself a Christian! What a wide-open opportunity to love these unloved souls into the Kingdom! Of course, it will always be the Gospel which finally brings a soul into the Savior's fold, but it will be the love of Christian people that brings the Gospel to those in need of love.

And how many people *within* the Kingdom are hungry for our love—people to whom we nod on Sunday morning but to whom we never speak and whose burden we have never shared. "Bear ye one another's burdens," the apostle tells us, "and so fulfill the law of Christ."

Have we been reaching out to our friends and fellow men with the helping, healing love of Christ? Many a person, perhaps on our street, perhaps in our own congregation, is waiting for just such a demonstration of our affection. We dare not let them wait in vain.

Are we living up to the model not only of Christian fellowship but also of Christian *concern* which the Bible enjoins upon us when it says: "Bear ye one another's burdens"? God grant that we are.

The Sanity of Saintliness

God hath not given us the spirit of fear, but of power, and of love, and of a sound mind. 2 Timothy 1:7

In the above passage the apostle Paul reminds his young pupil Timothy of the gifts that Timothy had received from the Lord: not only the gifts of boldness and power but also the gifts of love and of a sound mind. This last-named gift has also been translated "good judgment" and "wise discretion."

Unfortunately, the Christian church down through the centuries has frequently demonstrated more of its boldness and power than its love and soundness of mind—more of its militancy than its good judgment and wise discretion. Again and again zealous defenders of the truth have resorted to brutal force to maintain their positions, showing no sign of "love" or of "wise discretion."

There is nothing mutually exclusive about using our *heart* and using our *head*—about using the Spirit-given grace of Christian love and the Spirit-given grace of a sound mind. Love need not rule out "good judgment and wise discretion." Nor vice versa. Almost any believer in Christ would agree with that statement (in theory) but, oh, how often we have thrown good judgment to the winds—all in the name of what we have chosen to call Christian "love."

As believers in Christ, we will strive for the proper balance between boldness and love—between power and wise discretion. In the defense of our faith we will maintain our "soundness of mind." We will keep our balance and not fly off the handle. Our attitude and action will not cast doubt either upon the generosity of our mind or on the love that is in our heart. We will, rather, demonstrate the "sanity of saintliness." To that end, we pray:

Assist my soul, too apt to stray, A stricter watch to keep;
And should I e'er forget Thy way, Restore Thy wandering sheep.

Make me to walk in Thy commands, 'Tis a delightful road,
Nor let my *head* or *heart* or *hands* Offend against my God. Amen.

Baptized into God's Family

Ye are all the children of God by faith in Christ Jesus. For as many of you as have been baptized into Christ have put on Christ. *Galatians 3:26-27*

For a full understanding of this unusual text we must be familiar with the context in which it was written. Paul was writing to the Christian converts in Galatia, among whom a heated dispute had arisen. There were those who claimed that certain Old Testament rituals had to be observed (including circumcision) before one could become a Christian.

Against this error Paul contended vigorously, pointing out that we are no longer bound by Old Testament ceremonials and rituals but that we are saved alone by grace through faith in the saving work of Christ. In this context he went on to say: "Ye are all the children of God by faith in Christ Jesus. For as many of you as have been baptized into Christ have put on Christ."

This is a remarkable passage and worthy of study. Paul's first statement is abundantly clear: you and I are the children of God, not by natural birth, but by faith in the atoning work of Jesus Christ, our Savior. It was He who brought us back into spiritual fellowship with God—back into God's family.

Then notice the second sentence. "For as many of you as have been baptized into Christ have put on Christ." What does that mean? In the language of Scripture it means that, in Baptism Christ has removed from us the filthy garments of our own righteousness and has clothed us in the pure robes of His *own* righteousness. In the New Testament Baptism is not merely a ceremony, it is a sacrament, a means of grace. Through the divine Word that accompanies Baptism our sins are "washed away" (Acts 22:16), and we are empowered to lead the "sanctified" life (1 Corinthians 6:11) by the Holy Spirit working through the Word.

Do we really appreciate what God has done for us in Holy Baptism? Do we consciously cling to its blessings from day to day? Let us always remember that we are baptized Christians, forgiven, cleansed, and sanctified by our wonderful Redeemer.

Marked Men

I bear in my body the marks of the Lord Jesus. Galatians 6:17

In ancient times there was a specific class of slaves attached to the various heathen temples. To indicate their lifelong attachment to the temple to which they had been assigned, these slaves were *branded* with the name of the particular god or goddess whom they served.

Thus, for instance, a lifelong slave at the temple of Diana would bear the mark of Diana in his flesh, and no matter where he might be seen, he would always be recognized as a slave of Diana's temple.

To people who were acquainted with this custom the apostle Paul, who frequently referred to himself as a slave of Christ, writes: "I bear in my body the marks of the *Lord Jesus*." Just what these marks were, we are not sure. Most probably they were the scars which were left by the scourgings he received at the hands of his countrymen, by the stones which were thrown at him in Lystra, or by the rods with which he was smitten at Philippi. At any rate, Paul was a "marked man," and he was proud to wear in his body these marks of the Lord Jesus.

In a sense, *every* Christian is a marked man. He is marked as one of the slaves of Christ. No matter where he goes, if he is consistently devoted to his high calling in Christ Jesus, his marks are bound to show. His attitude, his speech, his habits, his behavior (his entire view of life and living) are bound, sooner or later, to reveal him as a marked person—a follower of Christ.

How have we been bearing that mark? Have we been ashamed of it? Have we tried to conceal it? Or have we proudly displayed it as a badge of honor? May we always be ready to confess unashamedly: "I bear in my body the marks of the Lord Jesus."

Ashamed of Jesus, that dear Friend On whom my hopes of heaven depend?
No; when I blush, be this my shame, That I no more revere His name.

Moving Mountains

If ye have faith as a grain of mustard seed . . . nothing shall be impossible unto you. Matthew 17:20

Someone has said that doubt *creates* mountains, while faith *removes* them. How true!

If it were possible for us to turn back the calendar just six short months, and from that point of vantage to look forward once more to today, how many mountains we would see along the road which were put there by our doubts!

The anxious mother spent many an anxious moment, worried about the family budget. The harried father tossed restlessly on sleepless pillows, fearing the responsibilities which awaited him at the shop or the office. The worried school child lost sleep over a test for which he had spent hours in conscientious preparation. All afraid of mountains which, for the most part, were imaginary and which, when they now look back, were surely the creatures of their doubt. Yes, it is true that doubt creates mountains.

But faith removes them. Not any kind of faith; not faith in ourselves; not faith in a general sort of "providence," not faith in a good-natured "man upstairs." But faith in that heavenly Father who has revealed His love to us by sending His Son into the world for our redemption. He has assured us that He will give us strength sufficient for the day. "As thy days, so shall thy strength be," He has told us.

In His strength we shall be prepared to move the mountains of discouragement, anxiety, frustration, and fear. In His strength we shall be able to emerge victorious, no matter how hot the battle. With Paul we can say: "I can do *all* things through Christ, which strengtheneth me." For it is in Christ, and in Him alone, that we will find that power which *must* prevail.

Heavenly Father, remove the doubts and fears that assail my heart and soul. Grant me that strength, joy, and triumph which you have promised me through faith in Jesus Christ, my Savior. Amen.

"Eternal Life" Insurance

I know whom I have believed, and am persuaded that He is able to keep that which I have committed unto Him against that day. 2 Timothy 1:12

We hear much about life insurance these days. After all has been said in favor of life insurance that could possibly be said, (and, surely, much *could* be said) we shall still have to admit that the protection it offers is not for the person who dies, but for those who are left behind.

For the person who dies it will be important that he has something far more solid, far more lasting, than a $20,000-life-insurance policy.

The apostle Paul had taken out a policy which he knew was absolutely reliable. In the evening hours of life he could say: "I *know* whom I have believed, and am persuaded that He is able to keep that which I have committed unto Him against that day."

Paul had committed his entire eternity to the safekeeping of Jesus Christ, his Savior. He believed with a certainty that all the arguments of men could never shake that Jesus is the Son of God. He believed with a conviction, as immovable as the mountains, that Jesus had paid the entire debt of sin for him. And so he could also believe, with an assurance as sure as God's own promises are sure, that he had been given a clear title to a mansion in the Father's house above.

That was Paul's "*eternal* life" insurance. And that is the eternal life insurance which God offers to every member of the human race—freely and without price. Have we made that insurance *Ours* by faith in the Redeemer?

I am trusting Thee, Lord Jesus, Trusting only Thee;
Trusting Thee for full salvation, Great and free.

I am trusting Thee, Lord Jesus; Never let me fall.
I am trusting Thee forever And for all.

Those Little Things!

We glory in tribulations also, knowing that tribulation worketh *patience*, and patience, experience, and experience, hope. Romans 5:3-4

A man who had hitchhiked from coast to coast, and who had walked many miles in the process, was asked what he had found the hardest to endure. To the surprise of his questioner, it was not the steep mountains or the dazzling sun or the scorching desert heat that had troubled him most, but—in the words of the traveler—"it was the sand in my shoe."

Frequently it is the little things that make the Christian life most difficult. Somehow the great trials of life—moments of critical illness, of death, and bereavement—have a way of raising us to higher levels and bringing us closer to the only Source of spiritual strength.

But those smaller trials! How they plague us! And how they succeed again and again in causing us to fall and stumble! Those little irritations in the home, those endless vexations at the shop or office, those petty quarrels at the church—those are the "sand in our shoe" which wear us down and which frequently wear our Christianity thin.

But they shouldn't! In the text quoted above, Paul includes these vexations, these "sand in the shoe" experiences, among the daily tribulations that fall to the lot of every Christian. And he says that these very tribulations should help us grow in Godly patience, adding that Godly patience will lead to "experience"—better translated "the ability to endure." It is as we cultivate a closer walk with Jesus that we will be able to take our daily irritations in stride.

Have we permitted the little things in life (the sand in our shoes) to get us down, to destroy our personal and family happiness? Then let us pray for pardon and ask for the grace of quiet patience in every circumstance of life.

This I Know

The Lord *knoweth* them that are His. *2 Timothy 2:19*

"I know not what the day may bring,
If sorrow, joy, or tears,
But I know Jesus will be there
To share my hopes and fears.

"I know He'll watch, though dark the way;
He never tires or sleeps,
But ceaselessly where'er I be
A tender vigil keeps.

"I do not know what he has planned;
His hand I cannot trace.
But daily I can hear Him say,
'Sufficient is My grace.'

"And 'In the time of trouble, call
On Me, I'll see you through.'
He often sends me joy through pain,
He'll do the same for you.

"It's good to know that He is near
By night as well as day,
To share our losses and our gains
And guide us all the way."

In the Bible meditation for today, Jesus tells us that we do not need to be anxious about our daily lives for our "heavenly Father knoweth." As long as we know that *He* knows our present and our future needs, our heart need know no fear.

In the Upper Branches

Walk in the Spirit, and ye shall not fulfill the lust of the flesh. *Galatians 5:16*

An elderly woman had been confined to her bedroom for several years. Each spring she watched from her window as the same robin returned and built its nest high in a nearby tree. One morning she called to her daughter and said nervously: "Look! Our robin is building her nest in one of the lower branches this year. I'm afraid the neighbor's cat can reach it."

Several days later she looked out of her window—to find the ground beneath that branch covered with feathers. The neighbor's cat had, indeed, found the lower branch within his reach—and the robin was dead!

As Christians we, too, have the choice of building our lives in the "upper branches" or in the "lower"—of living thrillingly close to God or dangerously close to the world. In fact, consciously or unconsciously, we *make* that choice much more often than we think—in the choice of friends we choose, the books we read, the entertainment we prefer, the movies we see, our habits of church attendance. In each case we are settling in the upper or the lower branches—closer to, or farther from the tentacles of temptation.

Similarly, we have the choice of living in the upper or lower branches by the kinds of thoughts with which we fill our minds, whether they be thoughts of kindness, goodness, love, and lofty aspiration—or thoughts of the mean, the low, the trivial, or even the frivolous or the filthy.

Let us ask ourselves: On what level has our life been moving—on the upper or the lower? Scripture admonishes us: "Walk in the *Spirit*," that is, live on the level of the things of God, "and ye shall not fulfill the lust of the flesh." Let us pray God to help us stay in the "upper branches"—far from those influences which have conspired to bring about our fall.

The Great Multiplier

There is a lad here which hath five barley loaves and two small fishes; but what are they among so many? *John 6:9*

There is a legend about the boy who gave up his five barley loaves and two small fishes so that Christ could feed the multitude. It tells how the boy hurried home, after all the fragments had been gathered, and told his mother about the exciting incident.

With eyes still big with wonder, he told her how his five little barley cakes and two dried fishes had multiplied in the Savior's hand until there was enough to satisfy 5,000 hungry people. And then, with a wistful look, he added: "I wonder, Mother, whether it would be that way with *everything* you gave Him!"

It is only a legend, of course, but the question that little boy asked deserves an affirmative answer. Yes, in a sense, it is that way with everything we give the Savior. He is still the great Multiplier.

Many a Christian can testify to the unsearchable arithmetic whereby Christ accepts a gift from the believer and returns it to him in double measure. Many a Christian mother who has been faithful in her stewardship, as she takes stock of the family budget at the end of the month, becomes gratefully aware of the Savior's multiplying hand. "How did we ever go so far on so little?"

The question confronts us: Are we willing to turn over a generous portion of our earthly loaves and fishes to the Savior's use? Are we willing to contribute generously, according to our means, that His purposes on earth may be accomplished? Omnipotent though He is, Christ looks to us (as He looked to the boy with the lunch basket) to help Him carry on His work. Surely, we dare not fail Him!

We lose what on ourselves we spend; We have as treasure without end Whatever, Lord, to Thee we lend, Who givest all. Amen.

Too Much Gospel?

A man is not justified by the works of the Law, but by the faith of Jesus Christ.
Galatians 2:16

Do we sometimes feel that the doctrine of justification by faith is being preached too *much* in our churches? Do we feel that the pastor has told us once too often that "the blood of Jesus Christ, His Son, cleanseth us from all sin" or that "He is the Propitiation for our sins"?

Sometimes it may *seem* so. It may seem that the minister could take this fundamental Bible truth for granted and go on to something else. But again and again the conscientious preacher has found that the Gospel of forgiveness through the blood of Christ is something which we dare never take for granted.

Again and again it happens that a lifelong member of the church, when brought face to face with death, begins to point to his many virtues—his years of service on the church council or his many years as elder, as though these were the things which would enable him to stand before the presence of his God. And just as often the mourners of a departed loved one will point to his many Christian virtues and say: "Surely, if *anybody* ever went to heaven, Uncle John did!"

That is exactly what the Bible denies! "A man is *not* justified by works"—"but by the faith of Jesus Christ." Not what *we* have done, but what *Christ* has done. Not our attainment, but Christ's atonement. Let us never tire of hearing that precious Gospel again and again. Let us cling to it. Let us cherish it so that, when we stand in the presence of the holy God on Judgment Day, we shall be able to say with a believing and trusting heart:

> All that I was, my sin, my guilt, My death was all my own;
> All that I am I owe to Thee, My gracious God alone.
> Thy Word first made me feel my sin, It taught me to believe;
> Then, in believing, peace I found, and now *I live, I live!*

Simple Concerning Evil

I would have you wise unto that which is good, and simple concerning evil. *Romans 16:19*

A Christian young man was being ridiculed by his worldly companions because he refused to go along with them to a place of sinful amusement. "How do you *know* it's so bad?" they asked, "you've *never* been there!"

To which the young man replied: "I don't have to fall into every mud puddle to see if it is dirty."

There are some things in life concerning which a Christian had better not have any firsthand knowledge, some things concerning which he need have no experience. In the words of our young man, we need not fall into every mud puddle to see if it is dirty.

Over against the sophistication of our age which would urge the Christian to sample every type of doubtful pleasure to see if it is really sinful, the Bible urges: Be wise concerning that which is good; be simple concerning that which is evil.

Cultivate the company, the companionship of that which is good; avoid the company of that which is evil! Our Savior has purchased us at a great price and for a great purpose: that we may "be His own, and live under Him in His kingdom, and serve Him in everlasting righteousness, *innocence*, and blessedness."

The Bible makes it very clear that those who acknowledge Jesus Christ as their personal Savior must also acknowledge Him as their personal Lord—that is, as Master of their everyday lives: their thoughts and words and actions. It is only natural that the redeemed child of God will want to live a life that is pleasing to his divine Redeemer.

Each of us must ask himself the question: "How could I refuse to shun Every sinful pleasure, Since for me God's only Son Suffered without measure?"

And then let us determine that with God's help, we will avoid every opportunity for evil and seek out every opportunity for good—in the name of Him who died that we might live.

A Christian Psychology

Thou wilt keep him in perfect peace whose mind is stayed on Thee. *Isaiah 26:3*

That text contains more positive "psychology" than a whole library of technical volumes on the subject. "Thou wilt keep him in perfect peace whose mind is stayed on Thee." But what does it mean to have one's mind "stayed on God"?

It means, above all else, that we place our entire confidence in God. We throw our whole weight upon *Him,* trusting that "underneath are the everlasting arms."

Into His hands we commit all of our *yesterdays*—all of our failures, our sins, our regrets, all of our guilty record. With St. Paul we can "forget those things which are behind," because we know that all has been forgiven through the blood of our Redeemer.

Into His hands we commit *today.* Tomorrow, today will be yesterday, and God will not remember its failures and shortcomings. "I, even I, am He that blotteth out thy transgressions . . . . and I will not remember thy sins," He tells us. Today, as yesterday, is a day of mercy and of grace.

And into His hands we commit *tomorrow.* His mercies which have been "new unto us every morning" will be just as new, just as sure, and just all all-sufficing tomorrow as they are today. His promises are sure. His compassions fail not.

It is true, the above is more easily said than done. Our frail human nature is much more inclined to fear than to faith. But our Lord has promised to send us His "Comforter." Literally, He has promised to send us One who will always "walk at our side." This, we know, is His Holy Spirit, who will strengthen and uphold us and guide us safely through all our yesterdays, all our todays, and all of our tomorrows.

> Come, Holy Spirit, come! Let Thy bright beams arise;
> Dispel the sorrow from our minds, The darkness from our eyes.
> Revive our drooping faith, Our doubts and fears remove,
> And kindle in our breasts the flame Of never-dying love.

The Inward Man

For which cause we faint not, but though our outward man perish, yet the inward man is renewed day by day. *2 Corinthians 4:16*

When John Quincy Adams was a very old man, he was met one day by a friend who greeted him with the familiar words: "How do you do, Mr. Adams?"

The elderly gentlemen replied: "John Quincy Adams himself is very well, thank you, but the house in which he lives is falling to pieces. Time and the seasons have nearly destroyed it. I think John Quincy Adams will soon have to move out. But he himself is very well, sir."

The apostle Paul put it another way: "Though our outward man perish, yet the inward man is renewed day by day."

For the child of God there is no dread in the rapid flight of time. The passing years may bring with them their multiplied reminders that "swift to its close ebbs out life's little day"—the waning strength, the fading vigor, the slowing step, the blurring vision—but they also bring with them the glorious assurances by which our inward man is renewed day after day.

Are we living on these assurances? Is our inward man being nourished and strengthened daily by the remembrance of that "love divine, all human love excelling"—the love revealed on Calvary's cross? Then, although our outward man may, indeed, be perishing, our inward man will constantly be lifted by the joyful hope of life eternal. With the poet we can say:

> Oh, for that choicest blessing Of living in Thy love,
> And thus on earth possessing The peace of heaven above;
> Oh, for the bliss that by it The soul securely knows
> The holy calm and quiet Of faith's serene repose!

With that undaunted faith down deep in our heart, our "outward body" may, indeed, be perishing, but our "inward man" (our sin-cleansed soul) will be strengthened day by day.

Turning Burdens into Bridges

Most gladly therefore will I rather glory in my infirmities, that the power of Christ may rest upon me. 2 Corinthians 12:9

A biologist tells how he watched an ant carrying a piece of straw which seemed almost too heavy for it to drag. The ant came to a crack in the ground which was too big for it to cross. It stood still for a time, as though pondering the situation, then put the straw across the crack and walked over on the straw.

What a lesson for us! We speak much about the burdens we must bear. But have we ever thought of converting our burdens into bridges, of having our burdens bear *us* up instead of us bearing *them* up?

The apostle Paul had learned the secret of being borne *up* by his burden, instead of being borne *down* by it. He had been given "a thorn in the flesh," a physical affliction, the exact nature of which we do not know. But once he recognized his affliction as a part of his Lord's good and gracious will for him, he found that even his "thorn in the flesh" had brought him into a richer experience of His Savior's love.

Even more! If we read the words quoted above in their larger context, we see that Paul's very "weakness" made him stronger for the Lord. His "thorn in the flesh" became a source of inner strength which enabled him to accomplish great things for the spread of the Gospel.

With God's help we, too, can turn our burdens into bridges— bridges that lead not only to deeper faith and brighter hope, but also to ever larger fields of service to our Lord and to our fellowman.

When we turn our burdens into bridges, we will always see our Savior standing at the other side of each bridge. The poet had this thought in mind when he wrote the lines: "Nearer, my God to Thee, Nearer to Thee! E'en though it be a cross That raiseth me!"

Burdens, disappointments, *crosses* are inevitable in the believer's life. Let us pray that *every* cross we are asked to bear will "raise us nearer" to the Lord who bought us.

God Has No In-Laws

We shall all stand before the judgment seat of Christ. . . . So then everyone of us shall give account of himself to God. *Romans 14:10-12*

A pastor was visiting in the home of one of his parishioners. The wife was one of his faithful members. The husband and children were not. Once comfortably seated, the pastor was about to begin his personal witness to the husband and father of the household. But he was cut short when the man stopped him with a smile and reminded him, both politely and awkwardly: "You remember, Reverend, I've always carried my religion in my wife's name."

Yes, the Pastor remembered. This time, however, he came back with an answer that gave the husband much to think about. After a moment's reflection the pastor replied: "Yes, Mr. Smith, I remember. But I've searched my Bible and nowhere does it say that God has in-laws."

The point struck home. The faith which Mrs. Smith had placed in Jesus as her Savior was a personal one—a relationship between her and Him alone. In no way would it avail for her husband. There was no way in which he could (as he said) carry his "religion in his wife's name." He would have to come to *personal* contrition, repentance, and faith, as would each of the children God had given him.

Paul makes it clear in the passage quoted above that we "shall all stand before the judgment seat of Christ" (as individuals) so that "everyone of us shall give an account of himself to God." We are saved not by our wife's religion, nor our children's, nor our in-laws'—but by our own *personal* relationship to God: that relationship into which we have entered by personal faith in Jesus Christ as Savior and Lord.

How about *our* family? Does each of us belong to Christ through Holy Baptism and by an active faith which shows itself in a Christian life? Remember: in the matter of salvation God has only sons and daughters; He has no in-laws. May God grant us all a living faith in Jesus Christ as Savior.

God STILL Is Love

Though He slay me, yet will I trust in Him. Job 13:15

Mr. Spurgeon, the great English preacher, was once riding in the country. His eye suddenly fastened on a weather vane on a farmer's barn. On the arrow of the weather vane were inscribed the three words: "God is love."

Alighting from his coach and walking up to the farmer, he asked: "What do you mean by that? Do you mean that God's love changes with the wind?" "Oh, no!" said the farmer, "I mean that whichever way the wind is blowing, *God still is love!*"

If only we Christians could always remember that! "Whichever way the wind is blowing, God still is love." When the sky is blue and the sun is shining and all is calm and quiet, it is a comparatively simple matter to agree that "God is love." But when the heavens frown, when the clouds hang low and dark and heavy, when the winds begin to beat against our little lives, then—how frequently we begin to *doubt* that God is love.

If ever there was a life in which the winds of misfortune blew stiff and strong, it was the life of ancient Job. Within a relatively brief time Job had lost everything that he possessed—wealth, wife, children, property, herds—and, added to it all, he experienced the painful agony of a severe case of sores and boils from the soles of his feet to the top of his head.

So desperate and so seemingly hopeless was his condition that his friends suggested to him that he "curse God and die.'" But what was Job's reply? "Though He *slay* me, yet will I *trust* Him!" He was convinced that "no matter which way the winds were blowing, God still is love!"

We who have seen the love of God poured out on Calvary's cross can never doubt that statement. "He that spared not His own Son, but delivered Him up for us all, how shall He not with Him also freely give us all things?"

Lord, You have shown Your love for me through Jesus Christ, my Savior. Grant me Your Holy Spirit so that nothing in life will ever cause me to doubt Your steadfast love. Amen.

Our Transforming Savior

If any man be in Christ, he is a new creature; old things are passed away; behold, all things are become new. *2 Corinthians 5:17*

Luther Burbank, the great naturalist, once said: "If I have made any worthy contribution to the world, it is the discovery of the great principle in botany that a plant born a weed does not have to *remain* a weed, or that a plant degenerated by conditions of nature does not have to *remain* degenerate."

That, we agree with Luther Burbank, was a great discovery. But a revelation of infinitely greater significance awaits the man who plumbs the depths of God's power and mercy as revealed on Calvary's cross. In the shadow of that cross the unclean are made clean, the dishonest become upright, and men and women with depraved tastes are suddenly transformed into children of light.

In a sense of which Burbank never dreamed, it is true that at the foot of Calvary's cross "a weed does not have to *remain* a weed . . . and a degenerate plant does not have to *remain* degenerate." "If any man be in Christ, he is a new creature: old things are passed away; behold all things are become new."

Most of us have learned these words as a "Bible passage"—perhaps in confirmation instruction, perhaps in Bible class or Sunday school. But have we demonstrated this basic Christian truth in our everyday behavior? Do we show by our faith and life that through Christ we have, indeed, become "new creatures"?

The power of the Gospel of Christ to transform the lives of men and women is the greatest miracle that God has revealed to man. Through faith in His atoning blood "the children of wrath" become "the children of God," and "the children of darkness" are transformed into "the children of light."

Standing, in spirit, at the foot of Calvary's cross, we pray:

Dear dying Lamb, Thy precious blood Shall never lose its power
Till all the ransomed Church of God Be saved to sin no more. Amen.

There Is Rest for Our Souls

Ye shall find rest unto your souls, for My yoke is easy, and My burden is light.
Matthew 11:29-30

"Rest." What did the Savior mean by that? He did *not* mean instant release from all the cares, trials and afflictions of life. Ours is an adverse and wicked world, and in our passage through it we will have to encounter many trying and painful experiences.

Ours is not to be a rest *from* trial—but a rest *in* trial. It is the rest and peace which come from the certain knowledge of sins forgiven; that calm repose which comes from knowing that we are at one with God, forgiven through the blood of Christ.

But what did Christ mean when He invited us to take His yoke upon us and then assured us: "My yoke is easy and My burden is light"? We must remember that He was speaking to people who had been brought up under the heavy yoke of the Old Testment Law. The laws which God had given His people through Moses made very stern demands, governing almost every action of their lives—not only in the exercise of personal morality, but also in the performance of external ceremonies, and even in the strict observance of political or civic obligations. To the Israelite his religion was an onerous recital of an almost endless series of "Thou shalt" and "Thou shalt not."

One of the first public utterances of John the Baptist was: "The Law was given by Moses, but *grace* and truth came by Jesus Christ." The yoke under which the New Testament believer is to live is the yoke of grace (grace meaning undeserved mercy). We are no longer under the yoke of the Law with its stern demands and its threats of punishment. Rather, we are under the yoke of love—love that has set us free from guilt, free from the fear of punishment, free to serve the Lord who bought us. It is in this freedom that we have found the "rest for our souls" which the Savior offers to all who come to Him in trusting faith.

"The Devil Made Me Do It"

Your adversary, the devil, as a roaring lion, walketh about, seeking whom he may devour. *1 Peter 5:8*

A famous television comedian never failed to get a laugh when he spoke the line: "The devil made me do it." While we thoroughly disapprove of the levity of this remark, we cannot disagree with its theology. The Sacred Scriptures clearly teach the existence of a personal devil, who is the source of every evil and who "makes" us do things that are contrary to God's will.

That is why Peter warns us to be "sober and vigilant" and to "resist" the devil in steadfast faith. In every moment of temptation we are to flee to Christ and His powerful Word for the needed strength to overcome the Evil One.

Dr. Martin Luther took the devil very seriously. He makes frequent reference to him in his theological writings. His great battle hymn of the Reformation includes the well-known lines:

> The old evil Foe now means deadly woe; Deep guile and great might
> Are His dread arms in fight; On earth is not his equal.

There is a subtle danger, however, that we shift the blame for all of the ills of the world (and the church) to the devil in an effort to absolve *ourselves*. We cannot escape the responsibility for what we do. Nor dare we forget that in every struggle that pits man against man, the devil is usually on both sides. He is a past master at insinuating himself into our motives, words, and actions, no matter how loudly we protest that we are "on the Lord's side."

Then, too, let us always remember that the old evil foe can even use the Holy Scriptures to lead us into false paths, as he tried to do when tempting the Savior. In that case he *twisted* the Scriptures to suit his own purpose. (See Matthew 4:5-6.)

Peter's language was not too strong when he warned: "Your adversary, the devil . . . walketh about, seeking whom he may devour." To which he adds significantly: "Whom resist steadfast in the faith." Lord, grant us such faith!

314

Reformation Day

If ye continue in My Word, then are ye My disciples indeed. John 8:31

Today is the festival of the Reformation. Whether or not we shall continue to enjoy the priceless blessing of Luther's Reformation—the doctrine of salvation by grace through faith—depends upon whether or not we live up to the one condition which the Savior lays down in the above: *"If ye continue in My Word, then are ye My disciples indeed."*

The Church is to continue in God's Word. And who is the Church? The Church is you and I. You and I are to continue in God's Word if we are to remain His disciples—if we are to preserve and profess the precious Gospel of full and free salvation through Jesus Christ, His Son.

What has our record been in this respect? Are we familiar with our Bible, or has it become a stranger to us? Are we regular, conscientious, and attentive in our use of the Word and the Sacrament as it is dispensed to us at church? How zealous have we been in our personal searching of the Scriptures?

We shall not long remain "free" if we neglect "the truth," and we shall not long remember "the truth" if we do not diligently continue in God's Word.

Luther once said that the Gospel is like a traveling shower: it does not remain long in one place. History has shown his words to be all too true. Let us on this day, then, rededicate ourselves to an unswerving loyalty and undying devotion to the precious Gospel preserved for us in the pages of Holy Writ—the Gospel which, by the grace of God, has truly set us free. Let our prayer still be:

Lord Jesus Christ, with us abide, For round us falls the eventide;
Nor let Thy Word, that heav'nly light For us be ever veiled in night.
Oh, grant that in Thy holy Word We here may live and die, dear Lord;
And when our journey endeth here, Receive us into glory there. Amen.

God's Minorities

If God be for us, who can be against us? Romans 8:31

During the time Noah was building the ark, he was very much in the minority—but he won. When Joseph was sold into Egypt by his brothers, he was a decided minority—but he won. When Gideon and his 300 followers put the Midianites to flight, they were an insignificant minority—but they won.

When Elijah prayed down fire from heaven and put the prophets of Baal to shame, he was in a notable minority—but he won. When David, ridiculed by his brothers, went out to meet Goliath, his confidence in victory was definitely that of a minority—but he won. When Martin Luther nailed his theses on the door of the Castle Church, he was a lonesome minority—but he won. And when our blessed Lord bowed His bleeding head in death on Calvary's cross, He was a conspicuous minority—but He won.

In our human shortsightedness we are frequently tempted to believe that God is on the side of the greatest numbers—that "the voice of the people is the voice of God." Nothing could be farther from the truth. Again and again God has chosen insignificant minorities as His spokesmen. Again and again He has achieved His greatest victories through individuals who had the courage to stand up against overwhelming odds. Of one of the church fathers it was said: "It is Athanasius against the world." And he won.

We are reminded of a sage remark which Abraham Lincoln is said to have made during the dark days of the Civil War. Some friends had asked him: "Are you sure that God is on our side?" To which he replied: "It is more important to know that *we* are on *God's* side."

Once we are on God's side, we can say with Paul: "If God be for us, who can be against us?" With Christ at our side, we need not be afraid to be numbered among God's minorities.

With might of ours can naught be done, Soon were our loss effected;
But for us fights the Valiant One, Whom God Himself elected.

Faith Alive!

Faith by itself, if it has no works, is dead. James 2:17 RSV

One must read the entire passage from which the above verse is taken (James 2:14-18) for a proper understanding of the point which James is making. He is not contrasting a genuine faith in Christ with genuine deeds of love. Rather, he is contrasting an *alleged* or spurious faith with genuine deeds of Christian virtue.

Notice, in verse 14 he asks: "What does it profit . . . if a man *says* he has faith but has not works?" Merely mouthing the words of a creed is not the equivalent of saving faith. Saving faith is a personal, humble, Spirit-wrought trust in Jesus as Savior and Lord. Such a faith, far from being a mere subscription to a formal creedal statement, is an ever living, ever moving, ever motivating force within the human heart. It loves and keeps on loving, because it knows that God loves and keeps on loving us.

Martin Luther put it eloquently when he said: "Faith is a divine work in us . . . . [It is] a living, busy, active, mighty thing, so that it is impossible for it not to be constantly doing what is good. Likewise, faith does not ask if good works are to be done, but before one can ask, faith has already done them."

True, as Paul so frequently tells us, we are saved by faith *alone*. Nor dare we ever waver in that conviction! But the significant fact is that genuine faith is never "alone." It always *shows* itself in good works. Jesus tells us: "By their fruits ye shall know them." Our good deeds dare never be a substitute for saving faith, but they must inevitably blossom and grow to full fruition as the genuine fruit of the faith that dwells within us.

How about us? Is our faith a dead one: one that we recite and never translate into action? Or is it a faith that is alive, ready to feed the hungry, clothe the poor, visit the sick, and minister to the needs of those who need our love and care?

Lord, grant me a "faith that worketh by love." Amen.

Love That Found Me

Herein is love, not that we loved God, but that He loved us. *1 John 4:10*

In the explanation of the Third Article of the Apostles' Creed we confess: "I believe that I cannot by my own reason or strength believe in Jesus Christ, my Lord, *or come to Him.*" This inability of natural man to come to saving faith by his own power is beautifully inferred in the parable of the lost sheep.

Far from the safety of the fold, beyond the reach of the shepherd's voice, entangled perhaps in a thorny thicket, the solitary lamb would have perished, had not the shepherd's devotion compelled him to go to the rescue. The lamb could not come to the shepherd; so the shepherd went out in search of the lamb.

That lamb is you—and I. Today we are feeding upon the green pastures, we are being led beside the still waters, we are safe in the Shepherd's keeping *Only* because God from eternity saw us out in the desert of sin and decreed that we should be brought into the shelter of His fold. We were lost and would have remained forever lost had not His mercy sought and found us.

The entire distance between God and man was covered by God; the combined efforts of all three members of the Trinity were used to bridge the gap between the sinner and salvation. The Father gave us His Son; the Son atoned for our transgression; the Holy Spirit sought us out and brought us to our Savior. Therefore John says: "Herein is love, not that *we* loved God, but that He loved *us.*" What an inexhaustible source of comfort in days of doubt, depression or despair, to root our faith firmly in this assurance of Holy Scripture and to say with the poet:

> Oh, the height of Jesus' love! Higher than the heavens above,
> Deeper than the depths of sea, Lasting as eternity.
> LOVE THAT FOUND ME—wondrous thought!
> Found me when I sought Him not. Amen.

Love That Will Not Let Me Go

They shall never perish, neither shall any man pluck them out of My hand. *John 10:28*

How can I be sure that I will continue in the faith until the end? I know that I am a Christian today, but how can I know with certainty that I will be a believer tomorrow? Or, what assurance do I have that I will be trusting in the Savior when my feet are wandering through the valley of the shadow? These questions enter the heart of every child of God at some time.

Fortunately, God Himself has answered them for us. He has answered them in every Gospel promise. As perfect as God's love is, so perfect is the Gospel offer. His love could not permit Him to offer us a salvation which would not "wear"; His love could not mock us with a counterfeit redemption which would fail us when we needed it the most. No, His love went all the way. Not only our coming to faith, but also our continuing in the faith and our dying in the faith are part of His plan for us.

"They shall never perish," says Jesus, "neither shall any man pluck them out of my hands." "Ye are kept by the power of God through faith unto salvation," says Peter. Not we, but God does the keeping. And He keeps us through faith—faith nurtured through His Word, faith strengthened by the Sacrament. What a blessed assurance! God has promised to sustain the arms of our faith, and He has given us His pledge that the strong arms of *His love* will never let us go. Because of our wonderful salvation we are *HIS* both now and forevermore.

Therefore each night, as we fold our hands in sleep, we can confidently pray to Him who stands at our journey's end:

Myself I cannot save, Myself I cannot keep;
But strength in Thee I surely have, Whose eyelids never sleep.

My soul to Thee alone Now, therefore, I commend.
Thou, Jesus, having loved Thine own, Wilt love me *to the end.*

Avoid Foolish Talk

Steer clear of foolish discussions which lead people into the sin of anger. *2 Timothy 2:16 LB*

There is a big difference between Christian witnessing and theological wrangling. Normally we engage in the former to win a *brother* or *sister*; frequently we engage in the latter to win a *point*. Unfortunately it often happens that in winning our point we lose our brother. We once knew a family who had a motto on the wall near the kitchen table which read: "Fight the Good Fight!" They followed its injunction at almost every meal. They fought.

St. Paul admonishes them and us: "Steer clear!" Avoid like the plague those "foolish discussions" which we know are sure to lead to the sin of ugliness and anger. There are times, of course, when a Christian will have to speak out in defense of the truth. Then let him speak with the charity, the "sweet reasonableness" of which the apostle Paul speaks in other passages.

It is perhaps one of the most serious scandals of the Christian church that it has frequently resorted to rancor and bitterness in the handling of "religious differences." In the name of God so-called defenders of the faith have insulted the very God whose name they claimed to be defending. Paul knew this demonic side of human nature and so he warns his pupil Timothy against any senseless talk that might only lead to anger.

We must get rid of the idea that the good fight of faith is carried out only with a sharpened tongue or a poisoned pen. "Love . . . is not irritable or resentful" (1 Corinthians 13:5 RSV). We pray God to steer us clear of all foolish talk, talk that leads to bitterness and anger, and we pray Him, for Jesus' sake, to forgive us for the many foolish conversations that mar our record.

Oh, grant, when in my place I must and ought to speak,
My words due power and grace Lest I offend the weak. Amen.

Do You Find It Difficult To Share?

Bring ye all the tithes into the storehouse . . . and prove Me now herewith . . . if I will not open you the windows of heaven. *Malachi 3:10*

There is no denying it—our sinful heart is opposed to sharing. Opposed to sharing our money and our material possessions with God and our fellowmen. It is afraid lest, having given up this comfort or that convenience, we will never be able to replace them.

And yet God's Word assures us again and again that He who gives unto the Lord will never be the loser. "Give, and it shall be given unto you," says Jesus; "good measure, pressed down, and shaken together, and running over, shall men give into your bosom" (Luke 6:38). And again: "He that hath pity upon the poor lendeth unto the Lord; and that which he hath given will He pay him again" (Proverbs 19:17).

Through the prophet Malachi the Lord, as it were, dares us to test these promises. "Will a man rob God?" He asks, "Bring ye all the tithes into the storehouse . . . and *prove* Me now herewith . . . if I will not open you the windows of heaven and pour you out a blessing that there shall not be room enough to receive it."

Are we afraid to accept the "dare"? Afraid to take God at His Word? Let us pray for faith and courage to trust His promise. Then let us dig down deeply into our earthly treasures and share them, not only in support of His Gospel ministry (as important as that is) but also in support of the poor and needy at our doorstep and in every section of the world.

Out of gratitude to him who bore our sins and shared our sorrows in order that we might share His heaven, let us resolve to share our blessings as He has asked us to do.

Grant us hearts, dear Lord, to yield Thee Gladly, freely of Thine own;
With the sunshine of Thy mercy Melt our thankless hearts of stone
Till our cold and selfish natures, Warmed by Thee, at length believe
That more happy and more blessed 'Tis to give than to receive. Amen.

Someone To Hold On To

I know whom I have believed. 2 Timothy 1:12

We are living in a world of almost cataclysmic change. Old values, old truths are not only being challenged, they are being uprooted and discarded. The whole human family, as it were, is being tossed about on a surging sea of uncertainty.

What does one hold on to in such a time of storm and stress? We do well to take our cue from Paul. Notice, he does not say: "I know *what* I have believed." Rather, he says: "I know *whom* I have believed," and then goes on to say: "and am persuaded that He is able to keep that which I have committed unto Him against that day."

While the "what" of our faith is very important, the "whom" is even more important. The supreme object of the apostle Paul's faith was Jesus Christ, his Lord and Savior. He had entrusted his life to the Good Shepherd, whom he had learned to know and love. And he remembered the Shepherd's promise: "They shall never perish, neither shall any man pluck them out of My hand."

Each of us must ask himself: "Am I putting my primary trust in a system or in a *Savior*—in a long catalog of doctrines or in the *Christ* who is the heart and center of those doctrines? Paul's basic confidence rested on a very personal relationship. "I am crucified with Christ," he said, "and the life which I now live I live by faith in the Son of God who loved *ME* and gave Himself for *ME*."

That is why in the midst of calamity he could exult: "I know *whom* I have believed!" Behind that pronoun stood the power, the love, the mercy that would see him through, whatever the future might hold. Behind that pronoun stood the very Son of God, who had pledged to be *with* him—all the way.

> I am trusting Thee, Lord Jesus, trusting only Thee;
> Trusting Thee for full salvation, great and free.

I Shall Not Pass This Way Again

As we have therefore opportunity, let us do good unto all men. Galatians 6:10

A French philosopher once wrote: "I expect to pass through this world but once. Any good therefore that I can do, or any kindness that I can show to any fellow creature, let me do it now. Let me not defer it or neglect it, for I shall not pass this way again."

What a *sobering* thought! "I shall not pass this way again." As we thread our way along the pathway of life, each today dissolves into a yesterday—and each yesterday dissolves into the irretrievable past. We can look back along a seemingly endless road of yesterdays, but we cannot relive a single one of them. We cannot undo what we regret, nor can we do those things we know we *should* have done. There is a sense in which the door to the past will remain forever closed.

"I shall not pass this way again." What a *motivating* thought for our Christian life! *NOW*, not tomorrow, is the time to do that charitable deed which we know needs doing. We have no assurance tomorrow will ever come.

That apology which we owe our loved one: Do it now! That hospital visit we have been putting off: Do it now! That word of kindness and encouragement our neighbor needs so desperately: Speak it now! That helping hand that would mean so much to our faltering sister or brother: Extend it now! That word of gratitude to a loved one who has stood faithfully by our side: Speak it now!

Now is the hour. Tomorrow may be too late. We shall not pass this way again. The good deeds we *intend* to do may never get done. How important that we do them *now*! The apostle says, "The love of Christ leaves us no choice." We must do good as He gives us opportunity.

Lord, if there is any special kindness I can show today, help me do it now.
I shall not pass this way again. Amen.

Where To "Find" Christ

The Word of the Lord endureth forever. And this is the Word which by the Gospel is preached unto you. *1 Peter 1:25*

Recently a confused and desperate teenager wrote us: "Would you help me? Oh, I need it very much. I love Christ, but I can't find Him!" The remainder of her letter revealed a life which indeed called for the power of the living Christ. Her plaintive plea about finding Christ reminds us of the hopeless sob of ancient Job: "Oh, that I knew where I might *find* Him!"

You and I know where we can always find our Savior—not by ransacking our heart, not by searching our conscience, not by measuring our life by the standard of His Law. In those directions lie only further guilt and condemnation.

In moments of desperation we can always find our Savior in His Word. His Word abides forever, "and this is the Word which by the Gospel [the Good News] is preached unto you!"

Nor does this mean that in every moment of seeming "lostness" we must run to our library and seek out our well-worn Bible and scramble through its pages for a passage that fits our present need. What the Lord once said to Moses He says to every well-instructed Christian: "The Word is very nigh unto thee, in thy mouth, and in thy heart." The Christian heart is full of remembered Gospel voices of the Savior—even if sometimes they seem like muted echoes. Each remembered Gospel voice says: "Here I am . . . come!"

Are you desperate? Are you crushed? Are you ashamed of your life? Take heart! Christ is at your side! Remember His promise: "Thy sins be forgiven thee." "Lo, I am with you." "You need not look for *Me*, I have looked for *you*, and I have found you." That is His answer to *every* desperate, penitent heart. That is why you and I can always pray:

> Love that found me! Wondrous thought!
> Found me when I sought Him not! Amen.

Therefore Will Not We Fear

God set Him [Christ] at His own right hand . . . and hath put all things under His feet. *Ephesians 1:20, 22*

Today is Luther's birthday. We cannot read about the life of the great Reformer without being impressed with his Christian optimism and cheerful confidence. Once he had launched upon the great work of the Reformation, he had no doubts as to the ultimate success of his great undertaking, nor did he heed the many personal dangers involved in the course which he had chosen.

Luther himself explained his unusual optimism by saying that at the right hand of God he had a Friend who was not only pleading his cause, but was also sustaining and protecting him. That was the secret of his confidence. He believed with all his heart the Scriptural assurance that the eternal and omnipotent Christ "is able to save them to the uttermost that come unto God by Him, seeing He ever liveth to make intercession for them."

Our life, like that of Martin Luther, may be beset by difficulties and discouragements on every hand. We, too, may be called upon to suffer persecution, ridicule, and bitter opposition. There may be days in which our wavering heart hesitates upon the precipice that leads into the valley of despair.

At moments such as those, we are to remember that we have a Friend at the right hand of the Father. He, who left His Father's home to come to earth to suffer and die in the place of sinners, is even now at the right hand of the Father and "rules all things." "God hath put all things [also our troubles and our enemies] under His feet." He is not only *willing*, but also *able* to uphold us in the hour of need. That was Luther's confidence. And that is also *our* assurance. Of our omnipotent Friend at the right hand of the Father we, too, can sing:

> He lives to silence all my fears,
> He lives to wipe away my tears,
> He lives to calm my troubled heart,
> He lives all blessings to impart.

When Tithing Becomes "Too Much"

Charge them that are rich in this world . . . that they be rich in good works.
1 Timothy 6:17-18

The Savior frequently spoke in parables in order to share a spiritual insight. We will follow His example in this brief meditation by telling a parable in order to bring out the full meaning of the text quoted above.

There was once a young man who knelt in prayer with his pastor as he committed himself to tithe his income to the Lord. Since his income was only $10 a week he promised to give $1 to the church.

Many years later he sent for his pastor who visited him that very same evening. For almost an hour they discussed the good old days, and then he came to the point. "Pastor," he said, "I'd like to be released from the promise I made many years ago to tithe my income." Awkwardly, he continued: "You see, it's like this: when I made that promise, my tithe was only $1 a week. I've done very well financially over the years—with the result that my tithe has risen to $100 a week. Frankly, I can't afford that much."

The pastor hesitated, thought a moment, then said: "I'm afraid you can't go back on your promise. But there *Is* something you can do. We can kneel together and ask the Lord to *shrink* your income until you need to give only "$1 a week." There was an embarrassed silence. Then the pastor asked: "Would you like to pray with me?"

This story is only a parable, but it does serve to bring out the full meaning of the text "Charge them that are rich in this world . . . that they be rich in good works." Rich or poor, may this be our prayer:

> We give Thee but Thine own, Whate'er the gift may be;
> All that we have is Thine alone, A gift, O Lord, from Thee.
> May we Thy bounties thus As stewards true receive,
> And gladly, *as Thou blessest us*, To Thee our first fruits give.

The Shadowy Figure—Can We See It?

Inasmuch as ye did it NOT to one of the least of these, ye did it NOT to Me.
Matthew 25:45

These words should send a shiver down the spine of many a Christian. The glorified Christ is seated on His throne of judgment. He says to those on His left: "I was hungry, I was thirsty, I was a stranger, naked, sick, and in prison, and you never lifted a finger to help Me!"

We shudder before the verdict: "Inasmuch as ye did it NOT to one of the least of these, ye did it NOT to Me." You turned your backs on Me.

We are living in a day of unprecedented hunger, starvation, disease, social dislocation, and almost criminal maldistribution of the bounties a gracious Lord has given us. Despite the advances of science and technology, there is more human misery in the world today than the human mind can grasp. The insanity of war, the insatiable avarice of the human heart, the ignorance and squalor which fester like spreading sores over large sections of our world—all present an inescapable challenge to those who name the name of Christ. The unnumbered hordes of sick and miserable people who crowd the world today are the ones whom the Savior calls "the least of these my brethren."

Our Lord, indeed, expects us to thank Him for our daily blessings. But He expects much more than thanks. He expects generous and loving hearts that will share His bounties with the poor, the dispossessed, and the minority groups who suffer want—wherever they may be. Behind each needy person there stands, as it were, the shadowy figure of the One who says: "You will do it—or you will NOT do it—unto Me."

We may not be able to go to the far ends of the earth to feed the hungry, tend the sick, and help the poor, but we can pray fervently and give generously to alleviate human need.

> And we believe Thy Word, Though dim our faith may be;
> Whate'er for Thine we do, O Lord, We do it unto Thee.

On Being Evangelical

I beseech you, therefore, brethren, by the mercies of God . . . . Romans 12:1

Paul had just completed the doctrinal portion of his marvelous Letter to the Romans (chapters 1 to 11), and now he was ready to speak to them about their everyday Christian life.

It is highly important that we notice the form and the tone of his transition: his bridging over from faith to life. He starts his 12th chapter with the well-known words: "I beseech you, therefore, brethren, by the mercies of God, that you present your bodies a living sacrifice."

Notice the evangelical tone of almost every word of the apostle. Having expounded the way of salvation in the first part of his letter, he opens the second part not with "I command you," but "I beseech you." Then comes the connective word "therefore," or, in view of everything that God has done for you. Then comes "brethren." He was addressing his equals, his sisters and brothers in Christ. And what was the authority behind the request he was about to make? He pleads solely "by the mercies of God."

Occasionally we make the mistake of trying to improve the Christian lives of our sisters and brothers by pounding away at the Law—or by quoting profusely from the rules and regulations of our congregation or church body. There is a proper place for rules and regulations, but not in motivating to Christian life. Not the leverage of the Law but the warming influence of the Gospel is the only genuine "moving force" for Christian love and virtue.

Paul carried no big stick. He pounded no podium. He shouted no threats. He besought. He pleaded. He pointed only to the crucified Christ as the motivation for Christian living. The Christian poet expressed the mind of Paul when he wrote:

> Thy life was given for me, Thy blood, O Lord, was shed,
> That I might ransomed be, And quickened from the dead.
> *Thy life was given for me: What have I given for Thee?*

Not Ours—But Us!

First [they] gave their own selves to the Lord. *2 Corinthians 8:5*

A noted evangelist was conducting services in a town in England. Upon returning to his friend's house in the evening, the friend inquired: "Well, how many were converted tonight?" "Two and a half," replied the preacher. "Why, what do you mean?" asked the friend. "Was it two adults and a child?" "No," replied the evangelist, "it was two children and one adult. The children have given their lives to Christ in their youth, while the adult has come with only half of his." Using only *time* as his measurement, the evangelist had made a valid point. There are other measurements, of course.

How much of *our* life have we given to the Lord? The question is not how much of our money, how much of our time, or how many of our talents we have placed at His disposal—although these, to be sure, are important.

Of the Corinthians we read that before they gave anything to the Lord, they "first gave their *own selves*." Have we, out of gratitude for our Lord's great mercy in Christ, thus subordinated our will to His? Can we say with Paul: "I am crucified with Christ; nevertheless I live; yet not I, but Christ liveth in me, and the life which I now live in the flesh I live by the faith of the Son of God, who loved me and gave Himself for me"? Paul had, indeed, given his *all* (himself) to the Lord who had bought him.

Let us do some earnest heart-searching. Has our surrender been complete and unconditional? Is the life which I now live being lived "by the faith of the Son of God, who loved me and gave Himself for me"? God grant that it is. And may our constant prayer still be:

> Take my life and let it be Consecrated, Lord, to Thee;
> Take my moments and my days, Let them flow in ceaseless praise.
> Take my love, my Lord, I pour At Thy feet its treasure-store;
> Take *myself*, and I will be Ever, only, all for Thee. Amen.

God's Evergreens

His leaf also shall not wither. *Psalm 1:3*

On a hillside in southern Illinois stood a mammoth evergreen. In the springtime, when other trees were dressing themselves in their Easter finery, this evergreen seemed a bit out-of-date, if not also a bit out of place.

In the noontide of summer it looked so much like the trees around it that it seemed to be lost in the landscape. And when autumn decked its neighbors in gorgeous garments of gold and red, it seemed to be the most drab of all the trees on the hillside.

But when *winter* had come and the other trees, stripped of their foliage, were waving their skeleton arms in the wind, then the humble evergreen stood out in all its verdant beauty. Even with the snow bending its graceful boughs, it was just as green as it had been in the full flush of summer.

The believer in Christ is one of God's evergreens. "His leaf also shall not wither." In the winter seasons of life, when the winds of adversity blow stiff and strong, when the dull gray skies of gloom and drabness shut out the rays of cheering sunshine, the Christian stands out among his fellows as one of God's evergreens.

His roots are sunk deep into the promises of God. And from these promises he draws strength to adorn his life with Christian virtues regardless of surrounding circumstances.

Are *we* one of God's evergreens? Was the psalmist speaking of us when he said: "He shall be like a tree planted by the rivers of water, that bringeth forth his fruit in his season; his leaf also shall not wither—[literally, not *fade*]"? Are we one of those trees that, no matter what the season, bring joy and gladness to the eye of the beholder?

Lord, make me one of Your evergreens, with roots sunk deeply in Your Word, and with branches of adornment that never fade or wither. In Jesus' name. Amen.

Who Found Whom?

The Son of Man is come to seek and to save that which was lost. Luke 19:10

In the timber mountains of the Northwest a five-year-old boy was lost. Night came. The citizens and rangers searched frantically every cave and mountainside. Snow began to fall. Blanket upon blanket covered the forest floor, but no Bobby could be found.

The next morning the father, fatigued from an all-night search, kicked against what seemed to be a log in the path. But when the snow fell loose, a small boy sat up, stretched, yawned, and exclaimed: "Oh, Daddy! I've found you at last!"

Now—*who* found *whom*? Men sometimes speak of finding God. Learnedly, they speak of the quest for God, the search for certainty, and the discovery of the divine. But it was not God who was lost, it was *we*. Nor was it *we* who found God, it was *God* who found *us!*

In this connection it would do us well to read Martin Luther's explanation of the Third Article of the Apostles' Creed once more. In the plainest of language he tells us exactly "Who found whom" and who it was that brought the lost one home.

Remember his words? "I believe that I cannot by my own reason or strength believe in Jesus Christ, my Lord, or *come* to Him; but the Holy Ghost has called me [awakened me] by the Gospel, enlightened me with His gifts, sanctified and kept me in the true faith. . . ."

Or to revert to the story of little Bobby: it was not *he* who came to his father; it was his *father* who came to *him*. It was not the youngster who in his own strength clasped his father's hand and strode victoriously, on his own, back to warmth and shelter; it was the father who bundled his "lost son" up, clasped him tenderly in his arms and carried him all the way. Even so, it is with us: we are safe in our Savior's keeping today only because *HE* sought us and *HE* found us!

Love that found me—wondrous thought! Found me when I sought Him not!

Here am I! Send Him! Send Him!

[Moses answered the Lord saying:] "But I'm not the person for a job like that!"
Exodus 3:11 LB

We all remember the dramatic scene when the Lord appeared to Moses in a burning bush in the land of Midian. Describing the pitiable plight of His chosen people in the land of Egypt, the Lord commissioned Moses to go down to Egypt, to confront Pharaoh, and to lead His people out of their captivity.

Moses' reaction was typically human. Immediately he came up with a string of excuses. He was sure he didn't have the necessary gifts—the gifts of speech and eloquent persuasion. Surely, someone else would be a better choice. *The Living Bible* quotes one of Moses' desperate excuses with the colloquial words: "But I'm not the person for a job like that!"

Sound familiar? How many of us, when confronted by our Lord's command: "Go . . . and make disciples of all nations" or His divine commission, "Ye shall be witnesses unto me," can summon up a catalog of shopworn excuses? How easy it is to say politely: "I'm just not cut out for that," or "Frankly, that's not my cup of tea."

The fact is, we *are* cut out for various types of Christian service. Paul tells us that we are God's "workmanship, created in Christ Jesus unto good works." In other words, we have been saved to serve. Not all of us have the same gifts, but all of us have some gifts which God expects us to use in His Kingdom. (See 1 Corinthians 12.)

Moreover, as in the case of Moses, the Lord has promised to equip us for the spiritual duties which are specifically ours. He has promised us His Holy Spirit's aid, and has put into our hands His converting Gospel and the Sacraments. Scripture tells us that, as soon as Moses heard the Lord's voice, he answered, "Here am I." We never read that he followed through with "Send me! Send me!" although we know that He finally went. The danger is that when *we* hear the command, we reply: "Here am I! Send him! Send him!" *May that not be said of us!*

A Life of New Beginnings

. . . even so we also should walk in newness of life. Romans 6:4

There is a popular motto which says: "Today is the first day of the rest of your life." A motto such as this may be dismissed as being merely a clever saying or a sentimental slogan with very little meaning. On the other hand, it can be taken seriously and invested with real significance. Suppose we read it once more: "Today is the first day of the rest of your life."

Isn't that what we as baptized Christians believe? For us *every* day is a new beginning for our Christian faith and life. Martin Luther tells us that the significance of our baptism lies in this "that the old Adam in us should by daily contrition and repentance be drowned and die with all sins and evil lusts and, again, a new man daily come forth and arise, who shall live before God in righteousness and purity forever."

Indeed, for the believer each day is the first day of the rest of his life—a new life, a life of spiritual growth, of purposeful activity, of greater sanctification, and an ever closer walk with Jesus Christ, his Savior.

The question is, Do we really look at each new day in that way? Or is each day, for us, just another *old* day in a long series of humdrum yesterdays which have shown no change, no growth, no advancement in our personal Christian faith and life? Have we fallen into the rut of making each new day *another old beginning*? How appropriate, then, that we heed the counsel below:

> With the Lord begin thy day, Jesus will direct it.
> For His aid and counsel pray, Jesus will perfect it.
> Every morn with Jesus rise, And when day is ended,
> In His name then close thine eyes; Be to Him commended.

No Room for "Bulldogmatics"

Let your speech be always with grace. Colossians 4:6

During the war in Southeast Asia an army officer issued the following communique: "We saved the village, but in doing so we had to destroy it."

A *paradox?* Yes, to most of the people who read about it in the newspapers. But not to the military man who had issued it. He had saved a strategic point in the overall battle design, but in doing so he had had to annihilate the entire village, its rickety little markets, its thatched huts, and all of its inhabitants. In military parlance he had saved the line.

There is a kind of Christian witnessing, of "contending for the faith," that involves a similar *paradox.* It preserves the faith but it destroys the very person we set out to save. It destroys because it is lacking in love, in kindness, in genuine personal concern.

This is not to say that the believer in Christ is not to be positive in the expression of his convictions, that he is not to be dogmatic in the best sense of the word. Indeed, he *must* be dogmatic, since the basic truths he is seeking to impart are eternal and unchangeable. But there is a dogmatism of the clenched fist and a dogmatism of the open hand, a dogmatism of the gracious spirit and a dogmatism of the bitter heart and biting word.

St. Paul on several occasions stressed the importance of a humble heart and gracious spirit in our defense of the faith. He urged that our speech "be always with grace." Dogmatic? Yes. But never "*bull* dogmatic"! Let our dogmatism always be that of the kindly spirit, the warm heart, and the open and inviting hand. Let us defend the faith, but let us also pray:

> O, let me never speak What bounds of truth exceedeth;
> Grant that no idle word From out my mouth proceedeth;
> And, then, when in my place I must and ought to speak,
> My words grant power and *grace* Lest I offend the weak.

Whatever Became of Sin?

The Scripture hath concluded all under sin. Galatians 3:22

Sin has become a very unpopular word in our 20th century culture. Men will resort to all sorts of euphemisms to get around it. They may commit a "wrong," a "mistake," an "indiscretion," but never a sin. That word "just isn't used any more." Small wonder that Dr. Karl Menninger, famed psychiatrist and cofounder of the world-renowned Menninger Clinic, wrote a book during his later years, entitled *Whatever Became of Sin?*

The Scriptures insist that sin is an inescapable fact of life: a malady inherited from our first parents. All of us are equally infected. "If we say that we have no sin, we deceive ourselves," says John. "The Scripture hath concluded [imprisoned] *all* under sin," says Paul.

In fact, if one were to catalog all of the passages of the Bible which either declare or infer the universality of sin in the world (including such an explicit statement as "there is no difference, for *all have sinned*"), one could have no doubt that the Bible sees the entire human race as being shut up in the prison house of sin.

But why? Paul answers that question in Galatians 3:22. The Bible "concludes" all mankind under sin so that all may receive the same Gospel promise—and receive it on equal terms. All are equally guilty in God's sight, but all are equally redeemed from sin, death, and the devil by Jesus Christ, His Son.

Do we take our sins seriously? Seriously enough? If so, we will rejoice all the more in the comfort of the Gospel: "Where sin abounded, grace did much more abound." It is gloriously true that "Christ Jesus came into the world to save *sinners*, of whom I am chief."

I lay my sins on Jesus,
The spotless Lamb of God;
He bears them all and frees us
From the accursed load.

I bring my guilt to Jesus,
To wash my crimson stains
White in His blood most precious
Till not a spot remains.

Read Acts 17:22-28

Is Your God Too Far?

Thou art near, O Lord. *Psalm 119:151*

Some years ago J. B. Phillips wrote an excellent book entitled *Your God Is Too Small*. In it he claimed that too many Christians had whittled God down to size—their *own* size.

Perhaps someone should write a similar book and entitle it *Your God Is Too Far*. How many of us, as we go about our daily work, think of God as a sort of absentee landlord living a billion light-years away, somewhere "way out there"?

There is no comfort in the contemplation of such a God. The Scriptures assure us that our Lord is as close to us as the very breath we breathe. In Psalm 139:3-5 David says: "Thou hast traced my journey and my resting places. . . . Thou hast kept close guard before me and behind and hast spread Thy hand over me" (NEB). David had put his trust in a personal God who was personally present with him every moment of his life.

At another time he wrote: "Whither shall I flee from Thy presence. . . . If I take the wings of the morning and dwell in the uttermost parts of the sea; even *there* shall Thy hand lead me, and Thy right hand uphold me." Wherever David went, his God was very *close*.

Our Savior meant it when He said: "Lo, I am with you alway, even unto the end of the world." The omnipresent Christ is with us at the breakfast table, at work, at the sickbed, in the hospital, in the operating room, in days of joy and in days of sadness. He has promised to be with us in every circumstance of life.

How easy it is even for "the best of Christians" to forget this. Well might we ask: Do we (really!) recognize and acknowledge His daily presence in our life—in all our joys and sorrows? Do we (really!) "walk with Him and talk with Him?"

Be near me, Lord Jesus, I ask Thee to stay
Close by me forever and love me, I pray. Amen.

Whose Church?

I will build My church and the gates of hell shall not prevail against it. Matthew 16:18

We are living in days when "men's hearts are failing them for fear, and for looking after those things" that are happening to the organized church. "Will the church survive?" they ask.

That all depends upon whose church we mean. Notice the pronouns Christ uses in the above passage. "*I* will build *My* church," He says. And against *His* church "the gates of hell shall not prevail."

It is not really we who are building the church. It is Christ, working through His Holy Spirit, according to His promise. And He is building His church on the sure foundation of Simon Peter's confession: "Thou art the Christ, the Son of the living God." It is on the rock-ribbed Word of God that He said He would build and preserve His church.

There is, of course, the constant temptation to equate the church with various types of human bureaucracies, with statistics, boards, committees, handbooks, even bankbooks—none of which in themselves are wrong, but none of which dare ever be confused with the church itself. The church is *believers*—believers down through the ages. To them has been given the promise of ultimate victory.

We may lament the passing of old and familiar customs, and our hearts may be saddened by the tearing down of scaffolding which we had mistaken for the church. But let us take heart. Christ *will* build His church. The church is His. No power in earth or hell can stop its progress. Until the end of time men will continue to hear the glorious confession of Peter: "Thou art the Christ, the Son of the living God."

> Mid toil and tribulation
> And tumult of her war
> She waits the consummation
> Of peace forevermore,
>
> Till with the vision glorious
> Her longing eyes are blest
> And the great Church victorious
> Shall be the Church at rest.

Thou, God, Seest Me

The eyes of the Lord are upon the righteous, and His ears are open unto their cry.
Psalm 34:15

A little boy, visiting in the home of an elderly lady, was intrigued by a colorful wall motto which had the text: "Thou, God, Seest Me." Noticing the child's interest, the elderly woman took the motto from the wall and began explaining to the child.

"Some people will tell you," she said, "that God is always watching you to see when you are doing wrong—so that He can punish you. I don't want you to think of this motto in that way. Every time you read these words, 'Thou, God, Seest Me,' I would rather have you remember that God loves you so much that He *cannot take His eyes off you*."

That is exactly what David meant when he wrote: "The eyes of the Lord are upon the righteous." As the loving mother cannot take her eyes off her newborn child, so the Lord "withdraweth not His eyes from the righteous." They are always the objects of His tender care.

If only we could live our lives in the full and constant awareness that God truly *does* have His eyes on us—and that, through Christ, His eyes have become the eyes of tender love and warm compassion. Again and again, throughout the day, may we lift our hearts heavenward and whisper the prayer: "Thou, God, seest me!"

More and more these words will become less and less a threat to our uneasy conscience and more and more an assurance of His loving presence. One day while walking the dusty roads of Palestine with His faithful few, Jesus pointed them to the carefree sparrows and reminded them that His heavenly Father had His "caring eye" on each of them. From His memorable words came the prayer which each of us may well repeat during our silent moments:

His eye is on the sparrow. And *I know* He cares for me!

Held by His Hand

The righteous . . . are in the hand of God. Ecclesiastes 9:1

On a cold winter day, when the sidewalks were all covered with ice, a pastor and his little boy were walking to church. It was the first time three-year-old Bobby was wearing an overcoat in which there were deep pockets. As they approached a slippery place, the father said: "You had better let me hold your hand." But the boy's hands were snug in his pockets—and he kept them there until he *slipped* and *fell!*

Somewhat humbled by his experience, he said: "I'll hold your hand, Daddy." And he reached up and took his father's hand in a feeble grasp. Soon they came to another slippery place—and down he went, for his tiny fingers had not been able to grip his father's hand with strength.

They resumed their walk, but after a moment's reflection Bobby looked up into his father's face and said: "*You* hold *My* hand, Daddy." And as they went safely on their way, it was the father's hand that kept the boy from further danger.

How often, when *we* have come to slippery places, have we had to learn that it was not *our* hold upon *God,* but *His* hold upon *us* that kept our feet from stumbling! We "are kept by the power of God through faith unto salvation," says St. Paul. It was this unshaken confidence that inspired the poet to write:

He leadeth me! O blessed thought! O word with heavn'ly comfort frought!
Whate'er I do, where'er I be, Still 'tis *God's hand* that leadeth me.

He leadeth me! He leadeth me! *My hand in His*—He leadeth me!
His stronger hand shall lead me on Until in heav'n my rest is won.

What a comfort to know that, as believers, we are in God's hand. He does the holding. Where He leads us, we will follow. With our hand secure in His we shall come some day to the far side of the valley—to His waiting "Father's house."

When the Lamp Burns Low

He will not . . . put out a flickering lamp. Isaiah 42:3 TEV

Recently a man who was guilty of a sinful habit and was terribly tortured by a guilty conscience wrote us for help: "I don't want to stop doing it," he said "but I *want* to want to!"

Perhaps we should read that last sentence again. Behind it may lie the flickering lamp of which Isaiah speaks above. The picture is that of a sputtering oil wick. It is burning so low and so uncertainly that we expect it to go out at any moment. But "No!" says our gracious God. "I will stand by it, I will nurse it, I will enable it to shine more brightly."

Even the smallest faith is a gift of God's Holy Spirit, and even the weakest faith can lay hold on His greatest promises. We are not saved by the greatness of our faith; we are saved by the greatness of our Savior. A precious diamond in the tiny hand of a two-day infant is worth just as much as it is in the strong hand of the full-grown adult. Not the hand that holds, but the treasure that is held, is the important thing. And in this case, the important thing is God's eternal promise: His promise in the Gospel of our Savior.

He who is alarmed by his sin, who is of a contrite heart, and has despaired of his own worthiness in God's sight, need but whisper, as did the dying man on the cross: "Lord, remember me . . ." For the moment that was faith enough!

Even a flickering faith is saving faith. Sometimes even "wanting to want to" is evidence of a moving of the Spirit. Each of us has days when the lamp of faith burns low. Thank God that we have a Savior who "will not break off a bent reed, nor put out a flickering lamp," but who will stand by us and nurse our wavering faith to health.

> Jesus, Thou my Strength in weakness, Let me hide myself in Thee;
> Tempted, tried, and sometimes failing— Let *Thy Cross* my victory be!

Love's Little Whiles

Ye shall be sorrowful, but your sorrow shall be turned into joy. John 16:20

When the Savior spoke the above words, He was referring primarily to the sorrow of Good Friday and to the holy joy of Easter. The little while of sadness was to be followed by an eternity of bliss.

In a sense the life of the Christian is but a swift succession of many of these little whiles. God permits sorrow to come our way, but our sorrows are separated from our joys by only "little whiles." "For a small moment I have forsaken thee," He says, "but with great mercies will I gather thee." "Weeping may endure for the night, but joy cometh in the morning," he says through the psalmist.

And life itself is but a "little while" in the calendar of God's eternity. Life's little while of sorrow will soon be swallowed up in the endless ages of pure delight in heaven. Lazarus spent but a "little while" in the company of dogs, but he is spending an eternity of bliss in Abraham's bosom. The malefactor spent but a "little while" suspended on the cross, but his sorrow has been turned into the endless joy of Paradise. Of these sorrows and joys Paul writes: "The sufferings of this present time are not worthy to be compared with the glory that shall be revealed in us."

Let us, then, accept these little whiles of pain and sorrow as preludes to a perfect day. We have our Savior's promise: Our sorrows shall be turned into joy; our shadows into sunshine; our little whiles of doubt and trial, of loneliness and sadness, shall be turned into eternal ages of joy and glory in the company of heaven.

It was a man who had trod the path of dark sorrow to bright joy who wrote those words of Christian triumph:

> Ye fearful saints, fresh courage take; The clouds ye so much dread
> Are big with mercy and shall break In *blessings* on your head.

The Opened Hand—at Thanksgiving Time

Thou openest Thine hand. *Psalm 145:16*

It is a familiar picture. Early on a summer morning, as the farmer, carrying a large container of chicken feed, approaches his chicken yard, the entire population of "chicken city" comes running toward him clucking and cackling in eager anticipation. They *know* what he is carrying in his hands.

What a picture of God's children in relation to their heavenly Father! The psalmist says: "The eyes of all wait upon Thee, and Thou givest them their meat in due season. Thou *openest Thine hand* and satisfiest the desire of every living thing."

It was a simple matter for Old Testament readers to see the parallel between the opened hand of the farmer and the opened hand of the heavenly Father who provided richly for their daily needs. Theirs was a largely *rural* society.

Most of us today are living in an impersonal, largely mechanized, urban environment. Our children (and sometimes we) consider the local supermarket to be the ultimate source of food and drink—and the department store or shopping mall the ultimate source of all of our necessities. Indeed, in our affluent secular society we are in danger of simply taking all of our material blessings for granted.

How important that we, during this season of Thanksgiving first, recognize with gratitude the Source of our daily sustenance, and, second, pass this knowledge along to our children.

We must constantly remind ourselves and those entrusted to our care to look *beyond* the supermarket, *beyond* the department store or shopping mall, to the opened hand of a heavenly Father who "so loved us" and still loves us, that He gave His only Son to live and die for us—and, with Him, continues "freely to give us *all* things" to support our body and life.

> Praise God from whom all blessings flow;
> Praise Him, all creatures here below;
> Praise Him above, ye heavenly host:
> Praise Father, Son, and Holy Ghost!

Read Matthew 15:21-28

November 28

The Silences of God

But He answered her not a word. Matthew 15:23

What the woman of Canaan lived through in several moments many of us spend a lifetime in going through. There are things we desire of God most earnestly, but our prayers seem to dissolve into empty silence. It would seem at times that God "answers us not a word."

In the case of the woman of Canaan, as in other passages of Scripture, we learn that there is always a loving purpose behind the mysterious (and sometimes perplexing) silences of God. A close reading of Matthew's account will show that Jesus remained silent a while in order to test the genuineness of her faith—yes, to test it severely. That is why, when He finally breaks His silence, He exclaims: "O woman, *great is thy faith!* Be it unto thee as thou wilt!"

We can be sure that the Savior heard the woman's plea the very first time she uttered it, but He had a gracious purpose in delaying His reply. Similarly, we can be sure that He hears our prayers before we speak them. But in His wisdom He always has a purpose either for answering us in seeming silence for a while or for granting our request according to *our* schedule. It is not for us to fathom or explain His purpose. It is rather for us to surrender and submit to it—in trusting faith.

As children of God, through Christ, we know that His purpose in our lives is a good and gracious one. We know this, because He has told us so. "I have loved thee with an everlasting love; therefore with loving-kindness have I drawn thee."

If God has told us *that*, need we worry about His silences? No. Rather let us use His silences as did the woman of Canaan. Let us use them to throw ourselves ever more completely upon His mercy. His loving Savior-heart can hear our faintest prayer—and since we know He loves us, we need have no fear.

> Beloved, "It is well!" God's ways are always right,
> And perfect love is o'er them all, Though far above our sight.

Chosen by His Grace

He hath chosen us in Him before the foundation of the world. *Ephesians 1:4*

The above passage contains a great mystery, but a most comforting one. We can argue about it and become lost in a maze of erudite theologizing, or we can simply trust it for what it says. Its language is crystal clear.

Someone has said that the mystery revealed in the above passage is included in a personal love letter addressed only to believers. Its message is normally confined to pronouns of the first person. In other words, the Lord is speaking to persons who have already come to know and love Him. Such persons accept His Word implicitly for what it says. And what it says is this.

God chose you and me to be His children, and He did so "before the foundation of the world." He did not choose us *en masse*. He chose us as individuals. He chose us by name. He chose us "in Him," that is, in Christ, or because of Christ. From all eternity God knew that Christ would die for us to restore us to His family. So He chose us "in Him."

St. Paul calls this "the election of grace." We were not chosen because of anything *we* would do, but because of something *Christ* would do. He died to make us "children of the Father." Our election, then, is solely a matter of grace—of God's undeserved mercy and love. This should be the source of greatest comfort to us.

Do we sometimes doubt that we are really God's children, that heaven will some day really be our home? Yes, we *could* doubt if the ultimate responsibility were ours. But God *chose* us; He chose us *in Christ*. We are "accepted in the Beloved."

Having been chosen by His grace "in Christ," we can sing with joy: "Since He is mine and I am His, What can I want beside?"

Advent—Our Lord Is Coming!

Lift up your heads, O ye gates; even lift them up, ye everlasting doors, and the King of Glory shall come in. Psalm 24:9

For centuries the magnificent hymn "Lift up your heads, ye mighty gates!" has been sung to usher in the Advent season. The hymn, written in 1642, was obviously based on the psalm of David quoted above. It is a stirring call to welcome the coming Messiah who would come to ransom and redeem His people.

The word "advent" means coming or arrival. Traditionally the church has devoted the Advent season to a meditation on the *threefold* coming of the Savior: (1) His coming in the flesh, (2) His spiritual coming into the hearts of men, women, and children through Word and Sacrament, and (3) His final coming on the Day of Judgment.

Within a few weeks we will celebrate His coming in the flesh, His human birth. It is altogether fitting and proper that we use these weeks to prepare our hearts to rejoice over the miracle of Christmas. In that miracle lies our highest hope for time and for eternity. In that miracle lies "forgiveness of sins, life, and salvation" for everyone of us.

We receive that miracle for our very own when the Savior comes into our hearts—through Word and Sacrament. And this is the second meaning of Advent. The Savior comes to us again and again—each time His saving Word is spoken. May the door of our heart always be open, that the King of Glory may come in.

Through faith in Him we need have no fear of His final advent—His coming at the end of time. In fact, we may look forward to His coming with glad anticipation. For us who have found forgiveness in His atoning death He will come *not* as Judge, but as the King of Glory, our Savior and our Lord. May ours be a blessed Advent season as we look forward to our Redeemer-King who is coming, coming, coming.

Hark the glad sound! The Savior comes, The Savior promised long;
Let every heart prepare a throne And every voice a song!

Joy

Rejoice in the Lord alway, and again I say, Rejoice. Philippians 4:4

For centuries the above Scripture passage, Philippians 4:4-7, was read in Christian churches on the Sunday before Christmas. Three essential ingredients of the true Christmas spirit are listed by the apostle: joy (verse 4), moderation (verse 5), and peace (verse 7). We will meditate on each of these ingredients in this and the following two devotions. First, joy.

The joy of which the apostle speaks is, of course, joy "in the Lord." During the present days it is the unbounded gladness which is ours in the "tidings of great joy" that unto us is born a Savior, which is Christ the Lord, the God-with-us, the Emmanuel! It is the joy over God's "unspeakable Gift" of Christmas.

Will Christmas day find that holy joy in our hearts and homes? Or only in our hymnbooks? Will Christmas morning find us ill-tempered at the breakfast table, at odds with father or mother or sister or brother? Peeved and pouty? Will our Christmas joy stop with the opening of the last Christmas gift?

No, the true joy of Christmas must be reflected in our lives. It must find expression over the coffee cups at the breakfast table, in our attitudes and conversations in the family circle, in our casual contacts with our fellowmen.

True Christmas joy is something which cannot be shut up in one corner of our heart where it will have no influence upon our thoughts, words and actions. It is a warm and glowing, radiant thing. It clamors for expression. "My heart for very joy doth leap, My lips no more can silence keep," says Luther. Let us open up our hearts to the full joy of Christmas, and then let us radiate the warmth, the cheer, the gladness which is ours. May our lips and our lives proclaim to one and all:

> *Joy to the world,* the Lord is come! Let earth receive her King!
> Let every heart prepare Him room And heaven and nature sing!

Moderation

Let your moderation be known unto all men. The Lord is at hand.Philippians 4:5

The word "moderation" in the above text has been translated variously as gentleness, kindliness, and reasonableness. It is that particular quality that makes velvet different from burlap. It is a willingness to yield, to give and to *forgive*. It is a disposition of kindly, sympathetic understanding.

How desperately the world and the church need this gentleness today—this attitude of deference, of reasonableness! It will do us no good to talk piously or wistfully about the gentleness of the saints, if we are not gentle ourselves. What has been our record in this respect? Are we clutching our petty prejudices, our smouldering hatreds, our silly little grudges to our heart, determined that we will never let them go? Do we insist, openly or subtly, on always paying back in kind? On keeping all scores even?

Are we willing to let our brother have his say? Are we willing to listen? *Really* listen? And having listened, can we disagree agreeably? Do we always have to have the last word? Perhaps the last angry word?

The apostle Paul had another word which came close to expressing the gentleness, the kindliness, of which we are speaking in this meditation. It is the word he repeats again and again in 1 Corinthians 13. It has been translated variously as love or charity. We quote only the following lines:

Love is patient and kind; love is not jealous or boastful; it is not arrogant or rude. Love does not insist on its own way; it is not irritable or resentful; it does not rejoice at wrong, but rejoices in the right. Love bears all things; [love] believes all things . . . [love] endures all things" (RSV).

How do we score in these *tender* Christian virtues?

Lord God, I ask in Jesus' name, forgive my sins of lovelessness; give me a gentle spirit. Amen.

Peace

And the peace of God, which passeth all understanding, shall keep your hearts and minds through Christ Jesus. *Philippians 4:7*

We shall hear much about "peace" during the coming days. Unfortunately much of what will be said and written will have nothing whatever to do with the peace of which the angels sang on that first night in Bethlehem. The "peace on earth" of which the angels sang was not a program of international good will, nor was it even primarily the peace of man to man.

It was, above all else, peace between *God* and man. The peace of reconciliation. "God and sinners reconciled!" It was the peace of soul, peace of mind, peace of conscience which comes from the knowledge that God, the very God whom we had offended by our sins, was in Christ—in that little Babe of Bethlehem—reconciling the world unto Himself, not charging our sins against us. It was the peace of which Paul spoke when he said: "Therefore being justified by faith, we have *peace* with God through our Lord Jesus Christ" (Romans 5:1).

This peace, says the apostle, "passeth all understanding." It is a supernatural peace, not attainable by human wisdom. Yet it is given fully and freely to all who kneel in humble faith at Bethlehem's manger and acknowledge the infant Savior as the Lamb of God who was born to bear the sins of the world.

Let this heavenly peace possess our hearts and minds in a special measure during the coming days as we hear the angels' song and listen to the Christmas story. Yes, let "the peace of God, which passeth all understanding, keep our hearts and minds through Christ Jesus." With that peace as our prized possession we can sing:

> Hark! the herald angels sing, "Glory to the newborn King;
> *Peace on earth* and mercy mild, God and sinners reconciled!"
> Joyful, all ye nations rise; Join the triumph of the skies;
> With the angelic host proclaim, "Christ is born in Bethlehem!"

There Is Only One Like Him

Search the Scriptures . . . they are they which testify of Me. *John 5:39*

The world has never known another person like Jesus Christ. The story of a man's life usually begins with his birth, but the story of the life of Christ begins several thousand years before He was born.

Already in the Garden of Eden God promised the world a Savior. Throughout the centuries that followed, this promise was repeated in various forms and to various people—the promise becoming clearer and clearer as the centuries wore on.

Jesus was to be born of the seed of Abraham, of the tribe of Judah, of the family of David, of a virgin mother, in the little town of Bethlehem. He was to die as the Lamb of God which would take away the sin of the world. All had been clearly prophesied by men at various points in time and in various stations in life.

The Savior Himself told the people of His day that these prophecies pointed to Him. These Old Testament Scriptures, He told the recognized Bible authorities of His day, "testify of Me." Again and again we see Him making an important decision or taking an important step "that the Scriptures might be fulfilled."

St. Luke tells us that on that first Easter Sunday, while Jesus walked along the road with the disciples of Emmaus, "beginning at Moses and all the prophets, He expounded to them in all the Scriptures the things concerning Himself" (Luke 24:27).

Surely, here was no ordinary man. Here was the Messiah, the promised Deliverer, the Savior, the Son of God. Well might we confess reverently every time we speak the Second Article of the Creed: "And [we believe] in Jesus Christ, His only Son, our Lord!"

Jesus, be Thou our Glory now And through eternity!

Read Matthew 1:21-23, Isaiah 7:14   **December 5**

What's in a Name?

His name shall be called Emmanuel, (which means, God with us). *Matthew 1:23* RSV

What does your name mean? Do you know? Today our names are frequently little more than identification tags. We are named after a relative, a friend, or some prominent person living at the time of our birth.

The Israelites took the choosing of names for their children seriously, frequently imploring God's special guidance. They wanted whatever name they chose to have special significance. Thus, the Hebrew word "Jesus" means "Savior." "Christ" means "the anointed one" or "the messiah." "Emmanuel" means "God with us."

The coming Redeemer whom Isaiah had foretold was given a number of names long before He was born. The name mentioned in our text above is Emmanuel, meaning "God with us" or, more explicitly, "the God who would dwell in human flesh."

That is why Matthew in the very first chapter of his gospel is eager to identify the infant who was to be born of the Virgin Mary as the Emmanuel prophesied by the prophet Isaiah. His Gospel was to be the story of the "God with us." And that is why John, too, in the very first chapter of *his* gospel, wastes no time before telling us that "the Word [namely, God's Son] was made flesh and dwelt among us." In other words, in Christ, God had become man and shared our life with us.

Why is this so comforting to us? For many reasons, but let us consider just one. It was this Emmanuel, this "God with us," who shortly before returning to heaven assured us: "Lo, I am with you always, even unto the end of the world."

Christ was not only "God with us" 2,000 years ago; He is still "God with us" today. Do we feel outmatched in the battle of life? Are our burdens too heavy? our foes too many? our days too long and lonely? Take heart. Whatever our lot in life may be, we have an omnipotent Friend beside us. Even today He is "God with us."

Oh, come to us, Abide with us; Our Lord, Immanuel!

Oh, Wondrous Love!

In this was manifested the love of God toward us, because that God sent His only begotten Son into the world, that we might live through Him. *1 John 4:9*

There is nothing in heaven or on earth that can be compared with the love of God. Angels have sung of it; men have marveled at it; and children's lips have dwelt upon its sweetness. But to sound the depths of that love or to measure its richness is beyond the furthest stretch of man's imagination.

The poet spoke well when he said: "O perfect love, all human love transcending!" This unspeakable love—whose "breadth and length and depth and height" the saints have contemplated but never comprehended—this matchless mercy, this immeasurable compassion—is once more the object of our special meditation as we move into the foreglow of the Christmas season.

Christmas is pre-eminently the festival of love. The fullness of time had come—the time that God had designated from all eternity. The clocks of heaven had struck. The cup of man's iniquity had been filled to overflowing. But instead of thunderbolts of judgment piercing through the skies—as men had every reason to expect—angel voices filled the midnight air with messages of peace on earth and God's good will toward men.

The world had given God a sordid record of rejection and rebellion. In reply God gave the world His only Son to be their Savior. The world had given God long centuries of sin. In reply God gave His ungrateful and rebellious children the full measure of His *grace*. Surely, the world has seen no greater love! May our contemplation of this wondrous love fill our hearts with peace and joy throughout the coming season.

> Love divine, all love excelling, Joy of heaven to earth come down,
> Fix in us Thy humble dwelling, All Thy faithful mercies crown.
> Jesus, Thou art all compassion, Pure, unbounded love Thou art;
> Visit us with Thy salvation, Enter every trembling heart.

The "Peace Accord" That Never Fails

He [Christ] is our peace. *Ephesians 2:14*

The world, especially in our century, has seen many "peace accords." Unfortunately, many of them were not worth the paper they were written on. Whenever the safety or self-interest of one of the parties to the accord seemed threatened, the stage was set for war. From the dawn of history permanent peace has been an elusive will-o'-the'wisp—something to be striven for but never fully attained.

Not so the "peace accord" which God has made with man. He has given us His signature in the birth, life, death, and resurrection of His Son. That is why Paul can say in the text above: "Christ is our peace"—the very Christ who is "the same yesterday, today, and forever." Down through the corridors of time we hear the changeless echo of Christmas, Good Friday, and Easter: "Peace on earth and mercy mild, God and sinners *reconciled!*"

Notice that final word in the above paragraph printed in italics. When we say that Christ is our Peace, we think primarily of that miraculous peace which He has established between heaven and earth—the peace of reconciliation between God and man. Heaven and earth may pass away, but the peace which Christ has won for us will last into all eternity.

It is noteworthy that the apostle Paul regarded this heavenly peace as one of the chief attributes of God. Again and again he refers to Him as "the God of Peace." Thank God that, when sin and guilt assail our soul, and when our accusing conscience fills our heart with deep and dark despair, we have a lasting "peace accord" with Him. Because of the limitless mercy and all-sufficient merit of His Son, our Lord and Savior, Jesus Christ, His promises will never fail us.

Bane and blessing, pain and pleasure, By the Cross are sanctified;
PEACE is there that knows no measure, Joys that through all time abide.

Christmas or Xmas—Which Will It Be?

Thou art careful and troubled about *many* things: but *one* thing is needful. *Luke 10:41-42*

If ever there was a season when the Christian is tempted to place first things last and last things first, it is the modern Christmas season. It seems that we can hardly escape it. The pre-holiday world in which we are living is moving faster and faster; the very air we are breathing is charged with a spirit of nervousness. Our homes are becoming restless, kitchens are becoming crowded, heads are being crammed, hands are being given more work than they can handle.

Our church, our school, our Sunday school activities, our programs, plans, and parties—all of them, if we do not get them properly subordinated, will so befuddle, so bemuddle our thoughts and minds that when the festive days are over and the haze of hurried excitement has lifted, we will find ourselves *not* spiritually stronger but only physically weaker. We shall have succumbed to the triple X of a pagan Xmas—the modern excesses of excitement, extravagance, and exhaustion!

Let us resolve, as we plan to celebrate another Christmas, that no matter how many externals crowd in upon us, they must not crowd out the "one thing needful." Let us determine to keep first things first. Let our souls bask in the starlight of Bethlehem, and our hearts fling wide their portals that the Christ Child may enter. Let us keep CHRIST in our Christmas, first, last, and always!

If we keep our hearts thus focused, then our hope and joy will not fade and dim with the dying Christmas candles. Then we will have found the one thing needful in the blessed days which lie ahead, and the joys of Christmas will not be taken from us. From now until that holy night may our heartfelt prayer be that of Martin Luther's cradle song:

Ah, dearest Jesus, holy Child, Make Thee a bed, soft, undefiled,
Within my heart, that it may be A quiet chamber *kept for Thee.* Amen.

Make Advent Time Revival Time

Wilt Thou not revive us again, that Thy people may rejoice in Thee? Psalm 85:6

The children of Israel had only recently returned from the land of Babylonia where they had been held captive for many years. From this Psalm it is evident that they were repentant for their sins and were eager to be accepted back into God's loving-kindness. Their hearts cried out for reassurance that the God Jehovah would "remember their sins no more" and that He would "revive" them (literally, give them life: specifically *spiritual* life) so that, once more, they might "rejoice" in Him.

There is a sense in which every Advent season is a season of penitence and of an eager looking forward to the joy of God's salvation. It is true that penitence cannot be turned on and off according to the season, but it is also true that certain seasons can be devoted to serious introspection which normally leads to penitence. The writers of the above psalm had come upon such a season, a time when they pondered their transgressions, and longed for the reassurance of God's love. The closing verses of this psalm tell us that the Lord *gave* them that assurance.

So, too, in this season of Advent it is altogether proper that we devote our thoughts to penitence, to our blemished record of the past year, and to our personal unworthiness of God's "unspeakable Gift," the anniversary of whose birth we are soon to celebrate.

Penitence and faith are not mutually exclusive. In fact, they go together. By the gracious operation of God's Holy Spirit penitence leads to faith—and faith to joy. Joy in the great salvation our Lord has wrought. As we look forward to that holy night ("when Christ was born"), we can bring penitent, believing, and joyful hearts to the Infant King and worship Him in true devotion.

Let us, then, look forward to the coming days both as advent time and as revival time—preparing our hearts for Christmas when *penitence will lead to faith* and *faith will lead to joy* unspeakable.

One Thing I Know

One thing I know—that, whereas I was blind, now I see. *John 9:25*

The above sentence is one of the most eloquent sentences of the Bible. Jesus had just restored sight to the blind young man. The leaders of the Jews, anxious to disprove the miracle, had subjected the poor young man to endless questioning. Finally, after relentless cross-examination, the young man exclaimed:

"Whether He [Christ] be a sinner or not, I do not know. *One thing* I know, that, whereas I was blind, *now I see!*" This was as much as to say that when it comes to long and logical arguments, I am no match for you professional theologians. There are many questions I cannot answer. But one thing I *do* know—and all your arguments will never change that fact. Yesterday I was blind! And today I see!

So, too, it is with every humble child of God. He may not know how it was possible for *God to become man,* but he does know that the God-Man, Jesus Christ, has shined into his heart and has given him the light of the glory of God.

He may not know how it was possible for the Son of God to redeem his life from destruction, but he does know that a heavenly peace has flooded his soul ever since he learned to believe that "the blood of Jesus Christ, His Son, cleanseth us from all sin." These things he *knows,* because God has opened his eyes to them!

How blest are those who, above all else, know but *one* thing: Jesus Christ is Savior and Lord!

Lord Jesus, as we prepare our hearts for the celebration of Your birth, may we say with confidence: "This one thing we KNOW! You are our only Lord and Savior." Amen.

My Prophet
(First in a Series)

If ye continue in My Word . . . Ye shall know the truth. *John 8:31-32*

One of the deepest cravings of the human heart is to know "the truth." The anxious mother's heart would give anything to know "the truth" about her wayward boy. The lover is hungry for "the truth" of his beloved. And the worried family tosses restlessly on sleepless pillows because they do not know "the truth" about a father, son, or brother who has been reported "missing" from the field of battle.

So, too, the heart of sin-troubled man is tossed upon the turbulent waves of a torturing uncertainty until it has learned "the truth" about God and His relationship to a world that seems to make no sense. We Christians can never sufficiently thank God that we know *that* truth! For us the suspense, the darkness, the despair of uncertainty about the fundamental issues of life has forever been dispelled. We know the truth!

Our Savior, "the Wonderful, the Counselor," "in whom are hid all the treasures of wisdom and knowledge," and "in whom dwelleth all the fullness of the Godhead bodily," has revealed the Father's mind to us. He has brought us the wondrous Gospel of a gracious God, the soul-reviving message of peace and pardon through His atoning blood. He has drawn the concealing curtain aside and opened up to us the tender kindness of the loving Father heart of God. That was the purpose of His becoming "the Word made Flesh."

If we but continue in *His Word*, as recorded in the Holy Scriptures, we shall always know the truth, and the truth shall make us free—free from the gnawing dread of doubt and certainty, free from sin and death and hell—*free* to enter the Father's House!

> O Word of God Incarnate, O Wisdom from on high,
> O Truth unchanged, unchanging, O Light of our dark sky,—
> We praise Thee for the radiance That from the hallowed page,
> A lantern to our footsteps, Shines on from age to age.

My Priest

If any man sin, we have an Advocate with the Father, Jesus Christ, the Righteous. *1 John 2:1*

As we read the high-priestly prayer of Christ, recorded in the 17th chapter of St. John, we are impressed by the frequent repetition of the pronouns "I" and "Thou" and "they." *"I pray for them which Thou has given Me, for they are Thine"* is but one of the many beautiful lines of the Savior's prayer, in which He pours out His heart to His Father on behalf of His friends.

"They," "Thou," and "I." In those three words we find the blessed meaning and the full glory of the Savior's priestly office. He is the eternal Mediator between the Father and the sinner. Throughout the endless ages He stands before the Father's throne, and the burden of His changeless plea is ever, only: "they" and "Thou" and "I."

"They have sinned, O Father," we can hear Him saying. "Thou mightest justly punish them for their immeasurable iniquity. But I have redeemed them by My death on Calvary's cross. And now *they* are *Thine*, O Father, even as *I* am *Thine*, for I have purchased them!"

It was this thought that prompted the writer of the letter to the Hebrews to reassure the newly converted Jews that Christ was, indeed, their divine High Priest (their Go-Between, their Spokesman) before the throne of God who "is able also to save them to the uttermost that come unto God by Him, seeing He ever liveth to make *intercession* for them."

What a marvelous comfort in days of weakness, in hours of doubt and despair, to know that we have a Mediator at the Father's throne who pleads our cause for us—to know that the Father's Son is the sinner's Friend and that through Him we have eternal access into the Father's house. "Let us therefore come boldly unto the Throne of grace, that we may obtain mercy and find grace to help in time of need."

Of our eternal Go-Between we sing:

> He lives to bless me with His love, He lives to plead for me above,
> He lives my hungry soul to feed, He lives to help in time of need.

My Pattern

Learn of Me. *Matthew 11:29*

As we contemplate the earthly life of our Lord in all its grace and beauty, we have no doubt often breathed the prayer of the Christian poet: "I long to be *like* Jesus, meek, loving, lowly, mild; I long to be *like* Jesus, the Father's only Child!"

It is right that this should be our heart's desire. With the aid of God's Holy Spirit we are to pattern our life after that of the Savior. "Learn of Me," He says. "I have given you an example, that ye should do as I have done." Peter writes: "Christ has left us an example, that we should follow in His steps." And John speaks clearly when he says: "He that saith he abideth in *Him* ought himself also so to walk, even as *He* walked."

It is true, we sinful mortals will never attain to the perfection of the Savior, whose holy life was without blemish and without spot. But we are to keep His shining example constantly before us—and we are to measure our life by His. His love, His lowliness, His selflessness!—what a tragic contrast between these and our bitterness, our pride, our selfishness, our petty meanness. How far short we have fallen of the Pattern!

What a blessed comfort in such a moment to remember that Jesus is *more* than our Pattern—He is our *Savior!* In Him our faults, our failures, our sins have been forgiven. In Him we find abundant pardon for every sin—and together with that pardon we find abundant power to pattern our life ever more closely after *His!* Who among us hasn't often prayed:

> I long to be like Jesus, Meek, loving, lowly, mild;
> I long to be like Jesus, The Father's holy Child.
> I long to be with Jesus Amid the heavenly throng
> To sing with saints His praises. To learn the angels' song.

Lord, grant me Thy Holy Spirit so that I may not only call Jesus Christ my God and Lord but may also pattern my life ever more closely after His. I ask it in His name. Amen.

My Pilot

Yea, though I walk through the valley of the shadow of death, I will fear no evil, for THOU art with me. Psalm 23:4

Few hymns in the English language have brought more comfort and strength to the heart of the Christian than the touching lines of Edward Hopper's "Jesus, Savior, Pilot Me." Perhaps no poet will ever surpass his closing stanza for its sublime portrayal of the Christian's confidence in His Savior during the fateful hour of death:

> When at last I near the shore, And the fearful breakers roar
> Twixt me and the peaceful rest, Then, *while leaning on Thy breast,*
> May I hear Thee say to Me: "Fear not! I will pilot Thee!"

When for us life's sun is setting and earth's bright lights are growing dim; when the heavy clouds around us are growing darker, darker, and sure destruction seems our doom—at that very moment we will feel the powerful hand of the Savior gently touching ours. Out of the gathering gloom we will see our heavenly Pilot coming, even as He came to His troubled disciples out of the gray mists of the Sea of Galilee. And we shall hear His reassuring voice: "Be not afraid! It is I. I have traveled this way before. I will lead thee safe to shore. Only trust Me. Only follow!"

What a glorious prospect for those who have come to God through faith in Him whose birth we are about to celebrate. They will set out upon that unknown sea—not in desperation, not in foretaste of the judgment, not bathed in beads of sweat or parched by the heat of a tortured conscience, not deserted and alone—but—*"while leaning on His breast,"* safe in the everlasting arms of Him who will come from the Father's house to meet us and who will lead us safely home!

> As a mother stills her child, Thou canst hush the ocean wild;
> Boisterous waves obey Thy will When Thou say'st to them "Be still!"
> Wondrous sovereign of the sea, Jesus, Savior, pilot me!

My Passover

Christ, our Passover, is sacrificed for us. *1 Corinthians 5:7*

Few Bible scenes are more dear to the Christian's heart than the scene of our Lord's Last Supper. The Savior and His disciples had just completed the ritual of the Passover meal. Their thoughts had dwelt on that night when, 1,500 years before, every family in Israel had painted their doorposts with the blood of the Passover lamb and had eaten its flesh with unleavened bread and herbs. Vividly they recalled how the blood of the lamb had insured the safety of God's people.

Then, after the meal was ended, the Savior reached for the fragments of bread on the table, gave them to His disciples, and said: "Take, eat, *this* is *My* body, which is given for you (no longer the body of a lamb). And then He took the cup, offered it to them, and said: "This cup is the *New* Testament in *My* blood, which is shed for you for the remission of sins (no longer the blood of the Old Testament lamb!). *Christ*, the eternal Passover, had come! There would no longer be any need for types and symbols.

There can be no doubt that our Lord was fully aware of the significance of the moment—the effective replacement of the symbol by the fact. Nor can there be any doubt that the disciples soon became aware of the divine mystery taking place before their very eyes. They were in the presence of the Pascal Lamb! The cradle of Christmas was soon to be overshadowed by the cross!

What a precious Gospel! "Christ, our Passover, is sacrificed for us," says Paul. We have been redeemed "with the precious blood of Christ, as of a Lamb without blemish and without spot," says Peter. His blood, sprinkled on our hearts by faith, has forever stayed the divine hand of avenging justice and won for us a complete salvation. "Not all the blood of beasts On Jewish altars slain Could give the guilty conscience peace Or Wash away its stain. But Christ, the heavenly Lamb, Takes all our sins away: A sacrifice of nobler name And richer blood than they."

My Proxy

The Son of God, who loved me and gave Himself for me. *Galatians 2:20*

There are few sentences more beautiful or few passages more comforting than these affectionate words of the great apostle spoken of his Savior. "He *loved* me and *gave Himself* for me." That was all Paul needed to know, but knowing that, he knew all!

And so we, too, find all that we need to know for time and for eternity in the simple sweetness of these tender words. Does the world hate me? He *loved* me! Do I find the way hard, the path dark, the night cold, the world friendless? He *loved* me! Does the shadow of tomorrow's burden haunt my every step and cause my feet to falter? He *loved* me—and His love goes with me all the way; His love is everlasting; it can never change.

Or is it my sins that seek to cause my heart alarm? My crimson record? My restless conscience? I need not fear. "He *gave Himself for me.*" He took my sins to Calvary's cross and bore my guilt. He paid my debt. He endured my punishment. He suffered all—He gave *Himself* for me! "Oh, the height of Jesus' love! Higher than the heavens above, Deeper than the depth of sea, Lasting as eternity!" The Infant Child of Bethlehem was born to be my proxy!

What a blessed, soul-reviving thought to inscribe across the threshold of each new day! Tomorrow morning, every morning, every hour of the week, in hours of toil and hours of play, let our hearts be echoing the glad refrain: MY SAVIOR LOVES ME! HE GAVE HIMSELF FOR ME! And with that song on our lips we shall walk joyfully down the pilgrim path that leads to the eternal mansions where we shall see our Savior and love Him and enjoy Him forevermore.

> Chief of sinners though I be, Jesus shed His blood for me;
> Died that I might live on high, Lived that I might never die.
> As the branch is to the vine, I am His and He is mine.

My Pledge of Life Eternal

Because I live, ye shall live also. *John 14:19*

Men of all ages have sought for pledges of immortality—for proofs of a life beyond the grave. In our day, for instance, it has become the fashion to point to the dying leaves of autumn and to the tender shoots of springtime as pictures of human death and resurrection—and as pledges of a life beyond the tomb.

But when the cold fingers of icy death come tapping at our shoulder, there will be no comfort in the fact that October is the time of falling leaves and that springtime is the season when the lilacs and the lilies bloom! At that moment nothing less will comfort our turbulent souls than the vision of our Savior, triumphant in the skies, with the seal of victory over death in His nail-pierced hands and a shout of assurance from His blessed lips: *"Because I live, ye shall live also!"*

His victory over the grave is our pledge of life eternal. His empty tomb proclaims to us that some day our grave, too, shall be empty. "Christ is the firstfruits of them that slept," says Paul. Just as the firstfruits are the forepledge, the foretaste, of a later and more general harvest, so Christ's resurrection is the guarantee and forepledge of *our* resurrection to life immortal—in that later, greater harvest!

For us death holds no terror. Our Savior has lifted the veiling cloud which hung heavily over what seemed to be our journey's end—and at the end of the road that winds up the far side of the valley we can see our Father's house.

That is why we can sing with fervent faith throughout this coming Christmas season the stirring words of the Christian poet:

> Praise God the Lord, ye sons of men, Before His highest throne;
> Today He opens heaven again And gives us His dear Son.
>
> He opens us again the door Of Paradise today;
> The angel guards the gate no more, To God our thanks we pray.

What Do You Want for Christmas?

One thing have I desired of the Lord, that will I seek after; that I may dwell in the house of the Lord all the days of my life. Psalm 27:4

Since early November we have been bombarded with enticing suggestions for "gifts for Christmas." To the accompaniment of nostalgic Christmas music department stores have become winter wonderlands filled with attractive gifts for every member of the family. Even television has invaded our homes with almost irresistible siren voices and gorgeous full-colored pictures of nearly every creature-comfort—all "ideal gifts for Christmas."

As Christians, we welcome every useful gift that our provident Father in heaven permits His children to enjoy. But, as Christians, we will also pray for the grace to keep every gift of heaven in its true perspective. What is it that we *really* want for Christmas?—Really?

In the psalm quoted above David was not speaking of the Christmas season. Yet his mind-set and his heart-set provide us with an example which all of us well might follow during these pre-Christmas days. He says: "*One thing* have I desired of the Lord, that will I seek after; that I may dwell in the house of the Lord all the days of my life." That was the gift that David wanted above all others: the peace and deep-down satisfaction that came from constant and intimate fellowship with his Lord.

Surely, all of us share this worthy desire with King David. But during this time of the year there is great danger that our focus become blurred—that we want "above all" the heavenly gift of the infant Christ, but that, somehow, we also want "above all" that new, large screen, color television set. Only a divided heart, however, can want two different gifts "above all."

As another Christmas approaches may we be given the single-hearted devotion of David who said: "One thing have I desired of the Lord." May that "one thing" be the Christ of our salvation.

Thee will I love, my Lord, my Savior. Thee will I love with all my heart. Amen.

The Profoundest Thought of All

Where is the wise? 1 Corinthians 1:20

The renowned theologian, Dr. Karl Barth, was spending an evening with friends when one of them asked him: "Tell me, Doctor, what is the profoundest thought that ever entered your mind?"

After a brief moment of reflection Dr. Barth replied very simply: "The profoundest thought I have ever known is the simple truth: 'Jesus loves me, this I know, for the Bible tells me so'"

How true! The depths of that statement will never be fathomed. Paul tells us: "Eye hath not seen nor ear heard, neither have entered into the heart of man the things which God hath prepared for them that love Him. But God *hath revealed* them unto us by His Spirit."

The profoundest insights that have ever entered the heart of man are those that are revealed in Bethlehem's manger and at Calvary's cross. There we find a God of love, of mercy, of infinite compassion; a God who redeems, forgives, restores for Jesus' sake; a God whom we can find nowhere else but in the "simple" Gospel of our Lord.

Paul was a man of great learning. "A college man," we might say today. Yet he is at great pains to remind his Corinthian Christians in the chapter that follows our text:

"When I came to you, brethren, I did not come proclaiming to you the testimony of God in lofty words or wisdom. For I decided to know nothing among you except Jesus Christ and Him crucified" (1 Corinthians 2:1 RSV). And he says very much the same thing to the Galatian Christians, extolling the love of Jesus Christ, "the Son of God who loved me and gave Himself for me." *That* was the one over-powering, overwhelming thought in his life.

Have we ever thought of it in that way—that our profoundest thought can be clothed in a Sunday school vocabulary: "Jesus loves me, this I know, for the Bible tells me so"?

Lord God, let me never become so "wise" that I neglect my Savior and His love. Amen.

Barging In on Christmas?

They [the shepherds] made known abroad the saying which was told them concerning this Child. *Luke 2:17*

It was a cold winter morning. Two women, their arms filled with bundles and their coat collars raised against the biting wind, were walking past the window of a large department store.

In the window was a life-size tableau of the scene of the Nativity: the Christ Child in the manger, Mary and Joseph, the kneeling shepherds, and the cattle standing nearby.

"Can you beat that!" one of the women was overheard to say. "The churches are even barging in on Christmas!"

To her the substitution of the Christ Child for Kris Kringle was an unwarranted intrusion by the religious people of the community. How ironic that the world should have drifted so far from the original significance of Christmas that the King of Kings should be accused of "barging in" on His own birthday celebration!

What the world needs today is more—and not less—of such "barging in" on the part of the church. During these weeks let Christians remember that the message of the season is in great part a missionary proclamation. "Behold, I bring you good tidings of great joy, which shall be to *all people*," the angel said.

"All people," including the millions of busy shoppers who are milling through crowded department store aisles these days, need to be told that unto them is born a Savior. They need nothing more than that the church "barge in" on their preoccupation with the toys and the tinsel of the season.

Of the shepherds we are told that they "made known abroad the saying which was told them concerning this child." What an excellent opportunity we have to follow their example during these pre-Christmas days! Through our Christmas cards, our caroling, and our holiday conversations we can spread the news that Christ, the Savior, is born.

Christmas is not to be merely a church celebration. Our Lord meant it to be a world celebration! "God so loved the world!" "Peace on *earth*, good will to men!" May each of us spread the message far and wide!

The Messiah!

And beginning at Moses and all the prophets, He expounded unto them in all the scriptures the things concerning Himself. . . . And their eyes were opened. *Luke 24:27-31*

Normally the above Scriptural account is read in Christian churches during the Easter season since the event it describes took place on the day of Christ's resurrection. But we do well to remember its essential aspect also during the season of Advent.

We recall that the Savior had joined the two despondent disciples who had left Jerusalem and were on their way to their home in Emmaus late in the afternoon of the first Easter Sunday. When He asked the reason for their despondency, they told Him of the death of their dearest Friend—a death by crucifixion.

It was at that point that Christ (still a stranger to them) began to "expound to them in all the Scriptures the things concerning Himself," ultimately revealing Himself to them as the promised Messiah. Step by step He showed them how His birth, His life, His suffering and death, had been accurately foretold in "Moses and the Prophets"—another way of saying "in the Old Testament."

As we prepare to celebrate the birth of the Christ Child, we must discipline our hearts and minds to go beyond and beneath the shallow sentimentalities which would merely ooh! and ah! about "the sweet little baby Jesus." We must see in the infant in Mary's arms Him concerning whom "Moses and the prophets" had prophesied—the promised Messiah, the divine Deliverer, the Son of God, the mighty Redeemer of Israel and of all mankind.

As we read the suggested Gospel portion indicated at the top of this page, we see that *Christ* identified Himself as the promised Messiah. (Christ is the Greek word for Messiah, both of which mean "the anointed One.") He who lay in Bethlehem's manger had been anointed from all eternity to be our Prophet, Priest, and King!

While we prepare to worship the infant Christ, may our hearts ring out: "Redeemer, come! I open wide My heart to Thee; here, Lord, abide. . . . Eternal praise and fame We offer to Thy name!"

Christmas Light

I am the Light of the world. John 8:12

Christmas and light! Ever since the brightness of heaven flooded the hills of Bethlehem and the twinkling of a star guided Eastern sages to their newborn King, Christmas and *light* have been intimately associated in the minds of Christian people.

Today the electrical capacities of large cities are taxed almost to their limit in order to make Christmas the time of light. But in many instances the fragile lights which were meant to be but symbols of the true Light of Christmas have come to be mistaken for the light itself! The symbol has been substituted for the substance: and the people's light is *darkness*.

CHRIST is the Light of Christmas. Christ is the Light of the world. Christ is the guiding Light of your life and mine. He is the Light of lights!

Remove from our heart every influence which has come to us from the Savior's Word—our Christian home, our Christian parents, our Christian training—erase from our memory every special providence, every comfort, every consolation, every hope-strengthening reassurance which has come to us as a gift of the Savior's love—and behold what dismal darkness remains.

Christ has been our Light! Every ray of heavenly cheer, every beam of brightness that has shined into our sin-darkened hearts has found its source in the true Christmas Light of Bethlehem. Let us therefore not permit the lights of Christmas to exclude the true *Light* of Christmas from our celebration, but let us draw ever closer to the infant Jesus, who again assures us: '*I* am the Light of the world; he that followeth Me shall not walk in darkness, but shall have the light of life."

Not only during the Christmas season, but throughout the year may we hear our Savior's voice ring loud and clear:

I am the Light, I light the way, A godly life displaying;
I bid you walk as in the day, I keep your feet from straying.
I am the Way, and well I show How you must sojourn here below.

Read Ephesians 2:1-9

Why Christmas?

I am come that they might have life. John 10:10

Take two sentences of the Bible, place them side by side, and you have the Bible's answer to the question: "Why Christmas?"

These two sentences are the words of the apostle Paul: "Ye were dead in trespasses and sins," and the words of the Savior: "I am come that they might have life."

Have you ever thought of what this world would be like without Christmas? Not the Christmas which is being celebrated by our department stores, but the Christmas which took place nearly 2,000 years ago in the quiet of Bethlehem's stable. What if there had never been a Christ Child?

Paul tells his Ephesian Christians that without Christ they were "strangers from the covenants of promise, *having no hope*, and without God in the world." He tells them, furthermore, that without Christ they were spiritually *dead*, utterly unable to turn a finger to win their own salvation.

But Christmas changed all that! With Christ new hope was born. "In Him was *life*," says John. In Him sin, death, and hell were vanquished forever, and forgiveness of sins, life, and salvation were won for all mankind. That is what the Savior meant when He said: "I am come that they might have *life*."

As we look forward to another Christmas, we might well ask ourselves: *WHAT IF?* What if there had been no Christ Child, no herald message: "Unto you is born a Savior"? Thank God, we need never contemplate that dreadful question seriously. Our Savior came—and with Him came life, life now and forevermore.

Rather, the question for us is: Now that the Son of God *has* come—to rescue us from sin and death and to give us life—how have we received Him? Have we taken Him into our hearts and lives, both as our personal Redeemer and as our Lord? God grant that we have.

Lord, we thank You for the new life we have found in Jesus Christ, Your Son. Renew us daily to live as He has taught us. Amen.

The Eternal Power of Christmas

Unto you is born this day in the city of David a Savior, which is Christ the Lord.
Luke 2:11

The hearts of Christians throughout the world are dwelling during these sacred hours upon the wondrous story of that first Christmas eve. And what a resplendent spectacle is unfolded before our wondering eyes in the simple language of that story!

Lowly shepherds in shepherds' garb, dumbfounded, stupefied, bewildered—*they* form the first Christmas audience. An angel of God, in all the glory and brilliance of heaven, the first Christmas messenger. A choir of angels, the first Christmas chorus. And the words, "Unto you is born this day in the city of David a Savior, which is Christ the Lord," the keynote of the first Christmas sermon ever preached to dying sinners.

It is the eternal power and divine eloquence of this simple yet tremendously important message which has perpetuated Christmas and which still electrifies the hearts of Christians whenever the glad tidings are repeated. Unto you is born a Savior!

Unto *you*, you who were born in sin, you whose life is a record of transgression and iniquity and are therefore under the wrath of an offended God; unto *you* is born this day in the city of David a Savior, a Redeemer, an Emancipator, which is Christ the Lord, the promised Messiah, the Emmanuel, the God-with-us, the Mighty God!

As long as that message remains true—and it will remain *forever* true—Christmas will never lose its power. Christmas will never cease to bring that peace, that hope, that joy of which the angels sang—that peace, that hope, that joy which—thank God—are ours today. Surely, no matter what our circumstances may be on this most holy day, we have every reason to lift our hearts in fervent prayer and say:

O holy Child of Bethlehem, Descend to us, we pray.
Cast out our sin And enter in, Be born in us today.
We hear the Christmas angels The great glad tidings tell;
Oh, come to us, Abide with us , Our Lord Immanuel! Amen.

For God So Loved the World—

... that He gave His only begotten Son, that whosoever believeth in Him should not perish, but have everlasting life. *John 3:16*

Once more the sun has dawned on Christmas day. Throughout the world wherever the name of Christ is known Christian people have gathered to celebrate the birthday of their Lord and King. Songs of praise and thanksgiving, anthems of adoration, and expressions of worship are echoing in millions of hearts and homes. For in these glad hours the eyes of untold multitudes are fixed on that blessed manger scene where lies the Christ, "the Star of our life and the only Hope of our eternity."

But why is Christmas a day of such unmixed joy? We need only remind ourselves of the plight of sinful man *had there been no Christmas!* Ever since the fall of our first parents, the human race had groaned under the lash of the most cruel taskmaster, enslaved under the power of the prince of darkness—spiritually without help or hope unless ransomed by the promised Savior! Then suddenly on that first Christmas night the heavens were torn asunder with the enthralling message of the angel: "Unto you is born a Savior!" *The ransom had arrived!*

The love of God, which sent a divine Redeemer to rescue a doomed humanity, is the source of today's unbounded gladness. For us who in humble faith accept the Christ Child as our Savior and Redeemer, Christmas spells the difference between an eternity in the company of the prince of darkness and a glorious eternity before the throne of God in heaven—in the company of Him who loved us and redeemed us to be His own forevermore. What a glorious festival, this Christmas! What a glorious message, this Gospel! What a glorious Savior, this Christ!

> Let us all with gladsome voice Praise the God of heaven,
> Who, to bid our hearts rejoice, His own Son hath given.
> To this vale of tears He comes, Here to serve in sadness,
> That with Him in heaven's fair homes We may reign in gladness!

Prayer for Christmas Day

Lord God, heavenly Father, we thank You on this day of gladness for the wondrous Gift which You have given us in the newborn Savior. How great is Your mercy! How unspeakable is Your love!

Forgive us our transgressions and the sins which have made us unworthy of Your kindness. Remove from our hearts the many temptations and distractions which would rob us of the abiding blessings of the Christmas Gospel.

Fix our thoughts upon the heavenly joys which are ours in the Christ Child. Like Mary, may we keep all these things and ponder them in our hearts. Like the shepherds, after having worshiped the newborn King, may we return to our several callings, glorifying and praising You—and making known abroad all that we have heard and seen.

May this be for us not merely a holiday, but a *holy* day, enduing us with grace and blessings which we may carry with us not only through this festive season but also out across the threshold of a brand new year.

May we embrace the Christ Child in the arms of faith throughout the days of our earthly journey—evermore praising Him and serving Him—until, in Your mercy, we join the great angelic chorus and sing eternal hallelujahs to Your holy name throughout the endless ages.

We ask it in the name of the Christ Child whom You have given us. Amen.

Christmas Means Faith

And it came to pass, as the angels were gone away from them into heaven, the shepherds said one to another, Let us now go even unto Bethlehem, and see this thing which is come to pass, which the Lord hath made known unto us. *Luke: 2:15*

Did you notice? The shepherds did not say: "Let us now go and see *if* this thing is come to pass." No, they said: "Let us now go and see this thing which *is* come to pass." They had heard the Christmas Gospel, and they believed it implicitly.

If only our modern world could throw away its doubt, its skepticism, its unbelief in the presence of the Christmas story! If only it could go and see and—*believe!*

The peace, the love, the joy of Christmas, can be taken into the human heart alone by faith. We can talk about the Babe in the manger, we can sing our Christmas carols, we can thoroughly enjoy our many Christmas television specials, we can join in the gaiety of the season, but if we have not accepted the Child of Bethlehem by faith, we have missed the heart and core of Christmas. Well has the poet said:

> Though Christ a thousand times in Bethlehem be born,
> If He's not born in thee, then thou art still forlorn.

Faith is the hand that reaches out across the years and brings the Savior with His blessings—the blessings of love, of tender mercy, and, above all, of divine forgiveness—into our hearts and homes. These are the lasting blessings of Christmas. Let us, therefore, reach out with the hand of faith and grasp the infant hand of our divine Redeemer, inviting Him tenderly:

> Ah, dearest Jesus, holy Child, Make Thee a bed, soft, undefiled,
> Within my heart that it may be A quiet chamber kept for Thee!

Unsearchable Love

And to know the love of Christ, which passeth knowledge. Ephesians 3:19

In this well-known passage from the Letter to the Ephesians, St. Paul exhausts the possibilities of human language in an effort to describe the love of Christ. He adds a fourth dimension to the usual three when he prays that "ye might be able to comprehend . . . what is the breadth and length and depth and height and to know the love of Christ which passeth knowledge."

The human mind simply cannot fathom a love so deep, so divine, that it could tear the eternal Son from the bosom of the Father and cause Him to come down to earth and to suffer and to die for a world of sinners. Such love, indeed, "passeth knowledge."

But we are not asked to understand it. We are asked to believe it! Men sometimes make the mistake of trying to understand the great truths of our salvation—the truth of God's love, of Christ's atonement, of full and free forgiveness through faith in Christ. But God does not ask us to understand the unsearchable mysteries of His divine revelation; He asks us only to believe and trust them.

The poet could not understand the height nor the depth nor the breadth of God's love. That is why in the well-known hymn he writes: "O perfect love, all human love transcending." No matter how far human love may reach, God's love reaches infinitely farther.

We need not understand the solar system to be warmed by the light of the sun. We need not know the chemical formula for a drop of water to be refreshed by a cooling spring. Nor need we fathom the mind of God to know that He loves us and that through Christ we have become His own. For that we need merely trust His Word.

Why Thou couldst ever love me so, And be the God Thou art,
Is darkness to my intellect, But sunshine to my heart.

"The Word Was Made Flesh"

In the beginning was the Word.... And the Word was made flesh and dwelt among us, (and we beheld His glory). *John 1:1, 14*

A nuclear scientist, speaking to a college graduation class, was making an urgent appeal for more graduates to study abroad so that they could interpret America's good intentions especially to the nations of the emerging Third World. Summing up, he said: "The best way to send an idea out into the world is to wrap it up in a person."

In a sense infinitely more sublime, that is what the Lord of heaven did on that first Christmas Eve. He had an "idea" which He was eager to convey to the entire human race, the message of His divine love, the electrifying Word of pardon, peace, and joy. In His unsearchable wisdom He took this "idea," which He was so eager to communicate to the human family, wrapped it up in a person, and laid it into a manger.

That is the eternal significance of Christmas. Paul writes to his pupil Timothy: "Without controversy, great is the mystery of Godliness: God was manifest in the flesh." John introduces Christ with the words: "The Word was made flesh and dwelt among us, and we beheld His glory, the glory as of the Only Begotten of the Father, full of grace and truth."

Indeed, God wrapped up the wondrous message of His love in the *Person* of His only begotten Son and sent that Son down from heaven to earth, so that all people everywhere might know what is in His Father heart—so that they might learn to know His good and gracious will toward all mankind, His mercy and compassion.

That is why in spirit we kneel before the manger bed and greet the heavenly Visitor:

> O Word of God Incarnate, O Wisdom from on high,
> O Truth unchanged, unchanging, O Light of our dark sky!

The Babe of Bethlehem is the Word of God incarnate—the Word made flesh—the message of God to man. Through His life, His teaching, His death, His resurrection, and His ascension He has revealed His Father's heart to us. Oh, come, let us worship and bow down before "the Word made flesh" lying in a manger!

Post-Christmas Depression?

The grass withereth, and the flower thereof falleth away; but the Word of the Lord endureth forever. 1 Peter 1:24-25

We read much these days about "post-Christmas depression." Psychiatrists tell us that the let-down which frequently follows the round of Christmas celebrations is rapidly becoming a national malady—in fact, suicides immediately after the holidays have shown an alarming increase.

Why should this be? There are, of course, a number of natural causes for a let-down feeling after the last Christmas carol has been sung—loneliness on the part of some; nostalgia which reaches back in time and fills the memory with sentimental moments that can never be recaptured; memories of departed loved ones; and the depressing realization that the joys of *anticipation* often do exceed the joys of *realization*, especially if our anticipation has been focused on the wrong things.

But there is a *Christian* perspective on the year-end holidays that can avoid (or, at least, alleviate) the malaise that frequently follows in the wake of December 25. The perspective is so simple that it may seem simplistic. As we sit beside the drooping tinsel of our fading tree and muse on the ephemeral nature of all the externals of another Christmas now past, let us fix our minds on the true *essentials*. No tinsel talk will do. Only the Word of our Lord as we hear it once again.

"For all flesh is as grass, and all the glory of man as the flower of grass. The grass withereth, and the flower thereof falleth away. But *the Word of the Lord endureth forever: and this is the Word which by the Gospel is preached unto you.*" The music may fall silent, the tree may droop its tired arms, the tinsel may tarnish. But the Gospel of Christ will abide *forever.* We can carry *that* Good News in our hearts not only until next Christmas but until we celebrate the *eternal* Christmas in our Father's house above. With that perspective, where is there room for prolonged depression!

Because and Therefore

Because Thou hast been my Help, therefore in the shadow of Thy wings will I rejoice. *Psalm 63:7*

If any man ever lived a dangerous life, that man was David. Indeed, there are periods of his life which read almost like pieces of exciting fiction. Again and again it seemed that he was walking into the jaws of inevitable death, but again and again he was delivered from the snares of his enemies.

As David looked back along the dangerous and adventurous path of his life, he could see the hand of his God at every turn. Looking *back*, he exclaimed: "Thou hast been my Help." Looking *forward*, he confidently asserted: "In the shadow of Thy wings will I rejoice."

Significantly, he connects these two assertions with the two little words "because" and "therefore." "*Because* Thou hast been my Help, *therefore* in the shadow of Thy wings will I rejoice." God's performance in the past was David's guarantee of God's performance in the future.

As we approach the close of the old year and the birth of the new, must we not say the same? He who has been our Help during the past year—in days of sickness and of sorrow, in days of trouble and of trial—surely He will keep His sheltering wings over us also in the year which lies ahead. Under the shadow of His wings we may confidently abide. With unshaken confidence we can say:

The Lord hath helped me hitherto By His surpassing favor
His mercies every morn were new, His kindness did not waver.
God hitherto hath been my Guide, Hath pleasures hitherto supplied
And hitherto hath helped me.

Help me henceforth, O God of grace, Help me on each occasion,
Help me in each and every place, Help me through Jesus' passion;
Help me in life and death, O God, Help me through Jesus' dying blood;
Help me as Thou hast helped me! Amen.

Abounding Grace

Where sin abounded, grace did much more abound. Romans 5:20

As we look back today over the path which we have covered during the past year, two great mountain peaks, as it were, loom up before our eyes: the mountain of our sin and the mountain of God's grace.

The past year, we confess it to our shame, has again been a year of sin—of many sins, of grievous sins—on the part of everyone of us. But the past year has also been a year of grace—of abounding grace—on the part of God. Let us thank our heavenly Father that towering high above the mountain of our sin is the incomparably higher mountain of His mercy.

Let us comfort ourselves with the unshakable assurance that in Christ the handwriting of the old year, which stood against us, has been blotted out, and that in Christ all the follies and the failures of the new year will also find their pardon and forgiveness. No matter how far we wander, His grace will follow and enfold us!

These are the Christian's thoughts on New Year's Eve. Yes, these are the thoughts of that *little* New Year's Eve service which we conduct each night when we fold our hands in sleep: absolute despair of our own record of accomplishments, and absolute and unwavering confidence in that Savior whose record of accomplishment has been written to *our* credit and who will be our Savior in the new year even as He has been in the old.

Our sins are great indeed! His love is even greater! It is this love which we shall carry with us out of the old year and across the threshold of the new. How assuring to know that the new year which lies ahead will be another year of *grace*.

As we look back upon the long road which lies behind us, with all its twists and turns, and as we look forward to the unknown and untraveled road that lies before us, we have every reason to stop—to ponder—and then to pray:

"Through many dangers, toils and snares I have already come;
'Tis *grace* has brought me safe thus far, And *grace* will lead me home." Amen.

Prayer at the Turning of the Year

At the close of another year, O Lord, and at the dawning of the new, we come before You with our prayers of thanksgiving. Throughout the past 12 months You have again been with us with Your boundless mercy, blotting out all of our transgressions in the blood of our divine Redeemer. We know that You will be with us also in the coming year, forgiving us our many sins because of the merits of the Savior.

O Lord, as we contemplate the unknown year which stretches out before us, we recognize our weakness. As we view its endless problems, we humbly confess: "With might of ours can naught be done." At this solemn hour we therefore bring the difficulties and perplexities of the coming year to You, imploring You, according to Your promise, to be with us and share our many burdens and finally lead us out of darkness into light.

Bless this year, O heavenly Father, to Your glory and to our good, for Jesus' sake. Amen.

Meditations
For
Special Occasions

Read Ephesians 5:25-33

The Wedded Couple's
First "Family" Devotion

Jesus also was invited to the marriage. John 2:2 RSV

The above words are taken from the Gospel story of the marriage feast at Cana, the details of which need no retelling here. The facts of preeminent importance are that Jesus was *invited*, that He *came*, and that His presence proved a *blessing*.

As you launch out upon your wedded life together, you will want to be sure that Jesus has been invited to your marriage, not only as a Guest but also as your constant Friend and Companion. Today He stands at the very threshold of your marriage and says: "Behold, I stand at the door and knock." May you resolve at this moment that the door to your hearts and your home will always be open to Him.

May you *always* be able to say: "Christ is the Head of this house, the silent Listener to every conversation, the unseen Guest at every meal." This will not happen without conscientious effort on your part. It will remain true only as you remain close to the Word of God, faithful in prayer, and regular in fellowship with Christ's holy people in the Christian congregation.

The young couple at the marriage feast in Cana were blessed in a miraculous manner. Not only did the Savior supply the needed wine when their original supply ran out, but when the festivities were over and all the guests had left, the master of the feast remarked, with great surprise, that the *best* wine (the wine that Christ supplied) had been saved 'til last!

How true of many Christian couples! Having remained faithful to their marriage vows, having reared their children in the nurture and admonition of the Lord, and having lived in daily close communion with their Lord and Savior, they see, as they approach their twilight years, that their Lord has saved "the choicest blessings to the last." In that faith we pray:

> Oh, blest the house, whate'er befall,
> Where Jesus Christ is all in all!
> Yea, if He were not dwelling there,
> How dark and poor and void it were!
>
> Then here will I and mine today
> A solemn covenant make and say:
> Though all the world forsake Thy Word
> I and my house will serve the Lord.

Read Matthew 19:13-15

At the Birth of a Child

Lo, children are an heritage of the Lord. *Psalm 127:3*

The arrival of a new, healthy child in a Christian family occasions excited joy and heartfelt gratitude. After months of waiting the precious gift has come—and it is yours to keep.

Our Father in heaven *wants* Christian couples to be excited, joyful, and grateful whenever a newborn infant joins the family. But in all of the excitement that attends the arrival of the latest member of the family, He also wants us to remember the words of the psalmist: "Lo, children are a *heritage of the Lord.*"

Exactly what does that mean? First, we are to remember that, without His blessing, your baby's crib would be empty. It is *He* who, in His power, love, and wisdom, gives (or withholds) the gift of children. Each child is, indeed, a *gift* of God's creative hand.

But more. Notice, the Bible uses the word "heritage." The original word is similar to our English word "inheritance," carrying two connotations: namely, that of great responsibility and that of great value. Surely, these two attributes apply to your new baby.

God has given you a great responsibility. You are responsible for your baby's needs both spiritual and physical. After he (she) has been brought to the Lord in baptism, you are to continue to bring him (her) up in the nurture and admonition of the Lord. This child is your "heritage" to keep and cultivate for Him who is the Lord and owner of us all.

But the word "heritage" also implies "great value." In the rural life of the Old Testament each new child had "great value" as a potential worker in the fields. Your child is of great value because of his(her) potential contribution to your family, your church, your community, and society as a whole. Yes, that chubby infant in your crib is of "great value" in *every* sense—a gift of God to be cherished, nourished, and given back to Him for a life of Christian service. To that end we pray:

With joy we bring this child, O Lord, Devoting him to Thee,
Imploring that, as we are Thine, So may our children be. Amen.

Read Psalm 100

Birthday or Anniversary in the Family

What shall I render unto the Lord for all His benefits toward me? I will take the cup of salvation and call upon the name of the Lord. *Psalm 116:12-13*

We have arrived at another significant milestone in the life of _____ , cherished member of our family. What do we say on an occasion like this? King David asked a similar question on a similar occasion. He asked: "What shall I render unto the Lord for all His benefits toward me?"

As David looked back over his eventful life, he saw the mighty hand of the Lord, always guiding and protecting, always shaping events so that they would result in ultimate blessing for the young shepherd boy who now was king. And so David could not suppress the question: What shall I give to the Lord as a token of my gratitude for the goodness which He has shown me?

His answer is most remarkable. May we be given the grace to follow his example. He answers: "I will take the cup of salvation and call upon the Lord." What did he mean? Because the Lord had filled his cup of blessing to overflowing with "blessing upon blessing," he would lift the "cup of salvation" (a symbol of Jewish temple worship). He would hold it aloft as a demonstration of God's *goodness* to him and he would sing praises to the Lord in the presence of the people.

In the language of our day, that means that I am going to show my gratitude to God on this very special day by humbly worshiping Him and drinking ever more deeply of the cup of His salvation. This is the *Lord's* day, and I am consecrating it to Him—with a heart that is full of thanks and praise for the salvation that is mine and for the providence that He still provides. My inmost prayer will always be:

Now thank we all our God With hearts and hands and voices,
Who wondrous things hath done, In whom His world rejoices;
Who from our mother's arms Hath blessed us on our way
With countless gifts of love, And still is ours today. Amen!

Read Isaiah 54:7, 8

In Days of Family Crisis

Who shall separate us from the love of Christ? . . . Nay, in all these things we are more than conquerors. *Romans 8:35-37*

In this sinful, out-of-joint world no family escapes its days of crisis. The important thing is that we know what to "hold on to" when the day of crisis comes. The apostle Paul knew that some of his struggling Christian families in Rome were living through trying times. And so in the middle of his lengthy letter to them he speaks words which every family, facing difficult days, might ponder. He says: "Who shall separate us from the love of Christ? Shall tribulation or distress or persecution, or famine or nakedness or peril or sword? . . . Nay, in all these things we are more than conquerors through Him that loved us.

"For I am persuaded that neither death nor life, nor angels nor principalities, nor powers, nor things present, nor things to come, nor height nor depth, nor any other creature, *shall be able to separate us from the love of God, which is in Christ Jesus our Lord.*"

So positive is Paul of the truth of his words that he resorts to poetic hyperbole in listing all conceivable crises. Today we might say: "I am persuaded that neither sickness nor death, neither poverty nor want, neither unemployment nor enforced idleness, neither an unfaithful spouse nor wayward children, neither family bitterness nor rancor, calamity nor disaster—*nothing* shall be able to separate us from the love of God which we have found in Christ Jesus, our Lord!"

Does this sound too abstract, too theological? By no means! When the crisis moment is upon us, when all human resources have failed, when all "helping hands" have proved devoid of help—how soul-sustaining it is to know that standing at our side is the loving, caring, omnipotent Redeemer, from whom nothing can ever separate us. When despair would overtake us, let us turn to Him; let us walk with Him and talk with Him. He will grip our hand more firmly and lead us where His love would take us. In Him is our salvation.

Read John 14:1-6; 11:23-26

Meditation for a Bereaved Family
"Far Better"

My desire is to depart and be with Christ, for that is far better. Philippians 1:23 RSV

The Lord, in His unsearchable wisdom, has taken our loved one to be with Him in heaven. Can we be sure of that? Yes, we can. The Holy Scriptures are full of such assurances. In our present devotion we shall meditate on the remarkable words of Paul recorded in the above text. He says (no doubt with a bit of homesickness for heaven): "My desire is to depart and be with Christ, for that is far better."

Paul was still in the prime of life, but he had seen and suffered enough to put his life in its proper perspective. He had learned to see his entire journey on this earth in the light of God's eternity. Although he worked untiringly to remain faithful to his calling as an apostle, he never for a moment forgot that "here we have no continuing city, but we seek one to come."

He was so sure of what lay beyond the sunset of this life that he could look forward longingly and say: "I have a desire to be with Christ." He knew where Christ had gone, and he yearned to be with Him. Christ had said: "Where I am, there ye shall be also." And he knew with unshakable assurance that to be with Christ in His Father's house above would be "far better."

Our greatest comfort in this hour is the knowledge that our loved one, like Paul, has gone to be with Christ—to be "forever with the Lord," and to sing His praise forevermore. Yes, our loved one, trusting in Jesus as his(her) only Lord and Savior, has answered the Savior's call to join Him in the mansions of His Father. Surely, though our mortal eyes cannot see it now, the eyes of faith assure us that being with Christ is, indeed, "far better." May we find our greatest comfort in the knowledge that our loved one is, indeed, in that blissful "better country"—forever with the Lord.

"Forever with the Lord!" Amen! so let it be.
Life from the dead is in that word, 'Tis immortality.

Prayers

Morning and Evening Prayers

Sunday Morning

Lord God, heavenly Father, we thank You at the beginning of another week for the privilege of worshiping at Your altar, of hearing Your Word, and of joining in the prayers and praises of Your redeemed as we gather once more on this holy day.

Prepare our hearts to receive Your Word. Remove from our minds all distracting thoughts. As we enter Your sanctuary once more, we pray with David: "May the words of my mouth and the meditation of my heart be acceptable in Your sight, O Lord, my Strength and my Redeemer."

Grant, also, that we may put to practice the message and the precepts of Your Word. Throughout the week that lies ahead may we translate into action what we hear today. May Your Holy Spirit attend us as we enter upon a new week of service to You and to our fellowman. May we be effective witnesses of all that we have "seen and heard." We implore your blessing as we launch out upon the week that lies before us. We ask this in Jesus' name. Amen.

Sunday Evening

Lord God, heavenly Father, we come to You at the end of another day of rest and worship. We ask Your blessing and Your guidance. May the Word we have heard today and the fellowship we have enjoyed be a source of strength to us throughout the week that lies ahead. May we be *doers* of Your Word and not *hearers* only. Help us to remember all who are in want, all who are lonely, all who are lying on beds of illness. Use us, O Father, to bring Your love and mercy to a world in need. May we be faithful stewards of the gifts and talents which You have given us. Having heard Your Word proclaimed today, may we say with the apostle Paul: "The love of Christ leaves us no choice"—no choice but to serve Him and to serve our fellowman. Amen.

Monday Morning

Lord God, heavenly Father, we thank You for Your protection during the night now past, and we pray for Your continuing presence during the coming day. Be with us to guide us and to guard us and to bless our labors undertaken in Your name. Keep us from sinning. If, in our weakness, we depart from Your will, forgive us, we pray, for Jesus' sake. May we love You above all else, and may we love our neighbor as ourselves. May we work both faithfully and diligently as we pursue our daily calling. May all that we think or say or do glorify Your name. We ask it, trusting only in Your Son who has emboldened us to step into Your presence, unworthy though we are. In His blessed name we pray. Amen.

Monday Evening

We thank You, O heavenly Father, through Jesus Christ Your Son, that You have graciously seen us through another day. Wherever we have done wrong, we ask for Your forgiveness; not because we deserve it but because we have learned to know You as our loving Father "full of compassion, and gracious, and plenteous in mercy and faithfulness." Enable us, O gracious Father, to forgive others as You have forgiven us. Let our "sweet reasonableness," enjoined in Your Word, be known among those who are close to us—at home, at work, at church, as well as to all with whom we come into contact. Guard our hearts and guard our lips so that all we think or say or do will reflect the great love that You have shown us in Jesus Christ our Lord. Amen.

Tuesday Morning

Lord Jesus, as we face the challenge of another day, we ask for the continuing gift of Your Holy Spirit. Fulfill Your promise, we pray, to send the holy Comforter to all who put their trust in You. We confess that we are weak and frail. By ourselves we would fall prey to the devil, the world, and our own sinful flesh. It is Your Holy Spirit that strengthens us in the hour of trial and gives us the power to overcome. We go forward into another day confident of Your Spirit's presence. May He guide and guard and keep us. We ask this special blessing because we know You as our gracious Lord and Savior. Amen.

Tuesday Evening

At the end of another day, O Lord, we come into Your presence with hearts full of praise and thanksgiving. We thank You especially, in this evening hour, for the gift of Your Word which has made us "wise unto salvation" through Jesus Christ our Savior. May we always treasure Your Word as a most precious gift. Guard us against the temptation to neglect it or to silence its voice through indifference. Let the message of Your Gospel continue to be a lamp unto our feet and a light unto our path, leading us ever onward and upward until we reach our home above. We ask it in the name of Jesus Christ, our Savior. Amen.

Wednesday Morning

Lord God, heavenly Father, You have kept us safely through another night and brought us to the dawning of a brand new day. May it be a day of opportunity: opportunity to serve both You and our fellowmen, particularly those whom You have placed beside us on our pilgrim path through life. May we always be willing to *serve* and not only to *be* served. Grant us Your Holy Spirit, so that by His leading we may be "the salt of the earth" and "the light of the world." Grant us grace so that we may see the open doors which You have placed before us: doors of missionary opportunity and doors of Christian service wherever it is needed. And having *seen* the doors which You have opened, grant us grace that we might *enter* them. This day and every day let us be found "at Your service!" In Jesus' name we ask it. Amen.

Wednesday Evening

Lord Jesus, we have completed another day on our pilgrim path to Your Father's house. May we never forget that in this present world we are merely transients—wayfarers headed for the homeland. May we live each day in the perspective of eternity, knowing that "here we have no continuing city, but we seek one to come." Grant that the constant vision of the eternal city that lies at our journey's end may give hope to our spirit, courage to our heart, and strength to our feet—as we continue on our pilgrim way. Amen.

Thursday Morning

Lord Jesus, You have brought us safely through another night and to the dawning of another day. In this morning hour we thank You for all the blessings of the past and ask You to accompany us throughout the coming day. Truly, we "need Your presence every passing hour; what but Your grace can foil the tempter's power?" Grant, O Lord, that we might always view each new day as a precious gift from You, and may we fill its hours with deeds that will truly glorify Your name. We ask this favor, trusting only in Your grace and loving kindness. Amen.

Thursday Evening

Lord, sometimes we are puzzled. Sometimes we are frightened. Sometimes we feel that we have lost our way. In a world of constant change and threatening horizons, grant that Your unchanging Word may always be our guide. May the revelation of Your love in Jesus Christ dispel the darkness that surrounds us. As we come to the close of another day, we commend ourselves—all that we are and all that we have—to Your gracious keeping. Be with us tonight, we pray, and bless us as we resume our appointed tasks tomorrow. In Jesus' name we pray. Amen.

Friday Morning

Lord God in heaven, we thank You for Your protection during the night now past and we implore Your continued presence during the day that lies before us. Fill our hearts with love for You and for our fellowmen. Where there is bitterness let us show kindness. Where there is strife let us speak peace. Where there is despair let us spread hope. Where there is sorrow over sin let us speak Your word of forgiveness through the merits of Your Son. Use us today, O Lord, as the instruments of Your good and gracious will. You have purchased us to be Your own. We are Yours and You are ours. May we always prove faithful to our calling as "the purchase of Your love." We ask it in the name of Him who is our Savior and Redeemer. Amen.

Friday Evening

In this evening hour, heavenly Father, we are mindful of Your many mercies and Your loving kindness which have attended us each hour of this day. But, O Lord, we are also mindful of our many shortcomings and our many sins. We have not walked in Your perfect way. Forgive us for the sake of Jesus, who went to Calvary's cross to make payment for our transgressions. Wash us clean, and heal us; fill our troubled mind with peace: the peace which only You can give. As we draw the curtain on another day, bless us with refreshing sleep so that we may arise in the morning ready to serve You in our appointed task. All this we ask in the name of Jesus Christ, our Savior. Amen.

Saturday Morning

Lord Jesus, once more we step into Your presence with a truly thankful heart. You have heard our prayers and have kept us safe during another night. As we enter this new day we pray: Send Your holy angels to keep us in all our ways. Guard us against temptation lest, in our weakness, we fall and sin against Your holy will. And if we fall, grant us true repentance and assure us of Your full and free forgiveness, won for us on Calvary's cross. Use us, Lord, as instruments of Your love and mercy as we serve the needs of our fellowmen—both by word and by deed. As we enter upon the tasks of this new day, may we confidently place our hand in Yours, knowing that You will lead us in the paths that we should follow. You are our faithful Shepherd, our Savior and our Lord. Amen.

Saturday Evening

Gracious Savior, Your boundless love has brought us to the end of another week. Forgive us, we pray, wherever we have strayed from Your path. Bless our household this night—and all our loved ones near and far. Be with them and with us as a mighty shield and fortress. Cause Your holy angels to encamp round about us while we sleep, and ward off whatever might hurt or harm us. Speak peace to our souls, O Lord, and let us spend this night in quiet, restful slumber. When the morning breaks, may we arise refreshed and in good health, ready once more to praise and worship You in the sanctuary of Your church in the fellowship of Your redeemed. We ask these blessings, trusting in Your promise to hear our prayers. Amen.

Seasonal and Special Prayers

Martin Luther's Morning Prayer

I thank You, my heavenly Father, through Jesus Christ, Your dear Son, that You have kept me this night from all harm and danger; and I pray You to keep me this day also from sin and every evil, that all my doings and life may please You. For into Your hands I commend myself, my body and soul, and all things. Let Your holy angel be with me, that the wicked foe may have no power over me. Amen.

Martin Luther's Evening Prayer

I thank You, my heavenly Father, through Jesus Christ, Your dear Son, that You have graciously kept me this day; and I pray You to forgive me all my sins where I have done wrong, and graciously to keep me this night. For into Your hands I commend myself, my body and soul, and all things. Let Your holy angel be with me, that the wicked foe may have no power over me. Amen.

Prayer for the Church

Lord Jesus, You are the Head and Bishop of Your holy Christian church on earth. We thank You for Your bitter suffering and death by which you have redeemed us and made us members of Your body, the church. Through the converting power of Your Word and through the Holy Sacraments You have made us partakers of every spiritual blessing proclaimed by Your saving Gospel, namely, the forgiveness of sins, life, and salvation.

Grant that by the faithful witness of Your church, its pastors, its teachers, its missionaries, its spirit-filled members of all ages, the precious news of the Gospel may be brought to all people everywhere so that the borders of Your kingdom may be extended to the ends of the earth. Preserve Your church both in the soundness of its doctrine and in the warmth of its love, and let peace prevail within its fellowship. Bless the labors of all who work diligently for the extension of Your kingdom, so that more and more souls may be won for You—until that blessed day when You will come to take Your church to dwell forevermore in glory. We ask this, trusting solely in Your promise. Amen.

Prayer for Missions

Lord Jesus, You have commanded us to make disciples of all nations, baptizing them in the name of the Father, and of the Son, and of the Holy Ghost. Grant that Your church may always be obedient to Your command. May it send forth consecrated men and women to proclaim Your Gospel to all the world.

You have also asked us, as individuals, to be Your witnesses in our daily lives, bringing the message of salvation to those whose lives touch ours. May Your Holy Spirit enable and embolden us to share the good news of the Gospel with those who do not know You to be their Lord and Savior.

Bless Your Word, we pray, as we speak it day by day that it may accomplish Your gracious purpose: the extension of Your kingdom of grace here on earth and a growing harvest of souls for Your kingdom of glory in heaven. We ask it, trusting in Your promise. Amen.

Prayer for Our Pastor

Almighty and gracious God, the Father of our Lord Jesus Christ, we come to You in this quiet moment, asking You to bless our pastor. Remember him in love and mercy and bless the labors of his hands. Grant him wisdom, strength, and courage as he seeks to be a faithful shepherd of the flock over which the Holy Spirit has made him overseer. May he feed both young and old with the bread of Your Word, holding forth the word of Your law and the word of your Gospel, each in due season. May the members of our congregation uphold his hands, support his efforts, and accord him the honor that is due his sacred office, so that he may perform his ministry with joy. We ask these blessings in the name of Jesus, the chief Shepherd of the flock, our Savior and Redeemer. Amen.

For a Proper Hearing of the Word

Blessed Lord, who has caused all Holy Scripture to be written for our learning, grant that we may in such wise hear them, read, mark, learn, and inwardly digest them, that by patience and comfort of Your holy Word we may embrace and always hold fast the blessed hope of everlasting life, which You have given us in our Savior, Jesus Christ. Amen.

Prayer for Pardon

Oh, Lord, hear the prayers of all who come to You in penitence and faith. Pardon their sins and remember their iniquities no more. Shower them with Your redeeming grace and tender mercy. Wherever we have done wrong, forgive us, we pray, and may Your Holy Spirit guard us against further transgressions of Your holy will. All this we ask because of Jesus Christ, our only Savior and Redeemer. Amen.

On Behalf of One Who Is Ill

Lord, we come before You on behalf of all those who are suffering, particularly _____ , who is ill. Be with them, we pray, in Your might and in Your mercy. Comfort them with the assurance that You are the Lord who has redeemed them, who has forgiven them all their sins, and who is mightily able to heal all of their bodily afflictions. Give wisdom to the physicians who attend them and to all who are ministering to their needs, both physical and spiritual. Do not let their faith give way to doubt or their courage give way to fear. May this cross draw them ever closer to You and to the unerring promises of Your Word. If it is Your good and gracious will, restore them to health and to soundness of body, mind, and spirit. Nevertheless, not our will but Yours be done. Whatever You ordain is good, Your love abides forever. We place all of them, particularly _____ , wholly into Your hands. You are their Lord, their Savior and Redeemer. Amen.

To Be Prayed by One Who Is Ill

O Lord Jesus, it has pleased You to visit me with bodily illness. I know that Your love and mercy will not permit anything to come to me unless it is for my ultimate good and blessing. Grant that I may rightly receive Your visitation and that through this cross I may be drawn ever closer to You. Forgive my sins because of Your never-ending mercy. Grant me strength to bear my cross with cheerful hope and trusting patience. I pray You to bless the work of the physician(s) and of all who are ministering to my physical needs. Bless the words of comfort spoken to me by my pastor and other Christian friends. If it is Your will, restore me to health. Nevertheless, not my will but Yours be done. I place myself wholly into Your hands. You are my Savior and Redeemer. Amen.

A Prayer for Guidance

Direct us, O Lord, in all our doings—in our daily decisions, both great and small. Grant us Your guiding light upon the twisting pathways of our life. Lead us according to Your wisdom and according to Your love so that we may do only such things as glorify Your name. And finally, by Your mercy, lead us to eternal glory. Through Jesus Christ, our only Lord and Savior. Amen.

A Prayer for Peace

O Lord of Might, look with mercy upon our bleeding world. Forgive our sins for Jesus' sake. Turn the hearts of people everywhere that they may cease from strife and that the calamity of war may be averted. Bless the endeavors of our government and of all people everywhere who are laboring for peace with honor, and crown their efforts with success. Protect our land, our homes, our schools, our church and all that we hold dear. Lord, we know that You hear when Your children call; therefore, we seek our ultimate refuge only in You, trusting solely in the merits of Your Son. Be with us, Lord, for Jesus' sake. Amen.

Prayer for Our Enemies

Lord, we pray that You will forgive our enemies and all who despitefully use us and work to do us harm. Change their hearts by Your Holy Spirit that they may cease their enmity toward us and be inclined to walk with us in meekness and in peace. We ask it through the mediation of Jesus Christ, Your Son, our Lord. Amen.

A Birthday Prayer

Lord God, heavenly Father, once more You have permitted me to observe another anniversary of my birth. For this I am truly grateful. I praise You not only for the wondrous miracle of my birth and for Your loving providence down through the years, but also for the unsearchable miracle of my *rebirth* in the waters of Holy Baptism. Through Your Holy Spirit You have preserved me in my baptismal grace to this very hour.

As I look back across the years that have brought me to this day, I can only say with the patriarch Jacob: "Lord, I am not worthy of the least of all Your mercies and of all the steadfast faithfulness that You have shown to (me) Your servant." Indeed, Your mercies have been new to me every morning and Your compassion has never failed.

As I look forward, I pray: Help me to grow in faith toward You and in love and service to my fellowman. Crown this new year with Your blessing, as You have done so graciously in the past. Be with me in the years that lie before me as You have in the years gone by. And bring me at last to the heavenly feast where I may sing Your praises throughout endless ages. I ask this in the name of Him who died for me that I might live. Amen.

Ash Wednesday

Dear Savior, with this day we enter the season when we contemplate the tremendous price You paid for our redemption. As we follow You from the Upper Room, to Gethsemane, and to the heartless trials You had to endure before Caiaphas, Pilate and Herod, and as we follow you in spirit on the Via Dolorosa out to the Mount of Calvary, may we never forget that it was *our* sin that brought this sorrow and this pain on You. May this season, then, be a time of penitence and prayer. But with our eyes of faith toward Easter morn, may it also be a time of praise and thanksgiving in which we bow in humble worship before You, our Lord, our Savior, and our King. Amen.

Good Friday

O Thou crucified Redeemer, we bow before Your cross in shame and supplication—in shame, because we know it was *our* sin that brought this woe on You, in supplication, because we plead for Your forgiveness. You have taken our place, assumed our guilt, paid our penalty, and have won for us divine forgiveness. May we never forget the indescribable love that drove You to make this unspeakable sacrifice for us. As we stand, repentant, before Your cross, our heart overflows with love, with praise, with gratitude, and with thanksgiving. Over and over we repeat the words of the poet: "Thousand, thousand thanks shall be, Dearest Jesus, unto Thee!" Amen.

Easter Sunday

Lord Jesus, as we gather around Your empty tomb today, our hearts overflow with praise and joy. As we stand in spirit at Your empty grave, we share with the apostle Paul the jubilant assurance that You were "declared to be the Son of God, with power, by the resurrection from the dead!" We know, with an assurance that will never waver, that we have a *living* Savior, mighty in the heavens. Help us to rise with You from sin, sorrow, death, and the grave, and to live lives that proclaim Your resurrection—lives that glorify Your name—until we and all the faithful see You face to face in the glorious mansions of Your Father's house above. Amen.

Ascension Day

Lord Jesus, in the hurry and scurry of our everyday life, we are sometimes inclined to overlook the tremendous importance of the festival of Your glorious ascension into heaven before the eyes of Your disciples. May we always remember Your ascension as Your triumphant return to Your heavenly throne, there to rule in grace and power. And may we draw fresh courage and comfort from Your promise that some day You will return to take us to the heavenly home where you have gone. We rejoice in Your promise: "Where I am, there you will be also." Therefore our hearts are filled with joy as we join with all believers in the prayer: "Draw us to Thee, For then shall we Walk in Thy steps forever And hasten on Where Thou art gone To be with Thee, dear Savior." On this Ascension Day we look forward to that glorious reunion in Your Father's house above. May Your mercy bring us there. Amen.

Pentecost

Lord God, heavenly Father, we thank You, together with Jesus Christ, Your Son, our Savior, for having kept Your promise to send the Holy Spirit upon the disciples on the Day of Pentecost. We know that "no man can say that Jesus is Lord but by the Holy Spirit." Of our own powers we could never have come to saving faith in the blessed Holy Trinity. Left to ourselves, without the Spirit's aid, we could never have put our total trust in the saving work of Jesus Christ, our Lord and our Redeemer.

But we know from Your Holy Word that the Holy Ghost has called us by the Gospel, enlightened us with His gifts, sanctified us, and kept us with Jesus Christ in the true faith. For this continuing gift of a "perpetual Pentecost" we thank You with all our hearts. May Your Holy Spirit continue His converting and sanctifying work in our hearts until Jesus comes again to gather all believers and to take them with Him into eternal bliss and glory. In Jesus' name we pray. Amen.